Becoming a Dynamics 365 Supply Chain Management Functional Consultant Associate

Optimize and streamline supply chain management processes to improve outcomes and reduce costs

Juan Bravo Vargas

Mariano Martínez Melo

BIRMINGHAM—MUMBAI

Becoming a Dynamics 365 Supply Chain Management Functional Consultant Associate

Group Product Manager: Alok Dhuri

Publishing Product Manager: Kushal Dave

Book Project Manager: Manisha Singh

Senior Editor: Nithya Sadanandan

Technical Editor: Jubit Pincy

Copy Editor: Safis Editing

Indexer: Subalakshmi Govindhan

Production Designer: Alishon Mendonca

Senior DevRel Marketing Coordinator: Deepak Kumar

DevRel Marketing Coordinator: Mayank Singh

Business Development Executive: Puneet Kaur

First published: November 2023

Production reference: 1201123

Published by Packt Publishing Ltd.

Grosvenor House

11 St Paul's Square

Birmingham

B3 1RB, UK

ISBN 978-1-80461-800-4

www.packtpub.com

For those who make wishes upon seeing a shooting star, especially when you are doing data migration with Excel templates ;-)

Foreword

Life is a school and there is always more to learn. You have now picked up a book to learn more about Microsoft Dynamics 365 Supply Chain Management, a solution that has gone through a long history of updates and improvements. What I can guarantee you is that there will be new capabilities and improvements in the future, but do not find this discouraging.

Learning the fundamentals of Dynamics 365 Supply Chain Management will help you build a baseline of how the product approaches the business requirements and make you a key player when engaging with customers, partners, and Microsoft. Not only that, but you will be a valuable asset to those around you who need your support and help to better understand the principles the product is built around. This should serve as strong encouragement to you as the reader, as the adoption of Dynamics 365 is very solid and strong and the need for well-rounded and skilled functional architects will be prevalent. It is fantastic to see functional architects dedicating effort to putting their stories and hard-earned experience into a book for you to read.

There is a plethora of sources for learning Dynamics 365 Supply Chain Management, from official documentation in various forms to community-driven content such as online articles and public videos, but my preference has always been learning through books. Even though I enjoy watching training material as videos and I often find solutions in online articles and Microsoft documentation, I still love to unplug from the computer and sit back and read from a book.

Soon enough, you will be jumping into Dynamics 365 and applying your newly earned skills to become a master of supply chain. As you grow as a senior architect, I hope you will also help anyone new to the same journey. Finally, I extend my congratulations to Juan and Mariano for their achievements. Thank you for curating this content and helping others by sharing your knowledge.

Tommy Skaue

Senior Solution Architect, Dynamics 365 FastTrack

Contributors

About the authors

Juan Bravo Vargas is an experienced Manager with over 18 years of expertise in the IT Industry. A decade ago, he transitioned from traditional IT roles to spearhead ERP implementations, embracing a new career trajectory. This shift ignited his passion for continual learning and improving customer project delivery. He achieved certifications as a Microsoft Dynamics 365 Supply Chain consultant and Microsoft Dynamics 365 Solution Architect Expert. As a Microsoft Certified Trainer, he has taught Microsoft courses across Europe and the US for the past four years.

I must express my heartfelt gratitude to my family, whose support has been invaluable.

To Jaquelina, my wife: your unwavering belief and wisdom have been my guiding light. Your strength and support have been crucial in every step of this journey.

To my mother: thank you for your lifelong teachings and unconditional love. Your values and sacrifices have shaped me profoundly, guiding me personally and professionally.

Diana and Max: your joy and curiosity inspire me daily, bringing a fresh perspective to my work and life.

Thank you for being my constant source of inspiration and encouragement.

Mariano Martínez Melo is a principal solution manager with over 15 years of experience in implementing software. Since 2013, he has implemented over 25 supply chain solutions on Microsoft Dynamics 365 ERP systems, including Dynamics 365 F&O, Dynamics Ax 2012, Ax 2009, and Ax 4.0. He's currently certified as a supply chain functional consultant associate, manufacturing consultant associate, and Microsoft solution architect for finance and operations. In 2020, Mariano became an MCT, and currently, he delivers training courses for supply chain consultants and solution architects. He also contributes heavily to the Microsoft community, giving conferences and creating content on his blog and YouTube channel: Consejos Dynamics.

I would like to express my enormous gratitude to my family.

To my beloved wife, Soledad, whose support, patience, and wisdom were crucial during this journey. You are an incredible human being who guides and inspires me every day.

To my work team, for being a constant source of knowledge and humanity.

To my doggies, whose joy of life renews me daily.

Also, thanks to the team at Packt, who gave us lots of support while we worked on this book.

About the reviewer

Rahul Mohta brings 20+ years of expertise in ERP consulting, implementation, and pre-sales, focusing on Microsoft Dynamics 365 F&SCM.

He has diverse and rich experience in working with customers and partners globally, enabling them to realize the full value of their future Dynamics 365 platform.

Rahul strives to work as a solutions leader and trusted advisor, playing diverse roles and working extensively in both the functional and technical domains.

Table of Contents

3

Getting Started with the Inventory Management Module   53

4

Procurement and Sourcing, the Start of the Journey   89

5

Working with Quality Control Processes – a Hands-On Approach   141

6

Setting up and Managing Sales and Customers   169

7

Warehouse Management Implementation – Best Practices and Strategies - Part 1 | 205

8

Warehouse Management Implementation – Best Practices and Strategies - Part 2 | 241

9

Transportation Management – From Planning to Execution   275

10

Master Planning Implementation – A Guide to Streamlining Operations   317

11

Master Planning Implementation – Advanced Scenarios   355

Preface

Dynamics 365 Supply Chain Management, a component of Microsoft's Dynamics 365 suite, revolutionizes manufacturing, distribution, and logistics through advanced analytics and IoT technologies. It enhances operational efficiency, product quality, and profitability.

In this landscape, the supply chain consultant emerges as a crucial figure. These experts customize Dynamics 365 to a business's unique needs, providing strategic planning, implementation, training, and support. Their involvement ensures efficient project execution, risk mitigation, cost savings, and informed decision-making.

A knowledgeable consultant is vital for leveraging Dynamics 365's full potential, optimizing supply chain operations, and preparing businesses for future challenges and opportunities.

In this book, you will learn how to create and configure several types of products and understand the complete sales and procurement processes: setting up warehouses and supply chain flows, designing and customizing warehouse inbound and outbound flows, and covering all transportation and shipping processes. You will also learn how to create and control quality assurance on these products ending with a master plan, which suggests when to acquire all the material to cover this supply chain flow.

Who this book is for

If you are a solution consultant working with Dynamics 365 Supply Chain Management or an IT professional who wants to know how to become an expert on supply chains in Dynamics 365, this book is for you. This book is suitable for key users, business analysts, solution architects, and PMs who are in touch with Dynamics 365 Supply Chain Management. You need to have a fundamental knowledge of navigating across Dynamics 365 Supply Chain Management to get the most out of this book.

What this book covers

Chapter 1, *Getting Started with Dynamics 365 Supply Chain Management*, is a general introduction to the system and its main modules and components.

Chapter 2, *Working with Product Information Management*, contains the essential setups and considerations to correctly manage the product items and services in Dynamics 365 Supply Chain Management.

Chapter 3, *Getting Started with the Inventory Management Module*, explores a clear guideline for implementing and managing the inventory module.

Chapter 4, Procurement and Sourcing, the Start of the Journey, delves into the end-to-end source-to-pay process and the system capabilities to seamlessly acquire goods in your organization.

Chapter 5, Working with Quality Control Processes – a Hands-On Approach, explains the advantages of a quality module in Dynamics 365 Supply Chain Management and the essential setups.

Chapter 6, Setting up and Managing Sales and Customers, provides a profound overview of the order-to-cash process and the sales capabilities.

Chapter 7, Warehouse Management Implementation – Best Practices and Strategies - Part 1, covers the best practices and strategies for adequately implementing warehouse management.

Chapter 8, Warehouse Management Implementation – Best Practices and Strategies - Part 2, delves into the inbound and outbound operations in WMS.

Chapter 9, Transportation Management – From Planning to Execution, explains TMS and workflows and provides a clear guide to understanding the most common tasks during the outbound transport process.

Chapter 10, Master Planning Implementation – A Guide to Streamlining Operations, dives deep into the most solid planning capabilities in the Dynamics 365 supply chain and the essential setups to master the planning process.

Chapter 11, Master Planning Implementation – Advanced Scenarios, dives deep into the most complex scenarios, such as intercompany planning and multi-site, multi-warehouse planning.

Download the images

We also provide a PDF file that has color images of the screenshots and diagrams used in this book. You can download it here: `https://packt.link/gbp/9781804618004`

Conventions used

There are a number of text conventions used throughout this book.

`Code/format in text`: Indicates code words in text, database table names, folder names, filenames, file extensions, pathnames, dummy URLs, user input, and Twitter handles. Here is an example: "The same happens for the field rate engine class as we need to enter the class of the new engine: `TMSSmallParcelShippingEngine.SmallParcelShippingRateEngine`."

Bold: Indicates a path inside Dynamics 365 Supply Chain Management. Usually, this will refer to a navigation per module into the system. An example is "To set up the procurement catalog, please use the following path in Dynamics 365 Supply Chain Management: the **Procurement and Sourcing** module > **Procurement categories**. From this page, we can create a proper structure with nodes and sub-nodes and then associate the products or services for each sub-node."

> **Tips or important notes**
> Appears like this.

Get in touch

Feedback from our readers is always welcome.

General feedback: If you have questions about any aspect of this book, email us at customercare@ packtpub.com and mention the book title in the subject of your message.

Errata: Although we have taken every care to ensure the accuracy of our content, mistakes do happen. If you have found a mistake in this book, we would be grateful if you would report this to us. Please visit www.packtpub.com/support/errata and fill in the form.

Piracy: If you come across any illegal copies of our works in any form on the internet, we would be grateful if you would provide us with the location address or website name. Please contact us at copyright@packt.com with a link to the material.

If you are interested in becoming an author: If there is a topic that you have expertise in and you are interested in either writing or contributing to a book, please visit authors.packtpub.com.

Share Your Thoughts

Once you've read *Becoming a Dynamics 365 Supply Chain Management Functional Consultant Associate*, we'd love to hear your thoughts! Scan the QR code below to go straight to the Amazon review page for this book and share your feedback.

https://packt.link/r/1804618004

Your review is important to us and the tech community and will help us make sure we're delivering excellent quality content.

Download a free PDF copy of this book

Thanks for purchasing this book!

Do you like to read on the go but are unable to carry your print books everywhere?

Is your eBook purchase not compatible with the device of your choice?

Don't worry, now with every Packt book you get a DRM-free PDF version of that book at no cost.

Read anywhere, any place, on any device. Search, copy, and paste code from your favorite technical books directly into your application.

The perks don't stop there, you can get exclusive access to discounts, newsletters, and great free content in your inbox daily

Follow these simple steps to get the benefits:

1. Scan the QR code or visit the link below

https://packt.link/free-ebook/9781804618004

2. Submit your proof of purchase
3. That's it! We'll send your free PDF and other benefits to your email directly

1

Getting Started with Dynamics 365 Supply Chain Management

The pace of the world today is vastly different from what it was 5 or 10 years ago, and even more so compared to the last century. Companies' and customers' demands have shifted toward agile solutions, and we now live in a fully connected world. Companies require the same connectivity and agility to keep up with these changes and ensure smooth operations.

Supply Chain Management (**SCM**) in Dynamics 365 encompasses much more than planning and logistics. It offers a unified platform for business intelligence, incorporating advanced predictive analysis, **artificial intelligence** (**AI**) technology, and the **Internet of Things** (**IoT**) to optimize performance, quality, and profits across all aspects of the supply chain – from planning and production to warehousing and transportation management.

In this chapter, we will cover the following main topics:

- Overview of Dynamics 365 Supply Chain Management
- Applications that compose the Dynamics 365 solution
- Quick overview of the main modules of Supply Chain Management

By the end of the chapter, you will be able to recognize the main modules of the solution and the primary purpose of each one. Also, you will have discovered how the modules are seamlessly integrated.

Overview of Dynamics 365 Supply Chain Management

Dynamics 365 SCM offers several valuable features to help you manage your organization effectively.

The warehouse management system provides valuable insights driven by AI, allowing you to manage your stock efficiently and streamline inbound and outbound delivery processes using Microsoft Power BI.

With supply chain optimization, you can comprehensively view your entire supply chain, including stock information from partner organizations, and streamline deliveries to reduce costs and improve accuracy through analytics.

Automation with real-time insights from IoT can help minimize downtime and boost margins while improving operational performance.

To ensure product quality, Dynamics 365 SCM uses predictive insights and IoT data to anticipate issues with equipment and machines and maintain consistent product quality.

With the Asset Management add-in, you can systematically plan asset maintenance routines to extend the life of your equipment and promptly identify repairs and replacements using telemetry data.

The centralized dashboard in Dynamics 365 SCM allows you to manage all relevant information, such as product images and attachments, in a single, easily accessible location.

Finally, the Planning and Inventory Management modules in Dynamics 365 SCM provide a unified view of the inventory, warehouse, manufacturing, service, and logistics to improve strategic planning. Predictive analytics transforms data into insights, empowering companies to make better strategic decisions.

For clarity and a better understanding of the content, we should get a clear picture of the entire Dynamics 365 solution.

These are the four applications that compose the finance and operations apps:

- Dynamics 365 Finance
- Dynamics 365 Commerce
- Dynamics 365 SCM
- Dynamics 365 Human Resources

This book will focus on SCM and the main modules that compose this app.

The modules that belong to the SCM part are the following:

- Asset Management
- Inventory management
- Master planning
- Procurement and sourcing
- Product information management
- Production control
- Sales and marketing
- Service management

- Transportation management
- Warehouse management

Let's review together the main features and characteristics of each module.

Asset Management

Asset Management is a sophisticated tool for overseeing assets and maintenance tasks within Dynamics 365 SCM. This module integrates smoothly with multiple finance and operations applications.

This module allows you to manage the entire life cycle of the assets in your organization.

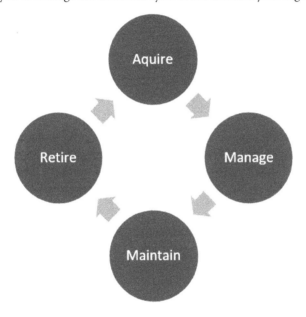

Figure 1.1 – Asset life cycle process in Dynamics 365

With Asset Management, you can proficiently oversee and maintain a wide range of equipment in your organization, including machines, production gear, and vehicles. This module provides solutions that cater to diverse industries.

Inventory management

Inventory management is a crucial component of any supply chain. It plays a vital role in ensuring that businesses have the right products in the right quantities at the right time. The Dynamics 365 SCM Inventory management module provides businesses with a comprehensive solution to manage and track their inventory.

This module helps businesses to accurately maintain and manage their inventory levels by providing real-time data on stock availability, sales trends, and purchase orders. The Inventory management module also enables businesses to create, manage, and monitor their stock levels and set up reordering rules based on their business requirements.

One of the critical features of the Inventory management module is the ability to track and manage the inventory of multiple sites and locations. This enables businesses to monitor their inventory levels across multiple warehouses, stores, or other locations and to make informed decisions about when and where to reorder products.

In addition to managing inventory levels, the Inventory management module also provides businesses with tools to manage their purchasing process. This includes creating and managing purchase orders, tracking orders' status, and managing the receiving process. The module also integrates with the Accounts payable module, allowing businesses to process invoices and payments to their suppliers directly from the Inventory management module.

The Inventory management module also provides businesses with tools to manage and track inventory costs. This includes operating standard and actual costs, tracking the cost of goods sold, and generating detailed reports on inventory costs.

Another essential feature of the Inventory management module is managing and tracking serial and batch numbers for inventory items. This enables businesses to track the history of specific items and to manage their inventory based on particular batch or serial numbers. This feature is handy for companies that sell perishable or time-sensitive products, as it allows them to track their product age and expiration date.

The Inventory management module within Dynamics 365 SCM provides businesses with a comprehensive and integrated solution for managing their inventory. With its real-time data, purchasing and cost management tools, and tracking capabilities, companies can improve their inventory management processes, reduce costs, and increase customer satisfaction.

Procurement and sourcing

The Procurement and sourcing module in Dynamics 365 SCM is a comprehensive solution for managing businesses' procurement and sourcing processes. This module provides businesses with the tools to manage the entire procurement process, from identifying the need for products or services to negotiating contracts and making purchases.

One of the essential features of the Procurement and sourcing module is the ability to manage and track suppliers. This includes creating and managing supplier records, monitoring supplier performance, and evaluating suppliers based on cost, quality, and delivery.

Another essential feature of the Procurement and sourcing module is the ability to manage and track purchase requisitions. This includes creating and approving purchase requisitions, tracking the status of requisitions, and managing the approval process for requisitions.

The Procurement and sourcing module equips businesses with the tools to manage and monitor purchase orders. It facilitates the creation and management of purchase orders, tracks the progress of orders, and oversees the receiving process for orders. The module is also compatible with the Accounts payable module, enabling businesses to handle invoices and payments to suppliers directly from the Procurement and sourcing module.

Another essential feature of the Procurement and sourcing module is the ability to manage and track sourcing events. This includes creating and managing sourcing events, managing the bidding process for events, and following the events' results. The module also provides businesses with tools to manage and track sourcing strategies, evaluate supplier responses, and decide which suppliers to use for specific products or services.

The Procurement and sourcing module also allows businesses to generate detailed reports on procurement and sourcing activities. This includes information on purchase requisitions, purchase orders, contracts, product data, sourcing events, and supplier performance.

Master planning

The Master planning module in Dynamics 365 SCM is a powerful tool for businesses to plan and manage their production and inventory processes. This module allows businesses to create and manage production plans, track production schedules, and manage inventory levels.

One of the critical features of the Master planning module is the ability to create and manage production plans. This includes creating plans based on demand forecasts, tracking production schedules, and managing the production process. The module also provides businesses with tools to manage and track production orders, progress, and schedules.

Another essential feature of the Master planning module is the ability to manage and track inventory levels. This includes the ability to track inventory quantities, track inventory movements, and manage inventory levels. The module also provides businesses with tools to manage and track inventory costs, track inventory transactions, and manage inventory balances.

The Master planning module also allows businesses to manage and track demand forecasts. This includes creating and managing demand forecasts, tracking demand trends, and making informed decisions about inventory levels and production schedules. The module also provides businesses with tools to manage and track demand patterns, evaluate demand drivers, and make informed decisions about demand forecasts.

In addition to these core production and inventory functions, the Master planning module allows businesses to manage and track product data. This includes creating and managing product records, tracking product costs, and managing the product approval process. The module also provides businesses with tools to manage and track product changes, product versions, and the product release process.

The Master planning module also allows businesses to generate detailed reports on production and inventory activities. This includes information on production plans, production schedules, inventory levels, demand forecasts, and product data. The module also provides businesses with tools to generate custom reports, track production and inventory metrics, and make informed production and inventory process decisions.

In this book, we will review more details about the planning optimization feature, which allows the system to run using an add-in that runs outside the supply chain and brings more efficiency and real-time execution with the ability to process large volumes of data in a few minutes, providing your organization the flexibility and speed to make faster decisions.

Product information management

Product information forms the foundation of SCM and commerce operations across all sectors. Product information management aims to centralize and streamline product information, such as product definitions, attributes, documentation, and identification. A consistent and uniform method of product information sharing must be utilized to ensure an accurate representation of products. Within the different components of a business solution, specific product information and configuration are needed to effectively manage the business processes tied to individual products, product groups, or product categories.

One of the key benefits of the Product information management module in Dynamics 365 is the ability to manage product information in a centralized location. This enables businesses to ensure that all relevant stakeholders have access to the same product information, reducing the risk of errors and inconsistencies. In addition, the module provides a platform for managing product documentation, attributes, and identifiers, ensuring that all product information is accurate, consistent, and up to date.

Another important aspect of the Product information management module is its integration with other modules in Dynamics 365, such as Sales and marketing, Procurement and sourcing, and Inventory management. This enables businesses to streamline the flow of product information across various processes and systems and ensures that product information is updated and consistent across the organization.

The Product information management module also offers a number of customization options, allowing businesses to configure the module to meet their specific needs and requirements. For example, companies can configure the module to support product-specific information and configuration, enabling them to manage business processes related to individual products, product families, or product categories. Additionally, businesses can define custom attributes and identifiers and configure workflows and data validation rules to ensure that product information is accurate and up to date.

Overall, the Product information management module in Dynamics 365 finance and operations provides a comprehensive solution for managing product information and ensuring that product information is accurate, consistent, and up to date. By streamlining product information management and integrating with other modules in Dynamics 365, the Product Information management module helps businesses to improve the efficiency and accuracy of their supply chain and commerce operations.

Production control

The Dynamics 365 SCM Production control module is a powerful tool that allows manufacturers to streamline their production processes and improve efficiency. This module lets users plan, schedule, and manage production orders, monitor work in progress, and track inventory levels in real time. The module gives users visibility into their production processes, enabling them to make informed decisions about resource allocation, inventory management, and production scheduling. Additionally, the module allows manufacturers to automate repetitive tasks and reduce the risk of errors, saving time and money in the long run. With its comprehensive features and ease of use, the Production control module is a must-have for any manufacturer looking to improve their production processes.

Warehouse management

The Dynamics 365 SCM Warehouse management module is a comprehensive solution that enables businesses to manage their operations efficiently. This module allows businesses to optimize their warehouse layout, manage inventory levels, and streamline their order fulfillment processes. The module provides real-time visibility into warehouse operations, enabling businesses to track inventory movements, monitor order statuses, and identify potential bottlenecks in their processes.

One of the key features of the warehouse management module is its ability to automate many warehouse tasks, such as inventory counting, replenishment, and put away. This helps businesses save time and reduce the risk of errors while increasing their inventory levels' accuracy. The module also supports various warehouse configurations, such as bin locations, zones, and cross-docking, allowing businesses to customize their warehouse operations to suit their unique needs.

The Warehouse management module also integrates with other modules in Dynamics 365 SCM, such as the Production control and Transportation management modules, enabling businesses to manage their entire supply chain from a single platform. This gives businesses end-to-end visibility into their supply chain operations, enabling them to make informed decisions about inventory levels, production schedules, and transportation routes. With its comprehensive features and ease of use, the Warehouse management module is a valuable tool for any business looking to optimize its warehouse operations and improve its supply chain efficiency.

Transportation management

The Transportation management module in Dynamics 365 SCM is a powerful solution that allows businesses to manage their transportation operations efficiently. With this module, businesses can plan, execute, and monitor transportation orders, track shipments in real time, and optimize transportation routes to reduce costs and improve efficiency.

The Transportation management module provides businesses with end-to-end visibility into their transportation operations, enabling them to track shipments across multiple carriers and modes of transportation. This helps businesses identify potential issues and proactively avoid delays and other problems.

Additionally, the Transportation management module integrates with other modules in Dynamics 365 SCM, such as the warehouse and production control modules, enabling businesses to manage their entire supply chain from a single platform. This gives businesses a comprehensive view of their operations, enabling them to make informed decisions about transportation routes, production schedules, and inventory levels.

Summary

In this chapter, we have gained a deeper understanding of the powerful modules that Dynamics 365 SCM offers. From Asset management to Inventory management, Procurement and sourcing, and Master planning, each module provides a comprehensive solution for various aspects of supply chain operations.

With these modules, businesses can enhance their processes, lower their costs, and ensure high levels of customer satisfaction. By utilizing the various features and tools these modules offer, companies can streamline their operations and achieve their goals efficiently.

In the upcoming chapters, we will explore the capabilities of each core module of Dynamics 365 SCM and explore practical examples that can make a significant impact during your implementation journey. Through a detailed examination of these modules and hands-on examples, you will better understand how to effectively leverage the features of Dynamics 365 SCM to optimize your business operations.

If you are struggling with the supply chain in your daily business operations, this book will provide you with a comprehensive understanding of Dynamics 365 SCM and how to improve your business processes with clear guidelines on the main functionalities.

2

Working with Product Information Management

Have you ever wondered how businesses keep track of all their products across different locations and legal entities? Well, that's where product information management comes in! It's a process that centralizes all the information about a product, such as its definition, categorization, and identifiers, so that it can be easily accessed and used by various departments within the organization.

Product information is essential for supply chain and commerce applications, and it includes everything from product names and descriptions to images, units of measure, and translations. This information is used to manage specific product or category business processes.

When defining a product, several factors exist, such as product type, subtype, dimensions, and configuration models. Product data can be imported from various sources, such as product life cycle management or product information management systems, and exported to other business applications.

In this chapter, we will cover the following topics:

- Understanding and creating products and product variants
- Identifying product types
- Creating a BOM and understanding all its details
- Designing product configurations by constraining their options
- Creating and handling hazardous materials
- Working with direct delivery products and learning about their capabilities
- Understanding product configurations about costs and pricing

Creating and managing products and product variants

In product management, it's crucial to establish clear and consistent product definitions that transcend individual legal entities. These definitions encompass core values such as product number, type, and name, which are shared across the organization. While some of these core values, such as the search name, can be customized at the legal entity level, other key attributes remain unchanged, forming the foundation of the product definition.

The approval process is super important when it comes to handling different versions of a product and making sure they're available within different parts of a company. This process is helped along by a release function, which lets users pick products that have different versions and make them available in one or more parts of the company. Thanks to this handy feature, companies can easily manage how different versions of a product are spread out and make sure they're available in the markets where they're needed.

Let's look at a couple of examples of product variants utilization in Dynamics 365 Supply Chain Management.

Clothing

Product: T-shirt

Variants:

Size: Small, medium, large, XL

Color: red, blue, green, black

Utilization

A customer wants to buy a medium-sized blue T-shirt. The retailer can use the product variant feature instead of having a separate product for each combination. The retailer can easily track inventory for each size and color combination, manage replenishments based on sales of specific variants, and offer promotions on specific sizes or colors.

Electronics manufacturer

Product: Smartphone

Variants:

Storage: 64 GB, 128 GB, 256 GB

Color: Silver, Gold, Space Grey

Utilization

A customer is interested in purchasing a 128 GB Gold smartphone. Using Dynamics 365 Supply Chain Management, the manufacturer can manage production runs based on the demand for specific variants. They can also analyze which variants are more popular and adjust their production and marketing strategies accordingly.

To further streamline the product management process, a decentralized approach is adopted. This enables the creation and maintenance of products directly from the **Released Products** page within the **Product Information Management** module. It's important to note that users must possess the necessary security role to carry out these actions. Specifically, these responsibilities are included in the Product Designer and Product Design Manager roles. By granting the appropriate access and permissions, organizations can empower their teams to effectively create and manage products, promoting a decentralized and agile product management approach.

When a product is created within a specific legal entity, it is worth mentioning that an automatic core product definition is generated in the shared products repository. This ensures that the product is accurately represented and shared across the organization, thereby maintaining consistency and eliminating redundant efforts.

Organizations can optimize their product management efforts by establishing clear product definitions, leveraging the authorization process, and adopting a decentralized approach to product creation and maintenance. This streamlined process enhances efficiency, promotes collaboration across legal entities, and fosters effective product design and distribution throughout the organization.

In Dynamics 365 Supply Chain Management, we can define a product by adding the following details:

- First, we need to define the product type, differentiating if it is an item or a service.
- The second important definition is distinguishing whether it is a product or a product master. The difference between them is that a product master will create product variants related to that product. For example, a T-shirt will have different sizes and colors. With a product master, we can define these variants under the same product number.

We can also define the categorization of the product – for example, a purchase category for office supplies.

The unit of measure of the product is an important definition to control in which unit the product will be handled, such as units, kilograms, liters, ounces, feet, and so on. We can also define the unit conversion if needed. This lets us know how many ounces a unit of this item has.

If the product is traded in other countries, we can input translations for the name and descriptions. This will allow documents to be printed in other languages. The system will allow us to upload an image or miniature of the product shown in related applications or documents printed on the system.

Also, we need to define the product variant model if we define a product master as the product type. This will include dimensions and dimension groups, the nomenclature of the variant, and the configuration model if needed. We will review these concepts later in this chapter.

It's important to note that product information changes frequently in dynamic organizations, so maintaining accurate and up-to-date data is crucial for business success.

Product data and sources

Now that we know how important it is to keep track of product information, let's talk about how that information is distributed and managed.

Firstly, product data can be created and managed within Supply Chain Management. But if you already have product information in other systems, such as product life cycle or product data management, there is no need to worry! You can import that data into Supply Chain Management too.

When working with multiple instances of Supply Chain Management, one instance is usually designated as the "master" for all the other instances. This makes it easier to manage product data across different locations.

Supply Chain Management also lets you use a tool called Microsoft Dataverse to share product data across different applications. You can export your product definitions from Supply Chain Management to Dataverse and then use that data to provision other business applications, such as **Dynamics 365 Sales**.

It's important to remember that product information constantly changes in dynamic and agile organizations. That's why it's critical to maintain accurate and up-to-date data. It's a business process that requires attention and effort to ensure your product information stays reliable and valuable.

Product masters and product variants

When it comes to creating products that meet customer demands quickly, being agile is key. To do this, product definitions are used to specify a set of generic products rather than distinct ones. Within Supply Chain Management, these generic products are called product masters.

Product masters encompass the guidelines and definitions that dictate the description and behavior of individual products across diverse business operations. These definitions enable the creation of unique products, referred to as product variants.

Products in the master list are linked to specific dimension groups and configurations, such as color, size, style, and configuration, to ensure precise implementation of business rules. This makes it easy for users to find and identify the products they need.

Configuration technologies for product customization

When it comes to configuring products to meet specific requirements, you have the option to choose among three different configuration technologies. Each technology offers distinct advantages based on your business needs. It is crucial to select the appropriate configuration technology during the implementation of Supply Chain Management since transitioning from one model to another after implementation is not feasible. Let's explore these technologies.

Predefined variants

The predefined variants configuration technology allows you to define product dimensions, such as color, style, and size, which determine the available options for customization. By specifying valid combinations of dimensions, unique product variants are created. This technology is suitable for businesses looking to offer predefined choices to customers, ensuring consistent and distinct product options.

Dimension-based configuration

The technology of dimension-based configuration is frequently utilized in production environments. This technique allows the configuration dimension to establish the **Bill of Materials** (**BOMs**). When a particular configuration is chosen, the system leverages the relevant subset of BOM lines for that configuration for strategizing and manufacturing. This method is often termed a universal BOM, given its use of a common BOM for all product configurations. It proves advantageous when you're overseeing intricate production procedures with diverse components.

Constraint-based configuration

The technology of constraint-based configuration employs a product configuration model to encapsulate all potential characteristics and elements needed to detail every product variant within a unified model. Attribute combinations are outlined using standard expressions or table-based limitations. Configuration models and configurators play a pivotal role in managing product information across a multitude of sectors. This technology is invaluable when navigating complex product configurations and facilitates extensive customization options.

Choosing the right configuration technology for your business process is vital to ensuring efficient and accurate product customization. Carefully consider your industry's unique requirements and the flexibility needed to meet customer demands. By making an informed decision, you can effectively enhance your Supply Chain Management implementation and deliver tailored products.

Now that we understand the concept of the products and their variants, let's start by configuring these options in Dynamics.

The Product Variant Model Definition workspace

The Product Variant Model Definition workspace serves as a comprehensive hub for managing product masters. It provides an overview of the product variants and their status in terms of release to specific legal entities. This workspace is designed to facilitate efficient monitoring and maintenance of released products.

By utilizing the Product Variant Model Definition workspace, organizations can effectively handle the release and maintenance of products, ensuring seamless coordination with specific legal entities and their unique requirements.

Let's review some more specific concepts related to products, especially at the legal entity level.

Released products

Products approved for distribution to a particular legal entity are released products. These products can be released individually or in bulk to one or multiple legal entities simultaneously. To cater to the specific requirements of each legal entity, additional properties and attributes may need to be assigned.

The Released Product Maintenance workspace

The Released Product Maintenance workspace empowers users to monitor and complete the necessary tasks associated with recently released products. It offers a centralized location to track and manage released products across various legal entities or sub-organizations within a legal entity. This workspace ensures streamlined released-product management, enabling efficient maintenance and monitoring processes.

Configuring the Released Product Maintenance workspace

To customize the Released Product Maintenance workspace and make it more efficient for your daily job, perform the following steps. By doing so, you will make it more friendly and effective:

1. **Customize the workspace**: Start by customizing the **Released Product Maintenance** workspace to your liking. This can be done by accessing the **Configure My Workspace** option from the menu.

2. **Select a category**: Choose a category hierarchy and a category that aligns with your specific needs. This will filter the workspace accordingly.

3. **Define time fences**: Set time fences, in days, for **Recently Released Products** and **Stopped Released Products**. This will help adjust the relevant product data within the workspace.

4. **Review product change cases**: Within the workspace, locate the list of product change cases related to products within the selected category hierarchy that are not yet completed or closed.

5. **Check the Recently Released list**: Look at the **Recently Released** list, which displays products released within the time fence you set in the workspace configuration.

6. **Validate items**: Note that each item in the list undergoes validation, and the validation status is presented. This status indicates whether the necessary configurations for the corresponding legal entity have been completed.

7. **Access pages for configuration**: From the list, navigate to various pages to complete the necessary product configurations. These pages include **Released Product Details**, **Product Attribute Maintenance**, **Product Category Maintenance**, **Default Order Settings**, and **Text Translations**.

8. **Complete configurations**: Upon directly accessing these pages from the list, efficiently fulfill the required configurations for the product, ensuring that the necessary adjustments are made for the specific legal entity.

By utilizing the configuration options available in the Released Product Maintenance workspace, you can tailor the workspace to your preferences, filter products based on category hierarchies, define time fences, and easily access relevant pages to complete product configurations. This empowers you to efficiently manage and configure released products, ensuring that the necessary adjustments are made to meet the requirements of the corresponding legal entities.

Manually creating a newly released product

Based on the company's operational procedures and regulations that dictate the use of this feature, you can manually generate a freshly launched product in one go. This functionality facilitates the development of an entirely new product and instantaneously releases it to the existing legal entity. To kick-start the creation process, you can opt to click on **Released Products** within the **Released Product Maintenance** workspace or on the **Released Product List** page:

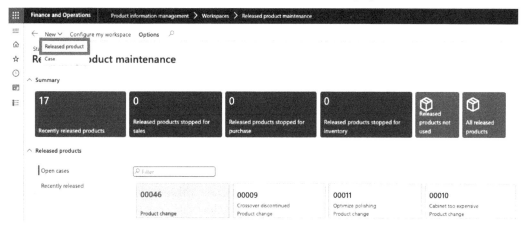

Figure 2.1 – Newly released product

Understanding product types in supply chain management

Let's start by explaining some definitions before creating our first product. In the realm of Dynamics 365 Supply Chain Management, products can be categorized into two distinct types:

- **Item**: Items are purchased products that can be used for consumption, distribution, reselling, or as components to produce other manufactured items (BOM). These products are crucial in supply chain operations, fulfilling various purposes and meeting customer demands.

- **Service**: Services are products that are utilized to quantify hourly services or other non-tangible offerings. These products differ from physical items as they represent intangible deliverables that are part of the service-oriented aspects of a business.

In *Figure 2.2*, we can identify the types we can utilize when we create a new release product:

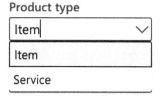

Figure 2.2 – Product types

After defining the product type, it is mandatory to define the product subtype. There are two distinct subtypes:

- **Product**: This refers to a uniquely distinguishable product that functions as the base model. It is characteristically unchangeable, meaning no additional product dimensions can be appended to its definition.

- **Product Master**: This comprehensive guide contains the definitions and regulations that outline how unique products are portrayed and operate within business procedures. From these foundational principles, unique products or product variants can be derived.

In Dynamics 365 Supply Chain Management, a Product Master is a crucial element that helps establish business rules and protocols. It is connected to a group of product characteristics and a configuration technology. These characteristics, such as color, size, style, and configuration, are used in Dynamics 365 Supply Chain Management to define and track how specific products behave. These characteristics make it easier for users to search for and identify products.

Think of a Product Master as a blueprint or prototype for different versions of a product. The different versions, also known as variants, can be pre-defined or created on the spot during sales situations using a product configurator. A Product Master is linked to one or more product characteristics, allowing for flexibility and customization:

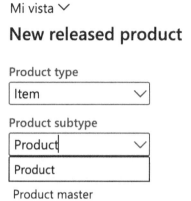

Figure 2.3 – Product subtype

Finally, as we've explained, if we define the product as Product Master, it is mandatory to define the product variants; let's review what these are:

- **Product variants**: A product variant is determined by the selected configuration technology. This variant can either be pre-established using the product dimensions of its parent product, the Master Product, or be configured with the assistance of a product configuration tool.

- **Product creation**: Let's review the most important steps to follow during the product creation process; formulating a new product entails the subsequent steps:

    I.   Design and detail the product.

    II.   Launch the product to legal entities.

    III.   Specify data particular to the legal entity.

When generating a new product definition, the primary attributes to include are the type and subtype.

To create released products, navigate to **Product Information Management** > **Products** > **Released Products**.

Product Type discerns whether a product is a tangible object (item) or an intangible service, while the subtype further classifies the product.

When we create a new release product, this will be the first field we must select based on the aforementioned criteria:

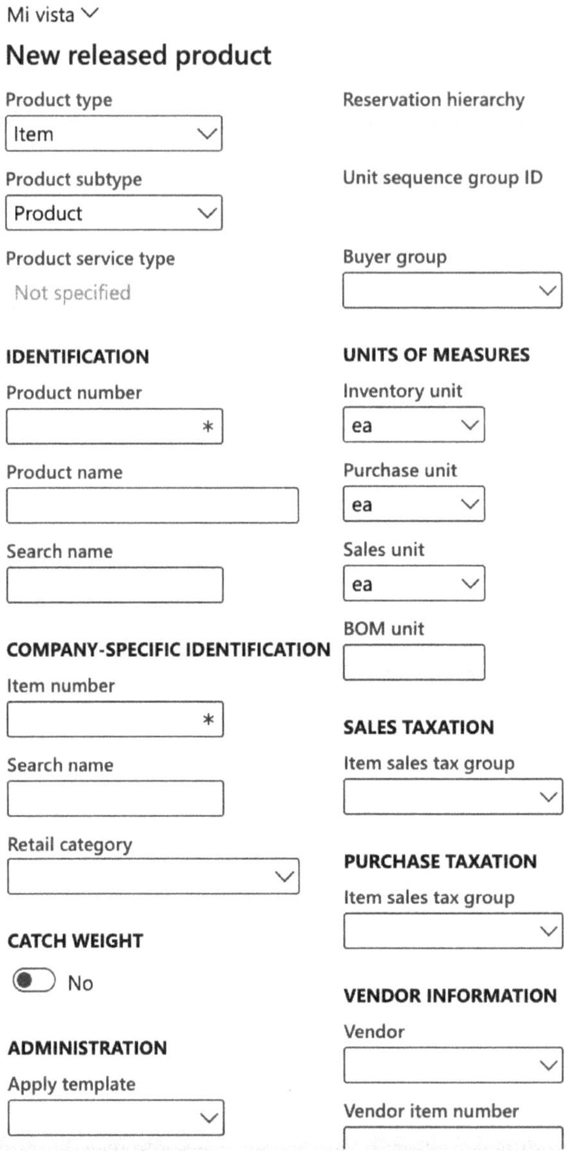

Mi vista ⌄

New released product

Product type

| Item   ⌄ |

Product subtype

| Product   ⌄ |

Product service type

Not specified

IDENTIFICATION

Product number

| * |

Product name

| |

Search name

| |

COMPANY-SPECIFIC IDENTIFICATION

Item number

| * |

Search name

| |

Retail category

| ⌄ |

CATCH WEIGHT

◉ No

ADMINISTRATION

Apply template

| ⌄ |

Reservation hierarchy

Unit sequence group ID

Buyer group

| ⌄ |

UNITS OF MEASURES

Inventory unit

| ea   ⌄ |

Purchase unit

| ea   ⌄ |

Sales unit

| ea   ⌄ |

BOM unit

| |

SALES TAXATION

Item sales tax group

| ⌄ |

PURCHASE TAXATION

Item sales tax group

| ⌄ |

VENDOR INFORMATION

Vendor

| ⌄ |

Vendor item number

| |

Figure 2.4 – The New released product dialogue

Product translation

The **Translation** feature allows for multilingual product descriptions. You can input product names and descriptions in numerous languages in this section. It's important to note that only the product number is mandatory, while the product name and description are voluntary. To access the **Translation** section, click the **Translation** button in the action pane of any product-related page or list.

Product translations primarily serve the purpose of being utilized in external documents. In contrast, the data values are always displayed in the system's default language when viewing product-associated pages and lists:

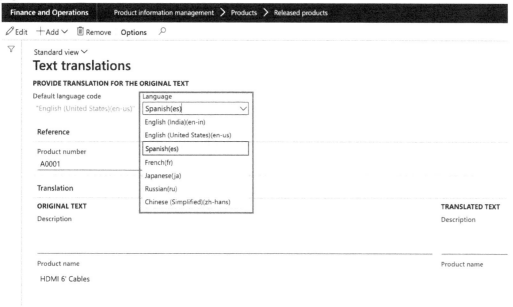

Figure 2.5 – Product translations

For external documents, the product name will appear in the company's chosen language or the customer's or vendor's preferred language.

Now that we've covered the product definition, let's discuss using a product in more than one legal entity.

Product setup authorization within a legal entity

Before you can use a Master Product in a transaction such as a sales or purchase order, you need to make sure the Master Product and at least one of its versions are available in the relevant parts of the company. This is especially important when the configuration technology is used to predefine versions. When it's time to release the product, there are many different combinations you can choose from to distribute to one or more parts of the company:

- You can release individual products or groups of products
- You can release a single version of a product or multiple versions
- You can release the product to one legal entity or several

The product release process allows users in the company to share product definitions with different parts of the organization. By releasing a product or a Master Product, you're connecting it to a specific part of the company and permitting it to be used in that area.

To proceed, navigate to **Product Information Management** > **Products** > **All Products and Master Products**. Upon clicking the **Release Products** button, select one or multiple products that you aim to authorize for one or more legal entities. This will allow you to utilize the product in processes such as inventory management, purchasing, sales, and production:

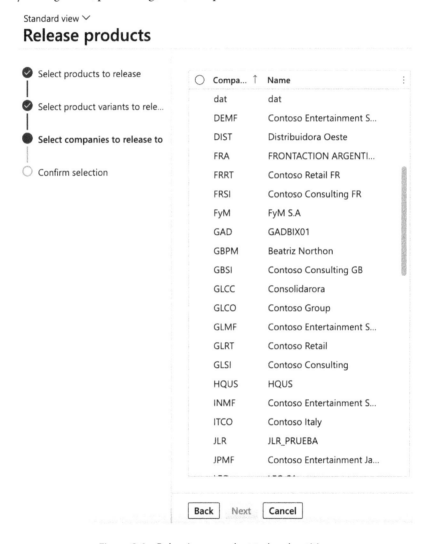

Figure 2.6 – Releasing a product to legal entities

Once a product has been released, we can finish by setting its final details.

Finalizing released products

After a product's release to a legal entity, finalizing its definition is paramount before it can be incorporated into transactions such as sales orders or purchase orders. The product definition needs to be fully completed in every legal entity to which it has been released. You can click on the **Validate** button in the product's action pane to check the finalization status of the product.

To complete a product, you need to provide some important information. You can fill in these fields by entering the details manually or using a pre-designed template.

The four main setups for a product to be set up are as follows:

- **Item model groups**: This defines how the item will be processed. Here, we set up whether the item is a stocked product or not and how to manage its costs by defining the inventory model.

  This setup is critical in terms of definitions; once you have defined it, it can't be changed if any transactions with the item exist:

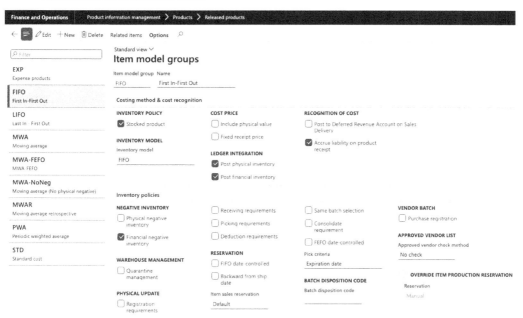

Figure 2.7 – Item model groups setup

- **Item groups**: This groups the item and defines its accounting on each transaction of every model – for example, which accounts will be used when the item is sold:

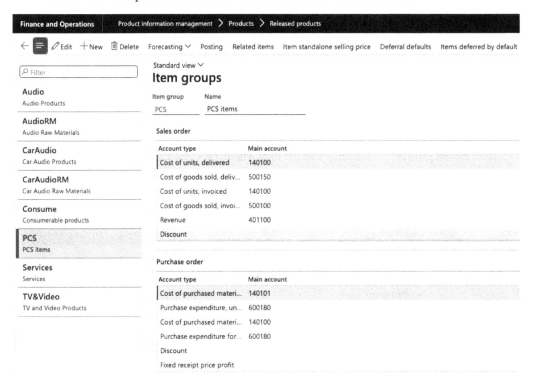

Figure 2.8 – Item groups setup

Storage dimension groups (if not already specified): Specify the dimensions related to storing the product, such as location or shelf. Also, one of the key setups here is if the items contained under this storage dimension group use a warehouse management process.

Deciding if the item will use WMS or will be a standard item is another decision to make before performing transactions with the items:

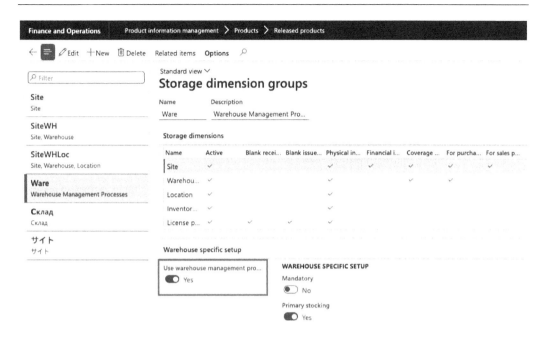

Figure 2.9 – Storage dimension groups setup

- **Tracking dimension groups** (if not already specified): Define the dimensions used for tracking the product, such as serial number or batch.

  Defining the tracking dimension group is another fundamental decision that must be made before any transactions with the item occur:

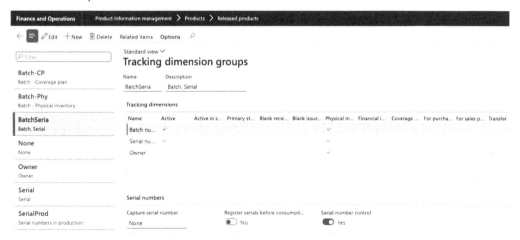

Figure 2.10 – Tracking dimension groups setup

The following are some other important setups:

- **Sales, purchase, inventory, bill of materials (BOM) units**: Determine the units of measurement used for sales, purchases, inventory management, and creating the bill of materials
- **Reservation hierarchy** (if using warehouse management procedures): Set up the hierarchy to manage inventory reservations effectively
- **Unit sequence group ID** (if using warehouse management procedures): Define the sequence group for units to maintain proper order in the warehouse

On the **Product Details** page, you'll find various tabs where you can enter specific information about each module and customize their settings:

- In the **General** tab, we can add or review any additional data related to the product.
- The **Purchase** tab lets us define details about the procurement process, such as pricing, and discounts on the purchase orders.
- The **Promote** tab controls whether the product can be linked to a coupon in commerce functions.
- The **Deliver** tab works with features such as Direct Delivery and applies specific rules for packaging the product.
- The **Sell** tab lets us define details about the sales process, such as pricing, and discounts on the sales orders.
- The **Manage Inventory** tabs let us define details about physical dimensions, handling and packaging requirements, and how the item is processed in the inventory management module.
- The **Engineer** tab contains all the detailed information about the manufacturing process, such as the item's production type, manufacturing measurements, and production specification.
- The **Plan** tab lets us associate the product with a coverage group that will be handled by the master planning module.
- The **Manage Projects** tab lets us associate the product with a project category that will be tracked by the project management and accounting module.
- The **Manage Cost** tab reviews all the cost-related information, such as cost price and cost group, and defines the ABC classification.
- The **Financial Dimensions** tab defines the default item financial dimensions that will be used when this product is accounted.
- The **Warehouse** tab relates to the warehouse management module and lets us set up the parameters specifically for products stored in warehouses managed by the Warehouse Management module.
- The **Retail** tab enables and sets values for the product's use within the Retail module.

- The **Transportation** tab relates to the Transportation Management module to enable this process for the product.

- The **Product Variants** tab is only applicable to Product Masters. You can specify default values for product dimensions such as size, color, style, and configuration, making it easier to manage different product versions.

> **Note**
> Once you've defined the unit of measure for an item, this can't be changed after you perform transactions in the system with the item. Defining the correct unit of measure is a crucial decision and needs to be planned carefully.

Country of origin classification

For enterprises that operate internationally, it's often necessary to provide details about the origin of the products they deal with. A specific field is available in the **Released Products** table to indicate the country of origin. You can find this under **Product Information Management** > **Products** > **Released Products** in the **Foreign trade** FastTab:

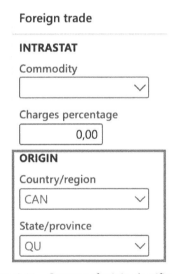

Figure 2.11 – Country of origin classification

Figure 2.6 demonstrates a rule that designates a specific product's destination and origin countries. This rule can be accessed via **Product Information Management** > **Setup** > **Product Compliance** > **Country of Origin** > **Country of Origin Rules**.

Occasionally, vendors supply a certificate (with an expiry date and certificate number) to their clientele. Armed with this documented information, customers can generate the requisite shipping documentation. Moreover, this data enables the customer to coordinate with suppliers when a certificate nears expiration.

Additionally, this data can assist a seller in verifying any specific details about a product headed to a country with requirements or tariffs, before concluding a sale.

Managing hazardous material product information

To ensure compliance with shipping and transport regulations, businesses involved in shipping hazardous materials must adhere to specific paperwork requirements. These additional documents are essential for classifying and managing dangerous goods during shipping. To streamline this task, Dynamics 365 Supply Chain Management provides a valuable feature known as the **hazardous materials** function.

This feature allows customers to store and access pertinent information about their released items conveniently. This stored information plays a crucial role in facilitating the preparation of accurate and comprehensive shipping documentation. However, it's important to note that while Dynamics 365 Supply Chain Management is a helpful tool in generating the required documents, organizations must establish robust processes and procedures for effectively managing the shipping of dangerous goods. By combining the power of Dynamics 365 and well-defined internal protocols, businesses can maintain compliance, enhance operational efficiency, and ensure the safe transportation of hazardous materials.

The first step here is to do the proper setup; it's crucial to maintain additional information about these products. This not only aids in compliance with regulations regarding shipping and handling but also ensures safety and efficiency. Additional setup options for these parameters can be found under **Product Information Management** > **Products** > **Released Products** in the **Manage Inventory** action tab:

Figure 2.12 – The Item hazardous material option

Documentation for shipping hazardous materials

The fields displayed on the **Released Products** screen can be configured under the **Hazardous material shipping documentation** menu item:

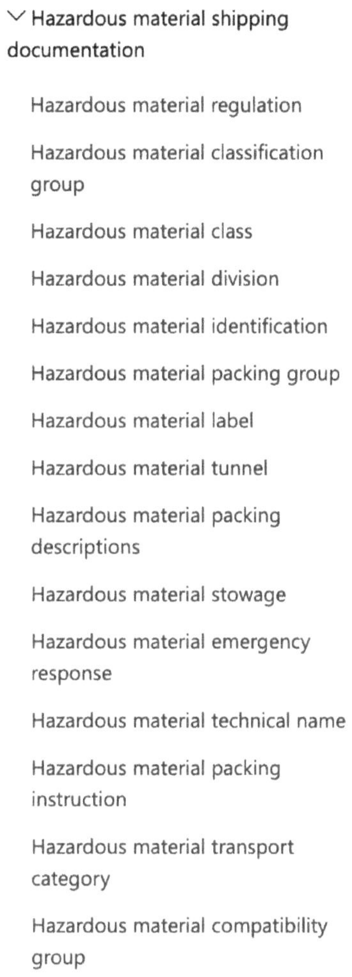

∨ Hazardous material shipping
documentation

    Hazardous material regulation

    Hazardous material classification
    group

    Hazardous material class

    Hazardous material division

    Hazardous material identification

    Hazardous material packing group

    Hazardous material label

    Hazardous material tunnel

    Hazardous material packing
    descriptions

    Hazardous material stowage

    Hazardous material emergency
    response

    Hazardous material technical name

    Hazardous material packing
    instruction

    Hazardous material transport
    category

    Hazardous material compatibility
    group

Figure 2.13 – The Hazardous material shipping documentation options

The key options in this list are as follows:

- **Hazardous material label**: This field specifies what's printed on the shipping label

- **Hazardous material identification**: This provides information about the nature of the hazardous material

- **Emergency response**: This field guides the correct response if the material interacts with a person or other items, helping prevent or mitigate damage

- **Hazardous material packing instructions**: This includes special packing instructions related to the hazardous material to ensure safe transportation and handling

Creating product masters with variants

Product dimensions, as opposed to product attributes, allow their values to be tracked across major processes, such as cost evaluation, inventory management, and analytical purposes. While product attributes can be linked with products and product masters, product dimensions are paired with product masters (excluding those configured using the **Constraint-based configuration** option) as they contribute to the distinctiveness of a product master's variations.

When creating a product master, you can decide which product dimensions are mandatory by choosing the corresponding product dimension group. To create product dimension groups, navigate to **Product Information Management > Setup > Dimension and Variant Groups > Product dimension groups**:

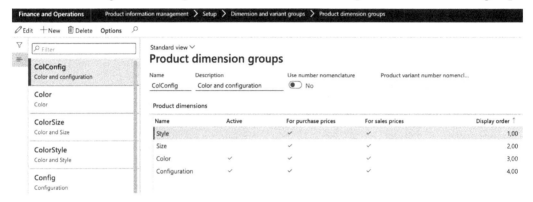

Figure 2.14 – The Product dimension groups screen

As product dimensions contribute to the uniqueness of a variant, several rules are to be followed:

- The dimension must be specified during the creation of product transactions, such as when a purchase or sales order line is initiated.

- The stipulated dimension is specific to the product transaction and cannot be modified – either wholly or partially – for related inventory transactions upon physical issue or receipt.

- Products are always reserved per each dimension. Reservations for product dimensions other than those specified in the active product transaction are not permitted.

Conceptualizing configurable products

To set up configurable products, access the **Product Information Management** section and navigate to **Products > Released Products > New**. This allows you to design products with different variations. When working with product masters, it's important to define how variations of a master product are created. Often, certain mandatory attributes need to be specified to generate a new variation.

The configuration technology, which is applied to the product master, determines how such variations are defined:

- **Predefined variant**: By selecting this option, you can model the product according to its dimensions, such as color, configuration, and size. This is the only method that enables you to directly set up product variants and allows for any combination of dimensions.

- **Dimension-based configuration**: With this technology, you can create different product variations by selecting specific values for the product dimensions. You can freely choose any combination of dimensions to make your desired variations.

- **Constraint-based configuration**: To use the Product Configurator, the product must have this mode enabled. This option can be selected if the **Configuration** feature is enabled for the product dimension group and no other product dimensions are activated:

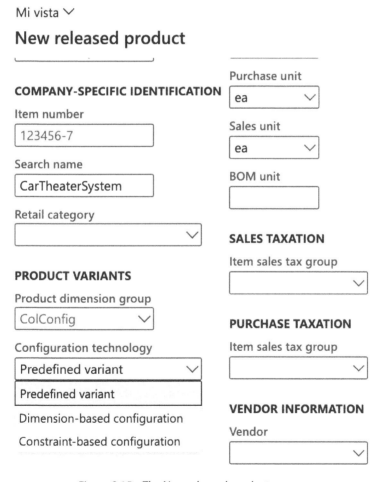

Figure 2.15 – The New released product screen

Setting up product masters and predefined product variants

When utilizing the predefined variant configuration technology, the uniqueness of each variant comes from the combination of one or more product dimensions applied to it.

Let's take the example of the USMF company, which sells refrigerators in different colors. Each color represents a specific product variant, containing the relevant details for that particular product. On the other hand, the product master retains default values that are common across all refrigerator models.

In the USMF company, you have the flexibility to create a released product as either a standalone product or as a product master, allowing you to define predefined variants.

The dimension group associated with the product master determines which product dimensions are mandatory when defining its variant(s). Once you select a product dimension group and create the initial product variant or assign dimension values, those choices become fixed and cannot be changed afterward:

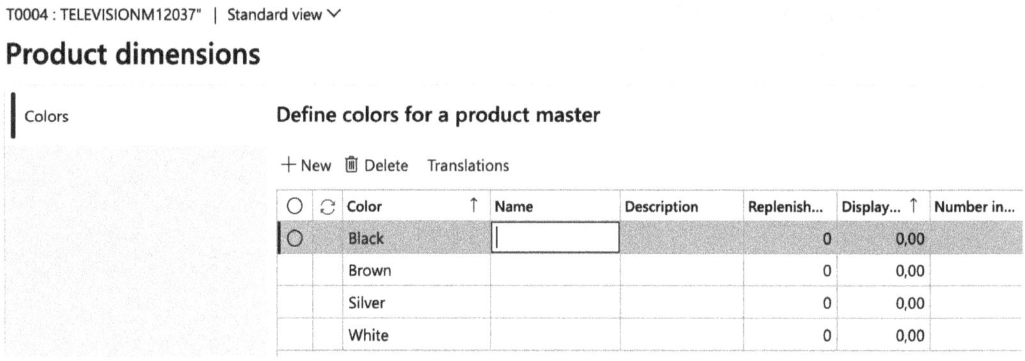

Figure 2.16 – The Product dimensions form

As shown in *Figure 2.11*, we can define each variant for a product dimension, on the related group for the item.

Product master and dimension-based configured product variants

Much like the predefined variants configuration technology, dimension-based configuration calls for using one or more product dimensions. The major advantage of this method is the ability to establish configuration rules and maintain configurations of **Bill of Materials** (**BOM**), simplifying the product configuration process during sales orders:

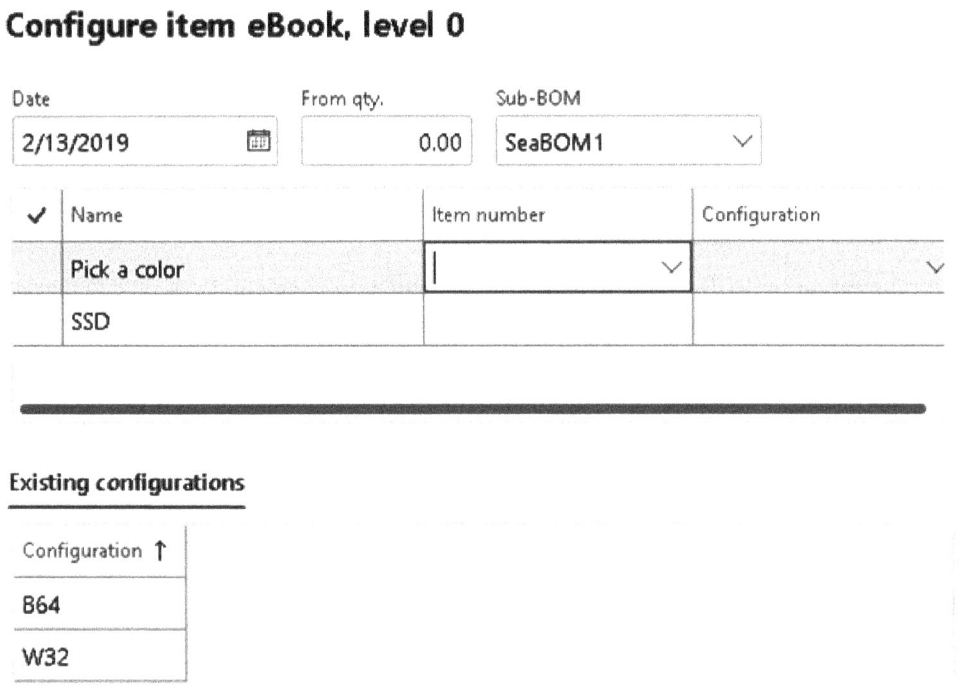

Configure item eBook, level 0

Date	From qty.	Sub-BOM
2/13/2019 📅	0.00	SeaBOM1 ∨

✓	Name	Item number	Configuration
	Pick a color	∣ ∨	∨
	SSD		

Existing configurations

Configuration ↑
B64
W32

Figure 2.17 – Defining a variant from a sales order

Figure 2.13 shows how we define a variant from a sales order, where we previously created the rules on which options we can select in this process. This example shows an SDD card sales process where we define a color and memory size. With dimension-based configuration, we can define that when the sales clerk selects different colors, different items in the BOM of the manufactured item will be used depending on that selection.

Dimension-based product configuration

Dimension-based product configuration offers a straightforward approach for deriving numerous product variants from a singular product master and its BOM. It is grounded in the following foundational concepts:

- **Product masters**: To initiate product configuration, the product master is the essential first step. With dimension-based product configuration, both the product master equipped with this technology and a product dimension group that includes the configuration dimension are imperative.

- **Configuration product dimension**: This feature allows for the distinction of product variations within a product master through dimension-based configuration. By entering a configuration dimension value, the user can identify and select specific product variants.

- **Configuration groups**: A central repository stores these groups that apply to all dimension-based product configuration models. They are linked to specific lines in the BOM and make sure that only one line from a group can be chosen for a single product variant.

- **BOM**: The BOM must be used to create product configurations based on dimensions. It must list all individual products that can be utilized in any variant of the product. Each line of the BOM must be linked to a configuration group, and any line that doesn't belong to a group must be included in all product variants.

- **Configuration route**: The order in which the configuration groups are presented to the user during product configuration is determined through the configuration route.

- **Configuration rules**: To ensure proper product configuration, it is crucial to follow these rules that dictate whether a product in one group of the BOM must require or exclude a product in another group within the same BOM.

In dimension-based configured products, the selection and creation of a variant for a product master are based on the choice made by the sales order taker, following the defined configuration rules.

Product configuration

A robust feature of Dynamics 365 Supply Chain Management, the product configuration toolset includes an interactive user interface that visually displays the product configuration model's architecture. It also offers a declarative constraint syntax that eliminates the need for traditional compilation, enabling companies to easily adopt configuration practices.

By using the product configurator, you can create and maintain configuration models.

For more information, see *Get started with product configuration in Dynamics 365 Supply Chain Management (*`https://learn.microsoft.com/en-us/training/modules/get-started-product-configuration-dyn365-supply-chain-mgmt/`*).*

Creating and managing product states in the life cycle of a product

Every product experiences a unique journey, embarking on a voyage from inception, through active use, culminating in its eventual sunset. Establishing these phases allows you to dictate which transactions – be it sales orders, purchase orders, or production orders – are permitted, and which are blocked.

The evolution of products, particularly in engineering, is intrinsically intertwined with the product's engineering version. Imagine orchestrating a scenario that utilizes a product dimension alongside a version – this setting enables you to use the life cycle state as a roadmap, guiding which transactions are permissible for each distinct version.

Establishing product life cycle states

To activate life cycle states, navigate to **Engineering Change Management** > **Setup** > **Product Lifecycle State**. Choose **New** to breathe life into a fresh life cycle or **Edit** to recalibrate the settings of existing states. In this form, you will find the following configurations:

- **Header**: Here, you need to add the name, the description, and the LifeState.

- **General FastTab**: This area presents two selections:

  I. **Default when released to legal entity**: Typically, this is for conventional products. You should choose **Yes** if you want the life cycle state to govern products when they're unveiled to legal entities. Select **No** if you plan to apply the life cycle state manually at a later stage. For engineering products, this option is moot, as their life cycle is cemented upon assignment to an engineering change category.

  II. **Is active for planning**: Choosing **Yes** for this function signifies that it will factor in products that reside within this life cycle state when performing computations for master planning and BOM levels. If **No** is your choice, products inhabiting this state will be excluded from these calculations:

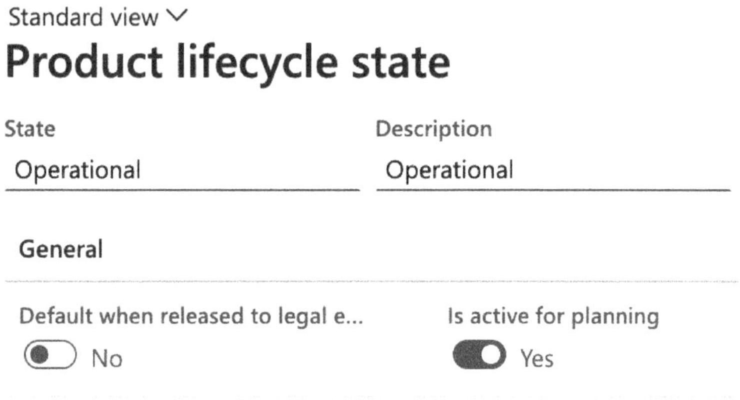

Standard view ∨

Product lifecycle state

State

Operational

Description

Operational

General

Default when released to legal e...

◉ No

Is active for planning

◉ Yes

Figure 2.18 – The Product lifecycle state form

Situated within the **Enabled Business Processes** FastTab, you'll find the **Process** column, which enumerates a pre-defined selection of potential business operations. The **Process area** column carries a default value that can be revised, though such a modification doesn't yield any tangible impact.

The **Policy** column introduces three options to choose from:

- **Enabled**: This selection greenlights the corresponding business operation.

- **Blocked**: If this is chosen, the specified business operation is barred. Any attempt to proceed with this operation will be halted by the system, exhibiting an error message. An illustration of this scenario would be an attempt to issue a purchase order on an item that's been classified as obsolete.

- **Enabled with Warning**: Opting for this introduces a cautionary measure. The system will flash a warning for certain circumstances, such as a production order employing a product that is currently in the design phase:

Enabled business processes

	Process	Process area	Policy
✓	Sales order	Sales ⌄	Blocked ⌄
	Sales quotation	Sales	Blocked
	WBS estimate for items	Planning	Blocked
✓	Item forecast	Planning	Enabled with warning
	Purchase order	Purchasing	Enabled
	Request for quote	Purchasing	Enabled
	Inventory transfer	Inventory	Enabled

Figure 2.19 – Enabled business processes

Product templates

Product templates serve as vital tools, enabling seamless duplication of information from a released product to other chosen released products. These templates are instrumental in streamlining the process of establishing legal entity-specific data for products, particularly when numerous values are identical across different products:

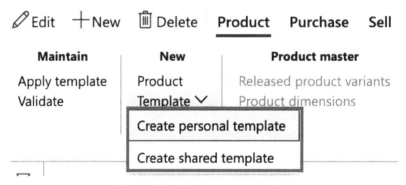

Figure 2.20 – New product template

Two categories of templates are at your disposal: personal templates and shared templates. A personal template serves as an exclusive tool for the creator, accessible only to the user who brought the template into existence. On the other hand, shared templates broaden the scope of accessibility, being available to any user within the system.

Designing and creating a BOM

A BOM is a list of all the important components needed to make a product. These components can include raw materials, partially finished items, or ingredients. Sometimes, even services can be included in a BOM. However, the main purpose of a BOM is to outline the materials required. When combined with a production plan that details the steps and resources needed to make the product, the BOM helps calculate the estimated cost of the product.

In this section, you will learn how to create BOMs and different versions of them using the BOM designer in Dynamics 365 Supply Chain Management.

You will need the following preconditions:

- Proficiency in supply chain management concepts
- Comprehension of how to generate products in Dynamics 365 Supply Chain Management
- Familiarity with inventory procedures within Dynamics 365 Supply Chain Management

Working with the BOM designer

The BOM Designer is a tool within Dynamics 365 Supply Chain Management that allows users to create and manage BOMs effectively. It provides a user-friendly interface and a range of features to simplify the process of defining and maintaining BOMs for various products. With the BOM Designer, users can easily add or remove components, specify quantities, define routing operations, and incorporate any necessary resources or services required for production. The tool helps streamline the creation of BOMs, ensuring accurate documentation of the materials and processes needed to manufacture a product.

Creating a BOM with the BOM designer

When you access the **Designer** page via the **Released Products** page, it reveals the hierarchy of active and approved BOMs for the chosen item, its default order site, and the current date. You can get there by going to **Product Information Management** > **Products** > **Released Products** > **Engineer** > **BOM** > **Designer**.

The BOM Designer consists of two main segments:

- **Tree**: This view provides a hierarchical view of the BOM structure.
- **Details**: This section offers detailed information on selected data. Selecting a node in the **Tree** view refreshes the FastTabs in the **Details** section to reflect that node, displaying relevant BOM line details, item data, BOM header, related route, and associated route operations.

The BOM Designer serves as a versatile tool for the following aspects:

- Constructing new BOM versions or modifying existing ones

- Editing and erasing BOM lines

- Validating BOMs for potential errors, such as BOM circularity

- Determining which BOM versions (if any) are linked to the selected BOM

- Tracking site assignments for BOM versions

- Printing BOMs and BOM lines for the chosen BOM

- Confirming the site linked to the BOM line

- Adding and editing BOMs and BOM lines

BOM lines or BOM functions can be utilized to alter BOM lines or the BOM itself. The functions available depend on the type of node selected in the tree. These functions can include editing BOM line attributes, deleting or adding BOM lines, creating new BOM versions, and more.

Here's a brief overview of the BOM creation process:

1. Create all products encompassed within all BOM versions that include the BOM itself.

2. Generate a BOM.

3. Construct BOM version(s), and then approve and activate them. This can be done either before or after adding the component products.

4. Include products to specify which items should be encompassed in the BOM.

5. If required, create configurations and associated rules for the BOM.

6. Generate site-specific BOMs/routes to allow for automatic selection of the appropriate BOM and route version, as well as item dimensions, when working with multiple sites.

Creating a basic BOM without linking any items or versions

In Dynamics 365 Supply Chain Management, it is possible to create simple BOMs without the need to include any items. This provides the flexibility to build and alter as many simple BOMs as needed.

Follow these steps to navigate to the right location:

1. Go to **Product Information Management** > **Bills of Materials and Formulas** > **Bill of Materials**.

   Here, you can initiate the process of constructing your simple BOM with ease:

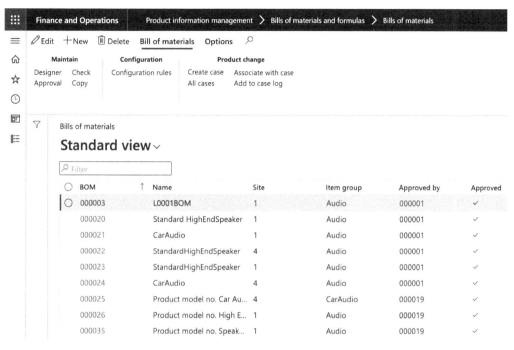

Figure 2.21 – The Bill of materials form

2. The BOM Designer page serves as your creative canvas for designing and managing tree structures for BOMs. By selecting **Setup**, you can customize different configurations and dictate the information that graces each line of your tree.

3. If you want to change the main selection in your view, simply click **Filter**. You can then choose to display only the specific BOM or route versions you want by selecting either **Selected/Active** or **Selected**. You also have the option to include non-approved and non-active BOM versions in your view if needed.

Keep in mind that if you access the BOM Designer from the **Bill of materials** list page, it won't show any route information. When you select a BOM or route version, it applies to all instances of the BOM Designer. So, the changes you make will be reflected universally.

Selecting a BOM and route

In the BOM Designer, you can adjust the filter for the BOM and route by using the **Filter** dialogue box. You can modify the following fields:

- **Configuration**: If the finished product is a product master, you can select the active product dimensions for the primary selection. However, if it's a non-product master, you cannot choose the product dimension selection in the **Filter** dialogue box.

- **Site**: You can modify the site represented by the BOM tree. By default, it shows the inventory site of the finished item.

- **Display principle**: This feature enables you to choose how BOM and route versions are presented in the current BOM structure. With **Active** or **Selected/Active** enabled, it shows the valid BOM or route version for the current date. With **Selected/Active** or **Selected**, you can select a specific BOM or route version by clicking **BOM** > **BOM versions** or **Route** > **Route versions**.

- **Version date**: You can indicate the date for the BOM and route version you want to use. This determines which BOM version is relevant for a specific date, based on the version dates established for the BOM versions.

- **From quantity**: You can filter the versions according to a specific "from quantity." Depending on this value, different BOM and route versions may be chosen.

- **Show valid only**: If you tick this option, the tree structure will only display BOM lines with valid dates. By right-clicking or double-clicking on a BOM line, you can open the **Edit BOM line** page, where you can see the validity dates of that specific BOM line.

When working with BOMs that include one or more levels of phantoms, the route associated with the top item often covers the entire BOM hierarchy. To simplify the view, you can lock the top-level route display by selecting **View | Lock route**. To unlock it, choose **View | Unlock route**.

If the **Resource consumption** checkbox is unmarked and the **Warehouse** field is empty, the picking warehouse defaults to that from the item master data.

BOM and formula versions

If you want to link a specific BOM or formula with a product that can be produced, you need to create a BOM or formula version.

These versions can have restrictions based on different factors:

- A specific time frame

- Quantity of the product

- The site of production

- Unique product dimensions

- And any other special requirements

Formula versions also have essential features, such as the following:

- The expected yield or output

- Information about coproducts and by-products

- Guidelines on how costs should be distributed within the formula

To tweak these settings, you'll have to go to **Product Information Management | Bills of Materials and Formulas | Bills of Materials**. Choose a product, then go to **Header**. It's like following a treasure map to find the hidden settings you need!

Figure 2.22 – Bill of materials detailed form

Approving and activating BOM and formula versions

Before incorporating a BOM version into your planning or manufacturing workflow, it's important to obtain prior approval. This approval functions like a stamp of approval that ensures the document is officially usable. Additionally, the BOM linked to the version can also receive approval at the same time, but this depends on whether the user chooses this option and has the necessary permissions.

Remember, a BOM version can only obtain its stamp of approval if the BOM it's linked to has already been approved. This is like a prerequisite in a course sequence where you must complete and pass the foundational course before advancing to the advanced one.

Activating the default BOM or formula version

To set a particular BOM or formula as the default version for master planning or production order creation, the version needs to be activated. Upon activation, the system verifies the version's exclusivity for given constraints such as period, site, or quantity. Should the activated version conflict with an already active version, you'll receive an error message. To resolve this, either deactivate the conflicting version or adjust the version constraints, typically the period, to avoid an ambiguous activation.

Product change with case management

The product change case offers an easy way to overview the BOM version constraints for approval and activation of new or altered BOMs and BOM versions. It also allows you to approve and activate all BOMs and formulas linked to a specific change for a certain activation date.

Alternative BOM versions

There may be times when you'd prefer not to use the active BOM version or formula version for forecasting, sales, or a parent product. In such cases, you can opt for a specific approved BOM as part of the requirement (be it a forecast line, sales line, or BOM line), provided an approved BOM version or formula version exists for the alternate BOM or formula.

When creating planned orders, production orders, or Kanbans, the planner or shop floor supervisor has the flexibility to use any approved BOM version that's valid on the requested planned production date to plan or produce a particular product. The BOM version that's used in this context isn't obligated to be activated as the default BOM version. It's like using a different recipe from the usual one when baking a cake, so long as it has been tested and approved, and is appropriate for the baking day.

For this, you must go to **Product information management** > **Bills of materials and formulas** > **Bills of materials** > **Lines**:

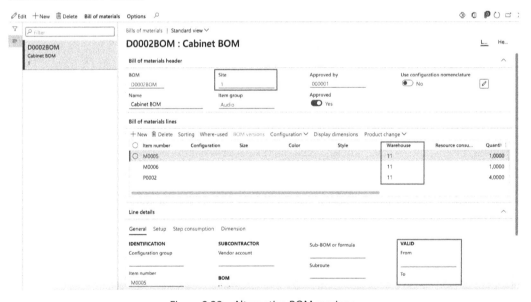

Figure 2.23 – Alternative BOM versions

BOM version control is crucial for accommodating ongoing changes to the item and employing various configurations, depending on the manufacturing circumstance. It allows for the phasing out of old components and the introduction of new ones.

Version control methods let you start and stop the production of select BOM versions. All BOM versions have an expiration date, but this can be avoided by approving and activating the new version. The system will then immediately start planning and purchasing based on the new active BOM version's details.

For example, a company could decide to initiate production of its best-selling subwoofer model at a second operational site. A new BOM version for this subwoofer model, identical to the main version but for a different site, is then created, approved, and activated.

In addition to activating or deactivating versions, Dynamics 365 Supply Chain Management offers several other ways to control which BOM version is used in production. These methods include control by date and quantity and site control.

Legal entities can create multiple BOM versions (identical in quantity and dates) produced at different sites. In such a case, a BOM version can be created on the BOM line page and the site for which the BOM version is valid can be specified in the **Site** field. If a site is not specified, the BOM version is valid for all sites.

Site-based version control enables you to control which BOM versions are ready for production depending on the site where they are produced. Legal entities can assign a BOM to multiple products or versions, depending on where it originates and if the product must undergo different manufacturing processes.

Copying BOM versions

When BOMs are similar in Dynamics 365 Supply Chain Management, the copy functionality can simplify the creation of new versions. You can copy existing BOMs on the **Copy BOM/route** page. After copying the BOM items, you can change or delete the BOM lines that do not align with the new version, and then insert new lines. If the existing BOM contains configurations, the system also copies the configurations, together with their rules and routes, to the new BOM.

Changing BOM versions

You may need to alter BOM versions due to component changes, shifts in the associated vendor, stock shortages, or necessary upgrades of the original item.

Here are the steps to change a BOM version:

I.   Create a BOM and a BOM version.

II.   Approve the new version.

III.   Specify the dates/site for the active period of this version and activate it.

IV.   Copy the BOM from an existing version.

V.   Make any required changes to the item or items in the new version.

BOM line types

Dynamics 365 Supply Chain Management provides a variety of BOM line types:

- For materials or services that are directly consumed and do not require further explosion or pegged supply, use the **Item** line type.

- If you want to create a sub-production, a BOM line event Kanban, or a direct purchase order for any product variant referenced by the BOM line, choose the **Supply** line type. The necessary item quantities are automatically reserved for the consuming production order when you estimate the production order.

- When you want to explode any lower-level BOM items included on the BOM line, choose the **Phantom** line type. Note that Phantoms are typically used to simplify the engineering process, but extensive use of phantom BOMs at many levels can affect performance. To improve performance, avoid deep hierarchies of phantoms and use pre-exploded production BOMs and routes instead.

- Use the **Vendor** line type if a subcontractor is involved in the production process and you want a sub-production or purchase order to be automatically created for the subcontractor.

Navigate to **Product information management** > **Bills of material and formulas** > **Bills of materials**:

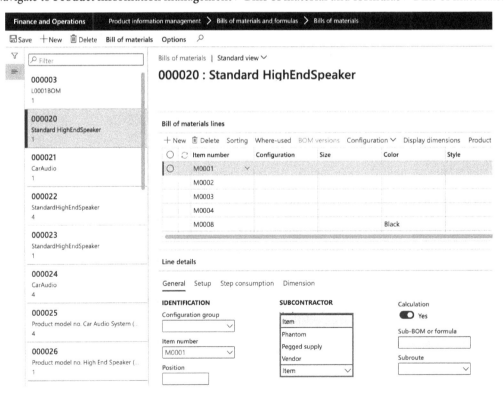

Figure 2.24 – Item line type options

BOM levels

BOMs outline the components necessary to produce a product. The complexity of these structures can vary:

- **Single-level BOM**: This type of BOM includes only the immediate components required to construct the product. It does not delve into the constituents of these components.

- **Multi-level BOM**: A multi-level BOM occurs when a BOM contains another BOM as a part of its composition. In this scenario, the subordinate BOM is considered the first level, and its components form the second level. Depending on the intricacy of the product being manufactured, BOMs can have as many levels as needed.

To access and manage these structures, navigate to **Product information management** > **Bills of materials and formulas** > **Bill of materials** > (select product) > **Maintain** > **Designer**:

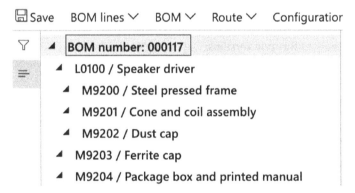

Figure 2.25 – BOM Designer

In the world of process manufacturing, a formula plays a crucial role in determining the materials, ingredients, and results of a specific process. It is accompanied by a corresponding route that outlines the entire process, which is used to plan and create products.

A formula usually contains one or more formula lines that identify the items or ingredients included in the formula. These lines can feature various items, including BOM items, formula items, catch weight items, purchased items, co-products, or by-products.

To create a new formula, you must start with the creation of a formula version before adding the formula line items. It is vital to have at least one version for every formula. Each formula version corresponds to one or more co-products and by-products that are produced alongside the final product.

Formulas come with unique features such as version control, graphical representation, formula size, formula multiples, yield, and quantity-dependent formula versions. Other features include total cost allocation, use for calculation, plan group, step consumption, and scalable lines.

These features provide advanced control and flexibility when managing formulas:

- **Version control**: Like BOMs, formula version control assists in phasing out outdated ingredients and incorporating new ones. It also allows for selecting alternative versions, depending on production or planning needs.

- **Graphical formula**: The formula designer allows you to visualize the formula structure in a graphical format. This graphic includes formula versions, co-products, and by-products.

- **Formula size**: The formula size, given in the **Per quantity** field on the formula lines, serves as a baseline. Modifying this field will update all **Per quantity** fields in the formula lines.

- **Formula multiples**: Formula multiples help determine the permissible batch order size for production through master planning or manual batch order. The formula size should meet the multiples requirement.

- **Yield**: You can specify a yield on the formula versions. The yield factor is applied to all formula lines when a batch order is created and is calculated as (actual output / theoretical output) * 100%.

- **Quantity-dependent formula versions**: Depending on the ordered amount of a formula item, you can choose different formula versions. For instance, for orders less than 500 kg, you might use **Version 1**; for orders over 500 kg, **Version 2** might be applied.

- **Total cost allocation**: This feature allows you to allocate the total production cost across co-products and the formula item. For planning items, the entire cost is allocated across the co-products.

- **Use for calculation**: This feature determines which formula size should be used if there are percent-controlled items to calculate quantity on the formula line.

- **Plan group**: Plan groups facilitate the substitution of items based on a priority ranking. Items within a group can be interchanged based on this priority.

- **Step consumption**: This functionality enables setting up complex (non-linear) consumption rules without the need for multiple BOMs or formulas.

- **Scalable lines**: This indicates whether a formula line is scalable based on the **Formula size** field or other scalable formula lines. If these quantities are updated, all scalable lines will adjust to maintain current ratios.

- **Approving and activating formulas**: Before they can be used for planning and production, formulas and formula versions need to be approved. Usually, formulas are activated before use. However, during production, a formula version that is approved but not activated can be selected.

The following are important mechanisms to ensure data integrity and maintain rigorous control over formulas and their versions:

- **Block Editing**: By activating this option, no fields on the formula lines can be edited or deleted once the formula has been approved. However, if the approval of the formula is removed, changes can be made to the formula lines. New formulas and new formula versions can also be created, regardless of this setting.

- **Block Removal of Approval**: When this option is selected, the approval of an approved formula or formula version cannot be removed. Nevertheless, the creation of new formulas and new formula versions is allowed, as is the removal of a formula version's activation.

- **Signature**: Utilizing the electronic signature functionality can enhance the security and control mechanisms in a system. If configured to necessitate an electronic signature upon formula approval, an interface requiring signature validation appears upon the formula's activation.

The user must possess proper electronic signing credentials, and the certificate must be validated successfully before the system commits any alterations. If the system fails to authenticate the signature, it denies the approval or reversal of approval, reverting all changes that initiated the respective processes.

These security layers assist organizations in maintaining precise and reliable records of their formula evolution. This traceability is paramount in regulated sectors where strict compliance and accountability are obligatory.

From a more technical perspective, a BOM is a comprehensive inventory of all the essential components, assemblies, and sub-assemblies required to fabricate a product. It often includes detailed procedures necessary for procuring and employing the requisite materials.

Now that we've reviewed the bill of materials functionalities let's dive into the product configurator functionality to extend those options.

Product configurator – purpose and advantages

A product configuration model is a system that allows manufacturers to manage various product variants in an organized manner. This model ensures products meet customer specifications, streamlines production, and reduces costs associated with carrying unnecessary inventory. The model consists of several key elements:

- **Components**: These are the building blocks of a product configuration model. Each component represents a portion of the product that can be defined and used multiple times in different product models.

- **Attributes**: These are properties associated with a component. The chosen attributes during the configuration process will determine the characteristics of the final product. They control inter-component and intra-component relationships and can influence the physical parts that make up the product.

- **Expression constraints and table constraints**: These constraints control the attribute values that can be chosen when configuring products for various types of orders. Users can build these constraints using either expression or table constraints, depending on their preference.

- **User requirements**: These represent specific needs or desires for the product configuration from the user's perspective. They contain all the elements of a subcomponent, but unlike a subcomponent, they're not bound to a product master. This means that any BOM lines or route operations defined within a user requirement are integrated into the parent component BOM structure or route, much like a phantom BOM.

A Phantom BOM is a type of BOM that represents a group of materials that are processed together but not stored as a single unit. This approach allows manufacturers to create and manage complex products more effectively.

These elements, together, enable a comprehensive and versatile product configuration model, giving manufacturers the ability to create a wide range of product variants without significantly increasing complexity or inventory costs.

Configuring catch weights

Catch weight is a key concept in industries where products vary in their weight or size, yet are packaged similarly. It allows for dual tracking in both an inventory unit and a catch weight unit. Here's a deeper explanation:

- **Inventory unit**: This unit of measure is how the product is usually stored or inventoried. For example, this could be by the number of bags, boxes, or packages.

- **Catch weight unit**: This unit of measure relates to how the product is sold or used. This could be by weight (kilograms, pounds) or volume.

A catch weight item has a specified range of inventory units, meaning each unit can vary in actual weight, but it stays within a set range. This helps accurately price items and allows for fair transactions, considering the inherent weight discrepancies.

Here are some examples in the food industry:

- **Fish**: Typically counted in inventory by the number of crates or boxes, but when sold, it is priced and weighed by the kilogram or pound.

- **Cheese wheels**: Stored and inventoried by the number of wheels, but when sold, they are priced and weighed by the kilogram or pound, as each wheel can vary in weight.

- **Bulk grains or seeds**: Stored as sacks or bags, sold by weight. While the number of sacks is inventoried, the weight of each sack can vary and therefore needs to be recorded.

To manage catch weight items, two methods can be employed:

- Partial visibility
- Full visibility

Let's take a closer look.

Partial visibility

In this method, the catch weight is known and visible only after the inventory unit is packed and ready for shipment or at the point of sale.

In certain industries, such as those dealing with bulk grains or seeds, the principle of partial visibility within catch weight management is profoundly beneficial. These industries typically employ machines to package containers, each holding a quantity of the product that falls within a specified weight tolerance. The collective weight of these manufactured containers holds significance, while the minute weight differences between individual bags do not warrant separate tracking.

For a catch weight item applying partial visibility, multiple inventory units can be grouped under a common batch or serial number. In this case, only the total value of the inventory unit is recorded, eliminating the need to log individual unit values. Therefore, for every transaction involving the inventory unit, the aggregate weight becomes a necessary input.

Given that individual container weights are not monitored, every inventory transaction, whether it be a transfer or shipment, necessitates recording the number of containers and their cumulative weight in the system for effective weight management.

When employing the partial visibility approach, if the entire catch weight quantity or dimension isn't earmarked, a portion equivalent to the minimum catch weight inventory will be set aside for that particular dimension. The gap between the physically reserved and the nominal quantity on order will remain on order until actual picking is conducted.

Consider, for instance, a scenario where three bags of bulk grains or seeds, all sharing the same batch number, arrive in the warehouse. During the product receipt process, a single transaction records both the quantity of bags and their combined weight. This total weight is an aggregation of all three bags and does not reflect the individual weights of each bag.

Full visibility

Here, the catch weight is known and tracked through all inventory transactions and stages of the product life cycle, starting from the receiving dock to the point of sale.

Full visibility is crucial in industries where the exact weight of a container must always be known, and this weight doesn't change once the container has been created – a prime example being wheels of cheese. Each wheel is produced and packaged, its weight precisely measured, and given a unique serial number. This known weight remains constant until the point of shipment, at which time it is invoiced to the customer.

Catch weight items with full visibility necessitate that every inventory unit is assigned a distinct serial number, and the specific weight of that unit is meticulously recorded. Thus, a unique serial number becomes intrinsically linked with the weight of the inventory unit.

The full visibility catch weight truly excels in certain conditions:

- When the weight of individual physical units, or handling units, needs to be tracked
- When finished products leave the factory or warehouse and do not require re-weighing, such as a 10 kg box of frozen chicken drumsticks
- When a variation in weight between individual handling units has implications for the cost and sales price of those units
- When the weight, once entered at a certain stage in the process, is expected to remain the same

Catch weight items serve several purposes:

- They allow for the creation of sales and purchase agreements in catch weight units. This is particularly handy for items priced per box, not by weight, such as boxes of oranges.
- They enable customer orders to be made in terms of boxes/packages, with the payment being based on weight.
- They make it possible to create purchase orders in catch weight units, which is ideal when ordering items priced per container.
- They provide the capability to view net requirements in catch weight units.
- They facilitate the creation of shipment staging in catch weight units.
- They aid in producing picking lists in catch weight units.
- They offer visibility into on-hand inventory in catch weight units.
- They permit the creation of formula lines in catch weight units when a whole container is used in a formula line.

The choice between partial and full visibility largely depends on the industry requirements, the nature of the product, and the information available at different stages of handling the product. Catch weight management helps companies improve inventory control, reduce waste, enhance product pricing, and increase overall operational efficiency.

Direct delivery products

Direct delivery presents an efficient method for users to craft a purchase order straight from a sales order, allowing the vendor to ship the order to the customer directly, thereby circumventing the need for the selling company to physically handle the goods. This streamlines the delivery process, diminishes delivery times, and mitigates the costs associated with maintaining inventory, as products are no longer required to be stored in your warehouse before being dispatched to the customer.

Setting up products for direct delivery

To designate a product for direct delivery, navigate to **Product information management** > **Products** > **Released products**. On the **Deliver** FastTab, slide the **Direct delivery** switch to **Yes** and define the warehouse for direct delivery:

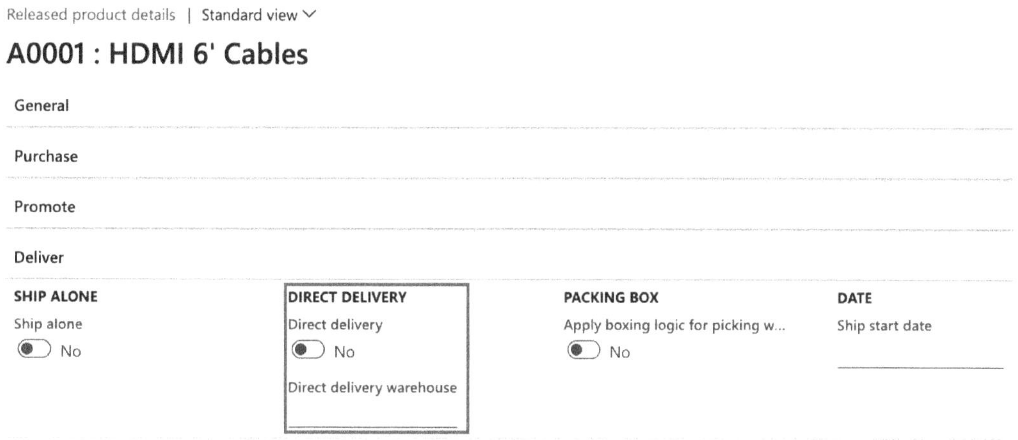

Released product details | Standard view ⌄

A0001 : HDMI 6' Cables

General

Purchase

Promote

Deliver

SHIP ALONE	DIRECT DELIVERY	PACKING BOX	DATE
Ship alone	Direct delivery	Apply boxing logic for picking w…	Ship start date
◉ No	◉ No	◉ No	
	Direct delivery warehouse		

Figure 2.26 – The Direct delivery flag

Executing the direct delivery process

Imagine you're at your desk, all set to organize some direct deliveries. You've got your trusty **Sales order** page open on your screen. First things first, you start a new sales order and make a list of order lines – it's a bit like writing a shopping list. Now, go ahead and look for the **Direct delivery** button. It's hanging out on the **Sales order** tab in the action pane. Click that button and start pointing out which lines on your list are meant to be a direct delivery.

This is when the magic happens! Your sales order lines that you marked for direct delivery are now linked with their matching purchase order lines. It's like they're two friends holding hands.

There's something you should remember, though. If some of the stuff you ordered has already been sent your way, you'll have to do a little bit of juggling with the leftover quantity. It's like splitting a pizza with friends after a few slices are already taken – you have to adjust. So, if you originally ordered 15 items and already got 5, make a new line for the remaining 10 items. Just don't forget to take this amount from the original line.

Once you've created this bridge of direct delivery between the sales order lines and the purchase order lines, you're ready to tweak the sales order with a packing slip. It's sort of like wrapping up a present and putting a bow on it – it just makes it look finished. From the purchase order, you can do a packing slip update or an invoice update. But remember, if you're doing an invoice update, you've got to do it from the **Sales order** page. And one more thing – the invoice update should not make the quantity on the sales order bigger than the amount you have received. After all, you can't claim to have more pizza than you received, right?

Understanding delivery dates and addresses

You've got your sales order line on your screen, and you decide to update the requested receipt date. As soon as you do this, the delivery date on the related purchase order line changes as well. It's like two twins who always want to match their clothes; you change one and the other one automatically updates!

Now, when you're dealing with a direct delivery, there's a twist. Normally, we'd use the company's address as the delivery address. But not this time. Instead, we write in the customer's address. It's kind of like sending a postcard to a friend – you write their address, not your own!

Let's say you need to change the delivery address on a direct delivery order line. Well, guess what? The sales order line is like a copycat - it will also update its delivery address to match. Just like when you tell your buddy you've moved house, they'd update your address in their contacts too. It's just that simple!

Handling deletions and warehouse requirements

Trying to remove a direct delivery sales order line is like trying to pick a card from a house of cards. The system alerts you because purchase order lines are linked to it, like cards in your tower.

And if some of the order is already on their way, you can't delete the sales order line or the linked purchase orders. It's like you can't take back a move in a board game once it's played.

Even though direct delivery items don't visit your warehouse, you still have to pretend and note down a warehouse on the sales order line. You might have picking rules for the item, but they're ignored for direct deliveries. It's like having a rule for a game that you don't use when playing a different version of the game.

Summary

At this point, we have gained a deeper understanding of the **Product Information Management** (**PIM**) module in Dynamics 365 Supply Chain Management, which has equipped us with a powerful suite of tools to design, centralize, manage, and optimize product data. By using PIM, we can ensure consistent and high-quality product information across multiple channels, streamline product introduction processes, and improve collaboration between different business units.

With this chapter, you should have gained a strong understanding of PIM and how crucial it is to comprehensively address various business processes and unlock the full potential of Dynamics 365. Now that you've acquired this knowledge, you will be able to effectively utilize the tool's capabilities. Instead of struggling with module customization or acquiring additional tools, many queries and challenges can be resolved through straightforward configuration adjustments or flag activation.

If you are still considering a change in your career path, having a strong proficiency in PIM not only makes you an invaluable asset to organizations utilizing Microsoft Dynamics 365 but also prepares you for diverse roles such as PIM Administrator, Product Manager, or Supply Chain Consultant.

In the next chapter, we will learn the most important topics related to Inventory Management in Dynamics 365 Supply Chain Management, Inbound Operations, Outbound Operations, and the internal operations required to maintain the stocks of our businesses in optimal conditions.

3
Getting Started with the Inventory Management Module

Inventory management is a critical element of every company that works with materials. With an inventory, companies can order, store, trade, and use raw materials and finished goods across multiple locations. Warehouse facilities have several daily operations, and Inventory management in Dynamics 365 **Supply Chain Management** (**SCM**) helps address these processes.

First of all, we must understand how a warehouse works and what these daily operations are. So, in this chapter, we'll learn about warehouse process flows, such as inbound and outbound operations, and how to configure inventory components and journals.

Here is what you will learn about in this chapter:

- The capabilities of the Inventory management module
- Designing and creating a warehouse and warehouse activities from a layout
- Performing inventory activities using journals
- Understanding and executing transfer orders between warehouses
- Performing inventory closing and understanding its impacts on the business

By the end of this chapter, you will have a better understanding of inventory management and be able to configure and perform core inventory processes in Dynamics 365 SCM.

Introducing Inventory management

To understand the Inventory management module, we need to first comprehend the daily operations and flows in a warehouse. We can separate warehouse activities into three main flows:

- **Inbound operations**: These activities let us bring materials into the warehouse
- **Outbound operations**: Here, we record which materials have left the warehouse
- **Internal operations**: These activities control the flow of materials inside the warehouse

We're going to simulate a real-world scenario in this chapter. Imagine we're working for a sportswear company and implementing the Inventory management module in a warehouse that works with sports shoe stock, such as running shoes and football shoes.

Inbound operations

This stage encompasses all activities related to bringing materials into the warehouse. These could be purchase orders, transfer orders, or returned sales orders that we need to handle to store those materials in the Facility.

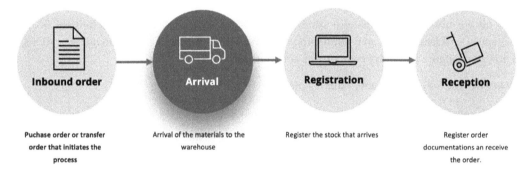

Figure 3.1 – Inbound operations example

In *Figure 3.1*, we see an inbound process flow of this example warehouse. First, we have the inbound order; this can be a transfer or purchase order planned to arrive at the inbound dock.

When, for example, the vendor delivers this order, the receiving clerk starts receiving it. That is, they unload all the goods from the truck and store them in their assigned locations. For example, all closed basketball shoe pallets go to a specific area in the warehouse.

With this activity, warehouse clerks must input all the required documents in the system, for example, packing lists, and register the purchase order as received.

Outbound operations

When we mention outbound operations, we might be talking about sales order picking or transfer orders, for example. Here, we need to search for the materials needed to load onto a truck and ship to a customer or another facility.

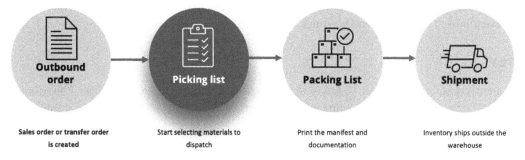

Figure 3.2 – Outbound operation example

In *Figure 3.2*, an outbound process for a sales order is described. Similarly to what happens on a purchase order, a sales order indicates a customer's wish to buy some of our products and initiates the process. In this case, a sales order is created, the stock is reserved, and a shipping date is confirmed for us to dispatch our material.

Once the shipping date is reached, the picking process starts. Here, the warehouse clerk locates the item to retrieve the exact quantity of the stock needed. Once the ordered item is picked up, the truck is loaded. Then, the required documents, such as packing lists, manifests, and shipping orders forms, can be printed. Then, the sales order is marked as shipped or delivered, and the invoice process can start.

Internal operations

In this last group of operations, we have the activities related to operations that control and handle inventory inside the warehouse. These include the following:

- **Transfer order**: This type of order is used when moving inventory between warehouses
- **Adjustment/movement**: This journal is used to correct inventory quantities
- **Counting**: Count inventory is a process that corrects virtual quantities by counting actual physical quantities
- **Transfer journal**: This is used when moving inventory between locations in the same warehouse

More warehouse processes are included in the manufacturing process, such as raw material picking and finished goods manufacturing.

Setting up our warehouse and inventory configurations

It's time to set up our warehouse. But first, let's break down the inventory structure. If we were to go to any warehouse, we would see that boxes and materials are stored in large and tall racks, and every location is named. This division and segmentation of the warehouse is called **inventory breakdown**. In Dynamics 365 SCM provides the ability to organize inventory based on site, warehouse, and location; let's review how to set them up in Dynamics.

Sites

Sites are storage locations and can be linked to a financial dimension in the general ledger. This means that a site is the main way of organizing inventory costs. SCM in Dynamics 365 creates at least one site, and all inventory transactions refer to a site.

However, depending on the company's logistics or business process, creating more than one site may be better. There are several cases where having two or more sites would be ideal. For example, if a company has more than one geographic location, the costs of the goods will differ from one location to another. Another example is if there is a manufacturing facility site in one place and a shared distribution center in another. We need to have separate sites to archive this distribution in Dynamics 365.

In these cases, a good analysis of the flow is needed to make a good decision on whether to create one or more sites.

To create a new site, we have to go to **Inventory Management | Setup | Inventory breakdown | Sites**. You will end up with a form as seen in the following screenshot:

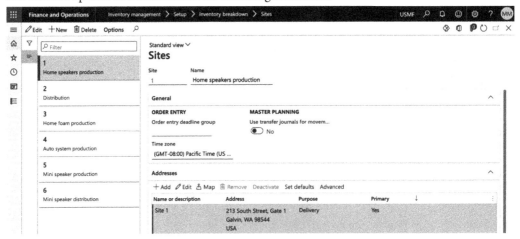

Figure 3.3 – Sites form

You can create an ID for the site and its name in this form. If you need to delete a site, you can only do it if it doesn't have a warehouse connected to it and has no on-hand inventory.

Warehouse

After creating a site, we need to configure a warehouse. A warehouse is a place in which we can store items. It's divided into locations for better organization of the inventory. Usually, a warehouse corresponds to a function of the company—for example, a raw material warehouse or a quarantine warehouse. So, for every implementation, there will be a need to create more than one warehouse.

Sometimes, we need to create virtual warehouses to have a different view and understanding of a company's goods. For example, if third-party operations need some of the company stocks, it's a good idea to create a virtual warehouse representing that vendor to register these transfer orders.

To create a warehouse, we need to go to **Inventory management** | **Setup** | **Inventory breakdown** | **Warehouses**. We'll end up in this form:

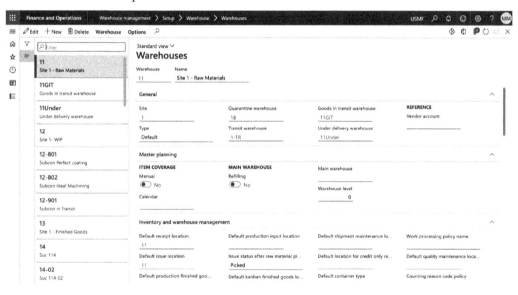

Figure 3.4 – Warehouses form

We can configure a warehouse in this form, but we must consider that there are different types of warehouses:

- **Default** is the typical, main type of warehouse. These are the warehouses where we can store inventory for general purposes.

- **Quarantine** is the type of warehouse for storing quarantine-controlled items. We can attach this warehouse to a default warehouse, and every quarantine-controlled item received in the default warehouse will automatically transfer to this. We can return the items to the default warehouse when the quarantine ends.

- **Transit** is used to represent that items are in transit between warehouses. When we ship a transfer order, the stock stored in the transit warehouse is attached to the default warehouse until received in the destination warehouse.

- The **Goods-In-Transit** warehouse type was introduced when the Landed cost module was released. It represents the transit of imported goods. When importing with this feature, it creates a receipt process to be invoiced before the physical arrival of the goods.

- **Under-delivery** represents the under-delivery transactions related to the default warehouse in the landed cost process.

As we can see, only a default warehouse follows the typical warehouse processes, and every other warehouse type has to be related to a default warehouse to extend its functions.

In this form, we can also enter information about the warehouse, such as the address or configuration for every module in Dynamics 365 that works with a warehouse. So, for example, in the **Plan** tab, we can set up master planning parameters related to this warehouse. But we will talk about this in more detail later.

Aisles and locations

Aisles and locations are the primary divisions of a warehouse. Walking inside a warehouse, we can see aisle after aisle, like in a supermarket. Every aisle contains racks to put the inventory with shelves and bins on each side. Each of them has a purpose. For example, we can have areas of entire racks and aisles that store palletized items. We can also have areas with superior levels of shelves for storing bulk items on that locations and lower levels of shelves for picking pieces. Here, we have an example of a warehouse layout:

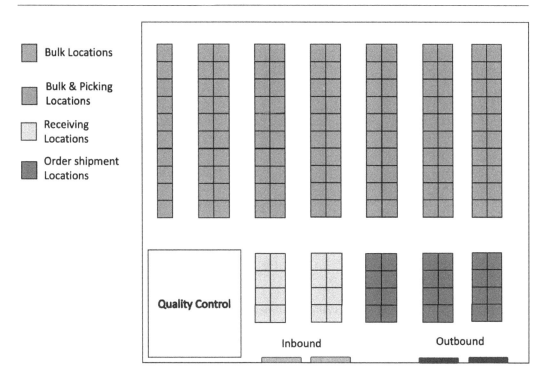

Figure 3.5 – Warehouse layout example

Looking at *Figure 3.5*, we can differentiate these areas and locations.

The first division in a warehouse is an aisle. These are used to group locations. An aisle is named with an ID, commonly an ascending number, and the first few digits of an ID indicate the aisle's location.

An aisle is divided into locations, which are the areas where the stock is stored and taken from. The location is the entity with the lower granularity level of the inventory, meaning that we cannot divide locations into other entities.

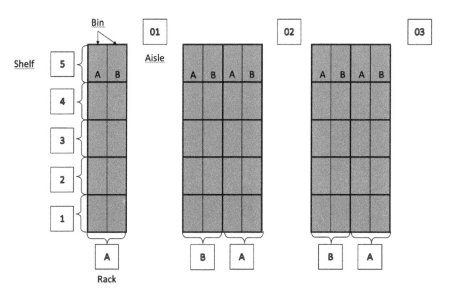

Figure 3.6 – Warehouse aisle division example

Commonly, a location has an ID that represents its coordinates in the warehouse. For example, the location ID "01B3A" tells us how to find that location inside the warehouse, with each part corresponding to a division in the warehouse: aisle (01), rack (B), shelf (3), and bin (A). Dynamics 365 can generate these names automatically, setting these values in the warehouse form under the locations tab, or it can be created manually.

Each location has attributes that define the way it works.

The size (height, width, depth, and volume) defines how many items or boxes fit into a location.

The position (aisle, rack, shelf, and bin) determines how it can be found.

The location type defines the use of the location:

- **Bulk**: This is the location to store bulked items. These items are still containerized or palletized and are used to replenish picking locations.
- **Picking**: Items stored here are ready to be picked for shipping. Workers select items to compose an order or shipment in this location more quickly because small quantities of items are stored. Usually, these locations are fixed for one item or product variant.
- **Inbound dock**: This is a location where the items are received.
- **Outbound dock**: This is a location where the items are shipped.

In Dynamics 365, there are two ways to create locations. First, go to **Inventory Management | Setup | Inventory Breakdown | Locations** and generate each location manually.

There is also a wizard to set up every location within a warehouse. So, back in the warehouse form (by going to Inventory management | Setup | Inventory Breakdown | Warehouse), select the warehouse for which we want to create the locations. We must set, in the location names tab, the name formats of each part of the location. Then, we can go to the **Warehouse** tab in the upper menu, then to the Maintain group and to the **Location wizard** option, and follow the wizard instructions to create the dock locations, bulk locations, and picking locations.

After configuring a warehouse, we can set up items to work with inventory management.

Item setup

It's possible to assign an item to a warehouse, and this is done by going to Product Information Management | Products | Released Products. Once here, we can select any product, and then under the Manage Inventory tab | the Warehouse group | Warehouse item, we can find the following form:

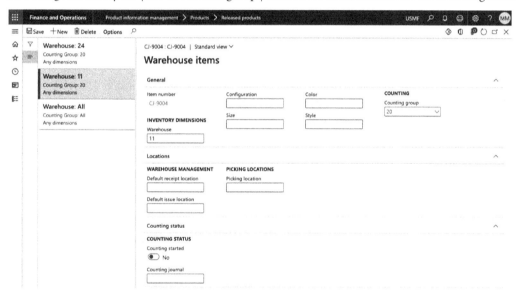

Figure 3.7 – Warehouse items form

Here, we can set up some parameters for the item related to a warehouse. This setup can be done once per warehouse. For example, we can find the following here:

- **Counting group**: Aggregates items into a group to define the frequency of the cycle counting
- **Default receipt location**: When receiving this item, it'll use this location by default
- **Default issue location**: When consuming this item, it'll use this location by default
- **Picking location**: Default location to pick this item from

ABC classification

Giving each item a logical importance in the inventory is essential for companies. For example, problems with a gold metal sheet will be different from problems with bolts. The first one could be more important or expensive than the latter, which can be differentiated by the ABC classification.

This analysis categorizes items into three levels of importance:

- A items will be highly controlled and counted regularly
- B items will be counted often and controlled
- C items will be measured least frequently

Having items classified in this way will help us organize inventory by importance, as it informs other business processes, such as procurement.

As various forms exist to work on this classification, Pareto's principle, or the 80/20 law, is usually used. This principle states that 80% of the result comes from 20% of the work. Applying this to items, we could divide our inventory like this:

- A: 20% of the inventory that represents the 80% of the total inventory value
- B: 30% of the inventory that represents 15% of the total inventory value
- C: 50% of the inventory that represents 5% of the total inventory value

This ABC classification can be done manually in Dynamics 365 by going to **Product information management** | **Products** | **Released products** and then to the **ABC CLASSIFICATION** field under the **Manage costs** tab. In this field, we can assign the A, B, or C group to an item.

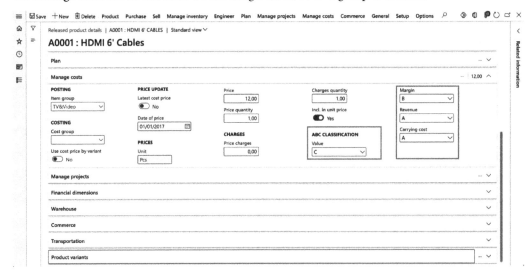

Figure 3.8 – ABC CLASSIFICATION field in the Released products form

As this is a manual classification, we rely on business experience to input those fields. But Dynamics 365 can calculate an ABC analysis based on statistical data. To analyze the data, we could use any of these four models:

- **Value model**: Specifies ABC items based on the inventory value

- **Margin model**: Specifies ABC items based on the marginal income

- **Revenue model**: Specifies ABC items based on sales

- **Carrying cost model**: Specifies ABC items based on inventory rotation

Considering this, we can go to Inventory Management | Periodic Tasks | ABC classification to analyze ABC items automatically.

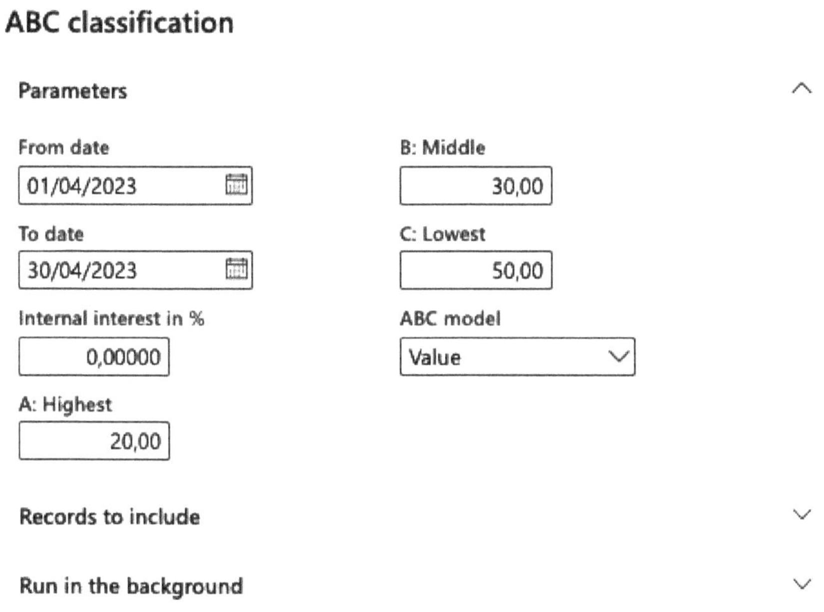

ABC classification

Parameters	^
From date	**B: Middle**
01/04/2023 📅	30,00
To date	**C: Lowest**
30/04/2023 📅	50,00
Internal interest in %	**ABC model**
0,00000	Value ⌄
A: Highest	
20,00	

Records to include   ⌄

Run in the background   ⌄

Figure 3.9 – ABC classification dialog

Here, we can specify the following parameters:

- **From date and To date**: Dates for the transactions this process will analyze

- **Internal interest in %**: Percentage of internal interest

- **A: Highest**: Percentages for the A classification

- **B: Middle**: Percentage for the B classification

- **C: Lowest**: Percentage for the C classification

- One thing to note is that A, B, and C percentages must add up to 100.

- **ABC model**: Here, we can select the Value, margin, Revenue, or Carrying cost option based on which ABC we want to calculate

This information will update the ABC classification on the Released product page. Suppose we need to analyze the calculations before the execution of the ABC classification job. In that case, a report can be found at Inventory Management | Inquiries and reports | Inventory value Reports | ABC Classification.

ABC classification
Contoso Entertainment System USA

Page 1 of 14
16/04/2023
16:14

From date	01/03/2021	To date	16/04/2023	Internal interest in %	0,00
A: Highest	20,00	B: Middle	30,00	C: Lowest	50,00
ABC model	Value	Total amount	210.120.529,57		

Item group	Item number	Product name	Current	Calculated	Amount
Audio	D0001	MidRangeSpeaker	None	C	5.723.289,88
Audio	D0002	Cabinet	None	C	136.696,66
Audio	D0003	StandardSpeaker	None	C	5.565,25
Audio	L0001	MidRangeSpeaker2	None	C	-49.853,99
Audio	P0001	AcousticFoamPanel	None	C	927,61
Audio	P0003	Foam remnants	None	C	0,00
Audio	D0004	HighEndSpeaker	None	C	24.581,73
Audio	T0001	SpeakerCable	None	C	-97.500,00
Audio	T0003	SurroundSoundReceive	None	C	-77.120,00
Audio	D0006	Speaker solution	None	C	0,00
Audio	D0007	Speaker Pro Kit	None	C	0,00
Audio	L0025	WLAN Radio software installed	None	C	0,00
Audio	L0026	WLAN Radio packed	None	C	0,00
Audio	L0002	Midrange Speaker Lean	None	C	0,00
Audio	1000	Surface Pro 128 GB	None	C	288.487,31

Figure 3.10 – ABC classification report

The bad news is that the ABC classification report cannot be executed from the ABC classification job. Therefore, to preview the calculated ABC classification, we must first execute this report and then input the same information on the ABC classification job again to update those levels.

Creating and posting inventory journals

Now that we have created the warehouse and the main parameters, we can start working with the inventory process and its journals.

Inbound operations

Let's bring back the inventory inbound process and dig into it. Then, we will describe how to incorporate that process into Dynamics 365 SCM.

Here we have an inbound example with the inventory status of each step:

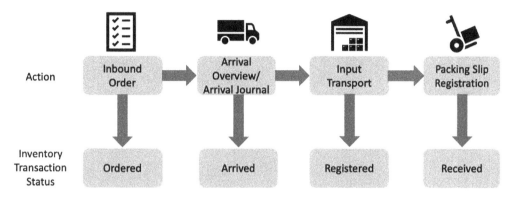

Figure 3.11 – Inbound process in Dynamics 365 SCM

In *Figure 3.11*, we can see that every inventory arrival process has an inventory transaction status associated with it:

1. When the order is created, the inventory has the ordered status, meaning that some stock will be received once the order is executed.

2. When the item arrives, and its arrival journal is created, the inventory status changes to **Arrive**. This means the inventory is physically in the warehouse.

3. After that, the inventory worker can register the arrival journal; this activity changes the status to **Registered**.

4. Finally, the inventory is changed to a Received status once the packing slip is updated.

This entire process could be done via the **Arrival overview** page. This form has an overview of every task regarding the arrival process. We can access this form from the Inventory Management | Inbound orders | Arrival overview menu:

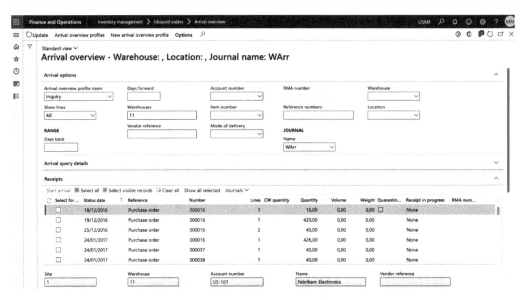

Figure 3.12 – Arrival overview form

On this form, we can view a list of orders expected to arrive on any date we set. In the first part of this form, **Arrival options** can configure profiles to filter the arrival information, and this filter will show orders in the **Receipts** tab. If we select an order from the **Receipts** tab, we could analyze the details of the lines in the **Lines** tab below.

If we need to create an arrival journal automatically, we can do so from the arrival overview screen, completing the journal name on the journal tab. When we do that, all specified values, such as warehouse and location, will be inherited by the lines, which is easier for business processes that do not require multiple workers to control each step of the process.

We will find the Arrival overview profile field in the arrival overview form. This will help us create and use filters to better view the pending inbound orders. For example, if we input Show lines "All," Days Back "30", Days Forward "0", Warehouse 11, the form will display all orders for the last 30 days that arrive at warehouse 11.

Once we select the arrival profile or manually modify those filters, the system will show all orders in the Receipts tab that match those filters.

Another visualization option in this form is to click on the **In progress** button to show all pending actions for the order lines that are yet to be posted.

Suppose we want to show only information related to a specific reference number in the overview. In that case, we can enter an account number in the Account Number field and an order number in the Reference Numbers field. Additionally, we can view all related receipt orders from the system date and to a specific number of days back from it. Also, we can filter all receipts of Warehouse 11, regardless of status.

So, as we can see, there are different options to control the information needed for the inbound orders that are waiting to be received.

It is possible for users to set up their profile to access it faster in the **Arrival overview profiles** form.

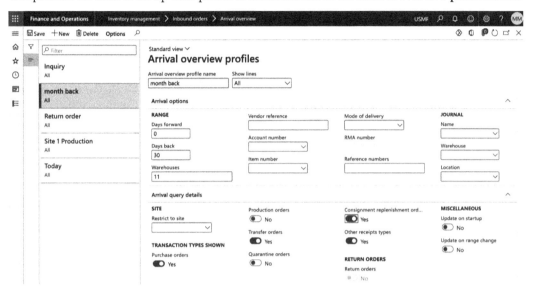

Figure 3.13 – Arrival overview profiles

After setting a descriptive name in the **Arrival overview profile name** field, we have to set whether we want to show all order lines or just the ones that are in progress or received in the **Show lines** field. In this case, it is set to **All**.

Then, in the Arrival options tab, we have to set the following:

Range: specify "Days forward" and "Days back." This is an interval of days from today when the orders must be received. In our example, Days back must be 30, and days forward must be 0. This will show the arrivals with zero days back from today and thirty days ahead from today.

In the Warehouses field, we set all the warehouses we want to include, in this case, warehouse 11. This form also has filters for Vendor reference, account number, and item number, which will filter orders with that information. Filling the **Journal Name** field with the journal name defined for the inventory arrival is a must because we cannot create journals automatically.

In the Arrival query details, we can filter which orders we want to be displayed. For example, we can activate and deactivate Purchase orders, Production orders, Transfer orders, Quarantine orders, consignment replenishment orders, and other receipt types. It can also include return orders.

Finally, it has two fields that control when the information for the **Arrival overview** form is refreshed. Update on startup will update information on accessing the form. Update on range change will update the data when the date ranges change.

Once the profile is created, we can select it from the **Arrival overview** page and set it as default.

Back to the **Arrival overview** form, let's register some arrivals.

We first need to start the arrival process. We have two ways to do it: from the receipt and the line.

Let's say we need to receive the purchase order PO-00001, which has two lines—one for two units of item A0001 and another for three units of item A0002. If we want to receive all lines of that order, we need to go to the receipt tab and then select order PO-0001 and then start arrival. This will create an item arrival journal for every line in the order. But if we only need to receive the second line for item A0002 after we select the order PO-00001 in the Receipt tab, we need to start the arrival for item A0002 in the Lines tab. Again, this will create an arrival journal but only for item A0002.

Sometimes, our vendor ships more than one order in one truck. In that case, the arrival journal overview lets us receive multiple orders in one arrival journal. So, what we need to do is select the orders that we are going to receive and then start the arrival.

At this point, the arrival of order PO-00001 has started. Now, we need to update the reception of the stock. To find this order more easily, we can go to the arrival options and modify the Show Lines filter to **In progress**. This will show us only the arrivals that are yet to be completed. So, after selecting the lines on the **Receipt** or **Lines** tab, we go to the Journals | Show arrivals from the **Receipts** menu. Here, we can access the arrival journal lines that we need to confirm.

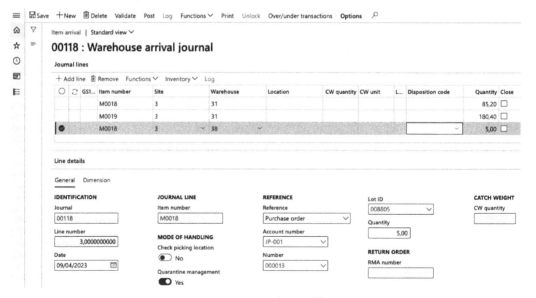

Figure 3.14 – Arrival journal lines

In this form, we confirm the quantities and the information of every line in the journal line tab. If any information has to be modified, this is the step where we can do it.

For example, if we need to reduce the quantity because less stock has arrived than expected, we go to the quantity field and lower it. This will decrease the quantity pending to be received and update the registered quantity of the order.

Here, we also create a batch ID in case the lot number is not created automatically. We can also send some quantities to Quarantine management from here.

To do this, we select Functions | Split under the Journal lines tab. Here, we input the quantity we want to be quarantined. And then, under the **Line details** tab, we set Quarantine management to **Yes**. This will modify the warehouse and prepare the items with a quarantine order, which we will cover in the next chapter.

Once we have set the relevant information, we can validate and post this journal using the buttons at the top of the form. This will enter the quantities in the locations informed in the journals and modify the inventory transaction status to **Registered**. Up to here, the **Receiving clerk** security role can carry out all of this process.

To finish this inbound flow, we need to process the product receipt. The Warehouse Manager or Purchasing manager can update the product receipt information because this is where the cost of the items is set. In the same Arrival Overview form, we can select Journals | Product receipt ready journals and find a list of arrival journals prepared to be received.

We need to go to the Functions | Product receipt menu, and a dialog screen will pop up showing the information posted in the purchase order.

This screen shows us some settings to complete, such as a posting option, which allows us to record the journal of the reception in the general ledger or register it as a pro forma receipt.

Also, the print option lets us print the receipt and use the print management parameters. Another printing option is to print products and shelf labels.

In the Overview grid, the purchase orders that will be received appear. There is an important field here, **Product Receipt**, which is mandatory to update. Usually, it is completed with the vendor packing slip number. If this information were completed in the arrival journal, this field would be updated automatically

Next is the **Lines** tab, which shows all the lines to be updated by this receipt. Again, most of this information came from **Purchase order**, but for our inventory process, there are a few fields that we can look up.

First of all, there are the vendor batch and expiry dates, which we can fill in to update that info for our batch. Close for receipt will update the remaining quantity to be received of the line to 0. This will block the line for any other arrivals.

Finally, the Details tab will show general information about the purchase order line; it will also let us update vendor batch information, such as vendor number and origin.

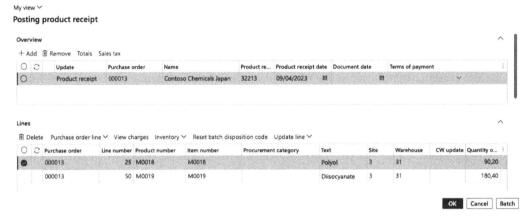

Figure 3.15 – Posting product receipt

When we are done updating this information, we click the **OK** button, and this will process the product receipt.

It will update the product receipt in the purchase order. In addition, inventory costs will be updated as physical ledger transactions waiting for the purchase invoice. It also modifies the status of the inventory transactions to Received, meaning that now the physical cost of the item is recorded.

Outbound operations

On the outbound side of the warehouse operations, as discussed earlier, are the activities that ship inventory outside our stock.

The following diagram depicts the activities of an outbound order and how the inventory status changes throughout the process:

Figure 3.16 – Outbound operations flows

Any output order initiates this flow. It could be a transfer order or a sales order, for example.

Once the order is placed in the on-hand inventory, we can see the inventory quantity reflecting the On Order transaction status. The inventory reserve changes the status of these on-hand quantities to Reserved and notifies to the sales order that the items will be shipped for that order.

When we generate the picking list, the shipment is automatically created and has a one-to-one relationship. Therefore, we can process the picking list and select all the items needed from the stock. At this point, the inventory transaction will be shown as **Picked**.

Following that process, we can send the shipment and update the packing slip information. At this point, the inventory transactions change their status to Deducted, and it records the physical cost voucher transaction in the general ledger.

Finally, in the sales process, we can generate the sales invoice. This will change the inventory transaction to the **Sold** status and create the financial transaction in the general ledger.

Let's go through the process of an outbound order and describe how these activities are handled.

The starting step of this process is to create the picking list. However, as it is an optional step, to do so, we need to set up some configurations first.

First, we will activate the picking route for sales and transfer orders. Go to Account receivable | Setup | Account receivable parameters, and in the Updates tab, we can select the picking route status.

If we set this field to Activated, the picking list lines must be manually updated. But if we set it to Completed, the picking process is made automatically when we generate the picking list. So, it depends on which method we use.

The same setup exists for transfer orders. Go to Inventory Management | Setup | Inventory and warehouse management parameters, and in the Transfer orders tab, we can select a value in the Picking route status field.

Following that, we need to activate the **End output inventory order** option. Go to Inventory **Management** | **Setup** | **Inventory and warehouse management parameters**, and under the **General** tab, you will find this option.

When warehouse workers process the picking list, the quantities are picked and reduced from the output order. If we set the **End output inventory order** option to **Yes**, the output order automatically ends, and the pending picking quantities are reported in the inventory order. But if it is set to **No**, then the output order is not closed, and we need to create another picking list for the remaining quantities.

With these two options, we can start our picking list process. So, let's go to a sales order under **Sales and Marketing** | **Sales Order** | **All sales orders**. Here, we need to select the order we want to ship and then go to the **Pick and Pack** tab, under the **Generate** group | the **Generate picking list** option.

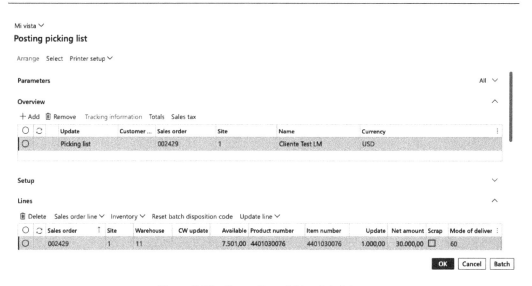

Figure 3.17 – Generating picking list dialog

Here, we generate the picking list. As we see in *Figure 3.17*, we have some options to explore:

- Under the **Parameters** group, we have the **Quantity** option, which we can associate with a previous sales process to relate the quantities we can pick; for example, the **Deliver Now** option takes the quantities from the Deliver Now field in the sales order. For this example, we set the **All** option, meaning all the ordered quantities will be picked.

- The **Reduce quantity** option, if set to **Yes**, automatically reduces the quantities from the available stock when we post the picking list. But if it is set to **No**, we must post a packing slip to reduce the picked quantities.

- In the **Print options** group, we can decide whether or not to print the picking list and use the print management options.

- The **overview** grid shows the orders this picking list includes. We can set it to more than one if we go to the select button at the top of this dialog screen. There, it will let us input a query to select more than one order or order line for picking.

- The **setup** tab shows important dates to set, such as picking list date, Payment terms base date, Due date, and document date.

- The **Line** and **Line details** tabs have information on each line and item to pick from the inventory. If we need to, we can decrease the quantities from the update field, and then it will select less from the stock.

By selecting **OK**, we will create the picking list. In the same sales order, we can go to the **Picking list registration** option, which will show us the picking route created for this shipment.

Selecting **Functions** and **Start picking route** will start the picking activity, and it will assign a worker to perform the picking activity.

In the lines tab, we can select the lines we want to pick, and then on **Functions | Update selected**, it will change the status to completed. If there are more lines, we can pick them one by one or update every line at once by going to **Updates** > **Update All** at the top of the form. As soon as we update all lines, the shipment will be completed.

These actions will register the picking list and the inventory transaction changes to pick the status. Also, if during picking list generation, we set the parameter **Reduce quantity** to yes, it will reduce the quantities from the on-hand inventory.

The final step in this output order is to post the packing slip. For example, a warehouse manager could go to **Inventory Management | Outbound Orders | Shipments**, select the shipment and then select the **Post packing slip** option to perform this activity. Likewise, a sales clerk or manager could navigate to the sales order under the **Pick and Pack** tab | the **Generate** group | **Post packing slip**.

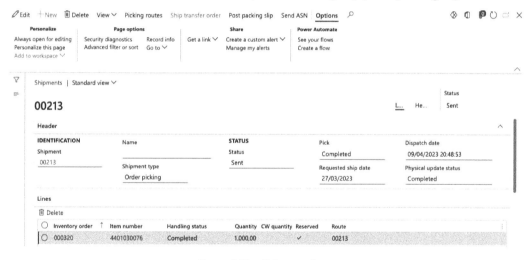

Figure 3.18 – Shipment form

Either way, we end up on the **Packing slip Posting** dialog screen, which has the same structure as the posting product receipt in the procurement process. Here, we can modify some information too.

We have the **Parameter** group in the **Parameters** tab with the same options as the picking list. But here, it is crucial to make sure that if we want to post this transaction in the general ledger, we set the Posting option to yes.

Compliance Documents show us options to print hazardous safety data sheets or prevent the completion of the process if a product's data sheet is expired.

In the **Overview** grid, we can see the packing slip information and the sales orders included.

The **Setup** tab shows important dates to know of, such as picking list date, Payment terms base date, Due date, and document date.

The **Line** and **Line details** tabs have the information of each line and item we picked from the inventory.

If we don't need to do the picking process on our implementation, we could easily start from the packing slip creation and select from here the quantities of items we will ship. That's why the **Parameter group** has a **Quantity** option. However, if you navigate to the Shipment, you'll see that this option is blocked because it relies on items being picked or reserved to perform this action.

When you click OK, a packing slip is generated, decreasing the on-hand stock (if not done on the picking list execution), creating the physical posting of the inventory, and modifying the status of the inventory order to Deducted.

Inventory journals

All Inventory management module transactions are based on inventory journals. These update and register the physical inventory transactions we can group into three inventory movements: increasing, decreasing, and moving from one location to another on-hand stock.

There are several inventory journals worth mentioning:

- **Movement**: This adds inventory and costs to an item but overrides the item group setup because we manually input the offset account. This inventory journal overrides the default accounts and imports the on-hand inventory as part of the implementation migration process.

- **Inventory adjustment**: This journal works similarly to the movement journal. It adds or decreases inventory and costs to an item. But this journal uses the default posting setup done in the item group. It is used when we need to register gains or losses to the inventory.

- **Transfer**: If we need to transfer items from one location to another, we could use this journal. Note that this journal is used when there are no financial implications. Otherwise, a transfer order is needed.

For example, if we need to transfer an item from warehouse A to warehouse B without cost or transit considerations, we use this journal.

A Transfer journal is a simple process that just requires filling in the from location and the to location and hitting Post journal. But in the background, it carries out two inventory transactions—an issue at the origin location and a receipt at the destination location:

- **Bill of materials (BOM)**: This journal is a production process made simple. If you have a BOM in place, you could report an item as finished with this journal. It generates an issue transaction of all the components in the BOM and a receipt transaction on the finished item. It is used in scenarios where an item needs to be produced, but we don't want to register a production order, or we don't need to consider the working times. For example, if we have a silo with liquid glue, we have to split it into 5-liter containers. Registering this type of journal rather than creating a production order is helpful for these cases.

- **Inventory ownership change**: This type of journal is associated with consignment orders and is used when we use the consignment inventory. This allows us to generate a purchase order for these items. The value of this inventory is charged to the company ledger accounts.

- **Item arrival**: This journal registers when an item arrives at a warehouse. Earlier in this chapter, we discussed the Arrival overview form in inbound order processing. The first journal created on that page is the item arrival journal, which could be manually created from this option.

- **Production input**: This is used when we need to receive items for a production order. This process could be initiated from the production order, but it can be created manually in this option.

- **Counting**: When we need to count items and control the on-hand inventory in the system versus the actual physical stock, we use this journal.

  We can set counting as part of the cycle counting process or count specific warehouses or locations in our inventory. When we create this type of journal, we can create its lines automatically by selecting the **Create lines** button, which has three different options: **On-hand** will look up to the on-hand stock and create lines based on that information. **Items** will look up to the released item's information and filter based on parameters we can set up. The **Expired batches** option will look up the expired batches to correct that inventory.

  In every case, we could filter by **Counting groups** and filter the items counted since a specific date.

  After creating this journal, we can print the counting list from the print menu, which allows the workers to have a copy of the locations and inventory they have to count. This counting list has options to be a blind counting or to show inventory quantities on the report.

When the quantities are updated, and all the count information is registered, we can post the journal; this will adjust the inventory, increasing or decreasing stocks and costs. The same principle for posting is used in the Inventory adjustment journal.

- **Tag counting**: We use this journal to count items by their tags. Each tag contains the tag number, item, and quantity. By creating this type of journal, we can scan or complete the tag number of each item and ensure that the product is in the inventory.

Each tag can be used one time and has three statuses:

- **Used**, meaning is counted
- **Voided**, meaning is not used anymore
- **Missing**, meaning is not in the inventory

So, when we post this journal, it creates a counting journal based on the tag counting lines, which allows us to register that quantity difference in the stock.

To create any journal, we have to go to the **Inventory Management | Journal Entries** menu. The different types of journals are divided into groups.

In the Items group, we'll find the groups related to **Items**, such as **Movement**, **Inventory adjustment**, **Transfer**, **Bills of materials**, and **Inventory ownership change**. Then, in the Item arrival group, we'll find journals related to the receiving process, **Item Arrival** and **Production input**. Finally, in the **Item counting** group, we'll find journals related to counting, such as **Counting** and **Tag counting**.

Setting up each of these journals is mandatory to create the journal names. The concept relies on pre-setup data being automatically populated on journal creation. For example, if we need to create a journal to register scrap month in a separate financial loss account, we could create a journal movement name for this and set it up with the proper offset account. This will allow the user to register only the quantities for that journal, not having to remember the bill every time and reducing the risk of typing errors.

Depending on the journal type, we can create these journal names by going to **Inventory Management | Setup | Journal Names | Inventory** or **Warehouse**.

Here, we can create a name and description and select a journal type. This type will be related to the process and part of the menu we will access.

In the voucher group, you will find the voucher series, when that number will be reserved, and on which date. Posting information will let us configure the level of detail we want to register in the General Ledger. The inventory group will control the way that we need to reserve the items before registration. Also, in the blocking group, we can maintain access to the journal only to a private group of users. Finally, we can associate the journal with an approval workflow. This will require complying with an approval process before the journal is posted.

Figure 3.19 – Inventory journal names

These approval workflows could be created by going to **Inventory Management | Setup | Inventory Management Workflows**. To set these workflows up, we must select which type of journal we will control with approvals.

There are approval workflows for the following: Counting, Ownership Change, Adjustment, BOM, Transfer, Movement, and Tag Counting.

To create one, take the following steps:

1. Click **New** and select the journal type you need. Then, a workflow editor app will be launched and installed on your computer.

2. Once the workflow is fully configured, you can save it and activate it to use it.

One thing to notice here is that workflows start working on the next created journal after we activate a workflow. This means that if we create a journal and, after that, activate a workflow, the journal won't enter into the approval steps. It also won't work for warehouse management processes.

To assign a workflow to a journal, in the **Inventory journal name** form, on the **Workflow** field, we can select the workflow from a drop-down list. It's also required to change the **Approval workflow** option to **Yes**.

Journals can be imported via the **Data Management framework**. This will become handy when working on the data migration process when initializing the inventory stock. If we import journal headers and lines, we need to make sure to use the same journal number in both entities, and the data created on the journal remains in that journal.

But to ease that migration process, two journals have composite entities, meaning we only need to migrate one entity to create a journal header and lines. But it will assume some things. So, for example, if we don't specify the number, it will create one every thousand lines. These entities are for **Inventory Adjustment Journal** and **Inventory Movement Journal**.

Working with transfer orders

A transfer order is a process by which we can move inventory from one facility to another. It considers when items are in transit from one warehouse to another. Its flow is part of the outbound and inbound processes in different sites or warehouses. Let me explain this in more depth.

When we need to transfer an item, we create a transfer order, and we will follow these steps:

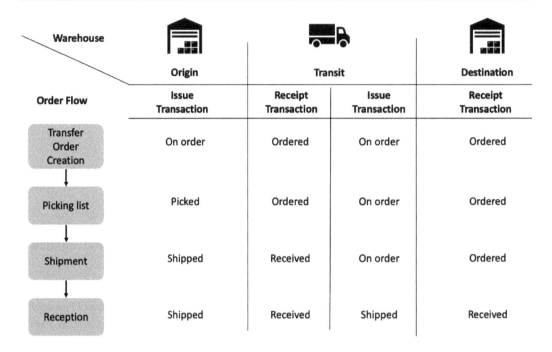

Warehouse	Origin	Transit		Destination
Order Flow	Issue Transaction	Receipt Transaction	Issue Transaction	Receipt Transaction
Transfer Order Creation	On order	Ordered	On order	Ordered
Picking list	Picked	Ordered	On order	Ordered
Shipment	Shipped	Received	On order	Ordered
Reception	Shipped	Received	Shipped	Received

Figure 3.20 – Transfer order flow and inventory statuses

1. Create the transfer order, indicating the origin and the destination warehouses and sites.
2. Pick the inventory from the origin warehouse.
3. Ship the items from the warehouse order to a transit warehouse.
4. Receive the items from the transit warehouse to the destination warehouse.

We could do the outbound process by generating a picking list, performing a picking list registration, and shipping the transfer order. The inbound process with the arrival overview receiving flow starts the arrival, posts the arrival journal, and receives the transfer order. This process could also be done with the **warehouse management system (WMS)** we will cover in *Chapter 7*.

It is essential to mention that transfer orders can also be done with the inventory transfer journal, but they have some differences.

A transfer order is a two-step process involving shipping and reception in two separate actions. In the middle of the process, the inventory is stored in a transit warehouse, waiting to be received. But a transfer journal is a single-step order because posting the journal will trigger the inventory to move to the destination immediately. A transfer order also could generate a printed document for fiscal control (in countries where this is needed).

We can create a transfer order by going to **Inventory Management | Inbound orders or Outbound Orders | Transfer order** to reach the following form:

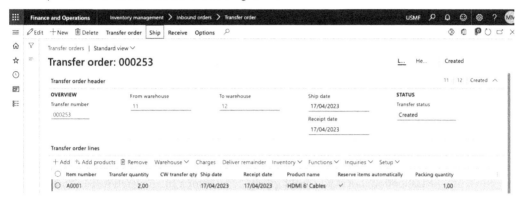

Figure 3.21 – Transfer order screen

Here, we hit new, and then fill the fields "from" and "to warehouse" to indicate the origin and destination of the materials. First, we need to ensure that the origin warehouse has a transfer warehouse set up in the Warehouse form, as we have seen before.

In the transfer order **Lines** tab, we must put all the items we need to transfer. For example, we could input a shipping and receipt date to plan when to move the stock. Also, we can reserve items automatically from the inventory by clicking on that option on every line, or we can do it manually from the **inventory | Reservation** option.

Once everything is set up, we can generate the picking list to manually pick items, as seen in the outbound process. Or we can skip that process and ship directly from the Ship transfer order option in the **Operations** group under the **Ship** tab.

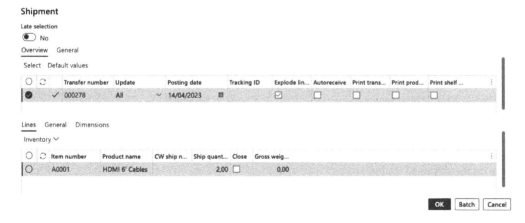

Figure 3.22 – Shipment dialog

This screen has several options to control how to transfer the materials. First, in the **update** field, we could select which quantities and lines we ship:

- **Ship Now** uses the **Ship Now** field in the Transfer order form; for example, if our line has 10 units to transfer and we input 5 units in the **Ship now** field, it will dispatch 5 units

- **All** will ship all units mentioned in the transfer quantity field

- The **Reserved Quantity** option will ship only the quantities we reserve for this transfer order

- **Available quantity** will ship only the available stock for the items in the transfer order

- **Picked quantity** will ship selected quantities via the picking list

These options depend on which actions and flow you are following. For example, to pick lists or WMS flows, you'll use the last option, but if you are shipping items from a small warehouse to an external one, it may be better to use the **All** or **Ship Now** option.

We can input the tracking ID in its field, if we have one, for informational purposes. It will be printed on the transfer shipment report.

There are also options to handle our items. For example, if we don't use a picking list, we could control which batch or serials are used for this process by clicking the Explode line check. This will allow us to manipulate each line's information by inventory dimension.

Auto receive check will automatically receive the items in the destination warehouse once shipped. This is useful for handling the receiving process in a third-party warehouse. For example, suppose we have a subcontracting vendor and we need to ship items to be manufactured by them. In that case, this option will handle that receiving flow by registering the reception automatically.

All these options could default to the **Default Values** option whenever we enter the ship transfer order menu.

Finally, we hit ok, and we can process the operation. Here, two transactions will be done: an outgoing transaction from the origin warehouse and an input transaction to the transit warehouse. Also, two movements are still pending: the output transaction from the transit warehouse and the receiving transaction to the destination one.

If all lines were sent, the transfer order status would change to **Shipped**.

To process this transaction, we can go to the **Receive** menu and, under the **operations** group, hit **Receive**.

A **Receive** dialog screen will pop up, showing which options we can select for this; they are similar to those on the shipment dialog .

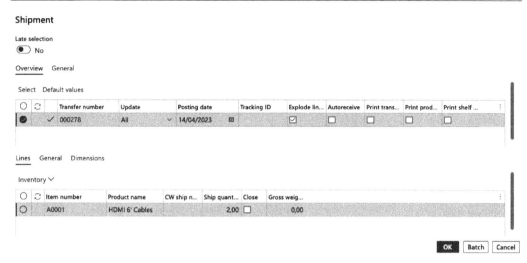

Figure 3.23 – Shipment dialog

In the update field, we have four options:

- **Receive now**: We will receive only the quantities for the lines for which we input a receive now quantity

- **All**: We will receive all quantities on the transfer warehouse we sent in this transfer order

- **Shipment**: We will receive the orders for one particular shipment ID

- **Registered quantities** that we picked for this specific transfer order

In the same way as before, if we select the **Explode lines** option, we can modify the receiving batches and locations for these items.

Once we are done, we can hit **Ok**, and it will process those two pending transactions.

There are some things to consider during this process.

The receiving process could be done on the arrival overview screen, which will also update this transfer order.

If we need to print a legal or informational document on this transaction, we could print the shipment details document under the **Ship** tab | the **View** group.

We could also process a load and a shipment with the WMS process if our warehouse is set up for those flows, but we will discuss these in this book *Chapters 7*, *8*, and *9* when we talk about WMS and TMS chapters.

It is important to note that there is no fixed, standalone flow for transfer orders; we could adapt this flow to best fit our implementation requirements.

Inquiries and reports

There are various inquiries and reports we can find in this module but we are just going to mention two of them.

The most used is the On-hand inventory, which we can find by navigating to **Inventory management | Inquiries and reports | On-Hand list**.

Figure 3.24 – On-hand List

In the on-hand list, we can review the inventory we have. When we access this form, it will provide the option to filter the information we want to view. Then, it will display the on-hand inventory, as shown in *Figure 3.24*. Information will be displayed in various columns:

- **Physical inventory**: Refers to the physically stored inventory.

- **Physical reserved**: Refers to the reserved inventory.

- **Available physical**: Refers to the inventory we can use. It is determined by subtracting the physical inventory from the physical reserved inventory.

- **Ordered in total**: Refers to orders that will increase the quantity of the inventory but have not been received yet.

- **On order**: Refers to orders that will use part of the inventory but are not reserved yet.

- **Available for reserve**: Refers to the inventory we can reserve for later use. Here, we have the projected receipts and consumption of the inventory.

- **Total Available**: Refers to the total inventory that will be available once pending orders are executed.

With this information, you can analyze the on-hand inventory. The beauty of this report is that you can modify the inventory dimensions, such as adding the location dimension to view inventory grouped by location or, for example, deactivating the warehouse dimension to view inventory group by site.

Another vital inventory query is the transactions inquiry. We can access it by navigating to **Inventory management | Inquiries and reports | Transactions**. We will find the following form:

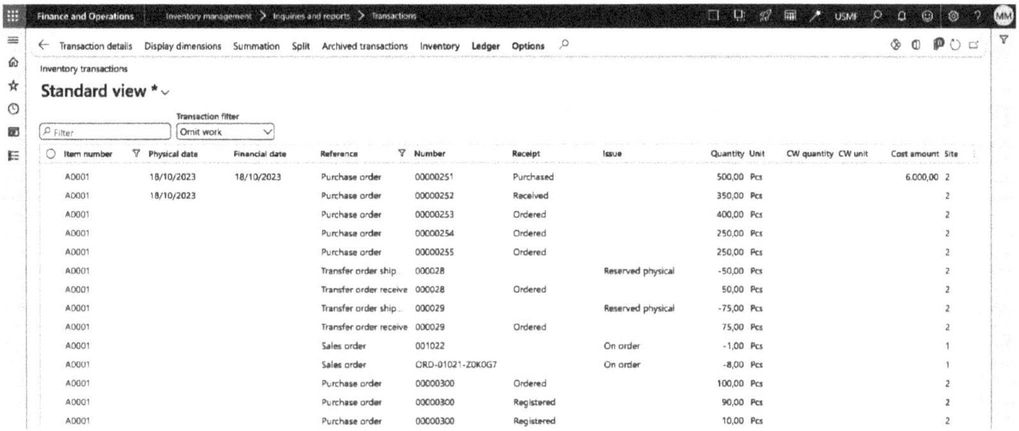

Figure 3.25 – Inventory transactions

As shown in *Figure 3.25*, the Inventory transactions query shows us all the inventory transactions in progress.

All transactions in this form have a status that tells us their progress. The status divides transactions into receipt and issue transactions. Receipt transactions have the following statuses:

- **Ordered**: Transaction is created
- **Registered**: Transaction has arrived but has not yet been received
- **Received**: Stock has been received and accounted for
- **Purchased**: Transactions have been invoiced

The same happens on issue transactions:

- **On order**: Transaction is created
- **Picked**: Picking list has been completed
- **Deducted**: Transaction has been shipped to the customer
- **Reserved physical**: Transaction has been reserved from the inventory
- **Sold**: Transaction has been invoiced

We can also view how much of the item has been requested and the total cost of the transaction. If we need more information, we can click on the transaction details to explore all the information related to that transaction.

All inventory reports can be found from the **Inventory Management | Inquiries and Reports** menu. You can find multiple inquiries and reports of this module segmented by its process.

Closing and adjustment

As part of the month-end or period-end closing activities, we need to ensure we process an inventory closing process. This process helps to reevaluate cost transactions and match inventory issue transactions with receipt transactions according to the inventory valuation method selected in the inventory model group of each item.

Usually, this process is run once per month, but it depends on each company's requirements. For example, some companies do it after each cycle count. But it is essential to run an inventory closing process regularly because it helps to ensure the costs of products are up to date. For example, Dynamics 365 SCM keeps track of the cost of each product using the weighted average dated costing method. the closing process reevaluates the transactions to the selected method for all items. For example, suppose we decide to use the First in, first out (FIFO) costing method. In that case, all transactions will be automatically recorded under the weighted average dated costing method. Once we close inventory, the transactions will be reevaluated using the FIFO costing method.

Date	Transaction type	Reference	Quantity	Price	Cost at posting	Cumulative cost	Cumulative qty	Weighted average cost		Cost price after closing	Cost price adjustment
Apr/01	Opening	On-hand	1	100,0	100,0	100,0	1,0	100,0			
Apr/10	Receipt (1)	Purchase order	1	90,0	90,0	190,0	2,0	95,0			
Apr/12	Issue (1)	Sales order	-1		-95,0	95,0	1,0	95,0	Inventory	100,0	-5,0
Apr/15	Receipt (2)	Inventory Adjustment	1	130,0	130,0	225,0	2,0	112,5	Closing		
Apr/17	Issue (2)	Sales order	-1		-112,5	112,5	1,0	112,5		90,0	22,5
Apr/20	Receipt (3)	Inventory Adjustment	1	150,0	150,0	262,5	2,0	131,3			
Apr/22	Issue (3)	Sales order	-1		-131,3	131,3	1,0	131,3		130,0	1,3
Apr/30	Closing	On-hand	1							150,0	

Figure 3.26 – FIFO costing example

In *Figure 3.26*, we can observe an example of all inventory transactions for one month. We have one quantity referenced as on-hand inventory, valued at 100 USD at the start of the month, and then we have a list of transactions. Each receipt transaction has a price of acquisition. As the days go by, the weighted average cost of the transaction changes because it divides the cumulative cost into the cumulative quantity. When an issue transaction is made, the cost will be recorded using the weighted average cost.

When we perform the inventory closing process, the system confirms the valuation method of the item, and it recalculates all issue transaction costing, matching the receipt transaction (or on-hand inventory) accordingly. For this example, on a FIFO method, match the opening on-hand value with the first issue. This creates a difference of -5 between the posted issue cost (95) and the FIFO cost (100). This is done for every transaction of every item. Once the process ends, it creates a closing posting with all the differences to the inventory account of every item, and it also makes an inventory transaction of inventory valuation.

Not all valuation methods require this closing. It isn't necessary for the standard costing method. This method has a default cost, so every inventory transaction will be valued at the standard cost. However, if a receipt transaction has a different value, this cost difference will be accounted for in a separate ledger account.

We must go to Inventory Management | Periodic Tasks | Closing and Adjustment to perform the inventory closing. It is also available under the Cost Administration workspace's Cost Management menu. Once there, we will see the following form:

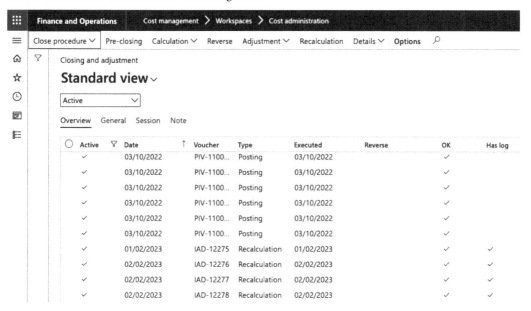

Figure 3.27 – Closing and adjustment form

Under the **Close procedure** option, we have three options. **Check open quantities** will show us a report with all transactions with physical costs but not financial ones—for example, a purchase order receipt without the purchase invoice. If we have some of these transactions, they won't be fully closed because the invoice's value could change the item's cost value. What will happen is that those transactions will remain open until the invoice is fully registered and we perform the subsequent inventory closing.

Check cost prices will print a report with the evaluation of cost prices until the expected closing date with a percentage variation. This will allow us to control every transaction that exceeds that threshold.

Close inventory is the action that will execute the inventory closing process. A dialog with options controlling the batch process will appear when we click that option.

The **period code** is the period that we are closing. If we don't use a period code, we could enter a date on which we close the inventory.

The **specification** is the level of detail that will be created in the voucher on the general ledger.

Knowing this is a time-consuming batch process, we have two parameters controlling endless iterations, and we must set them for better performance. **Max number of iterations per item** allows circularity on items, giving a better cost approximation but poorer performance. The **minimum amount allowed** gives a more approximated cost value but also jeopardizes the performance.

When we hit ok, it will start the closing process. Processing the batch job will take a while, so executing it during off-peak hours is recommended.

Once finished, it will block inventory transactions that have a date before the closing date. We can also view the **voucher** created for these adjustments on the **Details** option.

The **Details** menu also has a **Settlement** option showing which transactions were closed and adjusted.

We can also review the **log** for the closing process in the details option. We have warning and error messages about transactions that could not be processed or closed.

We can make some on-hand adjustments to the inventory closing process, allowing us to massively modify the closing cost value of the on-hand inventory. We can access the **Adjustment** menu and the **On-hand** option to do this. We can also adjust the calculated price of a receipt transaction by going to **Adjustment | Transaction**, but note that we cannot modify issue transactions this way.

If we need to reverse a closing operation, we can go to the Reverse option on this form, which will give us two options: reverse a voucher or all cost calculations. Once we execute a reverse, inventory closing will be canceled, allowing us to post inventory transactions in that period again. Remember that if you need to reverse an earlier closing, you must reverse all subsequent closings to reach the one needed.

Finally, there is an option to recalculate the inventory costs. This allows us to perform the costing calculations without a complete inventory closing process.

Summary

Inventory management is a robust module in which we control not only stock levels and how we store our inventory but also how we can process and validate information on the related supply chain processes, such as procurement and sales.

In this chapter, we've shown how to create and segment an inventory warehouse, defining its aisles and locations. We discussed how to work with inbound orders with the arrival overview option and inventory journals. In addition, we've seen the outbound orders flow and how to process transfer orders.

We also learned about inventory categorization with ABC classification and all the internal operations of a warehouse, such as cycle counts. Finally, we walked to the inventory closing process and updated the costs in our inventory using the costing method.

In the next chapter, we'll dive into the world of the procurement and sourcing module and learn how a company can request and purchase items and services.

Questions

1. A warehouse worker needs to transfer 10 units of cowboy boots from one picking location to another in the same warehouse. As a supply chain consultant, which of the following is the recommended activity?

    A. Transfer order with the **Auto receive** option enabled

    B. Transfer order with the **Auto receive** option disabled

    C. Transfer journal

    D. Movement journal

2. A warehouse manager asks you to recommend to him a suitable time to carry out inventory closing. He tells you that the finance department is closing periods once a month, but he has purchase orders that are not invoiced until one or two months later, so the costs of those transactions are not closed.

    As a supply chain consultant, which is the best option?

    A. Only do an inventory closing when the orders are fully invoiced

    B. Close inventory once a month, and if it is mandatory to keep costs updated, run an inventory recalculation in the open period

3. A warehouse worker has shipped an inventory transfer order. This order has two lines. He has only shipped the first line fully and the second line is still to be sent. What will be the status of the transfer order?

    A. Created

    B. Shipped

    C. Received

Answers

1. Option C

    An inventory transfer journal is recommended for transferring items between locations in the same warehouse. A transfer order works better for movements in different warehouses because it uses the concept of the transfer warehouse, and it has a shipping and receiving step.

2. Option B

    For the inventory transactions to be closed in the next periods is a better option to do an inventory closing once a month to update the GL transactions and also do an inventory recalculation to keep costs up to date when possible.

3. Option A

    It will be created because its status changes when all lines have the same status. To be shipped, all lines have to be fully sent. To be received, all lines must be fully received.

4

Procurement and Sourcing, the Start of the Journey

Procurement is the first step of our journey: learning how to purchase items and services from vendors. In this chapter, we will dive deep into the procurement-to-purchase process.

We will also review the end-to-end process, learn about the importance of purchase requisitions and purchase orders, navigate vendor rebates and contracts, and explore a beautiful feature for purchasing teams and vendors, the vendor collaboration portal.

Specifically, we will cover the following main topics:

- Procurement-to-purchase process
- Vendor collaboration portal
- Working with vendor rebates
- What about consignment inventory?

Let's go step by step and review the procure-to-purchase process in Dynamics 365 Supply Chain Management first.

Procure-to-purchase process

Think of the procurement process as a journey. It's a trip that your company takes to find the best goods and services it needs to keep things running smoothly. This journey is super important because you can save a lot of money and make your company more profitable if you do it right.

The first step of this journey is creating a **Request for Quotation** (**RFQ**). This is like inviting potential suppliers and asking them to tell you how much they'd charge for what you need. It's like shopping around to find the best deal.

Next, you'll start getting bids from suppliers. It's like receiving a bunch of different offers. Now, you must review these offers and decide which is the best. You're looking at more than just the price; you're also looking at quality, delivery time, and whether the supplier is reliable. This step is essential because making the right choice can save money and avoid headaches.

Once you've picked the best offer, you send the supplier a **Purchase Order** (**PO**). This is like your official agreement, saying you'll buy certain goods or services for a specific price. You must ensure this document is clear and accurate to avoid confusion or problems later.

When the goods or services are delivered, you check to ensure everything is as you ordered. If so, you accept the delivery and pay the supplier's invoice. This is the final step of the journey, and it's essential to ensure the invoice matches what you agreed to in the PO so you don't end up overpaying.

This journey can be much easier if you have the right tools. That's where Dynamics 365 Supply Chain Management comes in. It's like your trusty travel companion, helping you manage every step of the procurement process. It can handle RFQs, evaluate bids, create POs, and process invoices, all in one place. Plus, it can track deliveries, keep an eye on how healthy suppliers are, and even predict what you'll need based on what you've needed. With Dynamics 365 Supply Chain Management, your procurement journey can be smooth and successful.

In the following figure, we can see a short overview of the procure-to-purchase process and the relevant steps:

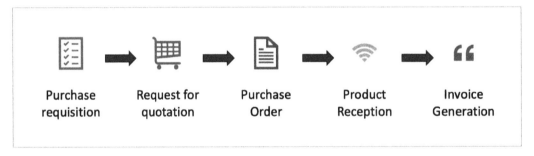

Figure 4.1 – Procure-to-purchase process

We will go through each step of the process in the next subsections.

Purchase requisition

Think of working with purchase requests like making an elaborate shopping list for your organization. When your company needs certain products or services, whether to keep the business running smoothly or to fuel growth, you jot down what you need on this list. This is also known as a **purchase request**. It's like having your own personal assistant, ensuring you get precisely what you need when you need it.

Now, not all shopping lists are created equal. Some organizations allow for various types of lists. One of these is the **replenishment** list – imagine it as your backroom grocery list. This list is for restocking items in specific places such as warehouses or offices. Once completed, the list gets whisked off to the master planner, who then puts their thinking cap on to determine the most effective way to fill the order. Once they give it their stamp of approval, the items are ready for delivery!

Next, we have the **consumption** list, a type of shopping list you use when you need to order items directly. This list comes into play for things the company will use internally – think office supplies or maintenance equipment.

And you can still compile a shopping list for these **indirect products** for those random items that occasionally pop up, unplanned – once-in-a-blue-moon purchases. This flexibility ensures nothing is left out and your operations run like a well-oiled machine.

Once your meticulously crafted shopping list is ready, it's forwarded to the purchasing department. They play the role of quality control, reviewing your list, and once it meets their criteria, they use your list to place the order with the vendors. It's like having a personal shopper!

If your organization allows it, you can order items directly from a supplier's website. You could be looking for the latest tech gadgets or scouring for a rare or unique item not found in any catalog. And, assuming you've been granted the proper access rights, you can also step in and make a shopping list for another colleague, helping to lighten their load.

Now, how do you keep track of all these shopping lists? Well, there's a predefined workflow process to keep everything in check. This process guides your list from when it's submitted, like a trusted chaperone, to approval and the final order being placed. You don't need to worry about losing track of your requests. There are two main types of shopping lists you'll come across:

- **Consumption lists**: Think of these as your internal shopping lists. They're for items or services that your organization will use internally. Once approved, an order is placed as quickly as a pizza delivery, ensuring you get what you need in no time.

- **Replenishment lists**: These are your inventory restocking gurus. If you need to ensure there's enough of a product to sell at a particular location and time, this is your go-to list. Depending on the situation, this list might be fulfilled through purchase, transfer, production, or even Kanban order.

Using a replenishment list means specifying the quantity of each item rather than the cost. This focus on quantity means that specific budget control and accounting rules don't apply, making it simpler and more efficient.

To effectively use a replenishment list, you must schedule to include request demand. The most efficient way to fill the order is then determined automatically, using a blend of the supply policies for the items in your organization and planning using master scheduling. It's like having a personal logistic manager ensuring everything runs smoothly.

Working with purchase requests means having an efficient, reliable system that ensures your organization always has the goods and services it needs right when it needs them, helping your operations to run seamlessly.

How to create a purchase requisition

Purchase requisitions can be created from the **Procurement and sourcing** module > **Purchase requisitions** > **All Purchase requisitions**.

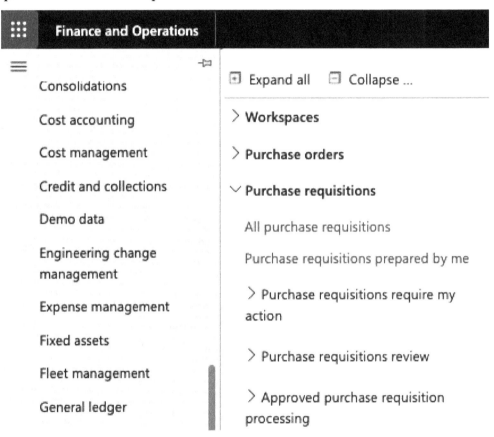

Figure 4.2 – Purchase requisition menu item

Think of this list as your superhero guide to all your shopping needs within the organization. It's like your personal organizer with the *who*, *what*, and *when* of purchase requests. It keeps track of the request number, who's supplying the goods, who prepared the request, and whether it's linked to any specific projects.

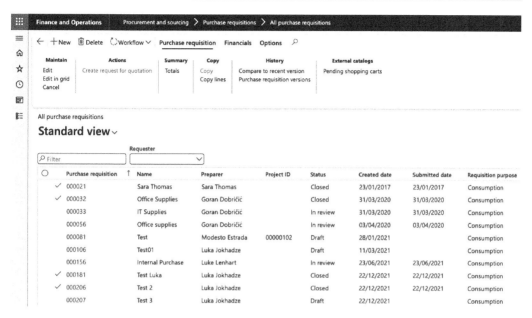

Figure 4.3 – The All purchase requisitions page

But wait, there's more! It also gives you a quick peek into how things are going, such as the status of the request (don't worry, we'll get to what these status terms mean in a moment).

All right, let's hit the pause button and focus momentarily on the **Status** column. Understanding these status terms will make creating a new request feel like a walk in the park. So, fasten your seatbelts; we're about to dive into the fun world of statuses of purchase requisitions.

Purchase requisitions statuses

As soon as a purchase requisition is created, this requisition receives a status. Likewise, every item or line you append to the purchase request also gets its own status. As soon as the purchase request gets submitted for validation via a workflow, the status of both the request and each item within it gets adjusted in line with their progression through the workflow process.

You have the flexibility to set up the workflow so that it channels the purchase request through the validation/approval process as a single entity. Alternatively, you can have each line on the purchase request independently directed to the suitable approver. If the lines of the purchase request undergo separate scrutiny, the status of each line gets modified as it proceeds through the examination process. Once all lines have successfully passed through the scrutiny procedure and no more assessment stages remain for the purchase request, the status of the entire purchase request is updated.

The following figure provides a snapshot of the various statuses of a purchase requisition and each line in the request received during the workflow approval process:

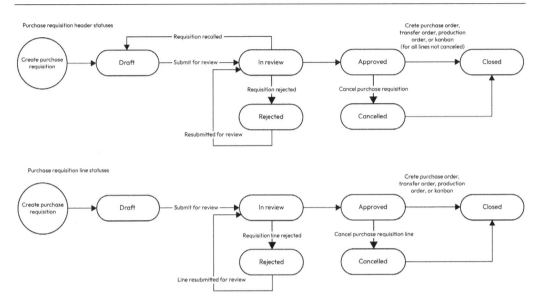

Figure 4.4 – Purchase requisition status map

Purchase requisition header and line status relationships

The status of each line influences the overall status of a purchase request. So, all lines within the request must complete their review journey before it can be thoroughly reviewed. The following table illustrates the various statuses of the request and the individual lines' experience navigating the workflow process.

Purchase requisition status	Purchase requisition line status	Description	
Draft	Draft	The purchase request and each line within it are ready to go but haven't been sent for review just yet. They're still in the **Draft** phase, which means you can tweak or adjust them as needed. If a request or line is recalled and hasn't been sent back for review, it also remains in the **Draft** phase. Keep in mind that you can send or pull back a whole purchase request at the document level. However, this doesn't work for individual lines within the request - you can't send or recall just one line.	

	In review	Suppose the workflow is set up to send each item in the purchase request to different reviewers. In that case, each item can carry an **In review** or **Rejected** status. The overall status of the purchase request is refreshed once the review starts.
		In review means that the items within the purchase request are under examination. Once a line in the request completes its journey through the workflow process, it retains the **In review** status. It continues to hold this status until every other item in the request has had its turn under the review spotlight.
In review	**Rejected**	**Rejected** means that a purchase requisition line has been rejected. Purchase requisition lines that are rejected can be modified and resubmitted.
		Remember, if you send back a line in your request that's been given a thumbs down (rejected), the review journey begins from scratch for all items in the request that are still waiting in the **In review** status
		Keep in mind that if you've already sent out a purchase request, you still have the option to bring it back. When you pull back a request, every line or item within it gets recalled too. And guess what? Any recalled item in your request can be removed if you no longer need it.
Rejected	**Rejected**	The entire purchase request and all items within it have been rejected. But don't worry! Rejected requests and any lines in them can dust themselves off and be sent back for another review round.
Approved	**Approved**	Every item in the purchase request has finished its review adventure, and all lines have been approved
		Approved means that the purchase requisition line has passed its review and is now approved.
	Canceled	**Canceled** indicates that an approved purchase requisition line has been nullified as it's no longer needed. Only the lines that received approval can receive this status.
	Closed	This means the purchase requisition line received approval and subsequent documents were produced based on its purpose.
		For consumption purposes, a purchase order is created.
		For replenishment purposes, multiple fulfillment documents are generated.

Canceled	Canceled	The entire purchase requisition, including all its associated lines, has been canceled.
Closed	Closed	The purchase requisition has been finalized, resulting in the generation of one or more fulfillment documents.
		Closed means that the purchase requisition line has received approval and subsequent documents were produced based on its designated purpose.
		If intended for consumption, a purchase order is created.
	Canceled	**Canceled** means that the approved purchase requisition line has been canceled due to a change in requirements. Only lines that have received approval are eligible for cancellation.

Table 4.1 – Approval status explanation

Now that we've gone over the various statuses of a purchase requisition and its lines, let's embark on the journey of creating a purchase request.

Purchase requisition creation

The following are the steps to create a purchase requisition:

1. To create a purchase requisition, we need to navigate to the **Procurement and sourcing** module > **Purchase requisitions** > **All Purchase requisitions** > **New**.

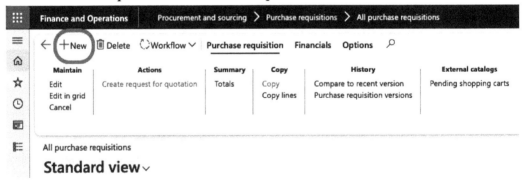

Figure 4.5 – New purchase requisition

2. From here, we will start our requisition journey, and the following screen will appear after clicking on the **New** button:

Create purchase requisition

Purchase requisition

PR002260

Name

Requested date

28/07/2023

Accounting date

28/07/2023

⬜ **SELECT DEFAULT PROJECT**

Buying legal entity

Project ID

Figure 4.6 – New purchase requisition creation

From here, we can give a name to our purchase requisition that represents what we are requesting. Also, we can associate the project associated with this request.

After we enter the minimal values for the purchase requisition creation, the next step will be to define a business justification in the header section, and a text field with the details where we can explain the purpose of our request.

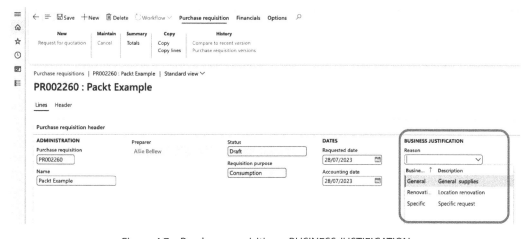

Figure 4.7 – Purchase requisition – BUSINESS JUSTIFICATION

Business justifications can be defined in a separate table at the following path: **Procurement and sourcing > Setup > Policies > Business justifications**.

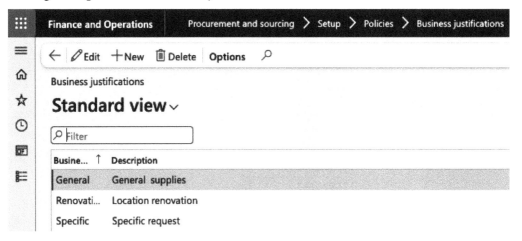

Figure 4.8 – Business justification table

1. Now, after we populate the business justifications, we can continue creating the draft of our purchase requisition and put the entire focus on the lines.

The lines can be added directly using the **Add line** button.

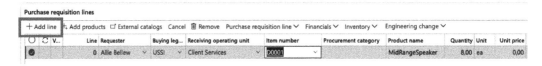

Figure 4.9 – Adding lines to purchase requisitions

Alternatively, we can do it using the **Add products** button, but here we will see a different screen showing our purchase catalog.

For top-notch service across our organization, I can't stress enough how important it is to craft a well-organized purchase catalog. When other departments liaise with the procurement team, this effort will be a massive time-saver for other business units.

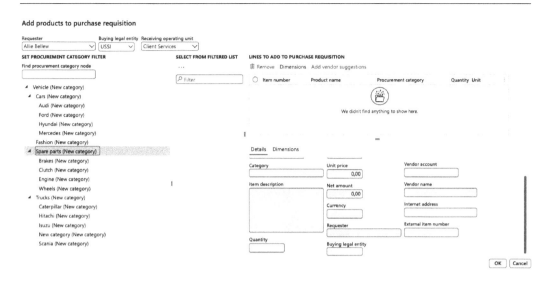

Figure 4.10 – Purchase requisitions catalog

To set up the procurement catalog, please use the following path in Dynamics 365 Supply Chain Management: **Procurement and sourcing Module** > **Procurement categories**. From this page, we can create a proper structure with nodes and sub-nodes and then associate the products or services for each sub-node.

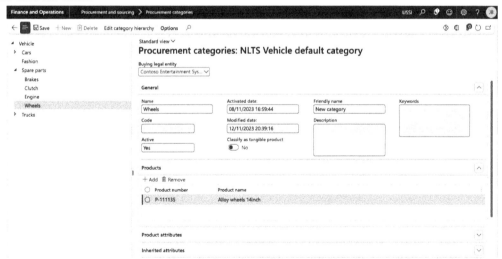

Figure 4.11 – Procurement categories menu item

4. After we have added the required lines to our purchase requisition, we can finally submit it for review/approval.

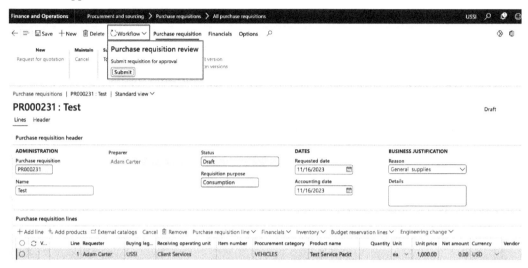

Figure 4.12 – Submitting the purchase requisition to the approval workflow

Once the purchase requisition reaches the final process of the workflow, we can continue to our next step in this journey. We can either create the PO immediately or go through the RFQ process.

Setting up purchasing policies helps to establish rules on whether a PO is automatically generated from a completed purchase requisition. How you've configured the PO and demand consolidation rule impacts how POs are created once a request gets the green light.

Unless a specific policy rule says otherwise, you must create all POs from the **Release manually approved purchase requests** list page. Once a purchase request hits the **Approved** status, you can automatically prepare the PO(s), with or without a batch job, or go old-school and do it manually. Let's now have a look at the RFQ process.

Setting up and carrying out an RFQ

The RFQ process invites suppliers to compete for your business by bidding on specific products and/ or services. It's like sending out an invitation when your organization needs to buy resources, asking various companies to put their best foot forward with competitive bids. This segment will guide you on how to put together quotation requests using our Supply Chain Management tools.

When you're in the market for something that multiple vendors can supply, you send a quotation request. The first steps are to create the demand, pick the vendors you'd like to see bids from, and then dispatch the request to them. Your quotation request will also include the deadline for their responses.

Here's what the RFQ process entails:

1. Crafting and dispatching a quotation request to one or more vendors

2. Receiving and logging the responses to your quotation request

3. Transferring the accepted responses to a PO

You can manually kick off the RFQ process from the **Request for Quotation** page, accessible from a list or details page. Or you can let the system automatically start it from a planned PO or a purchase request.

> **Important note**
> To start an RFQ from a purchase requisition, this request must be in a status of **In Review**; only then will the **Create request for quotation** button be active on the **Purchase requisitions** page.

Figure 4.13 – Creating an RFQ from a purchase requisition

After clicking **Create request for quotation**, we will see the following screen, asking to select the buying legal entity and the lines we want to transform into an RFQ.

Select the lines to copy to the request for quotation

Buying legal entity

UK04

	Purchase requisition	Item number	Product name	Buying leg...
✓	PR002257	3033	Entertaining UK Guests	UK04

Figure 4.14 – Selecting the lines to copy to the RFQ

After we accept the lines, we want to convert into an RFQ; the system will do the magic and will create our RFQ automatically. We should see a confirmation message like this:

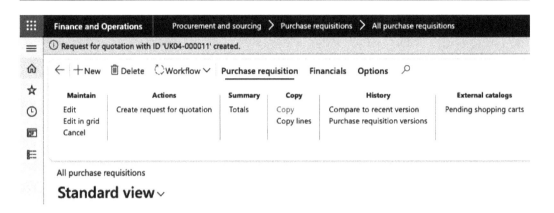

Figure 4.15 – RFQ creation confirmation message

Now, we can see our request for quotation created in the **Procurement and sourcing** module > **Requests for quotations** > **All requests for quotations**.

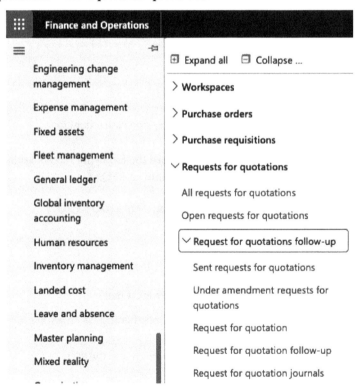

Figure 4.16 – The Requests for quotations menu item

From this menu item, we can see all the RFQs and the one we transform from a purchase requisition.

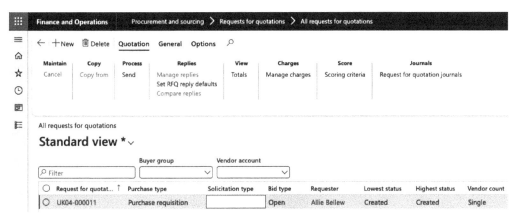

Figure 4.17 – All requests for quotations

In *Figure 4.17*, we can see the **Purchase type** column and, in this case, it clearly shows that this RFQ is coming from a purchase requisition. Let's look at the **Purchase type** options before we continue merging into the RFQ.

There are three possible purchase types when we create an RFQ:

Figure 4.18 – Selecting proper purchase types

In Dynamics 365 Supply Chain Management, we can issue an RFQ from three different sources:

- Manually or from planned POs
- From a purchase agreement
- From a purchase requisition, as we did before

RFQ statuses

As we reviewed before with purchase requisitions, RFQs also work with different statuses. Let's now explore the **Lowest status** and **Highest status** columns and let's navigate through these concepts in more detail.

The columns titled **Lowest status** and **Highest status** indicate the statuses of the order lines at their minimum and maximum levels, respectively. The order of statuses, from lowest to highest, is as follows:

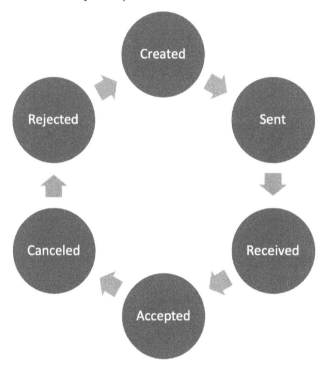

Figure 4.19 – RFQ statuses

Vendor count

Let's check another important column that could be relevant for this process. If we focus again on *Figure 4.17*, we will notice the **Vendor count** column; there are three possible values for this column:

- **None**: No vendor has been selected for this request
- **Single**: A single vendor has been selected for this request
- **Multiple**: Two or more vendors have been selected for this request

Now that we have done a general overview of the main fields and statuses of the RFQ, let's review the RFQ creation and sending process.

RFQ creation

Let's start by doing a manual RFQ. To do this, we will click the **New** button in the top bar, and immediately after this, we will see the following screen:

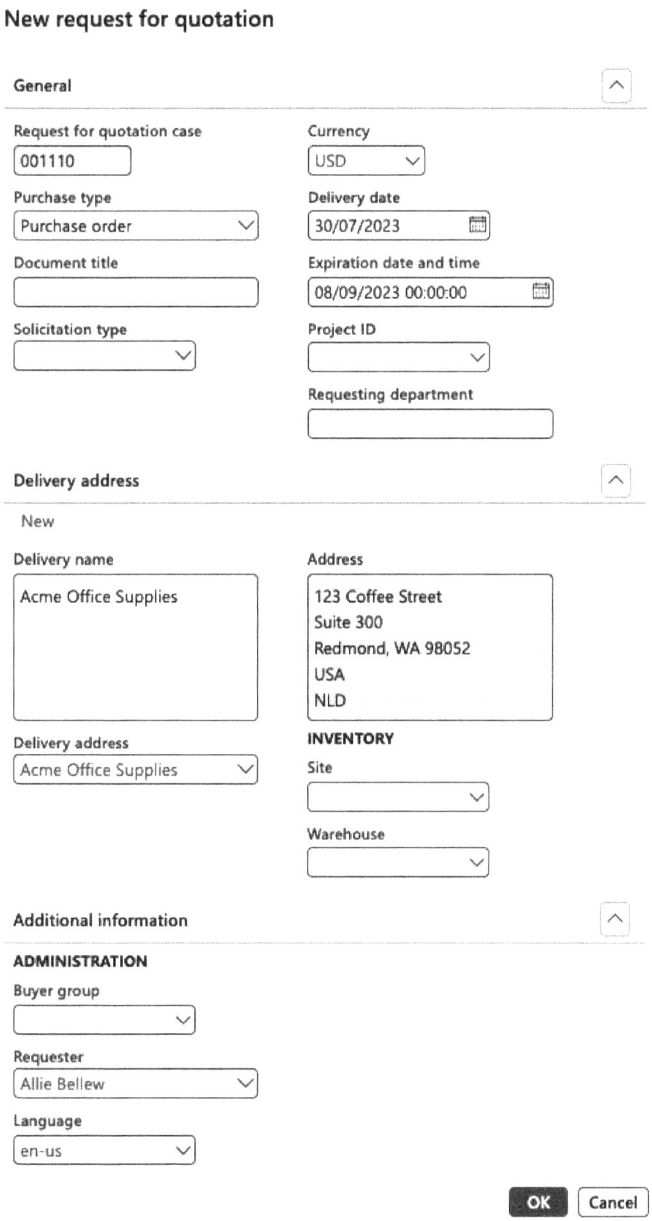

New request for quotation

General   ⌃

Request for quotation case   Currency
001110   USD   ⌄

Purchase type   Delivery date
Purchase order   ⌄   30/07/2023   📅

Document title   Expiration date and time
                                              08/09/2023 00:00:00   📅

Solicitation type   Project ID
                      ⌄   ⌄

                                              Requesting department

Delivery address   ⌃

  New

Delivery name   Address
Acme Office Supplies   123 Coffee Street
                                              Suite 300
                                              Redmond, WA 98052
                                              USA
                                              NLD

Delivery address   **INVENTORY**
Acme Office Supplies   ⌄   Site
                                                              ⌄

                                              Warehouse
                                                              ⌄

Additional information   ⌃

ADMINISTRATION
Buyer group
                      ⌄

Requester
Allie Bellew   ⌄

Language
en-us   ⌄

                                              OK   Cancel

Figure 4.20 – RFQ creation page

We must populate the field for our request with the significant possible details. Every field has a purpose and it is much better if we use them correctly.

The **Currency**, **Document title**, **Delivery date**, and **Expiration date and time** fields are relevant for our vendor; this information is like gold. Based on these values, our vendor could offer us different prices. So always be accurate when populating these fields.

> Solicitation type
>
> **Solicitation type** is mainly used to associate later scoring criteria. For more details on how to create a solicitation type and scoring criteria for an RFQ, visit the following link: `https://learn.microsoft.com/en-us/dynamics365/supply-chain/procurement/tasks/create-solicitation-types-scoring-criteria-rfqs`.

It is also essential to select the correct delivery address for our RFQ; our vendors might offer different prices based on the delivery location. If all fields are correctly populated, we are ready to click **OK** and continue our RFQ creation:

1. The first step will be to add our lines to our RFQ, adding the desired quantity in **Item number** in the **Request for quotation lines** section; the mandatory fields will be highlighted in red with an asterisk.

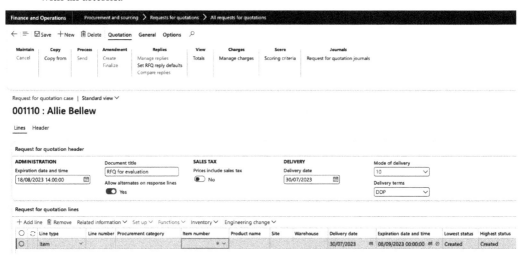

Figure 4.21 – Adding lines to the RFQ

2. After our lines have been added to the RFQ, we need to decide to whom we shall send our RFQ; for this, we need to go to the **Header** section of the RFQ and start adding our vendor. Remember, we can add one or more vendors to our RFQ.

This is the minimum essential to start sending our RFQ to our vendors.

In the following figure, we can see that two RFQs have been created for different vendor accounts:

Figure 4.22 – Adding vendors to the RFQ – the Header section

3. Once we have added vendors to our RFQ, the **Send** button on the top bar will become active.

Before we start sending this to our vendors, let's review the available options for replies.

Replies

One of the essential things to consider during the RFQ process is the replies from our vendors. For this, we have a dedicated space in our RFQ to manage the replies.

Figure 4.23 – RFQ Replies

Before we send our RFQ to our vendor, only the **Set RFQ reply defaults** option will appear as active; from this menu option, we can select the field we will consider valid to be used during the replies provided by our vendors.

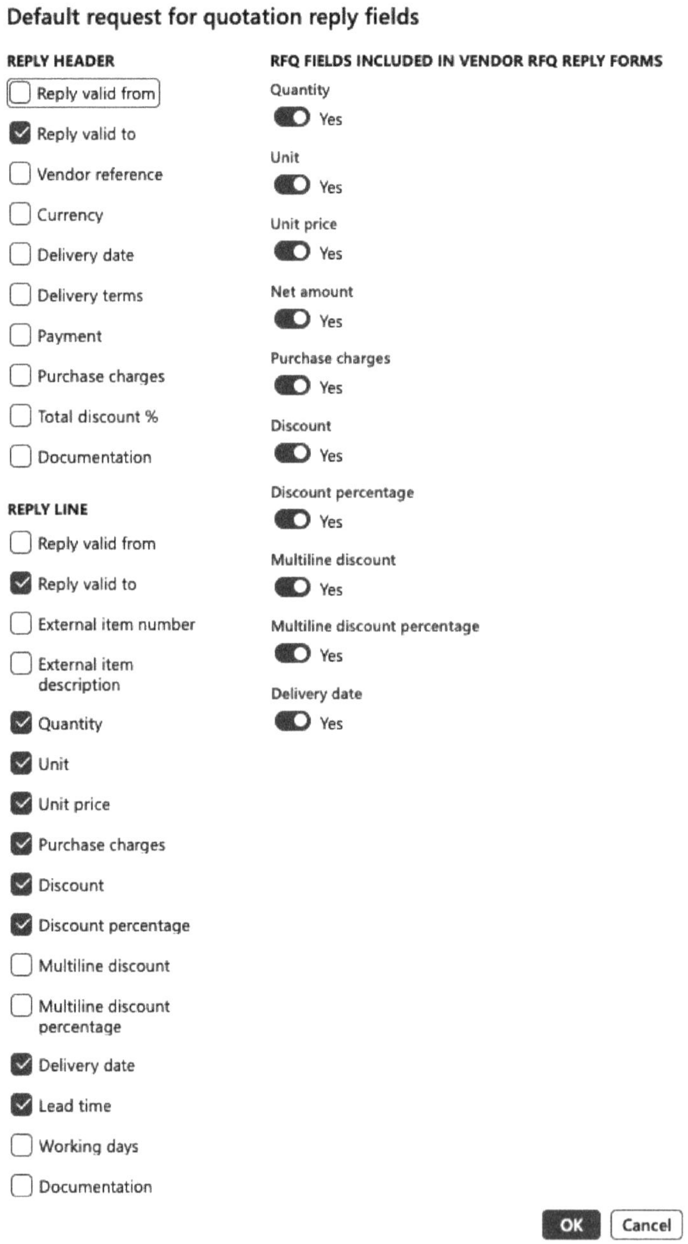

Default request for quotation reply fields

REPLY HEADER

- ☐ Reply valid from
- ☑ Reply valid to
- ☐ Vendor reference
- ☐ Currency
- ☐ Delivery date
- ☐ Delivery terms
- ☐ Payment
- ☐ Purchase charges
- ☐ Total discount %
- ☐ Documentation

REPLY LINE

- ☐ Reply valid from
- ☑ Reply valid to
- ☐ External item number
- ☐ External item description
- ☑ Quantity
- ☑ Unit
- ☑ Unit price
- ☑ Purchase charges
- ☑ Discount
- ☑ Discount percentage
- ☐ Multiline discount
- ☐ Multiline discount percentage
- ☑ Delivery date
- ☑ Lead time
- ☐ Working days
- ☐ Documentation

RFQ FIELDS INCLUDED IN VENDOR RFQ REPLY FORMS

Quantity
🔘 Yes

Unit
🔘 Yes

Unit price
🔘 Yes

Net amount
🔘 Yes

Purchase charges
🔘 Yes

Discount
🔘 Yes

Discount percentage
🔘 Yes

Multiline discount
🔘 Yes

Multiline discount percentage
🔘 Yes

Delivery date
🔘 Yes

[OK] [Cancel]

Figure 4.24 – Default request for quotation reply fields

Now that everything is set up, we can continue our process and press the **Send** button. Here, we will get a screen confirmation with the vendors selected for this bid and the items required to quote.

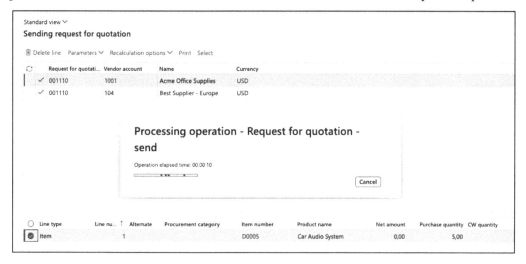

Figure 4.25 – Sending a request for quotation

Finally, after we have sent the RFQ, it can be printed or reviewed from **Request for quotation journals**.

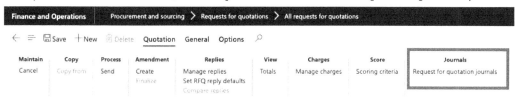

Figure 4.26 – Printing request for quotation from Journals

From here, we can review or print our RQF and formally send it by email to our vendors. For example, we have selected two vendors and, consequently, the system will generate two different RFQs, one RFQ for each vendor; as we can see in the following figure, the system has generated different RFQs by vendor account.

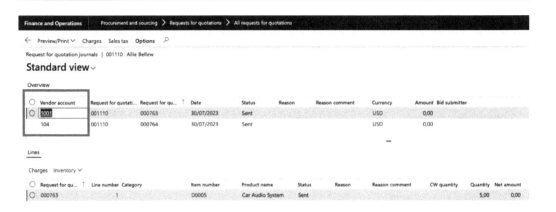

Figure 4.27 – Request for quotation journals

Contoso Entertainment
System USA
SWE

Request for quotation

Number	000763
Date	7/30/2023
Expiration date	8/18/2023 2:00 PM

Telephone	
Fax	
Registration	1234123400TT
Vendor account	1001

Acme Office Supplies
1234 Central Ave.
Charlotte, NC 28205
USA

Delivery address
Acme Office Supplies
123 Coffee Street
Suite 300
Redmond, WA 98052
USA
NLD

This text is from the request for
Quotation form notes

Category	Item number	Description	Expiration date	Delivery date	Quantity Unit	CW quantity CW unit
	D0005	Car Audio System	8/18/2023 2:00 PM	7/30/2023	5.00 ea	0.00
	Site : 4 Warehouse : 41					

Figure 4.28 – RFQ printout

Managing replies

After sending the RFQ to our vendor, the next logical step would be to start getting replies from our suppliers. The step we need to execute now is to register these replies in Dynamics 365 Supply Chain Management.

Let's review how the system manages this process and what options are available after getting all the replies.

If we go back to *Figure 4.26*, we will see the **Manage replies** button. From here, we can add the given replies from our vendors; if we do it manually, we can go into the following screen and, from the left filter, select our vendor and RFQ ID and edit the response provided by our vendor.

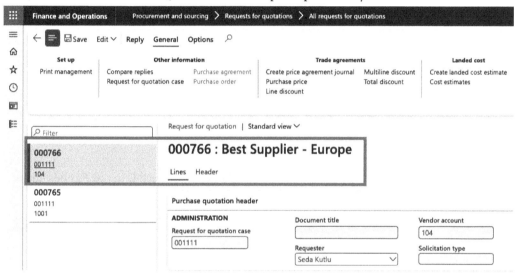

Figure 4.29 – Editing RQF replies

On the top bar, we have the **Edit** button with the **RFQ reply** drop-down option. Here, we can edit the selected field after sending the RFQ to our vendor. The most critical areas will be the quantity confirmed by the vendor, the unit price, the delivery date, and the validity of the offer. Per line, we can compare the values from our system against the ones provided by the vendor (*Figure 4.30*).

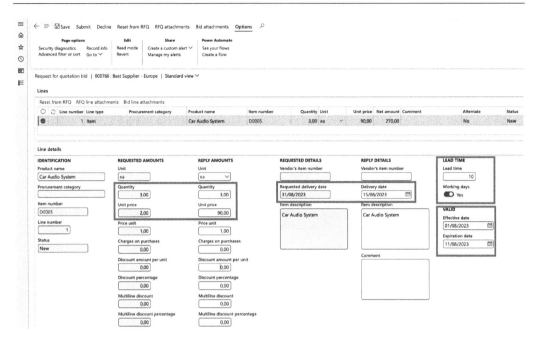

Figure 4.30 – Editing RQF reply lines

Finally, after we receive all our replies, we will have another option available in our **Replies** menu. This option is called **Compare replies**:

Figure 4.31 – Compare replies

From here, we can evaluate our vendor replies and decide which offer will win. Let's quickly explore the final step and how Microsoft Dynamics 365 can simplify our PO creation.

If we click the **Compare replies** option, we will see a list with the RFQ with information from our vendors. Now, we can start making decisions based on the most relevant values.

Figure 4.32 – Managing replies

In *Figure 4.32*, we can see one line with a lower unit price and another with a higher unit price. So, in this case, the decision will be easy. Of course, we can select based on lead time, delivery date, and any other factor in our RFQ.

To do this, we must select the line we want to accept or reject, and the respective options will become available for selection on the top bar.

Figure 4.33 – Accept or reject replies

When we click the **Accept** button, the magic is finally done, and now we can convert our accepted offer into a PO. At the same time, the system will propose a similar screen to reject the other RFQ.

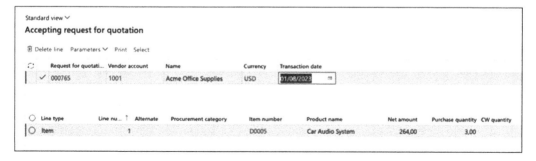

Figure 4.34 – Accept the RFQ and creating a PO

Finally, in the **Action center**, we will get confirmation that a new PO has been created:

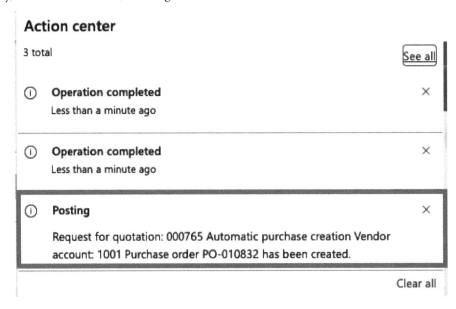

Figure 4.35 – Automatic PO creation message – Action center

In this exercise, we have seen how the purchase requisition process can be easily converted into an RFQ, which can then be transformed automatically into a PO.

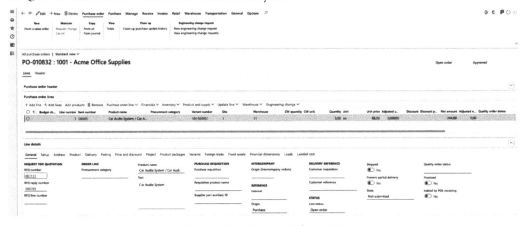

Figure 4.36 – PO created from RFQ

We have covered the manual process to understand how the system works, but this process can be easily automated. We will explore how to manage vendor collaboration later in this chapter in the *Vendor collaboration portal* section, especially looking at all aspects related to vendor communication.

POs

One tool shines brightly as a beacon of clarity and order – the venerable PO. Conceived by the buyer, this document represents the formalization of an official transaction, setting in motion the wheels to acquire goods. Upon receiving an affirmative nod from the vendor, this document undergoes a metamorphosis, emerging as a legally binding contract that both parties must adhere to.

A PO is akin to a comprehensive blueprint detailing the topography of the transaction. It encompasses various elements such as vivid descriptions of the goods, quantities involved, pricing structure, potential discounts, the terms and mechanics of payment, stipulated dates for delivery or performance, and other associated terms and conditions. It's a reference point, a compass pointing toward the specific seller participating in the transaction.

The beauty of POs is their versatility and adaptability. They cater to a myriad of roles and users, functioning as a dynamic tool to record and monitor the evolution of orders. An excellent example would be a procurement agent who deftly maneuvers POs to assemble a catalog of goods intended for acquisition from a particular vendor.

Every facet of the transaction, from pricing to delivery specifications and the detailed list of items, is meticulously chronicled in the PO. In addition to this, the procurement agent formulates a **Purchase Order Confirmation** document. This document is a professionally crafted notification transmitted to the vendor, heralding the upcoming procurement. When the items finally arrive at their destination, they are promptly inducted into the inventory, thus setting the stage for invoice creation. This well-orchestrated symphony of events marks the journey of the PO, an indispensable instrument in the orchestra of commerce.

> **Important note**
>
> POs can be created from different sources in Dynamics 365 Supply Chain Management; as we saw before, we can do it from **Purchase requisitions** or **Requests for quotations**, as well as the **Master Planning** module.

Now, let's review how to create a manual PO in Dynamics 365 Supply Chain Management:

1. Start by navigating to the **Procurement and sourcing** module > **Purchase orders** > **All purchase orders**:

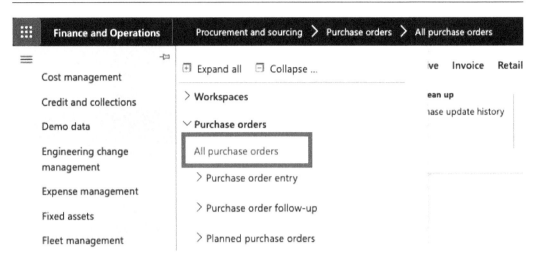

Figure 4.37 – Purchase orders menu item

2. Once on the **All purchase orders** window, click the **+New** button to create a new PO.

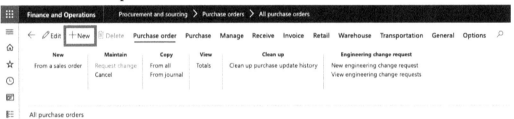

Figure 4.38 – All purchase orders

3. A form will open in which you'll start by populating the **Vendor** field. Type the name or ID of the vendor in the **Vendor account** field. Note that this vendor must be set up already in your system.

4. Now, define the **PURCHASE ORDER** details:

    *   **Purchase type**: Indicate the type of purchase. The options are **Journal**, **Purchase order**, or **Returned order**. In most cases, you'll select **Purchase order**.

    *   **Delivery date**: Enter the date on which you expect the items to be delivered. This is a key field for vendor performance tracking and for the system to anticipate inbound inventory.

    *   **Currency**: Choose the currency for the PO.

    *   **Site** and **Warehouse**: Indicate where the items should be delivered.

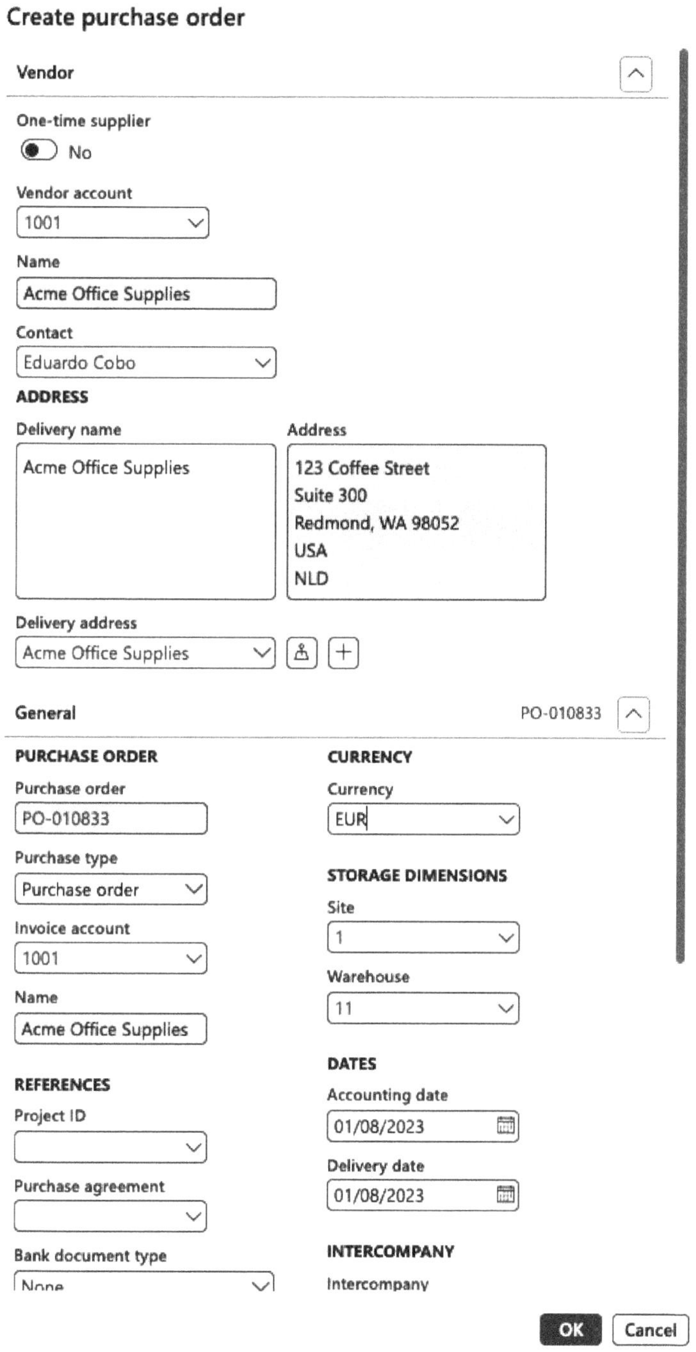

Create purchase order

Vendor   ⌃

One-time supplier

⬤ No

Vendor account

| 1001 | ⌄ |

Name

Acme Office Supplies

Contact

| Eduardo Cobo | ⌄ |

ADDRESS

Delivery name

Acme Office Supplies

Address

123 Coffee Street
Suite 300
Redmond, WA 98052
USA
NLD

Delivery address

| Acme Office Supplies | ⌄ | [⌗] [+]

General   PO-010833   ⌃

PURCHASE ORDER

Purchase order

PO-010833

Purchase type

| Purchase order | ⌄ |

Invoice account

| 1001 | ⌄ |

Name

Acme Office Supplies

REFERENCES

Project ID

| | ⌄ |

Purchase agreement

| | ⌄ |

Bank document type

| None | ⌄ |

CURRENCY

Currency

| EUR | ⌄ |

STORAGE DIMENSIONS

Site

| 1 | ⌄ |

Warehouse

| 11 | ⌄ |

DATES

Accounting date

| 01/08/2023 | 🗓 |

Delivery date

| 01/08/2023 | 🗓 |

INTERCOMPANY

Intercompany

OK   Cancel

Figure 4.39 – PO creation dialog

- **Enter line details**: You must add the line items for the PO. Click on the **+ Add line** button.

- **Item number**: Input the item number or browse the product catalog by clicking the drop-down arrow.

- **Quantity**: Indicate how many units you're ordering.

- **Unit**: The unit of measure will default from the product master data but can be changed if necessary.

- **Unit price**: Enter the agreed unit price.

- **Line amount**: This field will auto-calculate based on the quantity and unit price.

- **Delivery date**: You can also set a unique delivery date for each line if different items have different delivery dates.

- **Add additional details**: Each line also has tabs for **Delivery**, **Financial dimensions**, and **Price**. Here, you can add more specific information such as delivery terms, address, and various financial dimensions, including cost center, business unit, department, and so on.

- **Confirm and validate**: Once all the necessary fields are filled in and you're satisfied with the details, click **Validate** at the top to check for errors. If the validation is successful, the status of the PO will change from **Draft** to **In review**.

- **Submit the purchase order**: Lastly, click on **Confirm** to change the status from **In review** to **Confirmed**. This action sends the PO to the vendor.

Creating a manual PO can be a detailed process, but flexibility can be critical in many business scenarios. Once you're familiar with the core fields and strategy, managing your procurement effectively using Dynamics 365 Supply Chain Management becomes a swift task.

After sending the PO to our vendor, our next step will be to receive the goods or services we have acquired.

To receive a PO, this must have statuses of **Open order** and **Confirmed**, as shown in the following figure:

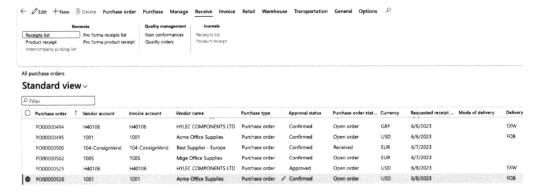

Figure 4.40 – All purchase orders view

In the top bar, we can see a tab named **Receive**, which contains the essential options to process our PO and make the stock available for usage in our warehouse.

Let's first review the **Receipts list**.

The receipts list is a handy document for the person handling the reception of the goods at the warehouse entrance.

To generate the receipts list, we should go to the screen's top section, select the **Receive** tab, and then the **Receipts list** option.

The following screen will appear; we must select the options highlighted in the red boxes to ensure we generate the document correctly.

Figure 4.41 – Generating the receipts list

After we have selected the **Document date** and **Terms of payment** options (usually, this must be aligned with the vendor transport note or vendor invoice), we can confirm and generate a document like the one shown in the following example:

Figure 4.42 – Receipts list example

The physical receipts list will allow the person doing the reception process to control the exact quantity received and also indicate a destination in the warehouse where the goods will be stored; this will be very useful for the next step.

Finally, we must align the physical process with the system information to conclude the receipt. Here, a personal recommendation is to do this in real time.

We will go again to the top section in the **Receive** tab and select the **Product receipt** option.

Now, it is important to register the exact quantity received in the warehouse; the following figure shows that we are entering the same stock quantity expected in the receipts list.

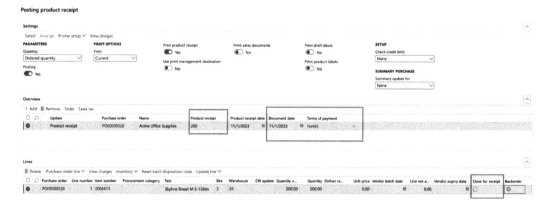

Figure 4.43 – Receipts list example part 2

If no more of the product is expected to be received in this PO, we can also click the **Close for receipt** option. This will mark the line as completed, and no more receptions will be allowed for this PO line.

And finally, to conclude the process, the final step is to register the vendor invoice in the system.

The moment we receive the invoice from our vendor, we must register the document in the system. This will make the document available to process the payment to our vendor.

We can do this from the top bar by selecting the Vendor **Invoice** tab and then the **Invoice** option.

The following screen will be presented, and we must fill in the marked fields carefully before posting the document.

Figure 4.44 – Invoice generation

The invoice identification and the date of the document are critical for the system and must be handled carefully.

Also, it is essential to review the prices in the invoice and investigate if a discrepancy is found.

We can post this document and complete the PO process if all the information is correct.

Of course, this may sound like a very manual handling process, but Microsoft Dynamics 365 Supply Chain Management also offers an outstanding possibility to automate our relationship with our vendors; let's review the vendor collaboration portal next.

Vendor collaboration portal

The vendor collaboration portal within Dynamics 365 Supply Chain Management is a web-based interface designed to streamline and enhance the collaboration between an organization and its vendors. It is a unified platform where the organization and vendors can access and manage orders, shipments, consignments, and other related activities.

Effective collaboration between companies and their vendors is pivotal in today's fast-paced business world. The vendor collaboration portal in Dynamics 365 Supply Chain Management emerges as a solution, offering a digital space where businesses and their vendors can seamlessly interact, manage transactions, and share information.

The process flow of the vendor collaboration is straightforward:

1. A PO or an RFQ is created for the vendor.

2. The vendor responds by accepting or rejecting the order.

3. Depending on the outcome, you can work with your vendors to correct the order until both parties are satisfied with the order.

Let's start by reviewing the PO life cycle to understand how the process is designed.

The PO life cycle on vendor collaboration

In the standard PO process, for vendor collaboration, we have six statuses that control the PO life cycle:

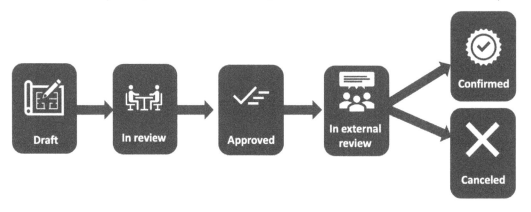

Figure 4.45 – Order statuses for vendor collaboration

1. When creating a PO, the initial status is set to **Draft** if working with change management. This means that the PO is currently being created.

2. After completion, the order can be sent for approval, which will change the status to **In review**. At this stage, the order is waiting for approval to be processed.

3. If approved, the status will change to **Approved**. This status is also the first one if change management is not being used and it means that the order is ready to be sent to the vendor.

4. After the order has been sent, the status will change to **In external review**. At this point, vendors have the ability to review, approve, or reject the PO.

5. If the vendor rejects or approves the order with changes, it will remain in the **In external review** status.

6. Once the order has been approved, it will move to the **Confirmed** status and can proceed with the normal purchasing process.

7. Canceling the order at any point in the process is possible, but vendor approval is required. If the cancellation is approved, the status will change to **Canceled**.

This means that when we send an order for vendor confirmation, the vendor has four available responses:

- The vendor accepts the order with automatic confirmation: The order status will change to **Confirmed**.

- The vendor accepts the order with no automatic confirmation: The order status will stay as **In external review**. We have to confirm it manually.

- The vendor rejects the order: The order status will stay as **In external review**. A vendor note is sent with the rejection.

- The vendor accepts with changes: The order status will stay as **In external review**, but the vendor sets change suggestions that we can accept.

Let's continue by configuring the vendor collaboration feature.

Setting up vendor collaboration

Now we're going to dive into setting up this functionality. There is a straightforward module to set up, so we will review the options we can activate on this module.

Unlike earlier versions, we don't need special licensing to activate this module, as in Ax 2012. This feature is activated and ready to use.

The first configuration we need to perform is to activate vendors to allow them to use vendor collaboration. To do that, we can navigate to **Accounts payable** > **Vendors** > **All vendors**, then select the vendor from the list we need to activate.

Under the **General** tab, we can change the **Collaboration activation** field to one of these two options:

- **Active (PO is auto-confirmed)**: This means that when this vendor approves the PO, it will change the order status to **Confirmed**

- **Active (PO is not auto-confirmed)**: When this vendor approves the PO, the status will remain as **In external review**, and we need to confirm the order afterward

Also, on the **Purchase order defaults** FastTab, we have the PO **prices/Amount** option. If activated, it will share the price information with the vendor.

Once the vendor is activated for vendor collaboration, we need to create vendor collaboration security roles. This is a vital step because if roles are not set up correctly, vendors might have access to sensitive information about the company. Let's navigate to **System administration** > **Security** > **External roles**:

External roles

Standard view ⌄

🔍 Filter		

↻ Security role	Description	Party role
Vendor admin (external) ⌄	Maintains vendor contact persons and vendor user requests	Vendor ⌄
Vendor contact (external)	Maintains vendor documents and responds to vendor inquiries in the vendor collaboration interface.	Vendor

Figure 4.46 – External roles setup

In this form, we can assign security roles to external parties of the company. By default, two security roles are provided for external vendors:

- **Vendor admin (external)** allows external vendors to maintain vendor contact information and request a new vendor contact to be provisioned.

- **Vendor contact (external)** allows external vendors to work with POs, and respond to and query information about orders. Also, they can maintain invoices, view the consignment inventory, respond to RFQs, and view vendor information.

You might want to add those two roles, or if your company has custom external roles, you can add them in the form, as shown in *Figure 4.46*.

Processing a PO on the vendor collaboration portal

We have thoroughly reviewed the PO creation process in this chapter. Once the order is created and approved, we can send it to the vendors for their review. To do so, on the PO form, select the PO with an **Approved** status, and inform the vendor that we want to collaborate. For example, in the demo data, you can test with the **Tailspin Parts** vendor (**US-104**).

In the **Purchase** tab, under **Vendor collaboration**, you have the **Send purchase order for confirmation** option. This will open a dialog screen to send the order to the vendor, as we can see in the following figure:

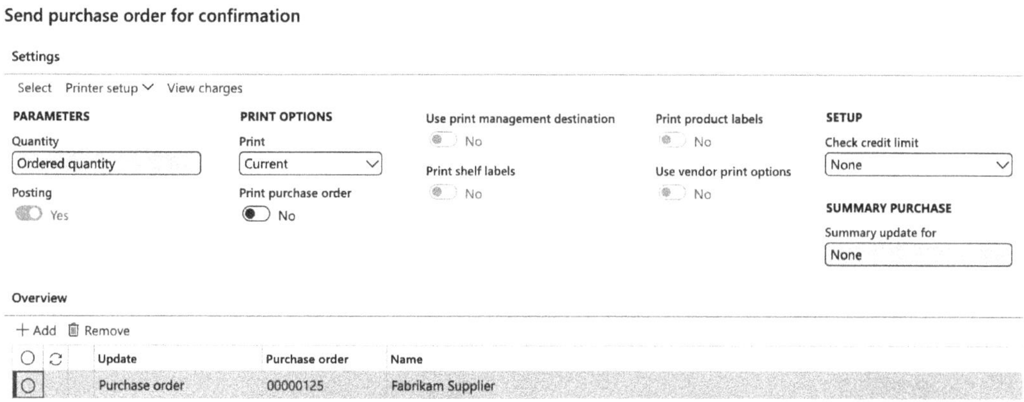

Send purchase order for confirmation

Settings

Select   Printer setup ∨   View charges

PARAMETERS	PRINT OPTIONS	Use print management destination	Print product labels	SETUP
Quantity	Print	No	No	Check credit limit
Ordered quantity	Current ∨	Print shelf labels	Use vendor print options	None ∨
Posting	Print purchase order	No	No	
Yes	No			SUMMARY PURCHASE
				Summary update for
				None

Overview

+ Add   🗑 Remove

○ ↻	Update	Purchase order	Name
○	Purchase order	00000125	Fabrikam Supplier

Figure 4.47 – Send purchase order for confirmation dialog

Here, we can select whether we need to print the PO or send it via email, with the **Use print management destination** option. Once we review those options, we can click **OK** and this will change the order status to **In external review**.

This vendor can see the order from the **Purchase orders for review** page under the **Vendor collaboration** module, as we can see in the following figure:

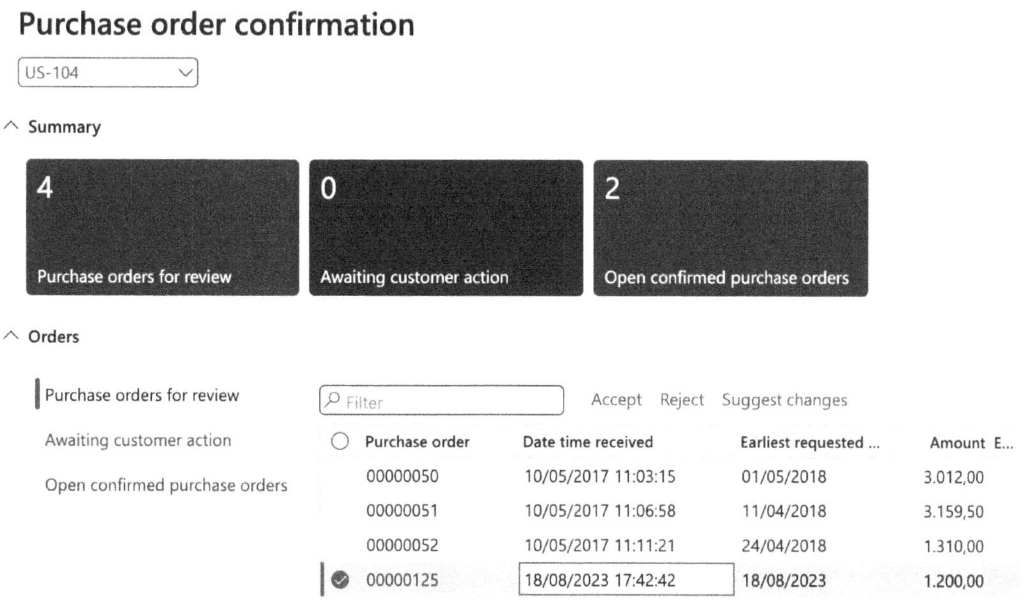

Purchase order confirmation

US-104 ∨

∧ Summary

4	0	2
Purchase orders for review	Awaiting customer action	Open confirmed purchase orders

∧ Orders

Purchase orders for review	🔍 Filter		Accept Reject Suggest changes		
Awaiting customer action	○ Purchase order	Date time received	Earliest requested ...	Amount E...	
Open confirmed purchase orders	00000050	10/05/2017 11:03:15	01/05/2018	3.012,00	
	00000051	10/05/2017 11:06:58	11/04/2018	3.159,50	
	00000052	10/05/2017 11:11:21	24/04/2018	1.310,00	
	✓ 00000125	18/08/2023 17:42:42	18/08/2023	1.200,00	

Figure 4.48 – Vendor view of the Purchase order confirmation workspace

As shown in the figure, vendors have a **Summary** tab where orders are divided into three groups: **Purchase orders for review**, **Awaiting customer action**, and **Open confirmed purchase orders**.

The same three queries are shown in the **Orders** tab. Here, vendors can accept, reject, and suggest changes. The vendor can also see the order information if they click on an order.

When the vendor accepts the order, the order will disappear from this view and can have two destinations. If the vendor has auto-confirmation, the PO will be automatically confirmed. But if not, it will be shown in the **Awaiting customer action** inquiries; we can see an example in this figure:

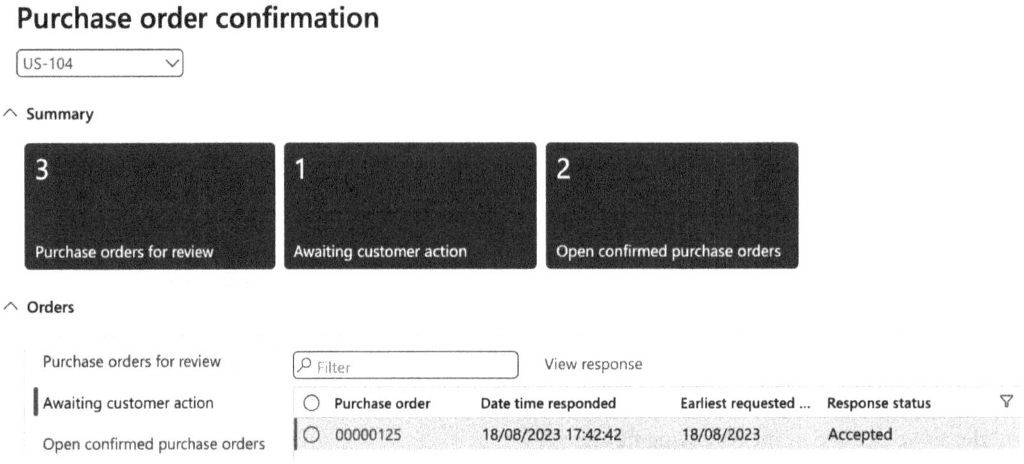

Purchase order confirmation

US-104

∧ Summary

3	1	2
Purchase orders for review	Awaiting customer action	Open confirmed purchase orders

∧ Orders

Purchase orders for review

Awaiting customer action	🔍 Filter	View response
Open confirmed purchase orders	○ Purchase order	Date time responded	Earliest requested ...	Response status	▽
	○ 00000125	18/08/2023 17:42:42	18/08/2023	Accepted	

Figure 4.49 – Order awaiting customer action

If this is the case, a purchase clerk of our company must confirm the order, and it will move to **Open confirmed purchase orders**. In the case of suggesting changes, it will also move to the **Awaiting customer action** inquiry, and a purchase clerk will have to correct and send the order to the vendor again. The vendor collaboration portal has other processes to collaborate with our vendors. For example, let's review the RFQ process.

Collaboration on RFQs

When we need to work with an RFQ, the vendor collaboration portal helps us to manage this process. Once the RFQ is created, we can ask vendors to place their bids in the portal.

Vendors can access the **Vendor bidding** workspace to view the RFQ placed. To access the workspace, vendors have to access the **Vendor collaboration** portal > **Bidding workspace** to reach the following form:

Vendor bidding

Figure 4.50 – Vendor bidding workspace

Here, requests for biddings will show up for vendors as new bid invitations, and they can respond to them by accessing them. When bids are responded to, they can follow the progress in this form.

Vendors have the following options when bidding on an RFQ:

- **Propose alternates**: If vendors do not work with a specific item, they can propose a substitute item on the bidding

- **Upload attachments**: Vendors can support their bids with attachments left in the header or lines of the bidding

- **Do Amendments**: Vendors can correct information and replace the existing bid with updated values

Once bids are confirmed, a PO will be created, whereas if bids are rejected, vendors will receive a notification on this form.

Working with vendor rebates

A **vendor rebate agreement** is a contract agreement between a company and a vendor that outlines the terms and conditions for the company to receive a monetary reward for meeting predetermined purchase targets. This means that when the seller effectively sells the goods, the buyer receives monetary compensation from the seller for that sale. Rebate programs manage rebates; the rebate programs are responsible for controlling when, how much, and under which terms.

We will dive into the process of capturing and calculating rebates provided by vendors, where you can significantly reduce supply chain expenses and enhance your product margins. Let's start by setting up this functionality.

Setting up

The first steps we need to do are in the **Procurement and sourcing parameters** form.

Navigate to **Procurement and sourcing** > **Setup** > **Procurement and sourcing parameters**. In the **Rebate program** tab, we will see the following form:

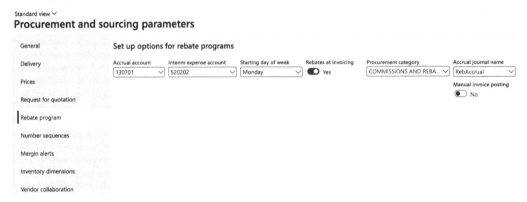

Figure 4.51 – Rebate program parameters

Here, we can see different setups for the rebate program:

- **Accrual account**: Input the account number for the vendor rebate accrual. This account will be debited once the rebate is approved and the accrual is posted.

- **Interim expense account**: Choose the account to be credited once the vendor rebate accrual is posted.

- **Starting day of the week**: This day will be the starting day to calculate vendor rebates if we accumulate them on a weekly basis.

- **Rebates at invoicing**: If set to **Yes**, a rebate claim will be created automatically upon invoicing.

- **Procurement Category**: This category will be used when posting the debit note against the vendor. In contrast to the other accounts, the credit account of this transaction will be set up in the **Procurement** category.

- **Accrual journal name**: Set a journal name where the rebate will be posted.

- **Manual invoice posting**: To process automatic rebate postings, this option must be disabled. If enabled, we have to do the posting manually.

Now, let's move on to rebate program types.

Rebate program types

Rebate program types handle the accounting configuration for each type of rebate that we have. Here, we can set up different rebate program types and change the accrual posting for each type.

By navigating to **Procurement and sourcing** > **Vendor rebates** > **Vendor rebate type**, we will reach the following form:

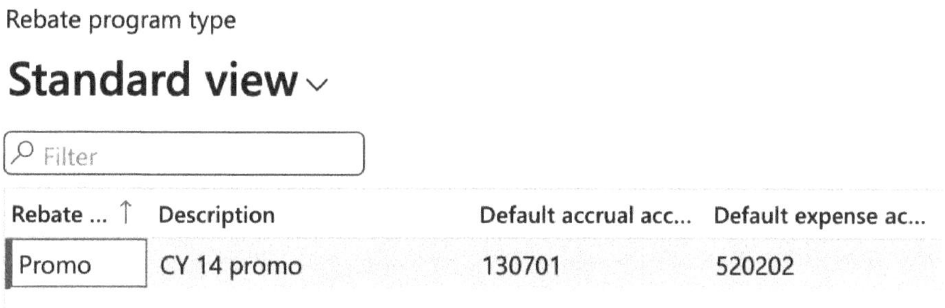

Rebate program type

Standard view ⌄

🔍 Filter

Rebate ... ↑	Description	Default accrual acc...	Default expense ac...
Promo	CY 14 promo	130701	520202

Figure 4.52 – Rebate program type

As shown in *Figure 4.52*, we can create any rebate program we want and assign it an accrual and an expense account.

Rebate groups

There are two types of rebate groups: **item rebate groups** and **vendor rebate groups**. These groups allow you to include multiple vendors and items in a single rebate program instead of creating individual programs for each one.

If we want to group items, we can find the rebate group form at **Procurement and sourcing** > **Vendor rebates** > **Rebate groups** > **Vendor rebate group** or **Item rebate group**.

Once vendor or item rebate groups are created, we can associate vendors and items individually in each master form. This setup is not required for the rebate to work but can be handled for categorizing vendors and items with the same agreement.

Rebate agreement

Here is the heart of the vendor rebate functionality. We can use rebate agreements to establish the specific details of a vendor rebate. This includes identifying the eligible item and vendor, determining the duration of the offer, outlining the conditions that must be met to comply with the rebate, and specifying how the rebate amount will be calculated.

To set this up, we will go to **Procurement and sourcing** > **Vendor rebates** > **Rebate agreements**:

Vendor rebate agreements

Standard view ⌄

Overview   General   Note   Dimensions

		Workflow approval...	Rebate program ID	Vendor code	Vendor selection	Item code	Item selection	Unit	Unit type		Minimum ...	Minimum ...	Start date	Expiry
○	⟳													
○		Approved	Promo	Table	⌄ US-101	⌄ Table	⌄ T0020	⌄ ea	⌄ Inventory unit	⌄	10	0,00	01/01/2017	▦ Never

CUMULATE	**PRICE**	**ACCOUNTS**	**CURRENCY**	**LINE BREAKS**	**VALIDATION**
Cumulate purchases by	Taken from	Rebate program accrual account	Currency	Rebate line break type	Validated
Month ⌄	Gross ⌄	130701 ⌄	USD ⌄	Quantity ⌄	⬤ Yes
Period type		Rebate program expense account			Validated by
		520202 ⌄	**APPROVAL**		000012
			Approval required		
			▭		

Lines

+ Add line   🗑 Remove

		Vendor code	Vendor selection	Item code	Item selection	Currency	Unit	Rebate line...	From value	To value	Value	Amount type	
○	⟳												
○		Table	US-101	Table	T0020	USD	ea	Quantity	10,00	20,00	15,0000	Amount per unit	⌄
		Table	US-101	Table	T0020	USD	ea	Quantity	20,00	0,00	30,0000	Amount per unit	

Figure 4.53 – Vendor rebate agreement

Here, we can create our agreement by clicking **New**. Once there, we must enter the rebate agreement information. In the top part of the form, we input under which conditions the agreement will apply. We have these fields:

- **Rebate program ID**: This is the rebate program we created earlier.

- **Vendor code** and **Vendor selection**: We can select **Table** to assign the agreement to one vendor, or **Group** to assign it to a vendor group.

- **Item code** and **Item selection**: The same happens with items. If we select the **Table** option, we assign the agreement to one item, but by selecting **Group**, we can assign it to a group of items.

- **Unit**: This is the unit of measure in which we will manage the agreement. If this unit is a requirement, ensure that the **Unit of measure** rebate option is set to **Exact match**. Otherwise, using the **Convert** option, it doesn't matter which unit we use in the PO. The rebate will apply. This is useful if we want to benefit certain types of packages among others.

- **Minimum quantity** and **Maximum quantity**: The quantity range between which the rebate will apply.

- **Start date** and **Expiry date**: This will control the dates on which the rebate will be active.

Then, in the middle part of the form, we can control how the rebate will be calculated:

- **Cumulate purchases by**: We set here the calculation of the rebate claim. This can be set by periods, for example, weekly, or by invoice value, which the value in the vendor invoices will determine.

- **Taken from**: Here, we specify the basis for the rebate calculation. Gross or net amounts can be used.

- **Approval required**: This will ask for approval before the rebate is accrued or paid.

- **Rebate line break type**: This defines the basis of the rebate. We have two options: **Quantity** or **Amount**.

In **Lines**, we can define different tiers to grant different rebates. As shown in *Figure 4.53*, the rebate line break is set to **Quantity**, and the tiers are defined from 10 to 20 units, which will pay 15 USD per unit, and from 20 units, it will pay 30 USD per unit of the item **T0020**.

Once the agreement is set up, we must click the validation button at the top of the form to make it active.

> **Note**
>
> If we need to work with dimensions, we have a button at the top to display the dimensions on the rebate. This allows us to work rebates from one warehouse or for a specific product dimension or both – for example, a T-shirt for a specific style in warehouse 24.

We can generate the rebate claims now that our rebate agreement is set.

Generating rebate claims

Now that our agreement is valid and approved, every time a PO is created with the vendor under the rebate agreement conditions, the system will identify that order line as a future vendor credit payment. The PO line will be marked, and we can view the details of the rebates applied to the PO line by entering the PO, selecting the line, and under **Purchase order line** > **View** > **Price details**, a vendor rebate will be shown, as we can see in the following figure:

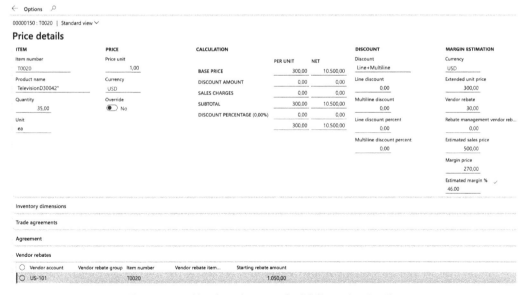

Figure 4.54 – Vendor rebates under PO line price details

> **Note**
>
> If you cannot access the price details, you must activate the **Enable price details** option in the **Procurement and sourcing parameters** form under the **Price** tab.

In *Figure 4.54*, we can see that this order line qualifies for a rebate claim, but it won't be generated until we invoice this PO to the vendor. Once that process is done, a vendor rebate claim will be automatically generated. To review that rebate claim, we can navigate to **Procurement and sourcing > Vendor rebates > Rebate claims**.

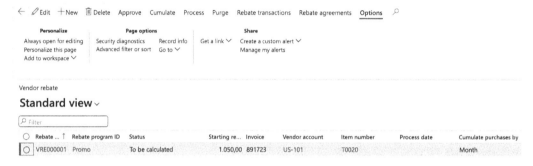

Figure 4.55 – Rebate claims

As shown in *Figure 4.55*, we can review and approve rebate claims. In this form, we can see each transaction related to a vendor invoice and which rebate program is applied to it. Those transactions have a status depending on the stage in which the rebate claim is.

To process the rebate claims, we can follow this process:

Figure 4.56 – Rebate claim process

1. Once a vendor invoice is generated, a rebate claim is given the status of **To be calculated**. This depends on the agreement created. If we select the **Invoice** option for **Cumulate purchases by**, the rebate claim will be created and calculated automatically. In any other case, for example, cumulating purchases by **Month**, we can cumulate rebate claims and calculate them all together in a unique document. To calculate rebate claims, we can select them and click the **Cumulate** button at the top of the rebate claims form (*Figure 4.55*), and filter by vendor or vendor group. This will change its status to **Calculated**.

2. Once claims are calculated, we can approve them, if we have set that up in the rebate agreement. To do that, we can click on the **Approve** button at the top of the form (*Figure 4.55*). That will change the rebate claim status to **Approved**. That process will also post a rebate accrual journal, debiting the expected vendor credit. We can see that voucher under the **Rebate transaction** button.

3. Now, we must process the rebate to move the claim to the accounts payable process. To do that, we need to click the **Process** button and filter by vendor or vendor group. This will change the status of the rebate claim to **Completed**.

4. The final step is to create the vendor invoice (credit note) for the vendor. If **Manual invoice posting** is enabled, we need to post the invoice manually; otherwise, a vendor invoice will be created automatically.

To see the postings of those transactions, we can see them in the **Vendor rebate transactions** section, as we can see in the following figure:

Figure 4.57 – Vendor rebate transactions

Postings will follow the setups we've done in **Procurement and sourcing parameters** and the vendor rebate agreements. This vendor invoice (credit note) generated by the rebate claims will be added to the vendor balance.

A final tip of this process is that the **Cumulate**, **Approve**, and **Process** actions can be executed by batch jobs and have this process fully automated.

What about consignment inventory?

Multiple companies have to ensure critical inventory in their facilities to reduce time and transportation costs, mostly because their manufacturing operations are too costly to stop them by inventory breakdowns.

To do that, companies store an inventory owned by vendors in their warehouses, and when they are ready to consume it, they take ownership of that inventory. This is called **consignment inventory**.

Consignment inventory process

The consignment process starts when a company brings a vendor's inventory into its warehouse. The company cannot create a PO because the inventory's owner is the vendor until this item is sold or consumed. If a PO is used, the company assumes the inventory value, which is unrealistic and will have financial differences.

The company must follow this process to perform a consignment in Supply Chain Management:

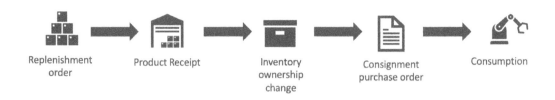

Figure 4.58 – Consignment process

In *Figure 4.58*, the consignment starts with a replenishment order made for the company to the vendor to bring the inventory into the company's facility. The difference with a PO is that the goods still belong to the vendor.

Once the order is in place and items arrive at the warehouse, we can post the product receipt, the inventory will be received, and the owner will be assigned automatically based on the vendor account.

When the company needs to use those goods, an inventory ownership change is used to take ownership of those goods. This will automatically create a PO automatically to the vendor, and the data of that order will be the information placed on the inventory ownership change journal.

The final step is to invoice that PO to the vendor and follow the account payable process. Now, we will review every step of the process in Supply Chain Management.

Initial setup

We need to configure a few parameters to start using this feature. As a first optional configuration, we can enable the vendor collaboration portal for our consignment vendor. This will allow us to share information when the consigned stock levels and the replenishment orders are in place. Remember that this setup is done in the **All vendors** form. First, we need to select a vendor, and under **Vendor collaboration**, set the field as **Active**.

Consigned items need to have a special setup. For example, the inventory owner of that item is a mandatory configuration to set up. To do so, we first must navigate to **Inventory management** > **Setup** > **Dimensions** > **Inventory owners** to create them.

This is a straightforward form. To create a new inventory owner, let's click on **New** and give it a name and an owner code. The most important field is the vendor account, which will link replenishment orders to a vendor.

To assign owners to items, we must have a tracking dimension group with the owner dimension enabled. Navigate to **Product information management** > **Setup** > **Dimensions and variant groups** > **Tracking dimension groups**, and you will access this form:

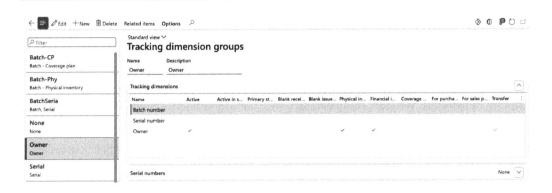

Figure 4.59 – Owner tracking dimension group

Create a tracking dimension group with the **Owner** dimension activated. This allows you to assign an inventory owner in the consignment process. When creating a new released product, if that item is a consigned item, you must assign the owner tracking dimension.

The last setup needed is to create an inventory ownership change journal from **Inventory management** > **Setup** > **Journal names** > **Inventory**. Here, we've got an example:

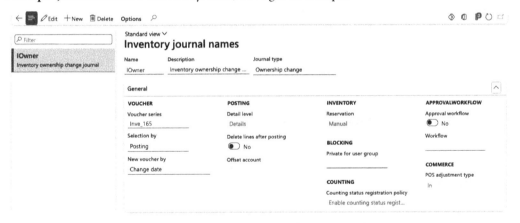

Figure 4.60 – Inventory ownership change journal name

Once this journal name is created, we can add it to the Inventory and warehouse management parameters under the **Journals** tab. This setup will default this journal name for every inventory ownership change.

Now that all parameters are set up, let's execute a consignment process.

Replenishment orders

To create a replenishment order, navigate to **Procurement and sourcing** > **Consignment** > **Consignment replenishment orders**. This form will show all consignment replenishment orders done, and to create one, we must click the **New** button. A dialog screen will open, asking us for the vendor account and the storage dimensions. We must complete them with the consignment vendor and the storage in which the items will arrive.

Once completed, we can click **OK**, and then a consignment replenishment order will be created, as we can see in the following figure:

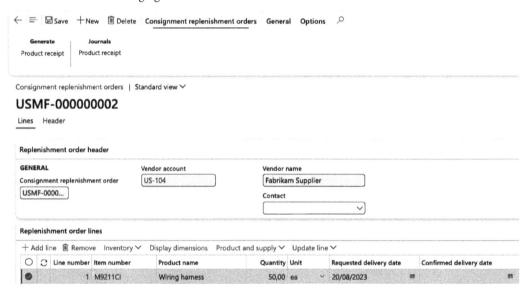

Figure 4.61 – Consignment replenishment order

As shown in *Figure 4.61*, under **Replenishment order lines**, we need to add the items the company needs to consign. When adding those items, ensure that the tracking dimension has the **Owner** dimension activated.

Once created, and when items arrive physically at the warehouse, we can post the product receipt in this form under **Receive** > **Generate** > **Product receipt**. The process is the same as we reviewed in the PO receiving process. Once done, the inventory will be on hand in the company's warehouse. But we can see in the inquiry that it will have the vendor's ownership:

On-hand | M9211CI

Standard view ⌄

Search name	Site	Warehouse	Owner	Physical in...	Physical re...	Available p...	Available p...	Ordered in...	On order	Ordered re...	Available f...	Total avail...
Wiringharness	2	24	US-104	50,00		50,00	50,00				50,00	50,00
Wiringharness	5	51	US-104	500,00		500,00	500,00				500,00	500,00

Figure 4.62 – Inquiry showing inventory ownership

Now that the inventory is in the company facility to consume, we need to create an ownership change journal.

Ownership change journal

To change ownership of the consigned inventory, let's navigate to **Procurement and sourcing** > **Consignment** > **Inventory ownership change**, click the **New** button at the top of the form, and in the dialog that appears, we can change the journal name, but let's keep the one that appears. The journal will be created as follows:

Figure 4.63 – Inventory ownership change journal

Here, we must add the items to change ownership. Usually, companies have a separate warehouse to store consignment products. This form allows us to not only change the ownership of the items but also do a transfer between warehouses or locations.

The most important part of this form is to indicate the **From owner** and **To owner** fields as being from the vendor to our company.

The **Quantity** field lets us change parts of the consigned inventory and not all of it simultaneously. It's important to check that field before posting, as this process will create a PO for the vendor automatically.

Once everything is okay, we can click the **Post** button. When this journal is posted, a PO is automatically created and received with all the information completed in this journal.

We can follow the process by creating the invoice related to that order and then follow the accounts receivable process.

Tips and recommendations

The items used in the consignment must have standard cost or moving average as costing methods. This is because there is no need to follow the cost of the items since there will be no GL transactions for them.

Another thing to notice is that those items cannot have a quality association because there is no consignment quality association type. If we create a purchase quality association for these items, it won't be triggered as they are not received on a purchase receipt process.

The consignment process has another limitation: this process does not work with advanced warehouse management functionalities.

Most companies work with consignment as a monthly process, in which replenishment orders occur daily but invoicing is done monthly. To support this process, it is recommended to group orders by month and invoice them automatically with a PO invoicing batch job.

Summary

In this chapter, we have reviewed all the procurement and sourcing processes, starting from the setup, creation, and execution of the purchase order process.

Then, we discussed purchase solicitation and the RFQ process, which allows vendors to quote for requirements made in our company and let the purchasing department compare the offers and select the best one.

After that, we learned about the vendor collaboration portal, which allows the company to communicate smoothly with vendors, optimizing processes that are usually handled by alternate forms of communication such as emailing.

Vendor rebates show us how to handle rebate contracts and process vendor invoicing in a controlled way. Finally, we closed this chapter by reviewing the vendor consignment process with all the dos and don'ts and recommended practices.

In the next chapter, we will review all the relevant information related to quality. Having reasonable control over the quality of our inventory, even from a sourcing and sales perspective, is essential for a business that wants to operate efficiently. Let's continue our adventure in the next chapter.

Questions

1. What is a purchase requisition in Dynamics 365 Supply Chain Management?

    A. A purchase requisition is one of the components of the procure-to-pay process that includes the solicitation of a product or service.

    B. A purchase requisition is sending various vendors an invitation to quote for their products.

    C. A purchase requisition is a component of the procure-to-pay process that allows the user to review and approve purchases.

2. You are implementing the **Procurement and sourcing** module. When working with vendor collaboration, a PO has a different life cycle. Which of the following statuses is only used in the vendor collaboration PO process?

   A. **In external approval**

   B. **In external review**

   C. **In external modification**

3. You are implementing the **Procurement and sourcing** module. You set up the vendor rebates correctly but when reviewing PO lines with **Vendor rebates** enabled, you cannot see rebate prices. Which of the following options do you need to review?

   A. In the PO line, under the **General** tab, activate the Rebates option.

   B. In **Procurement and sourcing parameters**, under the **Price** tab, activate the **Enable price details** option.

   C. In **Procurement and sourcing parameters**, under the **Price** tab, in the **Discount** field, select **Line + Multi Line**.

Answers

1. Option A.

   Microsoft Dynamics 365 Supply Chain Management offers a dedicated section to make this process easy for any employee in the organization, introducing approval steps and finally automating the PO creation.

2. Option B.

   In external review means that the vendor is reviewing the PO.

3. Option B.

   The Enable price details option displays detailed information about the prices, agreements, and trade agreements associated with the selected product in the PO line, and calculates discounts, rebates, margins, and royalties.

5

Working with Quality Control Processes – a Hands-On Approach

In today's competitive market, ensuring product quality is not just a necessity—it's a differentiator. As businesses strive to deliver top-notch products, the tools they employ play a pivotal role in achieving this goal. Enter Dynamics 365 Supply Chain Management, a comprehensive solution designed to streamline and enhance the quality control processes.

Quality control is the bedrock of customer trust. When customers purchase a product, they invest their faith in the brand, believing it will function as advertised. A lapse in quality can erode this trust, leading to lost customers and tarnished brand reputation.

Dynamics 365 Supply Chain Management offers a suite of tools tailored for quality control. From setting up quality parameters to managing quarantined products, Dynamics 365 provides businesses with the necessary capabilities to maintain and elevate product quality. This chapter aims to guide users through the intricacies of these tools, ensuring they can harness the full potential of Dynamics 365 in their quality control endeavors.

In this chapter, you will gain insights into the following:

- Configuring quality control and management settings
- Processing and managing quality orders
- Handling inventory blocking effectively

Join us as we explore the hands-on approach to quality control processes in Dynamics 365 Supply Chain Management.

The foundation of quality control

Before diving into the technicalities of Dynamics 365, it's crucial to understand the essence of quality control. Quality control is about consistency—ensuring every product meets the set standards every time. With Dynamics 365, this consistency is achieved through automation, real-time monitoring, and data-driven insights.

The quality control features are embedded into the **Inventory management** module simply because we want to ensure the excellent quality of our inventory items; these can be our raw materials, semi-finished products, and the end products that we will sell to our customers.

The quality management process in the Dynamics 365 supply chain consists of product testing and the management of non-conforming materials.

Managing quality management

To effectively oversee quality management, consider the following strategies:

- Initiate quality directives based on specific events, such as receiving a product for inbound tasks or collecting a product for outbound tasks.

- Record testing outcomes and evaluate whether they align with the predetermined testing standards and desired quality benchmarks.

- Incorporate document management to detail product guidelines and individualized notes, which can be referenced during the evaluation phase.

- Keep a record of products that don't meet standards, linking them with further details on discrepancies to trace back to the root issue.

- Note down the expenses associated with addressing discrepancies. These expenses might encompass items (e.g., replacement parts), various fees, and the labor hours needed for rectification.

- Plan rectification measures by connecting them to specific quality directives.

Setting up quality management

The quality management features within Supply Chain Management offer access to the essential settings needed to establish and oversee a company's quality evaluation standards.

Quality orders lay out a series of tests for an item, playing a pivotal role in quality oversight within **Finance and Operations**. These quality orders detail the quality criteria, an **acceptable quality level** (**AQL**), the relevant testing tool, documentation outlining the test, and various other aspects for each evaluation.

However, several mandatory and optional elements must be configured before initiating quality orders.

For the foundational setup of quality management, two key settings should be adjusted:

- **Use quality management**: This option turns on the quality management features and must be activated before accessing any of its functionalities. It's crucial to note that this setting is specific to each legal entity and doesn't extend to other entities within the organization.

- **Hourly rate**: An optional setting, it helps in estimating the time an employee invests in quality-related tasks. This rate isn't applied by default as it will be overridden by a trade agreement or price list from the **Project and Accounting Management** module.

You can locate these settings under **Inventory management** > **Setup** > **Inventory and warehouse management parameters** within the **Quality management** section.

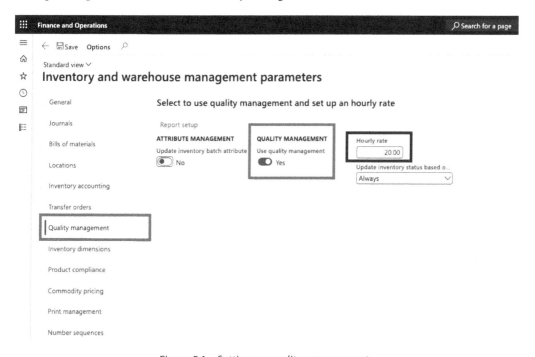

Figure 5.1 – Setting up quality management

Test instruments

Test instruments can be used to identify the necessary equipment for a test. Each test instrument designates a measurement unit, capturing the relevant measurement and decimal accuracy.

Setting up test instruments is an optional step. To access this, navigate to **Inventory management** > **Setup** > **Quality control** > **Test instruments**.

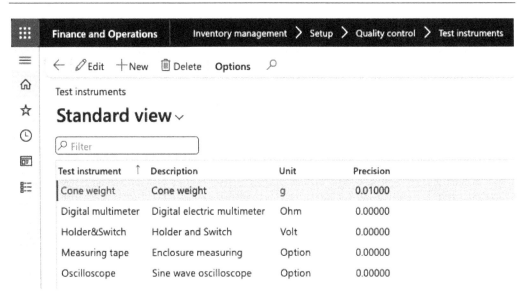

Figure 5.2 – Setting up test instruments

Tests

Tests can either be quantitative, where specifications and results are presented in numerical values with a designated unit of measure, or qualitative, where requirements and results are articulated through user-defined outcomes indicating a pass or fail.

Modifications to tests—whether additions, alterations, or deletions—are carried out within a quality directive. For a given set of tests, the quality directive outlines the overarching AQL, the sampling strategy and corresponding test volume, the necessity for destructive testing, and the order in which tests will be conducted.

Once test outcomes for each test within a quality directive are reported, initiate a verification procedure to allocate a pass or fail status, contingent on meeting the overall AQB. Subsequently, the quality directive must be finalized. During the test formulation phase, it's essential to specify permissible business operations during and after verification of the quality directive.

For instance, you can prevent the invoice update for a purchase order with associated stock undergoing inspection. Optionally, a discrepancy report is generated when a quality directive flags flawed material. This report serves as the foundation for further scrutiny after corrective tasks have been planned and remedial actions have been documented.

To create and manage tests, navigate to **Inventory management** > **Setup** > **Quality control** > **Tests**.

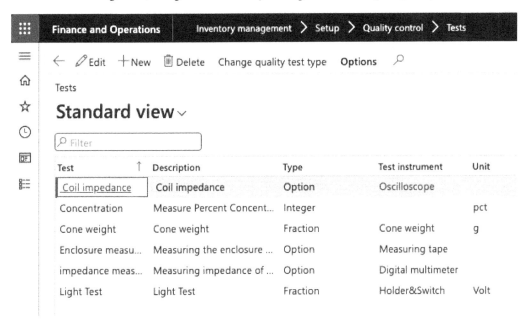

Figure 5.3 – Setting up tests

Item sampling

Sample item assessment refers to the number of items selected for evaluation during a test. This quantity can be a set number or a proportion. Such estimates are integrated with test clusters and quality affiliations.

For instance, consider a scenario where you're evaluating a batch of sample items. A business's protocols mandate a sporadic inspection of at least 20 units from every consignment received from a new supplier within the initial 60 days of collaboration. Establish a sample item assessment with a fixed count of 20 to fulfill this stipulation.

To determine a fixed count or proportion for items designated for quality directive evaluations, navigate to **Inventory management** > **Setup** > **Quality management** > **Item sampling**.

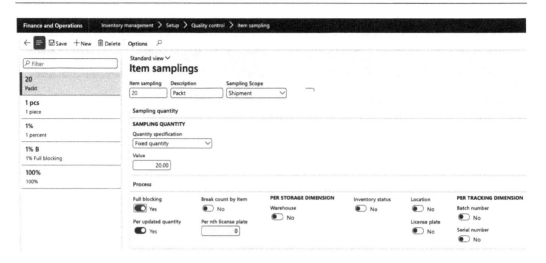

Figure 5.4 – Setting up item sampling

Test groups

Test groups are responsible for determining whether an item passes or fails the quality control; we can define the test groups from the following path.

Go to **Inventory management** > **Setup** > **Quality control** > **Test groups** to create test groups.

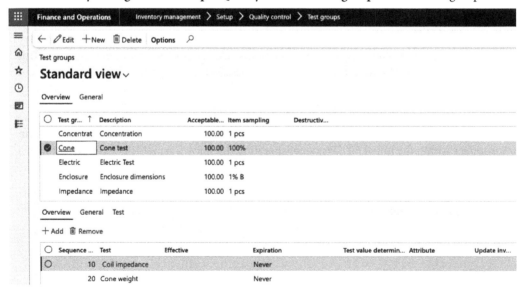

Figure 5.5 – Setting up test groups

Here, you can create new test groups, and view, edit, and associate the individual tests.

Quality associations

Think of quality associations as a set of rules in Dynamics 365 Supply Chain Management that help automate the quality check process. Here's a simple breakdown:

- **Automatic quality orders**: On the **Quality associations** page, you set up rules that tell the system when to create a quality order automatically—for instance, when you purchase or when items are quarantined, sold, or produced.

- **Where to find it**: Head to **Inventory management** > **Setup** > **Quality control** > **Quality associations**. This is your go-to spot to set up these rules and keep track of quality orders.

Figure 5.6 – Setting up quality associations

- **Grouping items**: Creating "item quality groups" is a good idea before diving into quality associations. Imagine you sell different types of nuts. Instead of setting rules for each class, you can group them as "Nuts" and put one rule for the whole group. It makes testing more organized!

During the definition of quality associations, here's what you can specify:

- **Transaction event**: When should the quality check happen (e.g., after a purchase)?

- **Tests**: What tests should be run on the items?

- **Quality standards (AQL)**: What's the acceptable quality level for the items?

- **Sampling plan**: How many items from a batch should be tested?

- **Variations**: Each unique scenario in your business that needs an automatic quality order should have its own quality association. For example, the rules for checking items from a new supplier might differ from those for checking returned items.

The **Quality associations** page has an excellent feature for businesses with multiple sites. If you specify a site, the system will only trigger the automatic quality order for that site.

In short, quality associations help ensure that your products maintain a consistent level of quality by automating checks based on rules you define. It's like having a vigilant quality control manager working 24/7!

In the quality association definition, one of the critical setups is the reference type; we can link our quality association to different business processes such as purchase orders, production orders, or sales orders.

Additional information

If you want to explore the full details of business processes and the possible variations you can define, please refer to the following documentation:

`https://learn.microsoft.com/en-us/dynamics365/supply-chain/inventory/quality-associations#working-with-quality-associations.`

In the following figure, we can see all the possible reference types from where we do a quality association.

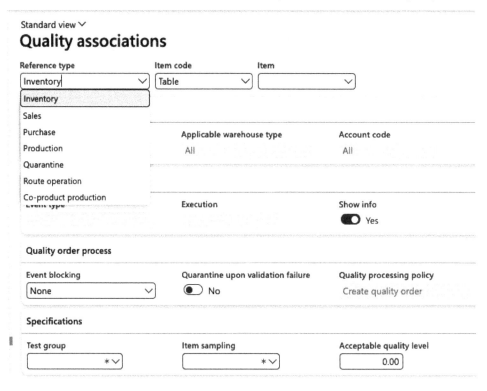

Figure 5.7 – Quality associations – Reference type

This means that we can, as an example, generate a quality association when a purchase order is received or before sending the goods to our customer into a sales order.

> **Note**
>
> If a quality order exists, the inventory quantities are blocked automatically for any use. This can be configured into **Item sampling** if we have selected **Full blocking**.

Example

A company is purchasing an item with some technical specifications regarding diameter and specific millimeters, as this product will be later used for equipment assembly.

The best setup here would be to create a specific association for this single item, setting the reference type as **Purchase order** and then setting the option per update quantity to **Yes**.

Each time a quantity is received against the purchase order, a new quality order will be generated according to the received quantity.

This will minimize any errors during the production assembly, and the specific item will be evaluated adequately upon the reception of the purchase.

Non-conformance in Dynamics 365 Supply Chain Management

In simple terms, **non-conformance** is like a red flag that says, "Hey, something's not right here!" It could be a product that didn't meet quality standards or even issues such as customer complaints or hiccups in production.

What's the source? Each non-conformance has a non-conformance type, which is the category of the problem. For example, was it a manufacturing error or a shipping issue?

Let's see the most relevant aspects to consider in the non-conformance:

- **Details, details, details**: When you create a non-conformance, you can add all sorts of helpful info such as its type, the nitty-gritty details of the problem, and what kind of problem it is (**Problem type**).

- **Setting up problem types**: You can define different problem types under **Inventory management** > **Setup** > **Quality management** > **Problem types**. This helps you categorize issues better. For example, you can have problem types such as **Material defect** or **Shipping delay**.

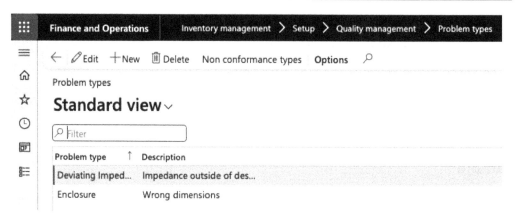

Figure 5.8 – Setting up problem types

- **Linking Non conformance and Problem types**: On the same **Problem types** page, you can specify which **Problem types** go with **Non conformance types**. This makes it easier to understand and resolve issues.

- **How to associate**: To link a non-conformance type for quality checks, just hit the **Non conformance types** button. It's like tagging the issue with a label so everyone knows what they're dealing with.

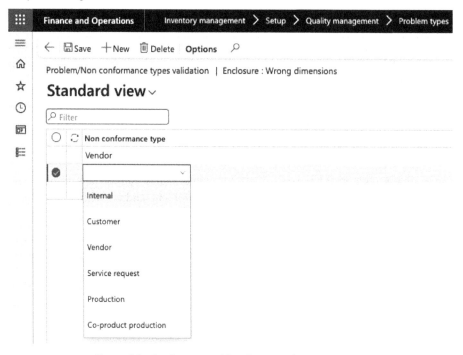

Figure 5.9 – Setting up problem/non-conformance types

So, non-conformance types help you spot and categorize quality issues, whether in products, customer service, or internal processes. It's a handy way to keep quality up to snuff!

When dealing with non-conformances, there are some additional settings you might need to consider:

- **Diagnostic types**: This helps you identify what kind of tests or checks are needed.

  Navigate to **Inventory management** > **Setup** > **Quality management** > **Diagnostic types**.

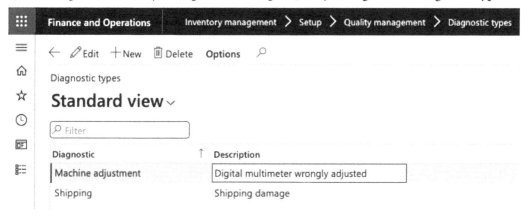

Figure 5.10 – Setting up diagnostic types

- **Quality charges**: If any costs are involved in fixing the issue, you set them up here.

  Navigate to **Inventory management** > **Setup** > **Quality management** > **Quality charges**.

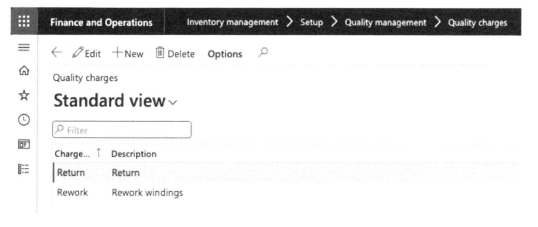

Figure 5.11 – Setting up quality charges

- **Operations**: This is where you define the steps involved in resolving a non-conformance.

  Navigate to **Inventory management** > **Setup** > **Quality management** > **Operations**.

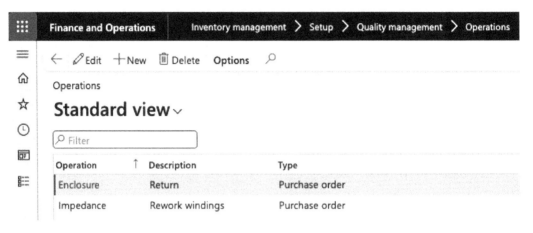

Figure 5.12 – Setting up operations

- **Quarantine zones**: These are designated areas where you keep items that didn't pass the quality check.

  Navigate to **Inventory management** > **Setup** > **Quality management** > **Quarantine zones**.

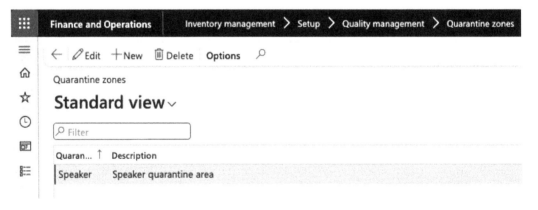

Figure 5.13 – Setting up quarantine zones

Until here, we have covered the most relevant setups for quality control and quality management; now, let's review some examples of non-conformance types.

Examples of non-conformance types

Different types of non-conformance require different kinds of information:

- **Customer**: Includes details such as customer account number or sales order number. For instance, if a customer complains about a product they received.

- **Service request**: For example, customer but specifically related to a service complaint. It might include the same customer and sales order details.

- **Vendor**: Involves vendor account numbers and purchase order details. For example, if a vendor is concerned about a part they supplied.

- **Production**: Includes production order numbers and is usually related to a specific batch of products made.

- **Internal**: Focuses on quality order numbers and could be related to internal tests or an employee's concern about product quality.

- **Co-product production**: This is a specialized type related to batch production orders for coproducts (made alongside the main product).

For example, if you're dealing with customer complaints, you might classify them under **Service request** non-conformances. On the other hand, if you're dealing with defects found during internal quality checks, those might go under **Internal** non-conformances.

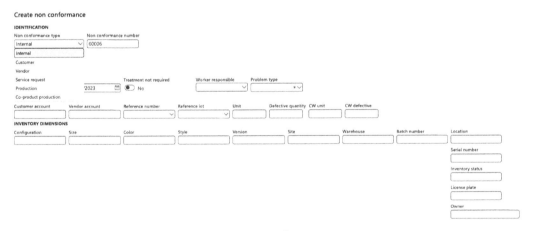

Figure 5.14 – Non-conformance types

So, these extra settings and types help you tailor your quality management system to handle all kinds of quality issues, making it easier to keep your products and services top-notch!

In summary, we have reviewed the most important quality control and quality management setups.

Let's have a visual look now at what we have covered.

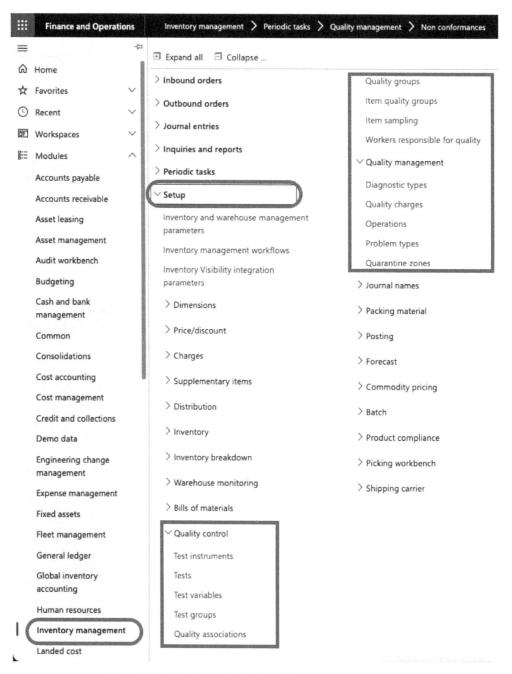

Figure 5.15 – Quality control and quality management setups

Remember that **Quality management** and **Quality control** features are available in the **Inventory management** module. Now we will review how to use the quality orders and the non-conformances.

Working with quality orders

Think of quality control as a particular check-up for your products. It ensures that everything is up to the mark. Here's how it works in Dynamics 365:

1. **Setting up tests**: You can list all the checks a product needs. This includes the following:

   - What standards it should meet
   - The tools to use for testing
   - Any related documents
   - How many samples to test
   - The AQLs

2. **Creating a quality order**: This is like a to-do list of tests for specific orders, be it a purchase, production, or even a certain amount of inventory. You can do either of the following:

   - Make this list yourself
   - Let the system create it for you based on set guidelines

3. **Setting guidelines**: For every business process, such as buying, producing, or selling, you can set rules. These rules help the system know when and what tests to run automatically, whether for products coming in or going out.

4. **Logging test results**: Once tests are done, you can do the following:

   - Note down the outcomes in the quality order
   - Check whether the results meet the set standards
   - Print a certificate showing the test results

Now, let's review how to create a quality order manually.

Manual creation of quality orders

To create a quality order manually, you will have to navigate to **Inventory management** > **Periodic tasks** > **Quality management** > **Quality orders**.

Here, we will be able to create an order for the specific inventory item and quantity, and we will also be able to run the specific test associated with the test group. The **Quality orders** page is your go-to spot for setting up quality checks. Here's what you can do:

- **Create a quality order**: You can manually make a quality order for different types of orders, such as the following:

  - Buying something (purchase order)

  - Making something (production order)

  - What you currently have in stock (physical on-hand inventory)

- **Test details**: When you create a quality order, you'll also specify the following:

  - How much of the item you want to test (test quantity)

  - What set of tests to run (test group)

- **Inventory-specific orders**: If you want to run tests on a specific number of items you have in stock, you'll need to create a quality order manually.

- **Set the AQL**: The system will automatically suggest an AQL based on your previous settings, making it easier to decide what's acceptable and what's not.

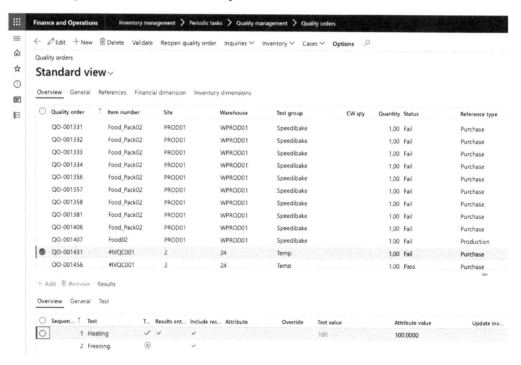

Figure 5.16 – Quality orders form

Non-conformances

Let's review now, in detail, the non-conformance orders in Dynamics 365, and let's check how the non-conformance can provide a structured way to address products or components that don't meet your standards.

Navigating non-conformance orders in Dynamics 365

Here's how to effectively manage them:

1. **Start with Non-conformance**: When you create one, it's labeled **New**, signaling that it's awaiting some action.

   The next step will be to make a decision with this newly created quality order.

2. **Make decisions**: Inside the non-conformances, we will find four different approval steps; here is a short and straightforward explanation of each step:

   - **Approve**: If the issue is valid and needs addressing, change its status to **Approved**.

   - **Refuse**: If no action is deemed necessary, update it to **Refused**.

   - **Close**: Mark it as **Closed** once you've tackled the issue.

   - **Reopen**: If further evaluation is needed, you can revert its status.

3. **Details for Approved issues**: Inside each quality order, it is extremely important to make a proper register and document the efforts made as clearly as possible:

   - List the corrective actions or operations to be done

   - Describe the rationale and the associated quality checks

   - Note any extra costs, items, and labor hours

   - The system will then show the total cost of addressing the issue

4. **Transitioning to quality orders**: If retesting or further quality checks are needed, you can create a quality order from the non-conformance. This new order will reference the original issue.

5. **Linking issues**: Dynamics 365 lets you connect related non-conformances or create a new one from an existing issue, showcasing the relationship between different quality challenges.

Consider creating a particular document type in the **Document type** section for your revisions. After that, swing by the **Report setup** area. Here, you can choose whether you want comments for this type to appear on your revision report. This nifty report will give you a peek into any mismatches and their related notes. Plus, you'll get a glimpse of the correction details and any messages tied to them.

Quality reports

Let's dive into the world of quality reports in Supply Chain Management. We're zooming in on three key reports: the non-conformance report, the non-conformance tag, and the corrections report.

In the following figure, we can see where we can access the report sections inside the non-conformances:

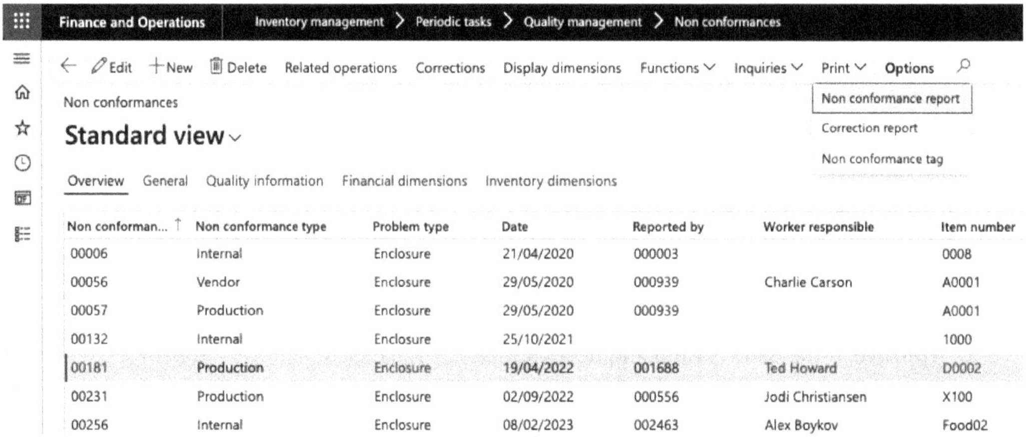

Non conforman... ↑	Non conformance type	Problem type	Date	Reported by	Worker responsible	Item number
00006	Internal	Enclosure	21/04/2020	000003		0008
00056	Vendor	Enclosure	29/05/2020	000939	Charlie Carson	A0001
00057	Production	Enclosure	29/05/2020	000939		A0001
00132	Internal	Enclosure	25/10/2021			1000
00181	Production	Enclosure	19/04/2022	001688	Ted Howard	D0002
00231	Production	Enclosure	02/09/2022	000556	Jodi Christiansen	X100
00256	Internal	Enclosure	08/02/2023	002463	Alex Boykov	Food02

Figure 5.17 – Quality reports

First up is **Non conformance report**. This report shows you all the essential details such as the issue number, the item involved, and the type of problem. You'll also see any related notes, depending on how you set up the report. You can customize the report to show only what you're interested in—whether by issue number, item, customer, vendor, or status.

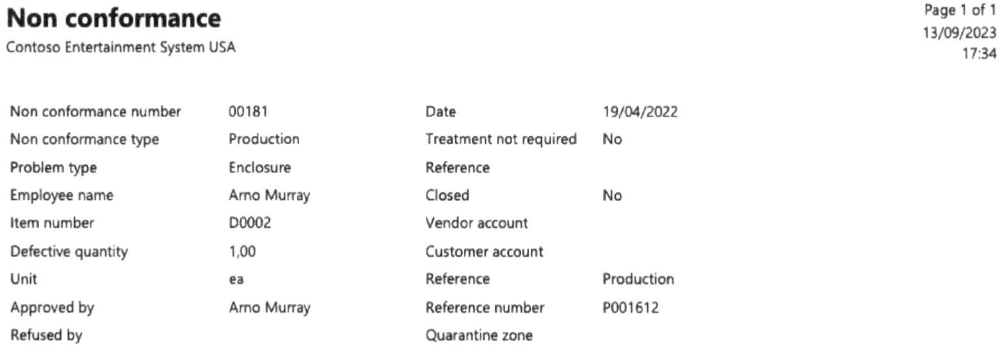

Figure 5.18 – Non conformance report

Next, let's talk about **Non conformance tag**. This tag also gives you the basics: the issue number and the item. It'll show you any related notes based on your setup preferences. Plus, it points out the quarantine zone and the type of restriction—such as whether the item is restricted for specific uses or completely unusable. This helps you decide what to do with the faulty material.

Non conformance tag
Contoso Entertainment System USA

Page 1 of 1
13/09/2023
17:36

Non conform product

Restricted usage

Item number	D0002
Product name	Cabinet
Date	19/04/2022
Vendor account	
Reference	Production
Reference number	P001612
Non conformance number	00181
Quarantine zone	
Defective quantity	1,00

Figure 5.19 – Non conformance tag report

Finally, we have the **Corrections report**. This one gives you a full rundown of the issue and related notes. It also tells you the corrective actions taken and any messages tied to those corrections. Like the others, what you see depends on how you've set up the report.

Corrections
Contoso Entertainment System USA

Page 1 of 1
16/11/2023
9:20

Non conformance number	00181	Date	19/04/2022
Non conformance type	Production	Treatment not required	No
Problem type	Enclosure	Reference	
Employee name	Arno Murray	Closed	No
Item number	D0002	Vendor account	
Defective quantity	1,00	Customer account	
Unit	ea	Reference	Production
Approved by	Arno Murray	Reference number	P001612
Refused by		Quarantine zone	

Created date and time	Employee name	Diagnostic	Correction priority	Planned date	Requested date	Completion date and time
19/04/2022 10:22:46	Charlie Carson	Shipping	Low	20/04/2022	03/04/2022	

Figure 5.20 – Corrections report

Certificate of analysis

Think of this as a seal of approval. It confirms that materials or products have been checked out and meet specific standards or specifications.

Do you need to create a certificate of analysis for a quality order? It's a breeze! Just head over to the following:

Inventory management > Inquiries and reports > Quality management > Certificate of analysis.
This is your go-to spot to prepare one manually.

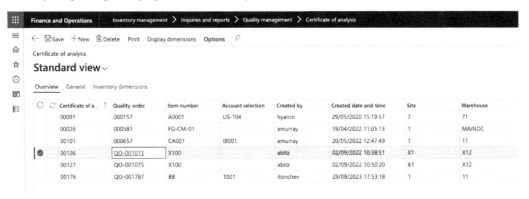

Figure 5.21 – Certificate of analysis form

Here is one example of what a certificate of analysis looks like:

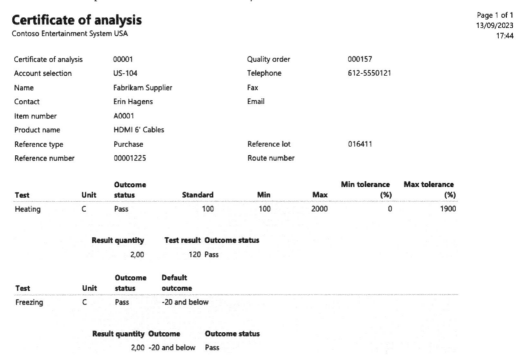

Figure 5.22 – Certificate of analysis printout example

Quarantine orders

Think of quarantine orders as a way to put a "Do Not Use" sign on your inventory. You may want to set some items aside for quality checks. When you do this, these items get a particular spot in a quarantine warehouse.

> **Quick tip**
>
> If you're diving deep into advanced warehouse management (found in **Warehouse management**), remember that quarantine order processing is specifically for return sales orders.

How to quarantine inventory items

You've got choices! You can either roll up your sleeves and set up quarantine orders by hand or let the system do the heavy lifting during inbound processing.

Want the system to handle it? Here's your path:

Inventory management > **Setup** > **Inventory** > **Item model groups**. Once there, tap the **Quarantine management** option under the **Inventory policies** tab.

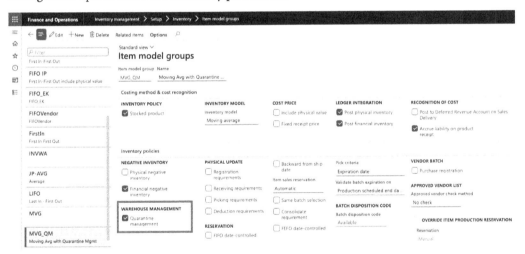

Figure 5.23 – Item model groups

Also, remember that you must define the default warehouse for quarantine. Go to **Inventory management** > **Setup** > **Inventory breakdown** > **Warehouses**.

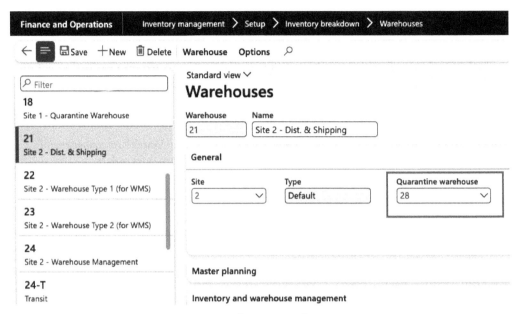

Figure 5.24 – Warehouse setup for quarantine

Whenever you log the physically on-hand inventory in a purchase or production order, any items marked for quarantine automatically get a new home in the quarantine warehouse. Why does this happen? Thanks to the quarantine order's status being switched to **Started**.

> **Here's a fun fact**
>
> If you're manually creating these quarantine orders, the item doesn't necessarily need to be pre-set for quarantine management in its item model group.

For this whole dance of quarantining, you'll need to pinpoint which on-hand inventory needs quarantining and choose the right quarantine warehouse. And to make things smoother, you can lean on the different quarantine order statuses to guide your steps.

Here's a quick peek at quarantine order statuses:

- **Created** – The initial stage when the order is made.

- **Started** – This is when the action begins, and items start moving to the quarantine warehouse.

- **Reported as finished** – The quarantine process for the items is complete.

- **Ended** – The order has been fully processed and closed out. When a quarantine order is marked as ended, the item is moved from the quarantine warehouse to the standard warehouse.

The movement back to the standard warehouse can be performed through an Item Arrival journal.

Quarantine order scrapping

During the quarantine order journey, scrapping some inventory is possible. When you decide to scrap, the inventory's status gets a minor update. It's marked as **Sold** through an issue transaction while still in the quarantine warehouse.

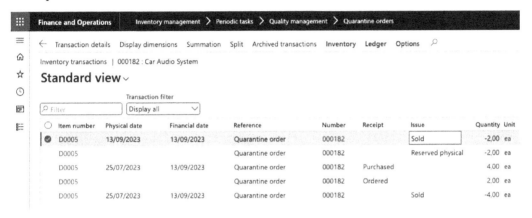

Figure 5.25 – Inventory scrap transaction

In simpler terms, think of it as decluttering your quarantine warehouse by marking certain items as **Sold** without them leaving the place. Handy, right?

Inventory blocking

Inventory blocking is like putting a "Do Not Touch" sign on certain items in your stock. You can block items in a few different ways:

- Manually
- By whipping up a quality order
- Through a process that auto-generates a quality order
- Using the **Inventory blocking** setting

Blocking items manually

To manually block some items, head to the **Inventory blocking** page and create a transaction. Keep in mind that you can only block items that are currently in stock.

You'll also need to decide whether to include expected items available after inspection. This option is turned on for items blocked through a quality order by default.

Delete the transaction at **Inventory management** > **Periodic tasks** > **Inventory blocking** to undo a manual block.

Blocking items with a quality order

You can earmark items for inspection by creating a quality order on the **Quality orders** page. The quantity you specify gets blocked. The sampling plan only dictates how many items need inspecting, not how many get blocked.

Auto-blocking items with a quality process

If a quality process calls for an item inspection, that item gets automatically blocked. The sampling plan tied to the auto-generated quality order will then decide how many items get blocked or inspected. If you've selected the **Full blocking** option at **Inventory management** > **Setup** > **Quality control** > **Item sampling**, the entire quantity of a purchase order line will be blocked during inspection, no matter the sampling quantity.

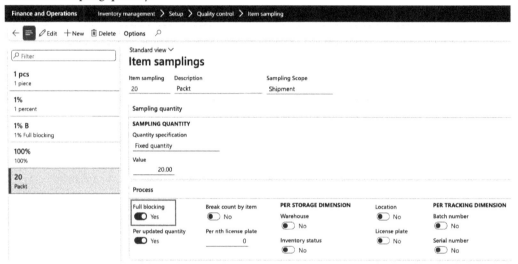

Figure 5.26 – Full blocking parameter in the Item sampling setup

Using the Inventory blocking parameter

Want to decide which inventory statuses act as blocking statuses? Head over to **Warehouse management** > **Setup** > **Inventory** > **Inventory statuses**. Here, you can set things up using the **Inventory blocking** parameter.

However, there's a catch! You can't use these blocking statuses for production orders, sales orders, transfer orders, outbound transactions, or when integrating with projects. For any outbound work, stick to items labeled with an **Available** inventory status.

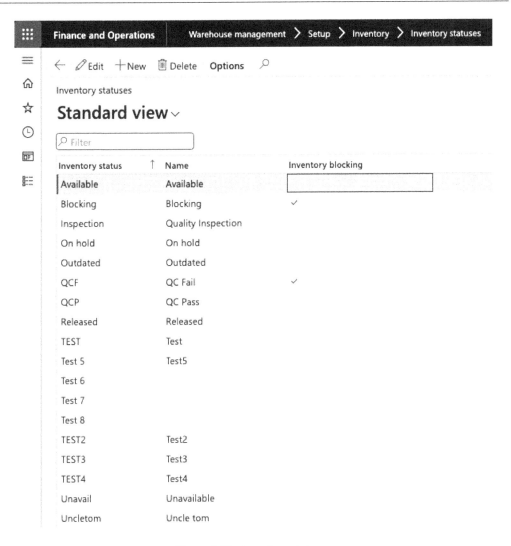

Figure 5.27 – Inventory statuses

Tips and recommendations

Here's a quick scenario. If items are tagged with a **Blocking** status, and you run master planning on them, the system will think these items are **missing in action (MIA)**. As a result, it'll automatically restock them.

With the quarantine order, we have covered how to exclude certain inventory from utilization and also avoid any mistake in the production or selling process; keeping something in quarantine is a significant advantage and also allows us to segregate and do proper management of our inventories.

Summary

As we pause at this chapter's end, let's take a moment to reflect on the exciting journey we've embarked on together. Dynamics 365 has been our trusty map, guiding us through the intricate terrains of quality control and management. We've learned, step by step, how to set up quality orders. Whether you're the kind who likes to roll up their sleeves and get hands-on or someone who leans on automation, there's a path for everyone.

Our exploration took us to the fascinating world of quality associations. Think of them as the unsung heroes ensuring that every product, every item, is just perfect. They're the behind-the-scenes magic that ensures everything's top-notch.

Then, we ventured into the realm of inventory. It's not just about counting items; it's also about making decisions. When to block, when to scrap, and most importantly, understanding the *why* behind each choice. It's like being a guardian of quality, ensuring only the worthy items pass through, while the rest are managed or set aside.

But remember, at the heart of all this tech and terminology is a simple goal: delivering excellence. With Dynamics 365 as our toolkit, we're not just meeting standards, we're setting them. As we gear up for the next chapter, let's carry forward all the insights and knowledge, ready to dive even deeper into the world of quality management. Here's to more learning and adventures ahead!

Questions

1. What's the difference between quality and quarantine orders in Dynamics 365?
2. What is a certificate of analysis in Dynamics 365 Supply Chain Management?
3. What options are available in Dynamics 365 Supply Chain Management for inventory blocking?

Answers

1. In Dynamics 365, quality and quarantine orders serve distinct purposes related to inventory management. A quality order is primarily used for inspecting items to ensure they meet specific quality standards before they enter the supply chain or are sold to customers. It often involves a set of tests or checks that the items must pass. On the other hand, a quarantine order is used to isolate items, usually in a separate warehouse, either for inspection or because they have already been identified as non-compliant. While quality orders aim to certify items, quarantine orders prevent potentially problematic items from entering the workflow until they are cleared or resolved.

2. In Dynamics 365 Supply Chain Management, a certificate of analysis confirms that materials or products have been tested and comply with predefined specifications or standards. It serves as a validation that the items meet the necessary quality criteria.

3. In Dynamics 365 Supply Chain Management, inventory blocking is a crucial feature that ensures items are not processed or consumed until they meet specific criteria. The options for inventory blocking include manual blocking, quality order blocking, automated blocking via a quality process, and **Inventory blocking** parameters.

6

Setting up and Managing Sales and Customers

The sales and marketing process is one of the most vibrant and dynamic components. It is the lifeblood of any organization, driving revenue, fostering customer relationships, and ensuring the steady flow of products and services to the market. At the heart of this process lies the dual responsibility of customer management and sales order processing. When executed effectively, these elements can elevate a business to new heights of success and customer satisfaction.

Dynamics 365 Supply Chain Management offers a comprehensive suite of tools to streamline and optimize these crucial processes. As we delve into this chapter, we aim to equip you with the knowledge and best practices to harness the full potential of Dynamics 365 in managing your sales and customer operations.

From processing sales orders to drafting contracts, every step is crucial in ensuring that the supply chain remains unbroken and efficient. But beyond the mechanics of order processing, there's the art of crafting sales agreements. When designed with precision and foresight, these agreements can be powerful tools to enhance sales, ensuring that the business and its customers reap maximum benefits.

In the following pages, we will embark on a journey to explore the nuances of sales order processing, delve deep into the intricacies of sales agreements, and understand how Dynamics 365 can be your ally in bringing out the best in your sales process. Whether you're a seasoned professional or a novice in sales and customer management, this chapter promises insights and guidance to pave the way for a robust and efficient sales operation.

Specifically, we will cover the following main topics:

- Order-to-cash process

- Sales groups and communications

- Intercompany trading

- Intercompany setup

Welcome to a world where sales and customer management converge seamlessly, powered by the capabilities of Dynamics 365 Supply Chain Management. Let's begin this transformative journey together.

Let's start from the process perspective in the sales world. The correct process to cover this area is the order-to-cash process.

Order to cash process

The **Order to Cash** (**O2C** or **OTC**) process refers to the end-to-end business process that covers the entirety of the order processing system, from when a customer places an order to the point where the company receives payment for that order. It's a crucial process for businesses, especially in the manufacturing and distribution sectors, as it directly impacts cash flow, customer satisfaction, and overall business efficiency.

Let's review the following diagram and the steps of the entire O2C process:

Figure 6.1 – O2C process

To better understand this process, we will immerse into each box and review how to handle this process in Dynamics 365 Supply Chain Management. Let's start!

In Dynamics 365 Supply Chain Management, the process can come from a sales quotation or create a sales order directly. To make the process simple and clean, we will start with the quotation process.

Sales quotation

Before creating our first sales quotation, we will do some basic setup in the system and define some default values. These values are relevant to the process, and we want to adjust three fields:

- **Days campaign expires**: When generating a quote, its expiration date is determined by adding the specified days in this field to the current date

- **Days before follow-up**: When generating a quote, its associated activity's follow-up date is determined by adding the specified days in this field to the current date

- **Quotation type customer**: This field will predefine if we want to create our quotation for a prospect or a customer directly; this can also be selected manually during the quotation creation process

To change these values, we can do it by going to the **Account receivable** module > **Setup** > **Accounts receivable parameters** and selecting the **General** tab:

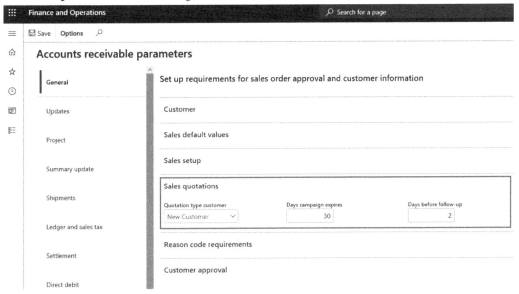

Figure 6.2 – Sales quotations default values

Now that our default values are defined, we can start creating our first sales quotation:

To create a sales quotation in Dynamics 365, we will navigate to **Sales and marketing** > **Sales quotations** > **All quotations**.

Here, we will be able to see the list of the quotations already generated in the system and the current status of each quote:

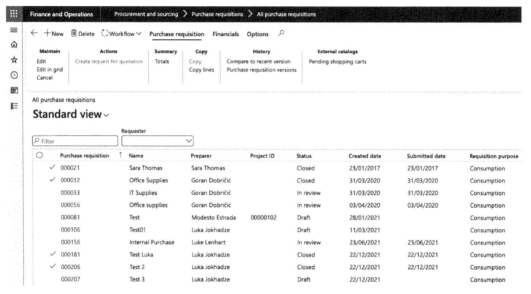

Figure 6.3 – All quotations

The sales quotation status

This can be very beneficial for the business to understand how many orders we, the business, manage to confirm and transform into sales orders and how many orders are lost.

We will also review how we can track the reasons for the lost quotations to get more accurate information. To create a new quotation, we will use the **+New** button from the top bar and fill in some basic information. Let's review it together:

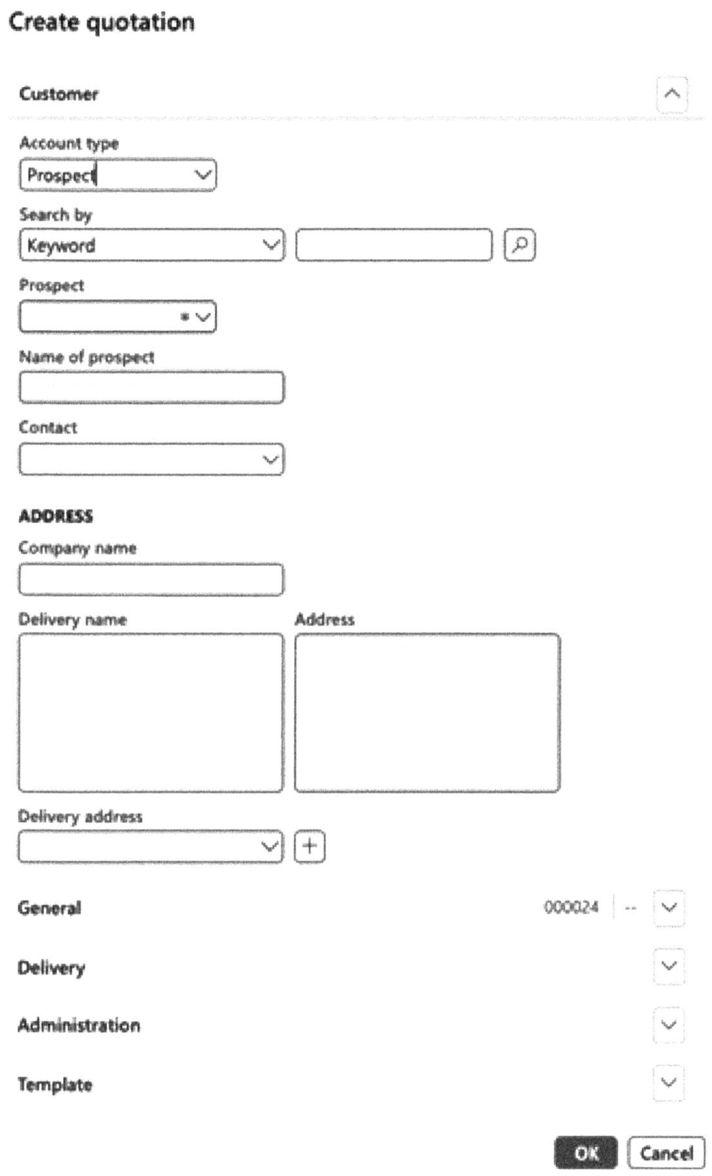

Create quotation

Customer   ˄

Account type

| Prospect | ˅ |

Search by

| Keyword | ˅ | | | 🔍 |

Prospect

| | * ˅ |

Name of prospect

| |

Contact

| | ˅ |

ADDRESS

Company name

| |

Delivery name   Address

| | | |

Delivery address

| | ˅ | + |

General   000024   --   ˅

Delivery   ˅

Administration   ˅

Template   ˅

OK Cancel

Figure 6.4 – Creating a new quotation

The first mandatory information to fill in will be **Account type**; here, the system proposes two options: **Prospect** and **Customer**. A prospect is just a potential customer, but we are not doing any business yet. It is simply an interested party to buy something from us who is interested in knowing details that can make them take the next step and become a customer.

If we select **Customer** in **Account type**, the **Prospect** field will be replaced by **Customer account**, and then we will only need to select the proper customer account:

Figure 6.5 – Creating a new quotation for the customer

If our master data is accurate, we will not need to do too much on the screen, and then we will be good to go to the next step. On the next screen, we will be able to add the lines and the items that we want to quote for our prospect or customer.

During the quotation process, what can really make the difference between winning or losing the quotation are the following three elements:

- Price

- Delivery date

- Available stock

Based on these criteria, we will prepare the line for our prospect/customer:

Figure 6.6 – Adding lines to the sales quotation

We will pick an item and define the appropriate site and warehouse and the price, and if required, we can offer a discount.

The discount can be entered as either a fixed value or a percentage of the unit price. The final part is the delivery date. If we expand **Line details** and go to the **Delivery** tab, we can change **Requested receipt date** and **Requested ship date**:

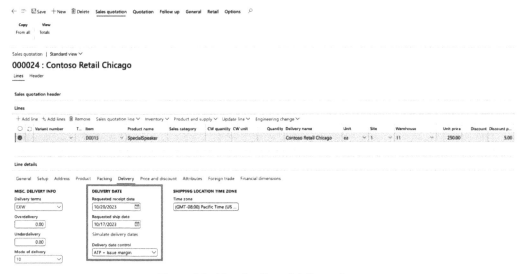

Figure 6.7 – Line details and delivery dates

Regarding the date, Dynamics 365 Supply Change Management has a lovely embedded feature: **Delivery date control**.

We will not discuss this right now, but we will touch on this topic again during the creation of sales orders.

Once we have entered all the lines and filled in the required fields, such as **Unit price**, **Discount**, and **Delivery date**, we are now ready to send our quotation.

To perform this action, we will go to the top bar in the **Quotation** tab and select **Send quotation**:

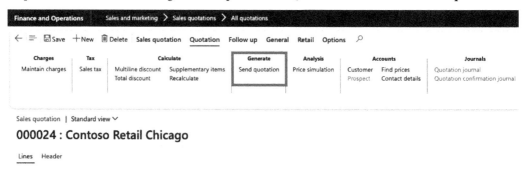

Figure 6.8 – Send quotation

From here, we will manage to generate our quotation in a printable format and send it to our customer. In the following quotation generated from the system, we will see all the relevant information from our prospect/customer and the validity of our quotation. Also, the requested item with all the details required to inform our prospect about the conditions, date, price, discount, and so on will be available:

Feilo Sylvania International Group Kft
123 Coffee Street
Suite 300
Redmond, WA 98052
USA

Telephone	
Fax	
Giro	
Tax registration number	1234123400

Quotation

Ship to:
Contoso Retail Chicago
Purple Road 234
Arlington Heights, IL 60004
USA

Page	1 of 1
Number	000024-1
Date	10/17/2023
Requisition	
Your ref.	
Our ref.	
Quotation deadline	11/16/2023
Payment	Net 10 days

Item number	Description	Ship date	Quantity	Unit	Sales price	Discount	Discount percent	Amount
D0010	Active speaker	11/17/2023	1.00	PL	1,350.00	0.00	5.00%	1,282.50

This text is from the Sales Quotation form notes

Currency	Sales subtotal amount	Total discount	Charges	Net amount	Sales tax	Round-off	Total
USD	1,282.50	0.00	0.00	1,282.50	0.00	0.00	1,282.50

Figure 6.9 – Generated quotation example

Now, logic tells us that we must properly follow up on the quotation and get a response from our prospect/customer.

Following this principle, Microsoft Dynamics 365 Supply Chain Management is prepared to reflect what is occurring in real business life into a systematic action. For this, we have another tab called **Follow up** in the top bar with three main actions:

- **Confirm**: We can confirm our quotation and, from here, convert it automatically into a sales order

- **Cancel**: We can cancel the quotation and stop progress with no action

- **Lost quotation**: We can mark our quotation as **Lost** and indicate a reason:

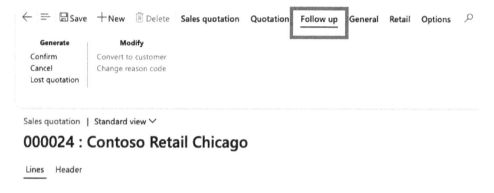

Figure 6.10 – Sales quotation follow up

Let's look at the **Lost quotation** action first to understand the scenario in the system and how we can customize the reasons for a lost quotation. When we click the **Lost quotation** action button, a new screen will appear asking for the reason for losing this quotation:

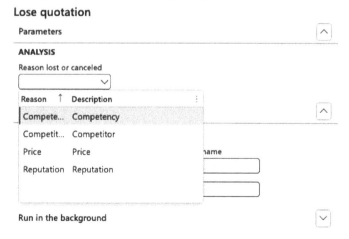

Figure 6.11 – Lose quotation reasons

These options can be customized in a table if we right-click on the **Reason lost or canceled** field and select **View details**:

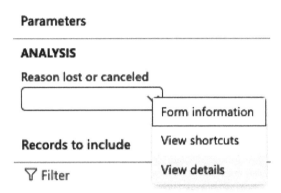

Figure 6.12 – Accessing the reasons table

Clicking on **View details** will guide us to the table where we can customize the possible reasons for lost quotations. We can customize this list based on the requirements captured from our business:

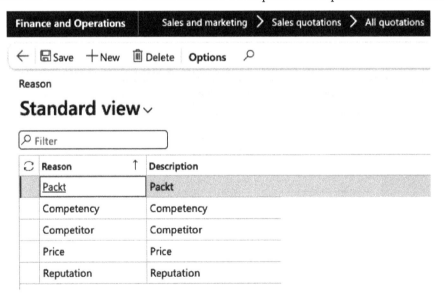

Figure 6.13 – Reason table for quotations

Having a clear reason for lost quotations can guide our future business decisions and improve how we quote our customers and what they demand from the business to be closer to their wishes.

Let's review now what will happen in the system if we mark the quotation as **Confirm**. Confirming the quotation in the **Follow up** tab will transform our quotation into a sales order. This is the first method to capture the demand from our customers in the system.

Upon confirmation of the sales quotation, the system undertakes these actions:

1. Generates a sales order.

2. Transfers all details from the sales quotation to the sales order.

3. Establishes a record in the quotation confirmation journal, accessible via **Sales and marketing** > **Sales quotations** > **Quotation update** > **Sales quotation confirmations**.

4. Records the current system date as the confirmation date in the sales quotation.

5. Updates the quotation status to **Confirmed**.

6. Locks the sales quotation, preventing further edits.

The other possible way to do it in Dynamics 365 Supply Chain Management is by creating the sales order directly without the need to pass through the quotation process. Now, let's review how to create a sales order in the system manually.

Sales order

The sales order process is a crucial and systematic sequence of actions that ensures the efficient delivery of products to customers. This process guarantees that the customer's requirements are met and that the company's operations run smoothly. The following subsections will offer a detailed breakdown of the steps involved:

1. Sales order creation

2. Addition of order lines

Sales order creation

This is the initial step where a sales order is generated based on the customer's request or purchase order. Different Dynamics 365 Supply Chain Management modules can generate a sales order. Here are some direct links to do it:

*   Module – **Sales and Marketing**:

    Sales Orders > **All Sales Orders** > **New+**

*   Module – **Accounts Receivable**:

    Sales Orders > **All Sales Orders** > **New+**

*   Module – **Retail and Commerce**:

    Customers > **All Sales Orders** > **New+**

- Module – **Revenue Recognition**

  The **Revenue recognition** module has been deprecated, and the functionalities are being transitioned to the new **Subscription billing** module.

For this guide, we will pick up the first one, **Sales and marketing** > **Sales orders** > **All Sales orders** > **New+**.

Once we click on **New+**, a new screen will ask for a few details:

Figure 6.14 – Creating a new sales order

The most relevant is to select the proper customer account. If our customer record is created correctly and we have all the master data in good shape, this process should be straightforward, and we should continue to the next step.

Also, it is essential to review the customer address carefully; remember that one customer can have multiple locations, so please consider the customer address as an essential field to validate before processing the order.

Addition of order lines

Now is the time to add all specific product details, quantities, discounts, and other pertinent information to the sales order, forming its line items:

Figure 6.15 – Adding lines to the sales order

One of the essential things for each line is the **Delivery** tab and the dates, which will be highly relevant for the end-to-end process in the Dynamics 365 supply chain process.

Now, let's talk about the dates in the sales order line and what is commonly known as **order promising**.

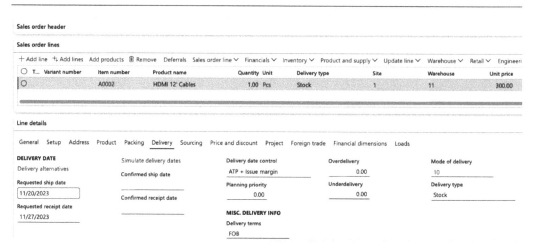

Figure 6.16 – Line details, delivery dates

In the sales order details, more specifically in the **Delivery** tab, we will see four different dates. Let's review the purpose of each and how to work with them; these are highly important and directly tied to how we promise to satisfy the customer:

- **Requested ship date**: This refers to when a customer expects an order to be shipped. It is used to prioritize downstream processes such as production and procurement. By considering the requested ship date, Dynamics 365 can increase the accuracy of customer order delivery dates.

- **Requested receipt date**: This refers to when a customer or a business expects to receive an order or shipment. It's the target date by which goods should be received after they have been shipped. This data is crucial for planning, as it helps businesses align their operations and logistics to ensure that goods arrive when needed.

- **Confirmed ship date**: This refers to the date confirmed with the customer of when the order will be shipped. This date might differ from the initial requested ship date based on inventory availability.

- **Confirmed receipt date**: This refers to the date a buyer or receiving party confirms that they will receive an order or shipment.

As we can see, the confirmed ship date and confirmed receipt date depend directly on the inventory availability. To avoid doing manual calculations, Microsoft Dynamics 365 Supply Chain Management offers a great functionality called **Simulate delivery dates**.

Let's see how this works and what setup is required.

To simulate the delivery dates, we need to understand what possible delivery control methods are available in Dynamics 365 supply chain management and, based on our business requirements, select the most effective to promise to our customers.

Microsoft Dynamics 365 supply chain management offers the following:

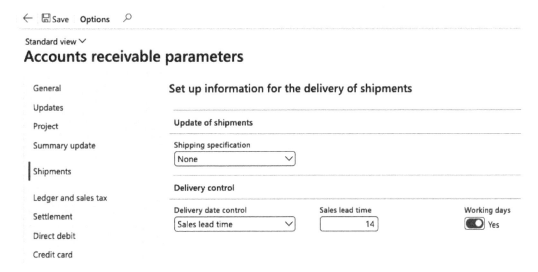

Figure 6.17 – Delivery date control methods

Let's review how they work and what we need to set up to use them properly:

- **None**: No delivery control method will be used, and we will manually select a date for the confirmed ship date and receipt date.

- **Sales lead time**: This refers to the duration between the initiation of a sales order and the shipping of the products. The delivery date estimation is determined by a predefined number of days and does not consider inventory levels, anticipated demand, or projected supply.

To predefine our sales lead time, we will do it from the **Accounts receivable** module > **Setup** > **Accounts receivable parameters** > **Shipments**, and in the **Delivery control** section, we can pre-define our **Delivery date control** method and **Sales lead time**; we can also specify whether these days will be working days or continuous days:

Figure 6.18 – Default Delivery control and Sales lead time

- **ATP** (available to promise): This represents the amount of a product that can be assuredly offered to a customer for a particular date. The ATP calculation factors include unused stock, lead times, planned receipts, and planned issues.

  For more details on the formula used and examples, please refer to the following link and QR code: `https://learn.microsoft.com/en-us/dynamics365/supply-chain/sales-marketing/delivery-dates-available-promise-calculations#atp-calculations`

Figure 6.19 – ATP calculation examples

- **ATP + Issue margin**: This works the same as ATP but includes additional days required to prepare the goods to be sent to the customer. This method can be very beneficial if the preparation process is complex:

Figure 6.20 – ATP + Issue margin setup

- **CTP** (capable to promise): Availability determination is done via explosion of all the components of a particular bill of materials. When utilizing planning optimization, the CTP delivery date control approach is not allowed. If chosen, it will trigger an error during the calculation. If planning optimization is enabled, enabling the below feature is highly recommended.

- **CTP for Planning Optimization**: By enabling this feature, we will add a **Delivery control** method to the system with the same name:

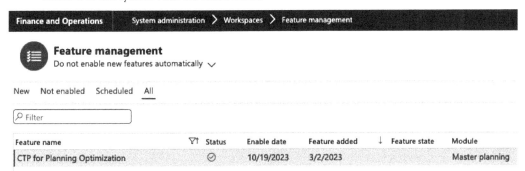

Figure 6.21 – Enabling the CTP for Planning Optimization feature

To have a deeper review of how **CTP** and **CTP for Planning Optimization** work, I highly recommend reviewing the official Microsoft documentation of this process; this also helps you to understand how master planning and planning optimization work. Of course, we will cover this in the master planning chapters later. Here is the link and QR code for the documentation: `https://learn.microsoft.com/en-us/dynamics365/supply-chain/master-planning/planning-optimization/calculate-delivery-dates-using-ctp`

Figure 6.22 – Delivery dates using CPT

All the preceding methods will provide us with a better and more accurate date to promise to our customers and keep them informed for better planning.

Confirming the order with the customer

Let's see now how this communication is made with the customer.

Once the order details are verified and confirmed, the sales order is formally acknowledged, signaling that the company is ready to fulfill the request. The requested items, prices, discounts, and dates are confirmed with the customer with the sales order confirmation.

Once we have entered all possible details in our order and there are no more changes, we generate the sales order confirmation and send it to the customer.

To confirm the sales order, we have two options in Dynamics 365:

- From the top bar, we can go to **Sell** > **Actions** > **Confirm now**. This will only generate the action of confirming the order and generating a sales order confirmation journal.

    We can go to the journal later and check what the system generated:

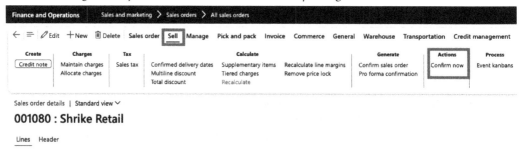

Figure 6.23 – Confirming the sales order

- The other alternative is, from the top bar, go to **Sell** > **Generate** > **Confirm sales order**. From here, the system will perform the following actions at the same time: mark the order as confirmed, generate the sales order confirmation journal, and display the confirmation journal on the screen:

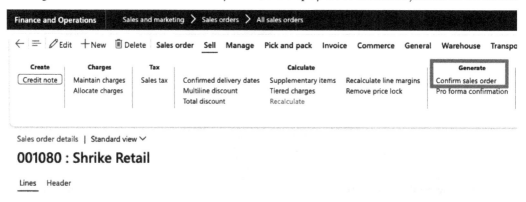

Figure 6.24 – Generating and confirming the sales order

After clicking the **Confirm sales order** action button, the system will display the sales order confirmation, and we can send it to our customer and keep them adequately informed that the order has been processed:

Figure 6.25 – Confirm sales order options

Here, we can finally see the generated output document to be sent to our customer:

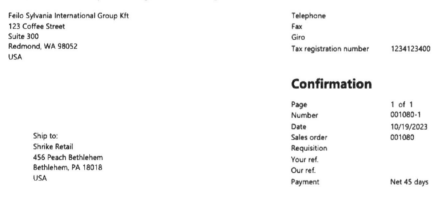

Figure 6.26 – Sales order confirmation example

The following steps are part of the O2C process but are not strictly lined with the sales process. The warehouse and finance teams usually handle these steps, but I will quickly summarize them to have complete visibility of the process:

1. **Generate a picking list**: A picking list is generated, which serves as a guide for warehouse staff to gather the required items for the order from inventory:

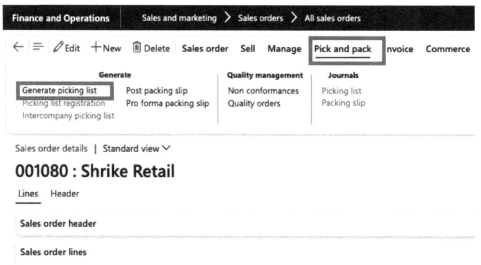

Figure 6.27 – Generate picking list

After clicking this option, the system will generate the picking list that can be used in the warehouse to collect the goods:

Figure 6.28 – Picking list printout example

2. **Picking list registration**: The items picked from the inventory are registered or marked off on the picking list, ensuring accuracy in order fulfillment:

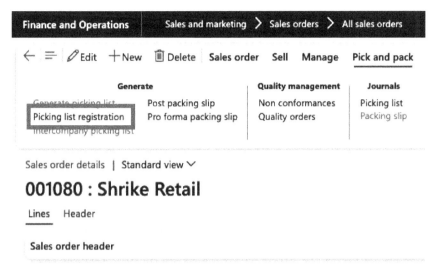

Figure 6.29 – Picking list registration

After the items are picked from their location, the warehouse operator will update the system to the right status, removing the stock from the location:

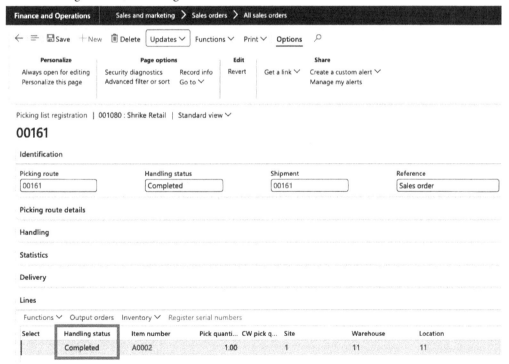

Figure 6.30 – Picking list registration process

3. **Generate a packing slip**: A packing slip is produced detailing the items in the shipment. This document accompanies the shipped goods and helps cross-check the contents upon delivery:

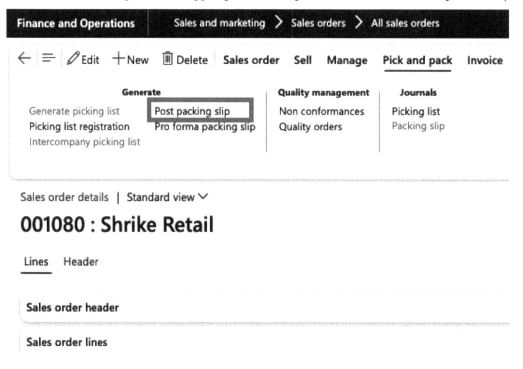

Figure 6.31 – Post packing slip

4. **Ship the items**: The packed items are dispatched to the customer using the chosen mode of transportation, be it air, sea, or land:

Feilo Sylvania International Group Kft
123 Coffee Street
Suite 300
Redmond, WA 98052
USA

Telephone
Fax
Giro
Tax registration number   1234123400

Packing slip

Page	1 of 1
Number	SPK-00002024
Version	SPK-00002024.1
Date	10/19/2023
Sales order	001080
Requisition	
Your ref.	
Our ref.	
Mode of delivery	Truck
Terms of delivery	Free on Board
Freighted by	Carrier
Customer account	US-023

Ship to:

Shrike Retail
456 Peach Bethlehem
Bethlehem, PA 18018
USA

Bill to:
Shrike Retail
456 Peach Bethlehem
Bethlehem, PA 18018
USA

Item number	Description	Ordered	Unit	CW quantity	CW unit	Delivered	Remaining quantity
A0002	HDMI 12' Cables	1.00	pcs	0.00		1.00	0.00
	Quantity : 1 Site : 1 Warehouse : 11						

This text is from the Sales Order Packing Slip form notes

Receipt : _____

Figure 6.32 – Packing slip example

5. **Generate an invoice**: After the goods are shipped, an invoice is generated and sent to the customer, indicating the amount due for the products and services provided:

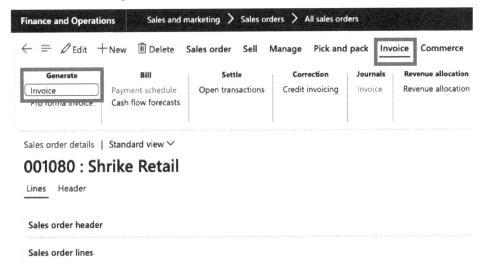

Figure 6.33 – Generating an invoice

Here, we can see the invoice generated for the customer:

Telephone	
Fax	
Giro	
Tax registration number	1234123400

Shrike Retail
456 Peach Bethlehem
Bethlehem, PA 18018
USA

Invoice

Number	CIV-00000751
Invoice date	10/19/2023
Page	1 of 1
Date and time	11/16/2023 5:56 PM
Sales order	001080
Requisition	
Your reference	
Our reference	
Payment	Net 45 days
Invoice account	US-023
Payment reference	

Contact

Packing duty license
number

Item number	Description	Quantity	Unit	Unit price	Discount percent	Discount	Amount	Print code
A0002	HDMI 12' Cables	1.00	pcs	300.00	3	0.00	291.00	

This text is from the Sales Order Invoice form notes

Sales subtotal amount	Total discount	Total charges	Net amount	Sales tax	Round-off	Total
291.00	0.00	0.00	291.00	0.00	0.00	291.00 USD

Due date   12/3/2023
Cash discount granted: 5.82 USD before 10/26/2023, 1.46 USD before 10/29/2023.

Figure 6.34 – Invoice example

6. **Receive payment**: The final step involves the customer paying based on the invoice. Once received, the sales order process is deemed complete, and the transaction is closed.

By following this structured process, businesses can ensure timely and accurate delivery of products, leading to enhanced customer satisfaction and streamlined operations. Let's now turn to something exciting when we talk about sales and customer management. Let's immerse ourselves in the world of commissions and customer groups.

Sales groups and commissions

Dynamics 365 Supply Chain Management offers a comprehensive solution for managing commissions, ensuring sales teams are appropriately incentivized and rewarded for their efforts. This capability is crucial for businesses that rely on sales teams to drive revenue and want to ensure accurate and timely commission payments.

The following are the key elements included in the solution:

- **Commission calculation**: Automated tools to calculate commissions based on predefined criteria, such as sales volume, revenue targets, or specific product sales

- **Tracking and reporting**: Detailed tracking of all commission-related activities, providing transparency to sales representatives and management

- **Integration with finance**: Seamless integration with financial modules ensures that commission payments are processed efficiently and accurately

- **Configurable rules**: The ability to set up and modify commission rules based on changing business needs or sales strategies

- **Dispute management**: Tools to handle any disputes related to commission calculations or payments

- **Forecasting**: Predictive analytics to forecast potential commission payouts based on sales trends

In this section, we will focus on the configuration of rules and sales groups and review how to calculate commission in Dynamics 365 Supply chain management.

One of the key elements for setting up the commission configuration is sales groups.

Sales groups

Sales groups in Dynamics 365 Supply Chain Management refer to categorizations or groupings of sales entities, which can be used to organize, manage, and report on sales activities.

These groups can be based on various criteria, such as product categories, geographical regions, sales channels, or specific customer segments.

By using sales groups, organizations can streamline their sales processes, set specific targets or quotas, and monitor performance against these targets. Additionally, sales groups can assign sales representatives or teams to specific customers or regions, ensuring that customers receive specialized attention based on their needs and preferences.

Of course, this categorization will help us to segment and calculate our commissions based on specific rules.

Let's review the setup of sales groups.

Setting up sales groups

To create or maintain sales groups, please navigate to **Sales and marketing** > **Commissions** > **Sales groups**:

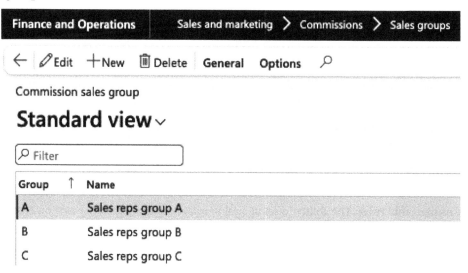

Figure 6.35 – Commission sales groups

Here, the setup looks relatively easy; we need to define a group ID and name.

After we create our new group, from the top bar, in the **General** section, we should select the **Sales rep.** option:

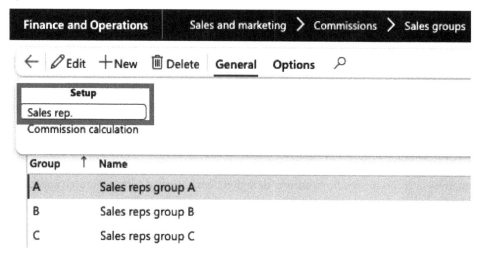

Figure 6.36 – Sales representatives

From this option, we will do the association with the sales representative, and we will indicate the commission share based on this sales group:

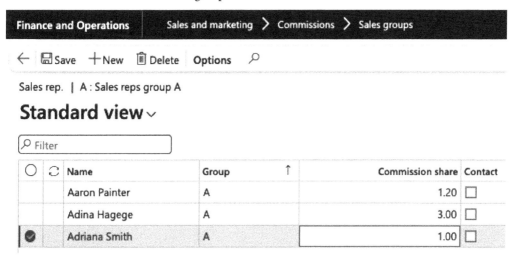

Figure 6.37 – Sales representative setup

Now, if we return to the previous screen and click **General > Commission calculation**, we will navigate to an area where we can define more specific rules:

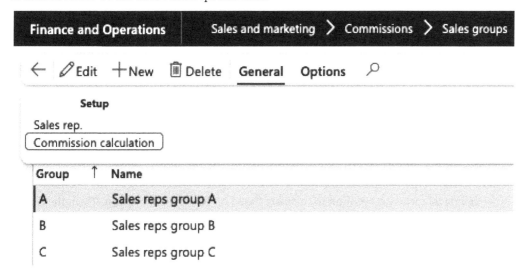

Figure 6.38 – Commission calculation

Here, we can create defined rules based on item associations. We can choose whether to do this association for a single item, a group of items, or the entire list:

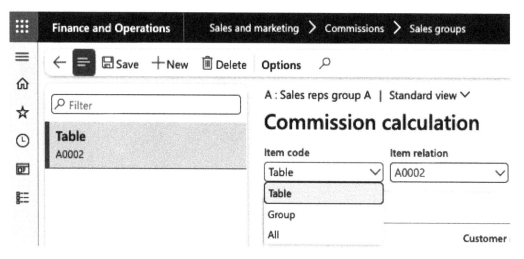

Figure 6.39 – Commission calculation item setup

Also, you can make a more profound link to customers based on the same criteria, a single customer group, or apply the rule to all customers.

Then, the final part of the setup will be based on how we want to calculate the commission percentage:

Figure 6.40 – COMMISSION BASED ON setup

The base for commission calculation can be one of the following:

- **Before line discount**

- **After line discount**

- **After total discount**

Also, we can decide whether we want to calculate based on **Revenue** or **Margin**. Then, the final decision is related to **PERIOD**; we can apply this calculation based on a very short period, months, or the entire year.

It is crucial to make this setup before we start making any sales or, if we do it after, consider that changes will be reflected only for future transactions. Now we have our rules defined, the commission will be calculated every time a new sales invoice is posted.

If you want to get additional details on registering sales commissions and some more examples, please refer to the official Microsoft Learn materials at the following link and QR code: `https://learn.microsoft.com/en-us/dynamics365/supply-chain/sales-marketing/tasks/register-sales-commissions`

Figure 6.41 – Register sales commissions documentation

Finally, one of the things we want to review is related to the capabilities of Microsoft Dynamics 365 Supply chain management to operate with other related companies; this process is called **intercompany trading**.

Intercompany trading

Intercompany trading often becomes necessary in the complex landscape of global businesses. Dynamics 365 Supply Chain Management recognizes this and offers robust capabilities to streamline and manage intercompany trade.

Organizations frequently act as a supplier or customers across different business units. For instance, a multinational organization might have several manufacturing entities that supply materials to its distribution entities within the same organization.

Dynamics 365 Supply Chain Management provides tools for intercompany planning, allowing businesses to integrate downstream intercompany demand into their demand forecasts. This integration ensures that inventory, capacity information, and other essential data are shared across companies, facilitating effective intercompany planning and operations.

When we talk about *intercompany*, Dynamics 365 supply chain management offers several integration points:

- **Intercompany demand forecasting**: Incorporate downstream intercompany demand into overall demand forecasts

- **Shared inventory and capacity information**: Promote transparency and collaboration by sharing inventory levels and production capacities across different business units

- **Optimized planning**: Utilize intercompany planning tools to ensure that resources are allocated efficiently and customer demands are met consistently

- **Seamless integration**: Ensure intercompany transactions are accurately reflected across all relevant business units, minimizing discrepancies and errors

Dynamics 365 Supply Chain Management can automate the creation and processing of intercompany sales orders, purchase orders, and other relevant transactions, reducing manual effort and potential errors.

Now, we will focus on understanding the required steps to configure and work with intercompany sales orders.

Before initiating intercompany trade configurations, determine which of your customers qualify as intercompany customers and identify the vendors that fall under the *intercompany vendor* category. For every legal entity within Microsoft Dynamics 365 Supply Chain Management, you must establish the trading policy that will govern the intercompany trading relationship with the designated customer or vendor.

You and your team must understand the intricacies of the intercompany parameters thoroughly.

Engage in discussions with the managerial personnel overseeing intercompany trade in each legal entity to understand the potential implications of the setup. Ensure that the correct values are established for every legal entity.

To understand intercompany trading, we can graphically see it as shown in the following figure:

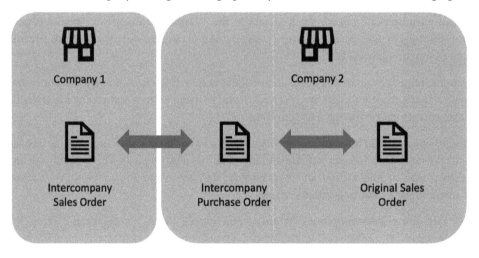

Figure 6.42 – Intercompany trading example

In the example shown in *Figure 6.42*, we are representing a *three-legged intercompany transaction* where a customer is placing a sales order, called **Original Sales Order**, which creates an intercompany sales order on the customer company that generates an intercompany sales order on the vendor company.

Intercompany setup

To set up a customer for intercompany trading, we will need to navigate to the **Customer master** list; we can do it from the following:

- **Accounts receivable** > **Customers** > **All customers**

- **Sales and marketing** > **Customers** > **All customers**

We need to select our desired customer from the list, then from the **Action** pane, select the **General** tab and then the **Intercompany** option, as shown in the following figure:

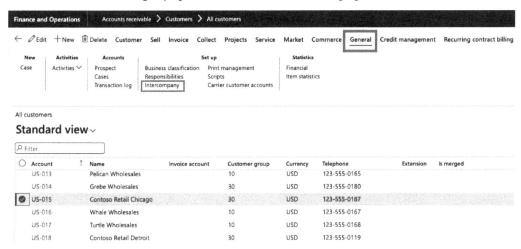

Figure 6.43 – Intercompany option on the All customers form

Then, we will see a new set of parameters that must be reviewed in detail.

The first tab is **Trading relationship**; here, we will generate a mapping with the sourcing legal entity and the corresponding vendor account:

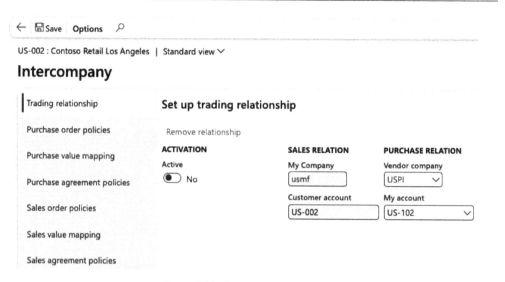

Figure 6.44 – Intercompany setup

It is important to set the **Active** field to **Yes** to start using intercompany trading between the related companies. Once the **Trading relationship** tab is complete, you can continue by defining the purchase order policies:

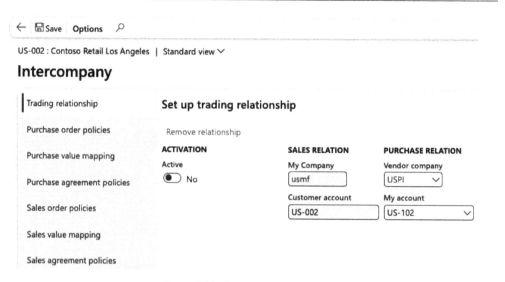

Figure 6.45 – Purchase order policies

The purchase order policies will define how the system will react at every process step. For example, you can decide whether you allow editing the prices or not. These parameters can heavily influence the business process; this needs to be tested carefully by the business.

We can divide them into three groups:

- **Process parameters**: Define whether packing slips and invoices are printed and posted automatically and whether you can bypass the vendor workflow for intercompany transactions

- **Price parameters**: Define whether you can edit prices and discounts of intercompany transactions

- **Synchronization parameters**: Define how information is shared between companies

Then, the next necessary setup is the value mappings; you can select whether you use **Our** values or a predefined **External** value from a table:

Figure 6.46 – Purchase value mapping

Once we complete our customer setup, it is essential to do the same setup for the requesting company; this time, we will do the same from a *vendor* perspective:

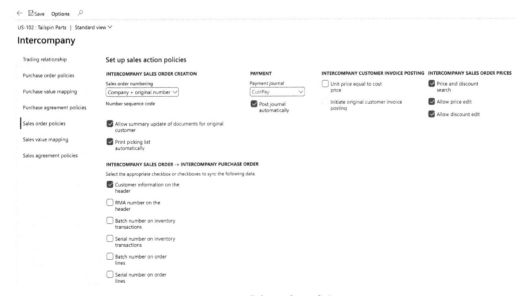

Figure 6.47 – Sales order policies

In this case, we have parameters to set the policies from a sales order perspective. We can divide them into five groups:

- **Process parameters**: How orders and picking lists are created.

- **Price parameters**: Control of prices and discounts can be modified here.

- **Payment parameters**: We can set up the payment journal and activate automated posting.

- **Intercompany customer invoice posting parameters**: Controls the sales order posting and which price is used for posting. If we activate a unit price equal to the cost price, we cannot use intercompany agreements.

- **Synchronization**: How information is shared between companies.

Finally, when the setup is ready, we can start creating a purchase order for one company. Then, automatically, the sales order with all the purchase order details will be generated in the selling company.

This is a tremendous advantage in terms of efficiency for companies that do internal sourcing/sales, and Dynamics 365 Supply chain management is ready to cope with this challenge. Remember that the items you want to buy/sell must be released to both companies.

Summary

During this chapter, we learned how to configure and work with quotations and sales orders; we reviewed the entire end-to-end O2C process from Microsoft Dynamics 365 Supply chain management. Also, we reviewed the delivery control methods and the list of possibilities that the system offers us to provide our customers with excellent service and quality during the selling process. We also covered the importance of confirmed dates and the process that follows after we confirm the sales order with our customers.

Also, we reviewed the capabilities of Dynamics 365 supply chain management to manage the commission calculations and the flexibility that it offers to create custom rules. Finally, we had a quick overview of how to work with intercompany sales orders that simplify the process between linked companies.

In our next chapter, we will continue by discovering another fantastic topic; we will immerse ourselves in warehouse operations and the best practices and strategies to handle our warehouse operations like a hero.

Questions

1. What are the essential configurations to work with quotations in Dynamics 365 supply chain management?

2. What are the delivery control methods available in Dynamics 365 Supply chain management?

3. What is required to set up intercompany trading?

Answers

1. Working with sales quotations requires predefining the default values for the following:

    *   **Account type**: We can choose between **Prospect** or **Customer** by default.
    *   Days campaign expires
    *   Days before follow-up

2. The following are the available delivery control methods:

    *   **None**
    *   **ATP**
    *   **ATP + Issue margin**
    *   **CTP**
    *   **CTP for Planning Optimization** (additional feature is required)

3. To set intercompany trading, you need to link a customer account with a vendor account from another legal entity and define the policies and the field mappings. Also, the items they want to trade should be available in both legal entities.

7

Warehouse Management Implementation – Best Practices and Strategies - Part 1

A **warehouse management system (WMS)** is a system that controls all warehouse operations and is oriented to leverage the performance of the warehouse, optimizing its process flows to achieve better times and dispatch orders faster. So, often, we relate these systems with a barcode scanner, but it is much more than that. Facilities that use WMSs in their warehouse design every step of a picking flow to optimize their business.

There are different types of WMSs, such as standalone WMSs, which we need to integrate with our ERP, or the Warehouse management module of Dynamics 365, which is part of the ERP; this allows us to easily connect with related modules, such as sales, procurement, and transportation. It also helps us manage warehouses for retail, manufacturing, or distribution companies.

Here is what you will learn in this chapter:

- Understanding warehouse management concepts and configuration
- Designing and setting up a warehouse layout
- Designing a mobile device menu and menu items for the warehouse management app

Warehouse management concepts and configuration

The warehouse management module is an extension of the inventory module we saw in *Chapter 3*. Every inventory process on the inventory module has flows and steps that could be extended using WMSs. We're going to review these concepts and setups in this section.

To begin using warehouse management, we must set it up. We will need several configurations, all of which we explained in earlier chapters, but we need to tune them.

Storage dimension groups

First, we need to create a storage dimension group. As we reviewed in *Chapter 2*, the storage dimension group controls how many dimensions will control our inventory. If we choose a site and warehouse, our inventory will only be able to work at the warehouse level, and we cannot control in which locations it will be stored.

Let's go to **Product Information Management** > **Setup** > **Dimension and variant groups** > **Storage dimension group**. Here, we'll find the following form:

Figure 7.1 – Storage dimension groups

Here, we can see the **Use warehouse management process** option under the **Warehouse specific setup** tab. This option will activate all five storage dimensions, allowing us to control WMS processes. In every transaction associated with an item with these storage dimensions, it will be asked for the basic dimensions, such as site warehouse and location, and then add two new dimensions:

- **Inventory Status**: This will control the status of the inventory. It controls two main statuses, **blocked** and **available**. However, we could use it to separate different business processes. For example, we could use this to block inventory for picking items. Still, if we need to restrict inventory for sales reservations, we could create a different inventory status, **Not for sale**, and prevent these items from being picked while they are not blocked.

- **License plate**: This dimension is used for tracking purposes in the warehouse. This could be a pallet, a bin, a box, and so on. It is used to track the inventory grouped in the same container.

Once we've set this up, we can move on to the reservation hierarchies.

Reservation hierarchies

This is a mandatory setup for warehouse management, and it controls which priority an item is reserved with. If we go to **Warehouse Management** > **Setup** > **Inventories** > **Reservation hierarchies**, we'll find this form:

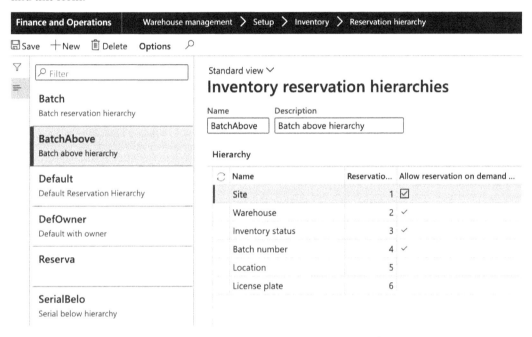

Figure 7.2 – The Inventory reservation hierarchies form

As shown in *Figure 7.2*, each reservation hierarchy we create sets a priority for inventory and tracking dimensions. Here, we can see that the site and warehouse are top priority, and then we reserve on inventory status; if it's available, we can reserve inventory, and then there is the batch number. This means that we can select a batch number on a sales order, regardless of the location that is stored, because it is a higher priority on our reservation hierarchy.

If we look up the **Allow reservation on-demand order** field, we can select a level of inventory reservation that we can reserve, regardless of the higher levels. So, for example, if we reserve a batch on our sales order, the upper levels will be flexible, automatically selecting the site and warehouse in which that batch is stored. But this reservation will override the location directives because a batch is reserved for this, and this batch cannot be changed by the user or the system when the picking work is being processed.

Lastly, when defining the reservation hierarchies, we must ensure that all inventory and tracking dimensions that are used by our item are listed and prioritized. If one or more dimensions are not on the list, we won't be able to use them for an item.

Unit sequence groups

When working with warehouse management items, we must define a sequence of units to work on every operation. For example, unit sequence groups manage the unit of measure that's used in a purchase order receipt or the units used in picking work or a cycle count. We can set it up by going to **Warehouse Management** > **Setup** > **Warehouse** > **Unit sequence groups**. The following screenshot shows an example of a unit sequence group:

Figure 7.3 – The Unit sequence groups form

Figure 7.3 shows a unit sequence group that converts the item into units, boxes, and pallets. In the line details, we can specify which unit is defaulted for cycle counting (each, in this example), for purchase and transfer (pallet), and production (each). This works as a defaulted unit, but if we need to change it to another unit in the execution of any of these processes, for example, we can do so manually.

There is also another critical field: **License plate grouping**. If it is activated and we receive a pallet, it will generate one license plate for the whole pallet; if not, it will create one license plate for every unit in the pallet. So, for example, if we receive a pallet of 10 boxes but **License plate grouping** is not activated, it will create 10 license plates, one for each box.

We can specify a default container for each unit in the **Default container type** field if we use containerization.

Inventory status

We talked about inventory status when we reviewed inventory dimensions. But to set up this dimension, we must go to **Warehouse management** > **Setup** > **Inventory** > **Inventory Statuses**.

Here, we can set up if an inventory is blocked or not activating the **Inventory blocking** field. We can create the inventory statuses we need and define which ones will block the inventory and which will not.

Inventory groups

As we reviewed in *Chapter 2*, item groups define the ledger accounts that an item will impact in every inventory transaction that's registered. But we can also define filters in this form. Filters help us categorize items and limit the vendors and customers to them. It also allows us to associate items with WMS process flows when we set up work templates or location profiles.

In the inventory group form, we can go to the bottom and set up the **Warehouse** tab, as shown here:

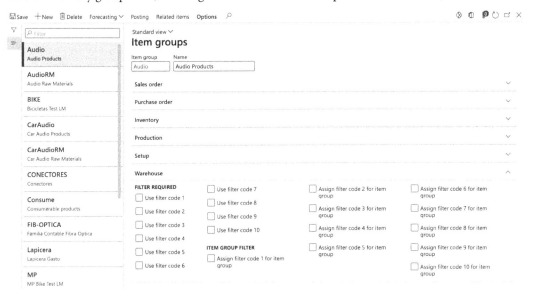

Figure 7.4 – The Warehouse tab on the Item groups form

We can use up to 10 different filter codes. If we activate the **Use filter code** option, we can activate the creation and assignment of these filter codes. The **Assign filter code** option will automatically assign a filter code to an item in the creation process.

Setting up items for warehouse management

Now that we've created all the needed configurations, we can design and set up an item to use warehouse management. Then, we can go to the **Released products** form to fulfill this.

The minimum configuration that's required to create an item that uses warehouse management is as follows:

- **Item group**: To set up their accounts and filter codes.
- **Item model group**: To set up their cost method and inventory behavior.
- **Storage dimension**: To control which inventory dimension we'll use. We'll need to activate the **Use warehouse management** option for warehouse management.
- **Tracking dimension**: To set up if we will track by batch, serial number, or none.
- **Reservation hierarchy**: To define in which order we'll reserve our inventory.

- **Unit sequence group**: To default units used for each warehouse process. We'll need to set up unit conversions if we use multiple units here.

- **Filters**: To define its filters and filter groups.

If we go to the **Warehouse** tab on this form, we can modify the item's behavior in the warehouse management processes:

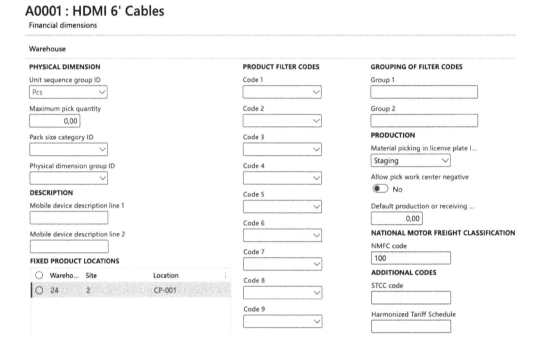

Figure 7.5 – The Warehouse tab on the Released product form

For example, we can set up the pack size category to associate this item with stocking limits. The **PHYSICAL DIMENSION** group lets us control the size and volume of the packing of this item – for example, the volume of a six-pack box.

We can extend the **DESCRIPTION** group of the mobile device with the mobile device description fields. We can also define the maximum quantity for picking and its behavior on production picking. Finally, we can see the item's fixed locations in each warehouse. In other words, we can control all item default behavior in the warehouse management module.

Setting up a warehouse for warehouse management

Now, it's time to set up a warehouse that controls warehouse management processes. In *Chapter 2*, we learned how to configure the inventory breakdown and its concepts, so in this part of this book, we will address them from the warehouse management perspective.

Let's remember Inventory management concepts. The stored inventory is divided into sites, warehouses, and locations. Site is the dimension that is linked to financial dimensions, and it is normally associated with a geographical division or when operational and handling costs change. A warehouse is where a company stores items. It is normally divided into areas and locations and numbered logically to give an understanding of where items are stored.

Configuring a warehouse for warehouse management

Before we cover parameters and setups, let's look at an example of a warehouse that follows WMS processes and flows. This example will help us understand and comprehend the best practices for designing and setting up a warehouse in Dynamics 365.

In the retail industry, a warehouse has many processes. They are very large places with many different zones and locations, and in some cases, with more than one floor.

So, let's think of a company that sells sportswear. We are working as solution consultants in this company and need to start setting up the warehouse for a **distribution center** (**DC**). This warehouse stores three main items: running shoes, football shoes, and sports T-shirts. They are divided into different zones because they have different packing and pallet sizes, so we must consider that.

Also, differently to other industries, we have to consider the processes that a retail warehouse has – for example, inbound and outbound **value-added service** (**VAS**) areas, in which the warehouse adds numbers and names to the football T-shirts or flow-thru that receive, sort, and ship products to stores in the same day.

We've received the following layout design from the warehouse manager:

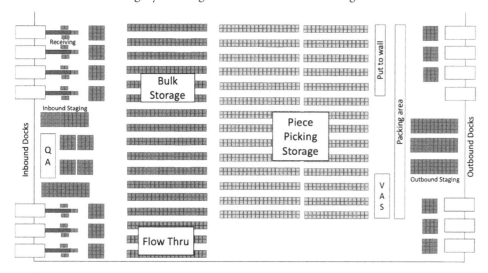

Figure 7.6 – Example of a warehouse layout for a retail company

In *Figure 7.6*, we can see areas designated for diverse flows and processes.

Starting with inbound docks, we have the receiving area and the inbound staging, where operators store pallets for a short time while trucks are unloaded. Here, we have the following:

- A **QA area** where items are revised.

- In green, we have the **Bulk storage** area, where we can store pallets of completed items.

- In orange is the **piece-picking area**, where items are stored in small containers and in small quantities. This allows workers to pick orders without having to look into a sealed pallet or higher-level stock.

- Then, there is the **outbound area**, where we have put-to-wall processes, where items are picked in any order, and the orders are organized by dynamic containers.

- There's also a **VAS** area where some picked T-shirts are customized.

- There's a **packing area** where every order is containerized and labeled properly.

- There's the **outbound staging and docks**, which is where orders are dispatched.

- There is also a **flow-thru area**, painted blue in the layout, where full pallets are stored and immediately shipped to the stores.

First, we need to break down all this information into a series of configuration steps because all the following setups are related:

1. Site and warehouse.

2. Location formats.

3. Location types.

4. Location profiles.

5. Zone and zone groups.

6. Locations.

Site and warehouse

Let's create our warehouse step by step. As we did in the inventory management chapter, we can create our WMS warehouse similarly by going to **Warehouse management** > **Setup** > **Warehouse** > **Warehouses**. This form is the same one we saw in *Chapter 3*. Going to the **Warehouse** tab, we need to activate the **Use Warehouse management processes** option to control the WMS in this warehouse:

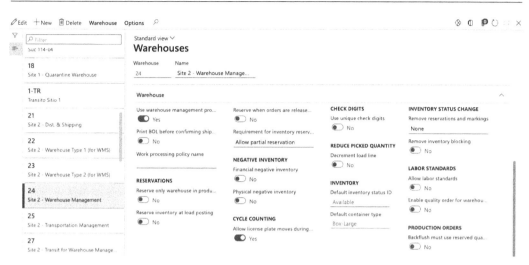

Figure 7.7 – The Warehouse tab on Warehouses form

This tab has several parameters to control how the warehouse works, such as controlling reservations. In the **Requirement for inventory** reservation, we can allow the release of an order with partial reservation or require full reservation of the demand. We can also activate negative financial or physical inventory. We could allow or not allow the movement of license plates in the cycle counting processes. Other important parameters are the labor standards, where we can set up a time for every work processing and then calculate our labor performance based on the work execution.

Once we've set up our warehouse, we have to move to the location format definition.

Location formats

By going to **Warehouse management** > **Setup** > **Warehouse** > **Location formats**, we can create the format for the ID number of each location. Unlike the definition we can make for standard inventory processes, here, Dynamics 365 allows us to define every part of the ID in the way we want. So, if we go that route, we will find the following form:

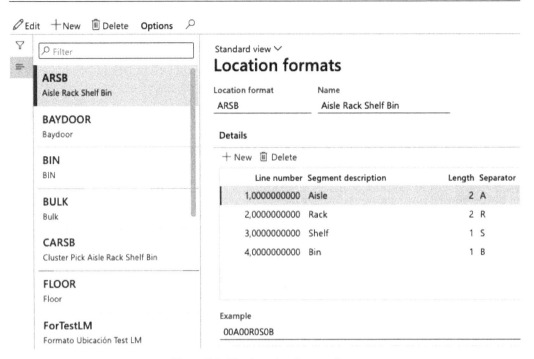

Figure 7.8 – The Location formats form

Here, we define a location format with a name, and then in the **Details** tab, we can set up how it will be codified.

In the example shown in *Figure 7.8*, we define four segments: **Aisle**, **Rack**, **Shelf**, and **Bin**. Each has a letter separator and a specified length, so in the example field, we could see how it will be numbered. As an example, `Aisle 01 Rack 03 Shelf 4` and `Bin 4` will be codified as `01A03R4S4B`.

This will be useful later when we number large quantities of locations with one click.

Location types

Now, we need to go to **Warehouse management** > **Setup** > **Warehouse** > **Location formats**. Here, we will define the location types needed for our warehouse, as shown in the following form:

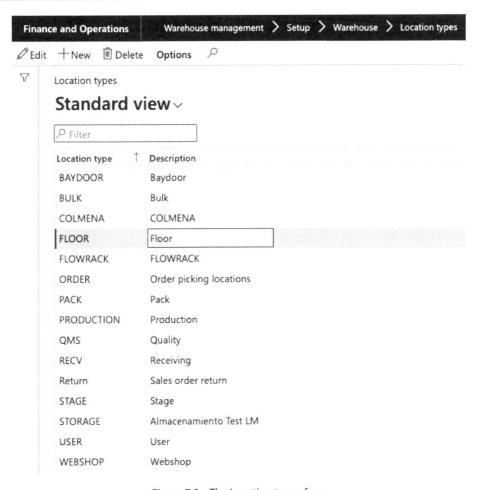

Figure 7.9 – The Location types form

As shown in *Figure 7.9*, this is a simple form where we can define our types of locations according to the business definition.

For example, if we look at *Figure 7.7*, which shows the example of a warehouse layout, we can define a flow-thru, a bulk, a bay door or dock, and staging. These types will help us later when we define the warehouse's different processes. A good example is a warehouse where we have specific types of products, such as frozen, dry, or fresh goods.

Location profiles

With the previous setups we've done, we can specify the location profiles to combine all this information. We can also apply other rules to control how a location will work. To reach this form, we must go to **Warehouse management** > **Setup** > **Warehouse** > **Location Profiles**:

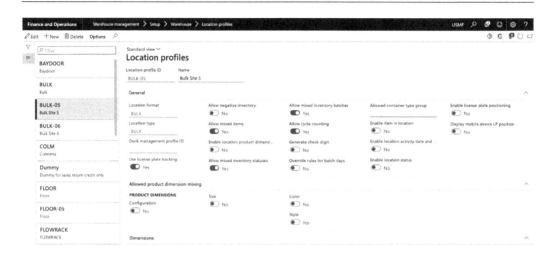

Figure 7.10 – The Location profiles form

In *Figure 7.10*, we can see a location profile example of bulk locations. The first thing to notice is the **Location profile ID** and **Name** fields, which identify our location profile.

Under the **General** tab, we specify the combination of our previously created **Location format** and **Location type**. This will work as a pattern for this profile's massive creation of locations. The **Use license plate tracking** option will allow our locations to track license plates and ask for them when entering these locations.

The **Allow mixed items** option will allow different items in one location. The same happens with the **Allow mixed inventory statuses** and **Allow mixed inventory batches** options. Another crucial parameter is **Allow cycle counting**, which can turn the cycle counting process on and off.

We have a tab here that allows product dimension mixing. For example, if we have T-shirts of different sizes and colors, we can activate product dimensions and allow mixing T-shirt variants.

Finally, in the **Dimension** tab, we can set up the location dimension, such as its height, length, and width, for a unit of measure or volumetrics. This will control how many items we can store. If we have different-sized locations, we need to create another location profile.

Zone and zone groups

We can zone our warehouse by defining different zones. This will group a series of locations and work to allocate products based on this categorization of locations. The zone group is the grouping of zones. For example, we can have the football and running shoe zones and group them into a sports shoe zone group.

We can set this up by going to **Warehouse management** > **setup** > **Warehouse** > **Zones and Zone Groups**:

Zones

Standard view ⌄

Zone ID	↑	Zone name	Zone group ID
BULK		BULK	BULK
BULK06		Bulk 6 for CycleCounting in WHS 61	BULK
FLOOR		FLOOR	FLOOR
PICKZONE1		PICKZONE1	FLOWRACK
PICKZONE2		PICKZONE2	FLOWRACK
PICKZONE3		PICKZONE3	FLOWRACK
Return		Sales return zone	Return
WEBSHOP1		Webshop 1 for Cluster Picking	WEBSHOP

Figure 7.11 – The Zones form

Locations

Previously in this chapter, we saw that locations are where we store our products. It is essential to consider the warehouse layout as the primary input or the physical layout for creating them in Dynamics 365. With this and all the previous configurations – location formats, types, profiles, zones, and zone groups – we can start creating our locations.

We need to go to **Warehouse Management** > **Setup** > **Warehouse** > **Locations**, where we will see the following form:

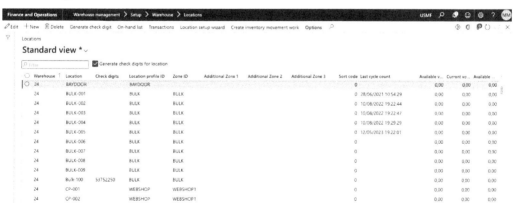

Figure 7.12 – The Locations form

Here, we can see and create locations for our warehouses. For example, in *Figure 7.12*, we can see locations for warehouse 24; every location has a name or ID, **Location profile ID**, and **Zone ID**. This is related to all the setups we've seen so far. We can manually click the **New** button to create new locations and start creating them individually, or we can use the location setup wizard. This wizard will create locations from given parameters, such as **Warehouse**, **Location profile ID**, and **Zone ID**, as shown here:

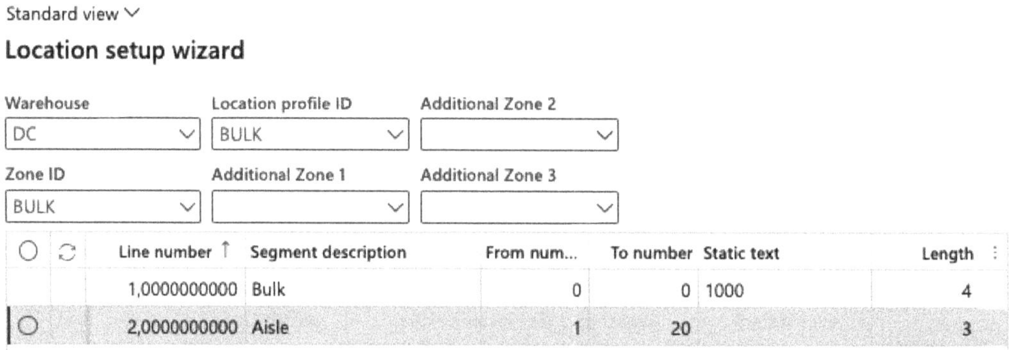

Standard view ∨

Location setup wizard

Warehouse		Location profile ID		Additional Zone 2	
DC	∨	BULK	∨		∨

Zone ID		Additional Zone 1		Additional Zone 3	
BULK	∨		∨		∨

	Line number ↑	Segment description	From num...	To number	Static text	Length	
	1,0000000000	Bulk	0	0	1000	4	
○	2,0000000000	Aisle	1	20		3	

Figure 7.13 – Location setup wizard

Once we've input a location profile, the segments will be displayed in the table. We must complete the from and to numbers of each segment to create these locations, but we can input a piece of static text that complies with the segment's length and fix it. In *Figure 7.13*, we've completed the formats with static text for the bulk segment and 20 different aisles for the second segment. When we hit **Create**, it will create locations 1000-01 to 1000-20 with the parameters we added in the header.

Another piece of information on the locations form is **Check digits**. This field creates a randomly generated digit that works as a barcode for the location. This means that when a user tries to input the location name manually, it will cause an error and will need to be scanned. This is useful to force workers who must walk and scan that location and mitigate location-switching problems.

If it is mandatory to consider storage capacities, we could set up location stocking limits. We can go to **Warehouse management** > **Setup** > **Warehouse** > **Location stocking limits** to reach the following form:

Figure 7.14 – The Location stocking limits form

Here, we can limit the number of units that are allowed per location or location profile (not both) in a warehouse. For example, in *Figure 7.14*, we've limited the number of pallets (denoted as PL here) in the floor location profile to 2. This is also useful for limiting the number of a certain item or pack size. This form allows you to limit stocks for product variants and container types. We could set up the capacity constraints at the location profile settings if we need volumetric restrictions.

Another way to control how items are stored in locations is by going to the **Fixed locations** form, which you can find by going to **Warehouse management** > **Setup** > **Warehouse** > **Fixed locations**:

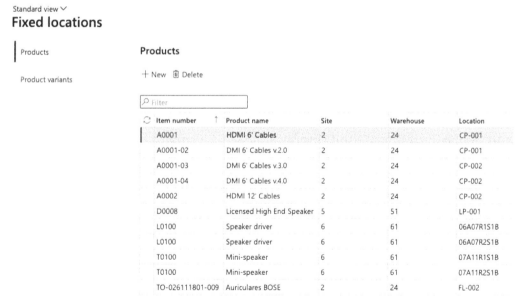

Figure 7.15 – The Fixed locations form

Here, we can assign an item to a location and store it if we've set up a fixed location for an item; we are defining that this location will be used for that item only. Defining items for picking locations is useful when we have high item demand.

With these three configurations, we can achieve an optimal warehousing process. For demand or mix/max replenishment, we can define fixed locations with stocking limits to control how much a replenishment process can transfer. We can control volumetrics (if we have different location sizes) for bulk locations or flow-thru processes, allowing Dynamics 365 to specify pallets with their correct location.

Now that we have finished our warehouse setup, we will switch gears and explain four basic concepts about the warehouse management module. These concepts will be the base for everything we will discuss from here on out.

Wave templates

Waves for warehouse management are a group of outbound demands to be released to a warehouse so that the picking process can start. When we create, for example, a sales order, these orders cannot be picked until we release them to the warehouse. This will create or use a wave, and therefore, a wave template, that will transform that demand into picking works that define specific criteria such as grouping certain types of orders.

There are three types of wave templates: **shipping**, **production order**, and **Kanban**.

We can create any number of wave templates, and Dynamics 365 will check them sequentially. If we set up a wave template on a higher sequence for shipping on warehouse 24 with only urgent orders and another for non-urgent orders, it will process the urgent orders first and then go on to other orders.

We will review these wave templates later when we cover outbound processes.

Work templates

Work is every step-by-step process that a warehouse contains. For example, to put away a pallet from a receiving dock, we need a work with at least two actions – one for picking the pallet from the receiving dock and another to put that pallet on the bulk location assigned.

To define these actions, we need to have work templates. We can find them by going to **Warehouse management** > **Setup** > **Work** > **Work templates**. Here, we can define which order type we're going to set up, the sequence, and the name and description, as shown in the following screenshot:

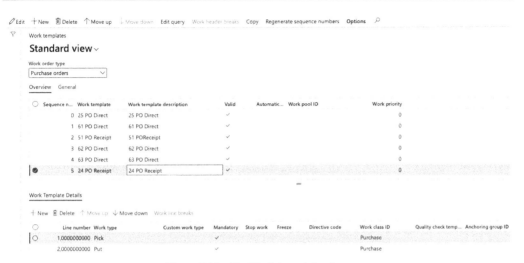

Figure 7.16 – The Work templates form

When setting up work templates, the first important step to take is to select their type. The work template's type refers to the type of movement or order we are configuring. There are the following types:

- Sales orders

- Purchase orders

- Raw material picking

- Finished good put away

- Co-product/by-product put away

- Transfer issue and receipt

- Inventory movement

- Cycle counting

- Replenishments

- Return orders

- Kanban movements

- Quality orders

There is an **Edit query** button at the top of the form that allows us to filter orders; for example, we can filter by warehouse or by order urgency.

In the work template details, we define every step of the work to a minimum of two lines; a pick and a put work type line are mandatory for the work to be valid.

They are tightly related to location directives so that we can set up a directive code for the location directives form.

It is crucial to notice that work templates have a sequence field that orders how templates are analyzed when works are created. Work templates with a lower sequence number are analyzed first. If they don't fit under the parameters set (query, warehouse, and so on), the following template is analyzed until it reaches the last one. If no work template complies with the order, an error message is displayed, and no work is created.

For example, looking at *Figure 7.16*, if a purchase order of warehouse 61 is received, the put-away work creation will review the first line with the 0 sequence number. As this line is for warehouse 25, it will pass to the next work template. The second line (sequence number = 1) is for warehouse 61, so a work will be created with the parameters of this second line.

Location directives

This form controls how the locations are automatically assigned to every work step. For example, here, we define that a sales order picking goes first to look up the fixed item locations in the picking locations of our warehouse, and then if it cannot find any, go to the bulk locations.

We can find this form by going to **Warehouse management** > **Setup** > **Location directives**:

Figure 7.17 – The Location directives form

As seen in *Figure 7.17*, the **Location directives** form has the same division of work order types. This form is divided into three parts:

- **Location directives**, where we set up the location directives parameters, such as work type, site, warehouse, and disposition code (the same as we set up in the work template form)

- **Lines**, where we set up the lines sequenced to divide works by quantity or if it has a unit of measure assigned (for example picking full pallets)

- **Location Directive Actions**, which control how Dynamics 365 assigns our locations – for example, first look at fixed locations and then into every other location

It is crucial to notice that, same as in the work templates, location directives have a sequence field that orders how directives are analyzed when works are created. Location directives with a lower sequence number are analyzed first. If they don't fit under the parameters set (query, warehouse, and so on), the following directive is analyzed until it reaches the last one. If no location directive complies with the order, work will be created but with blank locations.

Device menu and menu items

These two setups control the options and menus that the warehouse management app will have. Device menu configuration lets us define a menu to group out actions that the menu items will let us perform. For example, we could have an inbound device menu where we group all inbound menu items, such as purchase order receiving and put-away.

It's important to give a good definition of menus to ease the access of every worker to the tasks they need to do. Let's jump to the next section, where we will design the warehouse management app menus.

Warehouse management app and device setup

Dynamics 365 has an application to control the warehouse management process that we could download. It's called Supply Chain Management – Warehousing, and it can be downloaded on Google Play Store, Windows Store, and App Store. It is a standalone component, so we could easily download it on the device that's used for warehouse tasks.

The requirements are Android 4.4 or later, Windows 10 (UWP) October 2018 update 1809 or later, or iOS 13.0 or later, and once downloaded and installed, it is mandatory to configure it so that it can connect to an environment. If we set it up for a sandbox environment, we need to change its settings so that it points to a production environment later in the implementation.

Installing the warehousing app and setting it up for an environment

To do this, we need to follow these steps:

1. Create a web service application in **Azure Active Directory** (**AAD**).
2. Create a user account in Dynamics 365 Supply Chain Management.
3. Set up the application.

Creating a web service application in AAD

The application works with a web service on the Microsoft AAD tenant, so we must register it:

1. First, go to `https://portal.azure.com` and log in with your credentials. It is mandatory to have access to the Azure portal to create the application.

2. Once there, go to the left pane under **Azure Active Directory**. It is important to make sure that the AAD instance is the same one that's used for Supply Chain Management.

3. Then, go to **App registrations** and create a new application under **New application registration**. This will pop out a wizard that will guide us through the process.

4. Now, it will ask us for a name. Then, choose **Web application/Web API**. In the **Sign-on URL** field, we must write our Supply Chain Management URL, which ends with Oauth – for example, `https://example.dynamics.operations.com/Oauth`.

5. To finalize this, click **Create**. This will create our application and make it appear in the app registration list. Now, we need to select it and write down the application ID. We will need it later on in the app configuration.

6. Go to **Keys**, under the **Settings** pane, and create a key with a description and a duration. Click Save and write down this key. This is the client secret; we'll need this later in the app configuration step.

Create a user account in Dynamics 365 Supply Chain Management

We need to create and configure a user on the system to use this application. This will allow the application to create movements in Dynamics 365. We need to go to **System Administration** > **Common** > **Users** to do this:

1. First, create a new user; give it a name and a functional email. This email needs to be created in AAD. You could use an administrator user, but I strongly recommend creating a non-named user dedicated to the warehouse management app to comply with security best practices.

2. The only role that we have to assign to this user is the **Warehouse mobile device** user role.

3. Afterward, go to **System Administration** > **Setup** > **Azure Active Directory applications** to register the app. Click on **New** and input the previously created application ID under the **Client ID** field. **User ID** will be our recently created user. We can write a descriptive name as well.

With this configuration done, let's move on to the last step.

Setting up the application

The final step is to open the warehousing app on the device to connect it to our environment.

Once opened, hit **Connect** and then **Setup connection**. Here, we have multiple options:

Figure 7.18 – The Edit connection screen

Here, we need to set up various fields:

- **Authentication method**: Select the **Client secret** option.

- **Connection name**: Give the connection a descriptive name.

- **Azure AD client ID**: This is the Application ID we noted when we created the web service.

- **Active Directory client secret**: This is the client secret we noted when we created the web service.

- **Azure AD resource**: This is the root URL of our environment, but without the final slash – for example, `https://example.dynamics.operations.com`

- **Azure AD tenant**: This is the tenant that's used with the Supply Chain Management server – for example, `https://login.windows.net/example.onmicrosoft.com`. Again, apply this without the final slash.

- **Company**: This is the legal entity we need to connect – for example, "USMF."

Once you've filled these fields in, click **Save**. Now, we can connect to our environment.

Creating a menu and menu items

Before working with the warehouse management app, we need to configure two things:

- **Work classes**: These are used to categorize different types of work that the mobile device can process. We can set them up by going to **Warehouse management** > **Setup** > **Work** > **Work classes**:

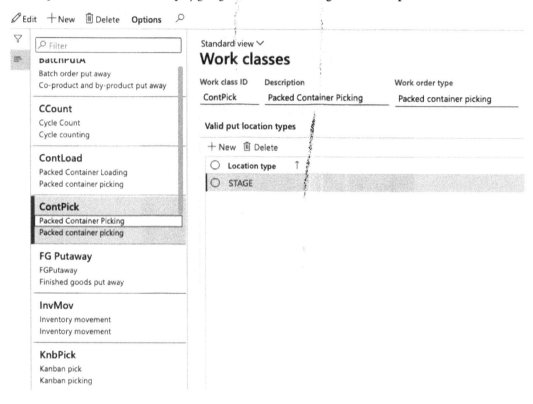

Figure 7.19 – The Work classes form

- **Device users**: These define the workers that are allowed to access the mobile device and their security access. We can set them up by going to **Warehouse management** > **Setup** > **Worker**:

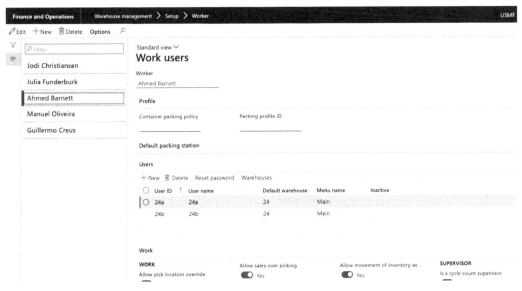

Figure 7.20 – The Work users form

Here, we associate a worker, and we can create as many users as the worker can access. We can associate all warehouses the user can access with the **Warehouse** button. We can control permissions to their actions in the **Work** tab, such as allowing pick or put locations override.

When we create a user in the **Users** tab, we can associate a default warehouse for its connection and a menu name that controls which menu that worker will have in its warehouse app.

These setups allow us to connect to the warehouse app successfully. Now, we can move on to creating device menus.

Device menus

The device menu contains a defined menu structure that allows users to complete their work successfully. We must design a menu while thinking about the user experience and make it as simple and accessible as possible. If a menu is too hard to comprehend, it may lead to issues and frustrated users.

We can define our device menus by going to **Warehouse management** > **Setup** > **Mobile device** > **Mobile device menus**, where we will find the following form:

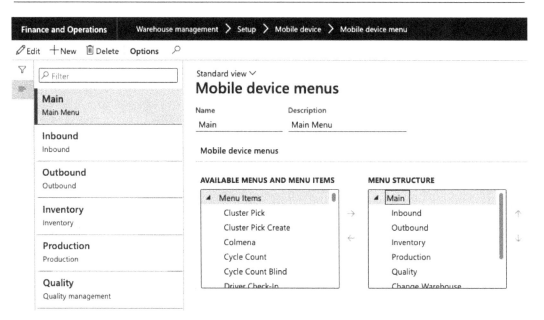

Figure 7.21 – The Mobile device menus form

Here, we can create every menu with the menu items that we created previously. For example, if we design a screen menu that starts in the inbound menu and inside the inbound option, we need to add the purchase receive and purchase put away, which is mandatory to create the following:

- Create purchase receive and put-away menu items

- Create an inbound mobile device menu

- Add the purchase receive and put-away menu items to the inbound device menu

- Create a main mobile device menu

- Add the inbound menu to the main menu

We will end up with a menu that looks like this:

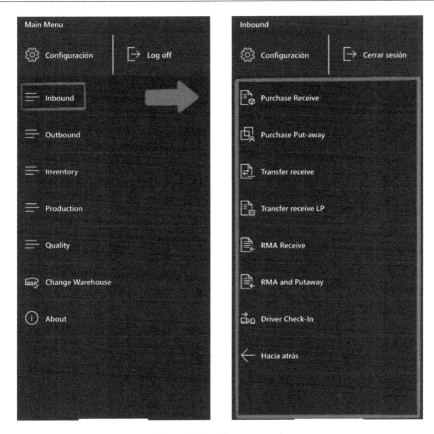

Figure 7.22 – Menu example

Once these menus have been created, we can create the menu items.

Menus items

Creating a menu item will vary, depending on the action we want to perform. We can categorize a menu item into three types:

- **Indirect**: These actions are unrelated to works – for example, change warehouse, location inquiry, and reprint label.

- **Existing work**: These actions are for completing works created by processes in Dynamics 365 – for example, sales picking, transfer order picking, and cycle count.

- **Non-existing work**: These actions create works, and be completed later on for another user – for example, purchase receiving

Let's give an example of the purchase-receiving process.

We need to perform three actions:

- The driver check-in and check-out to register the time when the driver arrives
- The purchase receiving to unload the truck to a receiving location
- The purchase put-away to move the items from the receiving location to the final location

Let's go to **Warehouse management** > **Setup** > **Mobile device** > **Mobile device menu items**. Once we're there, we can start creating our first menu item, **Driver Check-In**, as shown in the following screenshot:

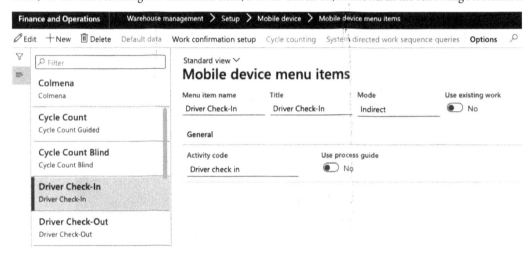

Figure 7.23 – Driver Check-In menu item example

To create it, we must click **New**, after which we'll be asked to provide a name and a title. The title is what will be shown on the mobile device. After that, we need to select the mode. In this case, we will select **Indirect** because it is a non-work-related action. Under the **General** tab, we have the activity code, which will change depending on the mode we selected.

The following is a list of all the indirect activities:

Activity	Description
None	This value does nothing. It is just a default value.
About	Gives information about the system, such as the app version, user, legal entity, and so on.
Change warehouse	Lets the worker change the warehouse only if it's allowed to.
Location inquiry	Gives information about items and quantities for a given location.
License plate inquiry	Gives information about items and quantities for a given LP.

Start production order	It performs the start of a production order from the mobile device.
Production scrap	For entering the scrap percentage of a production order.
Production last pallet	For entering the final pallet of items produced for a given order. You can also change the order status so that it reports as finished.
Item inquiry	Gives information about a scanned item, such as all locations and quantities.
Reprint label	To print an LP label again.
License plate build	Creates an LP that groups other LPs. In some cases, this helps move various LPs at the same time. But to pick items from this LP, we must break it first.
License plate break	Breaks up a build of LPs to pick items from there.
Driver check-in	To register a driver's arrival information and tie it with an appointment created by the transportation module.
Driver check out	To register a driver's departure information and tie it with an appointment created by the transportation module.
Flush number sequence cache	To delete the number sequence stored in the app cache.
Change batch disposition	Changes the disposition code specified for a batch.
Display open work list	Shows a list of work to select, but only of the specified work classes. To make this option functional, you must create a menu item with a user-directed existing work of the work classes needed first.
Consolidate license plate	Consolidates items from the same location under one license plate.
Register material consumption	Registers material consumption with times and quantity registration. This works for batch consumption scenarios where the item is not consumed at the same time in the production order (no pre- or back-flushing).
Remove container from group	Used for removing items or containers from a group of containers.
Empty Kanban	Changes the status of a Kanban to empty.
Cancel work	Used to cancel a work.
Outbound sorting	Uses the outbound sorting functionality to handle small containers and organize them into a pallet. When selected, you will be asked for an outbound sorting template.
Reprint single-wave label	Used to reprint a label for a given wave.
Reprint multiple wave labels	Used to reprint labels for multiple waves.

Assign to put-away cluster	Assigns one or more LPs to a put-away cluster.
Create transfer order form license plates	Scans various license plates and creates a transfer order to another warehouse.

Table 7.1 – Indirect activities

In our example, we will select **Driver check-in** from the list and then **Save**.

Now, we must create a purchase-receive menu item, as shown in the following screenshot:

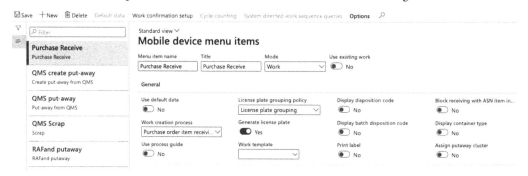

Figure 7.24 – Purchase-receive menu item example

Once we input the name and title, we must select the work mode and leave the **Use existing work** option set to **No** – when we receive a purchase order, we won't have a created work. Dynamics 365 will create a work to reflect the put-away once the receiving process is completed.

Differently from the indirect mode, we will have a work creation process field with a list of actions. Let's break them down.

In the first group, we have the inventory movement processes:

Work creation process	Description
None	This value does nothing. It is just a default value.
Movement	Moves items between locations that a worker specifies.
Quarantine	Puts items into quarantine to make them unavailable for other processes.
Movement by template	Same as a movement but uses a template to automatically direct the movement destination.
Warehouse transfer	Transfers items between warehouses.
Adjustment in	Increases an item's quantity. You must specify all inventory dimensions.

| Adjustment out | Decreases an item's quantity. You must specify all inventory dimensions. |
| Spot cycle count | Used to count a specific location. |

Table 7.2 – Inventory movement processes

Then, we can group the production processes:

Work creation process	Description
Report as finished	Reports production for finished goods and creates put-away work for another worker
Report as finished and put away	Reports production for finished goods and moves them to a put-away location
Kanban	Receives items for a Kanban and creates put-away work for another worker
Kanban put away	Receives items for a Kanban and moves them to a put-away location

Table 7.3 – Production processes

Finally, we have all the inbound receiving processes:

Work creation process	Description
Purchase order line receiving	Receives and stages items from a purchase order line and creates put-away work for another worker
Purchase order line receiving and put away	Receives items from a purchase order line and moves them to the put-away location
Purchase order item receiving	Receives and stages items from a purchase order by item number and creates a put-away work for another worker
Purchase order item receiving and put away	Receives items from a purchase order by item number and moves them to a put-away location
License plate receiving	Receives an inbound load using the LP number
Return order receiving	Receives and stages items from a return order by RMA number and creates a put-away work for another worker
Return order receiving and put away	Receives items from a return order by RMA number and moves them to a put-away location
Transfer order item receiving	Receives and stages items from a transfer order by item number and creates a put-away work for another worker

Transfer order item receiving and put away	Receives items from a transfer order by item number and moves them to a put-away location
Transfer order line receiving	Receives and stages items from a transfer order by line number and creates a put-away work for another worker
Transfer order line receiving and put away	Receives items from a transfer order by line number and moves them to a put-away location

Table 7.4 – Receiving processes

As you can see, many movements have different options, depending on the definition of the process. If we look at the warehouse layout in *Figure 7.6*, we can see an inbound staging location. In this case, we have an inbound process that first receives and stages the inbound orders, and then another worker that will execute the put-away.

So, we can select the **Purchase order item receiving** option, which will allow our worker to indicate the purchase order number and the item received. But if the process is different, we can receive by load or purchase order line, for example.

The form will change once we select the **Purchase order item receiving** option and will show multiple fields. These are the most important fields that can appear:

- **License plate grouping policy**, which defines how license plates are created.

  - **None** will create only one LP per reception
  - **License plate grouping** will group according to item unit sequence group, meaning that it will create a license plate grouping units of measure that has activated the license plate grouping in the unit sequence group
  - **User-defined** will group license plates according to the quantities and units of measure selected upon reception

- **Generate license plate**, if activated, will automatically create an LP number. If not, we must specify one. This is useful when we have pre-printed pallet barcode labels.

- **Work template**, where we can associate our menu with a specific work template.

- **Display disposition code and batch disposition code**. This will show the option to input a disposition or batch disposition code for the receiving process, which will allow you to redirect the destination of an item or a batch, for example, if it is broken to a quality inspection.

  You will notice that when you select different options, other fields appear. It is crucial to check them out before you finish setting everything up as they could modify how the warehousing app works from this menu.

Finally, we must create a menu item to process the put-away work for these purchase orders. Differently from the purchase receive menu item, a work exists to process the put-away work. To capture it, we must select the **Work** field and activate the **Use existing work** option, as shown in the following screenshot:

Figure 7.25 – Purchase put-away menu item example

When we activate the **Use existing work** option, this option will control the access to created works of the selected work classes under the **Work classes** tab. It will also bring different fields to the form.

The **Directed by** field controls how the works are processed. It has several options:

- **System directed**: Works under this menu item are automatically assigned. When we select this option, it will allow us to open the **System-directed work sequence queries** menu, where we can filter and re-sequence all works, giving them a different order.

- **User-directed**: This allows the worker to select the work by scanning the LP or work ID.

- **User grouping**: This allows the worker to select and group various works or LPs to move various items simultaneously.

- **System grouping**: The system automatically groups work based on the following parameters:

  - **System grouping field**: Select the field to scan to group works

  - **System grouping label**: Input a description that will be shown on the app to inform the worker which field to scan to group the work

- **Validated user directed**: Allows the worker to select the work based on an entity – for example, a load or shipment. Once this option has been selected, we must set up the following fields:

  - **Validated user-directed field**: Select a field to scan to group the work

  - **Validated user-directed label**: Write a description to inform the worker which field to scan

- **Cluster picking**: Allows the worker to work into clusters. Workers will pick items from a single location for multiple works simultaneously.

- **Cycle count grouping**: Allows the worker to group cycle counting work by selecting a zone, work pool, or location.

Besides this field, we can activate **Allow splitting of work** to allow workers to split picked quantities in more than one LP. This is useful when an LP is full, and the worker must use a new LP to complete the work. With this option, the worker can click the full button in the app, indicating that the LP is full. Then, the app will stop receiving picking work and indicate the put location for the full LP. The remaining work will be left open in the original work.

The **anchoring** option allows workers to anchor the remaining put-away work to a staging location. This is useful when a worker needs to put away work on a dock but can't because previous work is not completed. The worker could specify another dock as the staging location, and all remaining work will be directed there.

We need to specify **Cluster Profile ID** if we use cluster picking. In the profile, we define the cluster settings, such as how many locations will use the names and positions of the location, if they will create locations automatically, and so on.

There are several display options to show or not information in the menus. **Display inventory status** will show the inventory status dimension of the items. **Display disposition code** will allow you to input a disposition code on, for example, the receiving process of a return order. A worker can select and analyze the status of the goods and assign a proper disposition code for the items. **Display summary of pick screen** will show a summary of the selected work until the work is processed.

Generate license plate will create a new license plate number based on the number sequence. This option is useful when we're printing new labels for storing goods and we need to inform LP numbers.

The **override target license plate** option allows workers to modify the destination license plate for another. It is useful when we're reusing pallets, for example.

As we can see, many options and setups exist to control how workers must handle work and orders. If we have different ways to handle the same type of work, we can create different menu items and menus and assign them to the workers to separate not only permissions but also procedures.

We can also require workers to confirm information when they pick items. From the menu, we can choose **Work confirmation setup** to require a confirmation of location, items, variants, or quantity. This will be useful for workers to control and confirm what they are inputting into the works. In this form, first, we need to select the work type and then activate which information workers need to confirm; for example, if we select put work and tick location, workers must confirm locations on put works of this menu item.

App labels and field priority

Sometimes, some processes are deeply fixed in the company culture and are difficult to change in an implementation project. For example, the license plate concept is not descriptive for warehouse operators and is usually called **pallet** or **bin**. The warehouse management app lets us change those labels, making it easier for the workers to adapt to another platform.

We can go to **Warehouse management** > **Setup** > **Mobile device** > **Warehouse app field names** to reach this form:

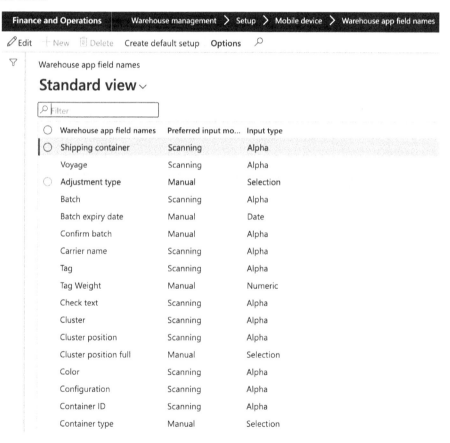

Figure 7.26 – The Warehouse app field names form

For new implementations, this list will be empty. We can generate data by clicking on the **Create default data** button. This will bring in the metadata of the warehouse app, where we can edit it.

We can modify the **Warehouse app field names** in the first column to change the standard label for another. Also, we can change the preferred input mode to **Scanning** or **Manual**, depending on each case. The **Input type** column specifies the type of input that should be used for the specific field. For example, for the license plate, we can select the numeric option if it will be a number sequence with only numeric characters. In the warehouse management app, a numeric keyboard will be displayed when entering that field.

If we navigate to **Warehouse management** > **Setup** > **Mobile device** > **Warehouse app field priority**, we can group the fields and priorities shown in the mobile app.

For example, let's say we define the following:

- Priority 10:

  - Item

  - Quantity

  - Unit of measure

- Priority 20:

  - Sort Position ID

  - Cluster ID

- Priority 30:

  - Product name

  - Item description

When a worker is performing work, and the warehouse app wants to show the information about the item, quantity, item description, unit of measure, and product name, it will be shown in the following order, based on its priority:

- **First row**: Item, quantity, unit of measure
- **Second row**: Product name, item description

All other information, such as location, won't be shown on the screen. We can see it if we click on the details page of the work.

Summary

In this chapter, we reviewed the foundations of the warehouse management processes that we can implement with Dynamics Supply Chain Management, starting with how we can design and configure a warehouse while breaking down zones and aisles into locations.

Then, we reviewed how to connect and configure the warehouse management app and design its menus and menu items for a smooth user experience.

After that, we looked at the three foundation blocks of the warehouse management module – work templates, wave templates, and location directives – and how to combine them to set up almost every use case scenario.

This chapter covered all the possible setups that can be done in warehouse management to follow the defining inbound and outbound processes that will be discussed in the next chapter.

Questions

Answer the following questions to test your knowledge of this chapter:

1. You are implementing the warehouse management module and you need to design the appropriate menus and menu items to have inbound workers and outbound workers with separate menus. Which of the following approaches is correct?

    A. Create separate inbound and outbound menus and add them to the main menu. Create the workers associated with the main menu.

    B. Create one main menu with all menu items included. Create the workers associated with the main menu. Filter the menu items via security administration.

    C. Create separate inbound and outbound menus. Create workers associated with the inbound menu and workers associated with the outbound menu.

2. You are implementing the warehouse management module and must create the warehouse locations. The warehouse manager must ensure that the locations' barcodes differ from the location ID. How can you address that requirement?

    A. By filling in the barcode number in the location profile.

    B. By generating check digits for location in the locations form.

    C. By creating separate zones for locations.

3. You are implementing a warehouse management module for a wine company. During the discovery process, you detect workers call "Casks" to the "License plates." You need to include that term in the mobile app to ease user adoption. How can you address that?

    A. Create new labels via development to modify the labels in the warehouse management app.

    B. Modify the warehouse app field names from "License Plate" to "Cask."

    C. Create a new mobile device menu item called "Casek Picking."

Answers

Here are the answers to this chapter's questions:

1. Option C: We can create a warehouse worker associated with any of the menus created from the worker's menu. This will filter the options that the worker can access.

2. Option B: Check digits allow us to generate a barcode automatically for the location.

3. Option B: Warehouse app field names allow us to modify labels on the mobile app for ease of user adoption.

8

Warehouse Management Implementation – Best Practices and Strategies - Part 2

In the previous chapter, we explored the different configurations and possibilities presented in the Warehouse module. In this chapter, we will concentrate on how to manage inbound and outbound operations in the warehouse.

Here, we will dive into the receive, store, and dispatch process while covering various options and use case scenarios.

To start, let's take a moment to recall the procedures we defined in *Chapter 3* when we delved into inventory management since the **warehouse management system** (**WMS**) is an extension of that module.

Here is what you will learn in this chapter:

- Working with the inbound process and stock allocation
- Executing internal warehouse processes such as cycle counting, replenishment, and transfer orders
- Working with the outbound process while focusing on shipments and wave releases

Inbound operations

In previous chapters, we reviewed that inbound operations refer to all processes where we enter inventory into our warehouse. Let's work with an example. Imagine that we need to create a receive purchase order for a pallet of running shoes. We want to make sure that the purchase order will be processed in the following way:

1. The stock arrives at the warehouse. A warehouse worker receives it in the app by entering the purchase order number and scanning the item's barcode. Then, the pallet is stored in a temporary receiving location.

2. A barcode for the LP is printed and given to the received pallet.

3. Another warehouse worker scans the barcode and executes the put-away work, storing the item in a bulk location if it's a full pallet or in a fixed product location if it's not a full pallet.

The first step is straightforward. As we define the mobile device menu, we can receive a purchase order by entering the inbound menu and then in the purchase receive option. Once there, we must enter the purchase order number, item, and quantity we are receiving.

The item will be stored in the receiving location defined in the warehouse parameters. This can be seen in the following screenshot:

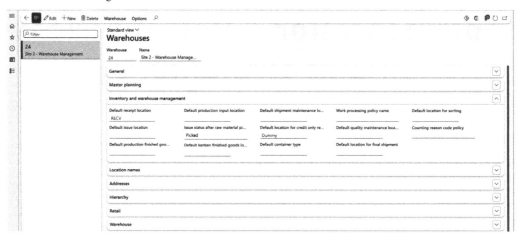

Figure 8.1 – Warehouse 24 default locations

> **Important note**
>
> Remember that if we set up a different menu item (such as purchase line receiving), it will ask for different information, such as purchase order and line or load ID. This process can be different for some warehouses inbound, so we must ensure we understand the flow before setting up the menu items properly.

Finally, another warehouse worker must do the put-away work. Setting up the work templates and location directives is important for this process to work properly.

Let's review the work templates for purchase orders:

Standard view∨

Work order type

| Purchase orders ∨ |

Overview   General

○	⟳	Sequence ...	Work template	Work template description	Valid	Automatic...	Work pool ID	Work priority
		0	25 PO Direct	25 PO Direct	✓	☐		0
		1	61 PO Direct	61 PO Direct	✓	☐		0
		2	51 PO Receipt	51 POReceipt	✓	☐		0
		3	62 PO Direct	62 PO Direct	✓	☐		0
		4	63 PO Direct	63 PO Direct	✓	☐		0
◉		5	24 PO Receipt	24 PO Receipt	☑	☐	∨	0

Work Template Details

+ New   🗑 Delete   ↑ Move up   ↓ Move down   Work line breaks

○	⟳	Line number	Work type	Custom work type	Mandatory	Stop work	Freeze	Directive code	Work class ID	Quality check temp...	Anchoring group ID
		1,0000000000	Pick		☑	☐	☐		Purchase		
○		2,0000000000	Print	∨	☑	☐	☐		Purchase ∨		
		3,0000000000	Put		☑	☐	☐		Purchase		

Figure 8.2 – Work template for purchase orders on warehouse 24

As shown in *Figure 8.2*, work templates are divided into warehouses. This is defined via the **Edit query** button. For example, for **24 PO Receipt**, if we click the **Edit query** button, we will see that it is filtered for warehouse 24.

In the work template lines, we have defined that the worker must do a pick, print the label, and, finally, put away the stock. These are the three steps that the worker must do for the put-away work. Look at the **Location directives** form shown in the following figure:

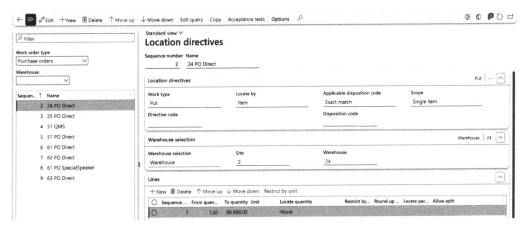

Figure 8.3 – Location directives for purchase order warehouse 24

Here, we can divide our lines into actions. In this case, we're creating a first sequence to detect if the worker receives full pallets by activating the **Restrict by unit** option. Here, we can input the PL unit of measure, and every time the worker receives pallets, it will activate the location directive actions shown in the bottom part of the form, which will be stored in a bulk location, as defined after clicking the **Edit query** button of the **Location directives** tab.

But suppose the worker is not receiving in pallets. In that case, it will move to the following sequence number and activate the location directive actions to store first in a fixed location for the item and, if that location is full, in another location.

It is important to understand how **Work templates** and **Location directives** work together. Work templates are the step-by-step part of the work, while location directives tell the system how we can find locations for every step of the work.

Following the last part of the example, when the second worker goes to the inbound menu, then to the purchase put-away menu item, this will do the pick work for them on the receiving location. Then, it will print a label for the PI, and finally, it will ask to move the pallet to a bulk location.

> **Important note**
> As before, the put-away work could be user-directed, as shown in this example, or system-directed, where the system automatically assigns the worker to do picking work.

To execute this purchase order receipt, the warehouse worker must log into the warehouse management app, and navigate to the **Purchase Receive** menu, as shown in the following screenshot:

Figure 8.4 – Purchase Receive

Once there, the worker must input or scan the purchase order number and item. The system will show the following screen, asking for the quantity:

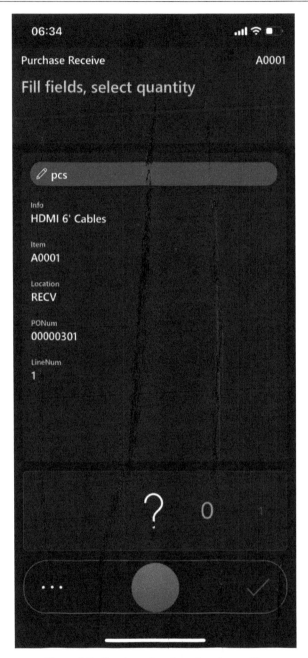

Figure 8.5 – Purchase Receive – input quantity

After inputting the quantity, the system will show a **Work completed** message. This will create the put-away work in Dynamics 365, as follows:

Standard view ⌄

☐ Show closed

Overview   General   Blocking reasons

	Work prior...	Locked by	Work ID	Work status	Site	Warehouse	Work pool ID	Target license plate ID	Work order type	Order number	Description
○					▽						
○	50	Mm	USMF-000119	In process	2	24		000USMF-0000000574	Purchase orders	00000301	

Lines   General

Transactions   User actions   Custom data   Cancel work line   Display dimensions   Quality check results

	Work status	Work type	Location	Item number	Product name	Work quan...	Remaining	Unit	User ID	Stop trans...	Mandatory	Work class...	Configuration
○	Closed	Pick	RECV	A0001	HDMI 6' Cables	50,00	0,00	pcs	Mm		✓	Purchase	
	In process	Put	FL-001	A0001	HDMI 6' Cables	50,00	50,00	pcs	Mm		✓	Purchase	

Figure 8.6 – Purchase order put-away work

This work is meant to move the received items from the inbound dock or receiving location to the final destination – in this case, location FL-001.

To perform this process, the warehouse worker must navigate to the purchase put-away menu item and scan or enter the work ID or license plate. The system will show the following menu:

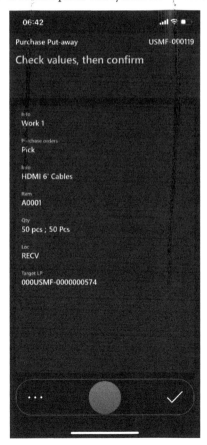

Figure 8.7 – Purchase Put-away

As shown in *Figure 8.7*, the system asks the worker to pick 50 pieces from the receiving location (RECV) of item A0001. The worker picks the pieces, after which Dynamics 365 asks for confirmation by scanning the barcode of the location or the item and asks the worker to move the items to the destination, as shown in the following figure:

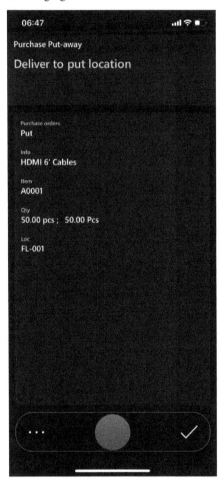

Figure 8.8 – Purchase Put-away – Put step

Once the worker delivers the pieces to the destination and confirms this, the system will show a "work completed" message.

There are other options for this purchase-receiving workflow that we can set up:

- Purchase order put-away clusters
- Purchase order put-away with a quality check
- Purchase order put-away with a quality order

Let's take a closer look.

Purchase order put-away clusters

Clustering allows the worker to group more than one put-away work into a cluster and then do the put-away in different locations. This will speed up the put-away process, but we need to set up a few things for this process.

- **Create Cluster profiles**: This is the configuration of the cluster.

  We can set this up by going to **Warehouse management** > **Setup** > **Mobile device** > **Cluster profiles**:

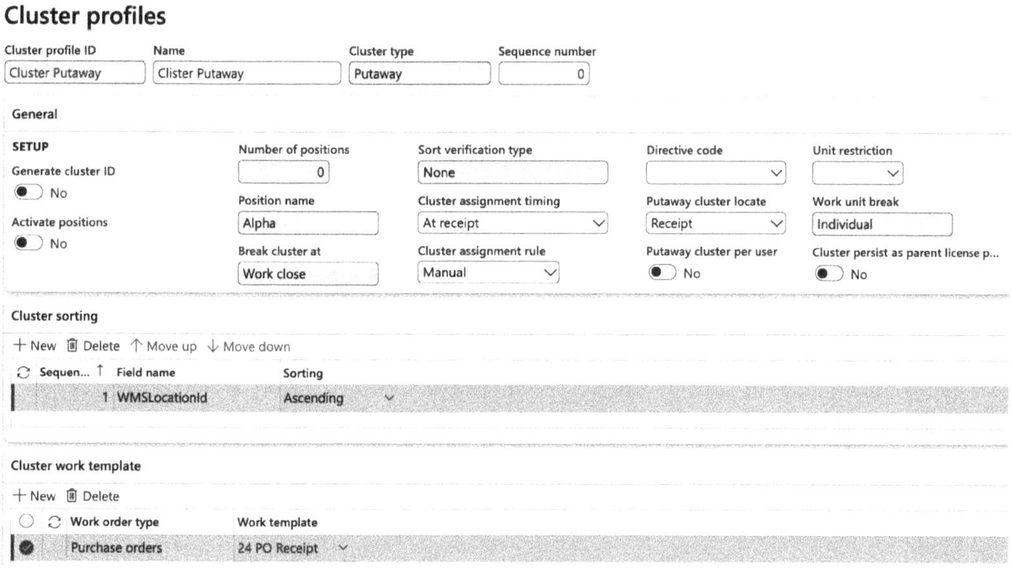

Figure 8.9 – The Cluster profiles form

As shown in *Figure 8.8*, we have options to control how the cluster works; in this case, it will define that we must assign the cluster at receipt. In the **Cluster sorting** option, it will be sorted by location ID. It will work with the 24 PO Receipt work template.

- **Activate option**: Assigns a put-away cluster.

  We must activate the assign put-away cluster option in the purchase receive device menu item.

- **Create put-away cluster menu item**

  We must create a put-away cluster menu item in the **Mobile device menus** item form. To do so, we must select **Work** mode and activate the **Use existing work** option. Finally, in the **Directed by** option, select the **Cluster putaway** option.

  Finally, in the **Work classes** tab, select the work class ID for the purchase order works.

- **Add the new put-away menu item to the inbound device menu**

  The last setup step is to add the previously created put-away menu item to the inbound menu in the **Device menu items** form.

During the receiving process, license plates will be assigned to a cluster location one at a time. Then, we must close the cluster and enter the put-away menu item. The system will direct the worker to the put-away locations for every license plate in that cluster.

Purchase order put-away with quality check

Often, on-purchase receiving is mandatory to do a quick inspection of the items the workers receive without creating a quality order. To do so, we need to do the following:

1. Go to **Warehouse management** > **Setup** > **Warehouse** > **Locations** and create a quality check location. This location will be used to move the items that failed the quality check.

2. Then, in **Warehouse management** > **Setup** > **Work** > **Work classes**, create a work class for the quality check.

3. Going to **Warehouse management** > **Setup** > **Work** > **Quality check template**, create a new template, set the **Prompt user** option to **Acceptance policy**, and create work only as **quality processing policy**. This will ensure the creation of only the work, not the quality order.

4. Now, in **Warehouse management** > **Setup** > **Work** > **Work template**, we need to create a **quality in quality check** work order type template. So, hit **New**, create a pick, and put actions for lines with the work class ID we created previously.

5. We also need to add a new step to the purchase order work template in the **Work template details** tab for quality check works. Make sure you add the template name in the **quality check template name** field.

6. To assign a location, we need to create a location directive for quality under **Quality check work**. Create a new one and assign it to work. In the **Actions** tab, add a line referring to the location you created in the first step.

7. Finally, add the work class ID for the quality check under the **Work classes fast** tab in the **Purchase Put-away** mobile device menu item.

With this setup, once the worker processes the put-away work, the system will prompt a quality check for the items; if the check passes, the app will direct the user to the put-away location. If it doesn't, the put-away work will close, and it will create a new work for taking that item to the quality check location.

Purchase order put-away with quality order

It is common for companies to process quality orders when receiving purchase orders, but as we saw in *Chapter 5*, quality orders occur in the inventory management module. There is a feature to connect quality management with the warehouse management process.

Once enabled, this feature will automatically generate the work as part of the purchase-receiving process and move the inventory required to a quality control location to execute the quality orders. Once the quality order has been validated, the quantities will be moved to a defined location, depending on the quality order's result.

This process will use two work order types:

- **Quality item sampling**: Create work that moves inventory to quality control
- **Quality order**: Create work that moves inventory from quality control to the destination location

To set this up, we need to do the following:

1. Go to **Warehouse management** > **Setup** > **Warehouse** > **Warehouse** and select our warehouse. Then, in the **Warehouse fast** tab, activate the **Enable quality order for warehouse processes** option. This will allow us to control the quality associations in this warehouse.

2. Create a **Quality location** area for the warehouse. When receiving, items will be moved to this location when needed for inspection.

3. We must select the quality association to activate in the **Quality associations** form under the inventory management module. In the **Conditions** tab, under the **Applicable warehouse type** field, select **Quality management for warehouse processes only**. You should only select this option if the reference type is purchase or production. Make sure the quality association is well created, as shown in *Chapter 5*.

4. Create a **work class** value for quality management.

5. Create a **work template** value for the **quality item sampling** order type. Create the pick and put pair in the work details tab and select the work class we created in *Step 4*.

6. Create a location directive for **quality item sampling**. Create it as a put work type, and in the **Location directive actions** tab, click on the **Edit query** button and filter to the location we created in *Step 2*.

7. In the **Purchase Put-away** mobile device menu item, add the work class ID we created in *Step 4*.

With this setup, once the worker receives a purchase order, the system will automatically move the item sample to the quality location and create a quality order.

Receive items at a different warehouse

Sometimes, companies redirect loads or items at a warehouse different from those specified in the original order. Dynamics 365 will prevent this from happening because every worker has to be logged in to the warehouse where the order arrives.

However, let's suppose we need to activate this option. In that case, we can go to the **Warehouse management** > **Setup** > **Warehouse** > **Sites** form, and under the **Warehouse** fast tab, we can activate the option to allow users on mobile devices to receive at another warehouse.

Now that we reviewed the inbound processes and understood the setups needed to create and process works, we can move on to the internal warehouse processes.

Internal warehouse processes

Once the items are received and stored, several activities regarding warehouse organization occur. From transfer orders to cycle counts, we will review the mechanisms to perform those activities and how to set them up in the warehouse management module. This section will review a warehouse's internal operations processes and flows.

Transfer orders

Transfer orders are used to move inventory from one warehouse to another. It consists of a two-part process: shipping and receiving the items. This section will review the shipping process since the *Inbound operations* section describes the receiving process.

As we reviewed in *Chapter 3*, transfer orders are managed in the transfer order form located in the inventory management module. Here we extend this activity by controlling its picking process with the mobile device app.

One thing to notice here is that even though this process works for inventory management and warehouse management, dynamics has no problem moving inventory from the WMS warehouse to a non-WMS warehouse and vice versa.

To set up the transfer order outbound process with warehouse management, we have to set up the following parameters:

- Mobile device menu items for pick and receive transfer orders.
- Work templates to specify how to create the work for pick and receive.
- Location directives to determine which locations will be used in every step of the work templates.
- Wave template to define how the work will be generated when a wave is processed.

For location directives and work templates, we've talked about in the previous section, so now let's work with the wave templates. To determine how the system creates the outbound work and enables the release to warehouse process.

Wave templates

To process outbound work, we need to create a wave template; we can find this option by going to **Warehouse management** > **Setup** > **Waves** > **Wave templates**. Here, we need to create a shipping wave for warehouse 24, as shown in the following screenshot:

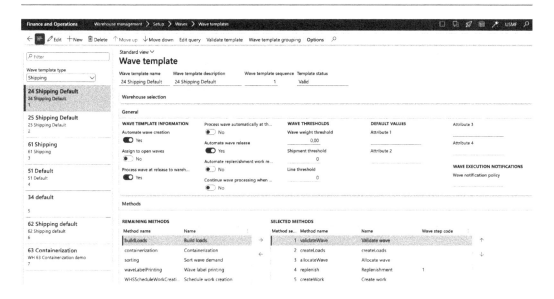

Figure 8.10 – The Wave template form

As shown in *Figure 8.10*, a wave template describes how we process the outbound work. In this case, shipping work for warehouse 24 is going to be created by this wave. When we release to the warehouse for picking, these steps must be completed to create work:

1. **Create wave**: This will create the wave.

2. **Assign to a wave**: Orders released to the warehouse must be assigned to a wave.

3. **Process the wave**: The wave is processed. This will process the selected methods assigned to the wave – for example, validate the wave, create the loads, allocate the wave, and create the work.

4. **Release wave**: Work that's created by the wave will be released to the warehouse so that workers can start picking.

In the wave template information under the **General** tab, we will set up whether or not those steps are automatically created. For example, in *Figure 8.5*, the **wave creation** is set to **Yes**, the **Process wave at release to warehouse** option is set to **Yes**, and **Automate wave release** is also set to **Yes**, which means that when we release to the warehouse, the wave will be created, processed, and released automatically.

This is useful when we're working with urgent orders that need to be processed fast, but normally, a warehouse works with time-slotted waves. For example, every order from 8 A.M. to 1 P.M. will be released and picked up after 1 P.M. In that case, we must automate wave creation and assign it to open waves. But the processing and release must be done manually or by a batch job after 1 P.M.

Like the work templates, we have an **Edit query** button to filter orders or shipments. In the examples given, we can have a wave template for urgent orders on sequence 10 and then the normal orders on sequence 20. It is important to have the most specific templates higher on the sequence and the others down below as this will ensure we validate the most specific work first.

Replenishment

Replenishment is a strategy that brings the stock to picking locations when the stock is decreasing to ensure that we won't run out of inventory when preparing an outbound order.

Dynamics 365 Supply Chain Management controls four replenishment strategies:

- **Wave demand replenishment**: This strategy creates replenishment work when the waves create picking work. When a location does not have the quantity needed, it automatically creates the replenishment and blocks the picking work until the location has the required stock.

- **Min/max replenishment**: This strategy uses minimum and maximum quantity values to replenish the inventory at the picking locations. The min/max replenishment templates control this; when an inventory is lower than the minimum, it will create replenishment work. This is the main strategy to maintain optimal stock levels and can be complemented by wave demand replenishment.

- **Load demand replenishment**: This strategy summarizes all the released loads and creates replenishment work for the required picking locations.

- **Immediate replenishment**: This strategy creates immediate replenishment work when location directive allocation fails.

To set up any of these four strategies, we need to create a template by going to **Warehouse management > Setup > Replenishment > Replenishment templates**:

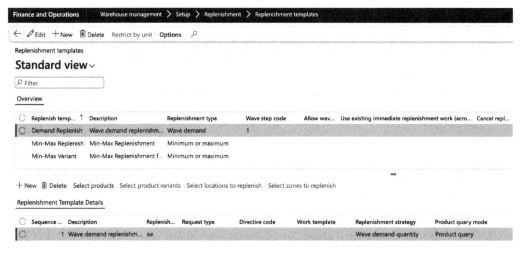

Figure 8.11 – The Replenishment templates form

Figure 8.11 shows an example of a wave demand replenishment with a wave step code of 1. This wave step code has to be assigned in the respective wave template that was assigned to this replenishment.

We must set up the unit of measure and the strategy under **Replenishment Template Details**. Then, under **Select products**, we can filter the items that will be replenished this way.

Warehouse slotting

Slotting is a technique that replenishes inventory before releasing it to the warehouse.

The demand that's needed to replenish is calculated by the demand of the outbound orders. We must create a slotting template by going to **Warehouse management** > **Setup** > **Replenishment** > **Slotting templates**:

Figure 8.12 – The Slotting templates form

Figure 8.12 shows an example of a slotting template for warehouse 24. It will calculate replenishment based on the demand of the ordered sales orders for warehouse 24. For **Demand strategy** and **Demand type**, we can define if it came from sales or transfer orders and if it's from ordered or reserved quantities. In the **Details** tab, we can sequence which items and the minimum and maximum quantities we want to replenish. The **Edit query** button allows us to filter down that information and make all the necessary exceptions to replenish the required items.

Once this template has been set up, we can click the **Generate demand** button to see what quantities are needed. This can be seen next to the **Slotting demand** button. Then, we can click the **Locate demand** and **Run replenishment** buttons to create the picking work for that replenishment.

Cycle counting

Counting processes is a vital part of a warehouse for companies to control regularly if the inventory in the system is accurate and correct and the virtual stock has real quantities.

This process can be done automatically in two ways. First, we can use a cycle count plan, where we run periodic counting for the warehouse workers to do. Second, we can define a threshold that, once reached, will automatically create the counting work.

The full options and processes of cycle counting can be seen in the following diagram:

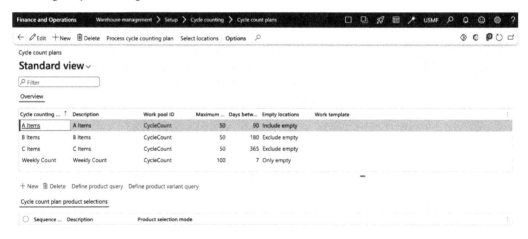

Figure 8.13 – Diagram of cycle counting options

We have the creation, process, and resolution steps of the counting work. It could be created automatically by placing thresholds or cycle counting plans or created manually based on locations or item settings. Once the work has been created, workers process the counting work, physically count quantities, and input that information in Dynamics 365. Finally, the differences between virtual and physical inventory are raised, and a supervisor can resolve the discrepancies.

Another option is to create a spot counting where a worker sees a difference in a location and creates and counts that particular location. This is done manually, and a supervisor must resolve discrepancies. The setup for cycle counting plans can be done by going to **Warehouse management** > **Setup** > **Cycle counting** > **Cycle count plans**:

Figure 8.14 – Cycle count plans

Here, we will create a cycle count plan with an ID and a description. Then, we can assign them a work pool ID to segregate counting for different zones or items and keep the counting groups distributed in worker groups. The **Days between cycle counts** field specifies the number of days between inventory counts. For example, in *Figure 8.9*, the **A Items** cycle count plan will create counting works every 90 days.

Lastly, in **Empty locations**, we can include or exclude locations without stock to be counted as part of the counting works. We can create product queries for the cycle counting plan to filter any product. For example, in *Figure 8.9*, we can filter **A Items** to be counted every 90 days and **C Items** every 365 days since **A Items** are more expensive than **C Items**, and we want to control them more regularly.

With this setup done, we can execute plans by clicking the **Process cycle counting plan**. Here, we can define a batch job to execute those planes every day. It will automatically create works when the days between each count pass.

On the other hand, the setup for the cycle count threshold can be done by going to **Warehouse management** > **Setup** > **Cycle counting** > **Cycle count thresholds**:

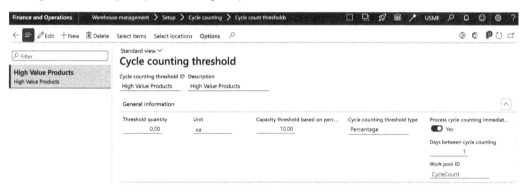

Figure 8.15 – The Cycle counting threshold form

Figure 8.14 shows an example of high-value products. This threshold can be set up by quantity or percentage of the stock. This example is set up by percentage, meaning that when the inventory of this location drops under 10% of the stock, it will automatically create a counting work for that location in the warehouse, and it will evaluate the threshold every day because the days between cycle counting is set to 1.

We must create the device menu items to process the cycle counting work. We can create a menu item to create a guided cycle count, where the system directs the worker to each location that needs to be counted. In the mobile device menu items, create a new menu item for the guided cycle count and set the existing **Work** field to **yes**. For **Directed by option**, select **System directed**, and finally, in the **Work classes** tab, add a work class for cycle counting.

Another option is to set the cycle count blind, meaning the worker cannot see quantities when counting. We can create another menu item or modify the one we created for cycle count. We must click on the **Cycle counting** button, after which we can select the following options:

- **Number of attempts**: The number of tries the warehouse worker has before confirming
- **Display item number**: If active, it will show the item number in the app
- **Display license plate**: If active, it will show the license plate in the app
- **Display batch number**: if active, it will show the batch number in the app
- **Display serial number**: if active, it will show the serial number in the app

With these parameters, we can control how much information the worker can see in a cycle counting process.

Once counting has been processed, we need to resolve discrepancies. This can be done by going to **Warehouse management** > **Cycle counting** > **Cycle counting work pending review**. Here, we will see all counting work that needs to be reviewed. We can select the work and click on **Cycle counting** to see the discrepancies between the system quantities and counted ones. Then, we can accept or reject the count. If we accept the count, a journal will automatically adjust the inventory difference. But if we reject it, it gets canceled, and nothing is adjusted.

The last option is **Spot counting**; this is where the worker may find a difference and correct it immediately. For example, let's say a worker is doing put-away work in an empty location and finds that the location is full. They can execute a previously created menu item to do spot counting and then continue with their put-away work.

Outbound warehouse processes

The outbound processes cover all the inventory flows that move inventory outside our warehouse. In this group of processes, we can count the transfer and sales orders. However, warehouses can have multiple ways of picking to address these processes. In some cases, it is straightforward, and a sales order could be picked and shipped, but in other cases, we may need to pick from different zones with more than one worker, put it in a staging location, and pack the goods before loading them in a truck.

The system has four entities (which we reviewed earlier) that intervene in the outbound process:

- **Location directives** control where to pick inventory and where to put it. For outbound, we need a minimum of two location directives – one for picking and another for put-away.
- **Work templates** control how to do the outbound work. At a minimum, we must have a pick and a put pair.
- **Menu and menu items** control the menus to process the picking and put-away work. They can be configured as user or system-directed.

- **Wave templates** define releasing all the shipping work to the warehouse. We can define waves as short scheduling where we can assign groups of work and release them together to execute parallel activities by various workers.

Sales order picking

When working with sales order picking, there are many possibilities we could set up. The first case we will review is direct sales order picking, where the sales order is released, and the picking work leads the worker to a picking location, after which the worker puts the picked item into a bay door location.

In this case, we need to set up the following:

- **Work template**: We must create a new work template with a pick and a put pair in the **Work Template Details** tab. Remember to add a work class ID for sales order work:

Standard view * ⌄

Work order type

| Sales orders ⌄ |

Overview   General

○	⟳	Sequen... ▽	Work template	Work template description	Valid	Automatic...	Work pool ID	Work priority
○		12	24 Direct SO	Direct Sales order	☑	☐	⌄	0

Work Template Details

+ New   🗑 Delete   ↑ Move up   ↓ Move down   Work line breaks

○	⟳	Line number	Work type	Custom work type	Mandatory	Stop work	Freeze	Directive code	Work class ID	Quality check temp...	Anchoring group ID
○		1,0000000000	Pick ⌄		☑	☐	☐		Sales ⌄		
		2,0000000000	Put		☑	☐	☐		Sales		

Figure 8.16 – Direct sales order work template

- **Location directive**: First, create a location directive for the picking work of the warehouse we work for. In the location directive actions, create an action, click on the **Edit query** button, and filter the location or location profile ID to a picking location or picking location profile. Then, we must create another location directive to put work in the loading location for the same warehouse. In this case, by clicking the **Edit query** button, we can filter the location profile ID to the bay door location profile.

- **Menu item**: In this case, we can create a system-directed menu item for sales picking. Remember to activate the **use work** option since all outbound processes work with created works.

- **Wave templates**: Create a shipping work template to process the work automatically. To do this, we must activate the **automate wave creation**, **Process wave at release to warehouse**, and **automate wave release** options.

When we create and release a sales order with a reserved inventory, the system will automatically do the following:

1. Create the wave.

2. Process the wave, creating the work.

3. Release the wave to the workers so that they can start picking.

Once work has been released and created, the worker will start picking in this way:

1. Enter the menu item for sales picking.

2. As they are conducting system-directed work, the created work for this sales order will automatically appear.

3. Perform the picking at the picking location.

4. Perform the put at the bay door.

> **Important note**
> Remember that we can modify this process based on the workflow of our warehouse. For example, workers can choose or scan the work ID to start this picking, which is done by changing the menu item to **User Directed**. Another example is to process waves manually, which is done by changing the options on the wave.

Sales order picking with staging locations

In this process, the picking is done in the same way as the direct sales order picking, but instead of putting the items at the bay door, workers put them in a staging location first. This is useful for more complex warehouses that, for example, bubble wrap their boxes and then move the wrapped boxes to a bay door.

The workflow is as follows:

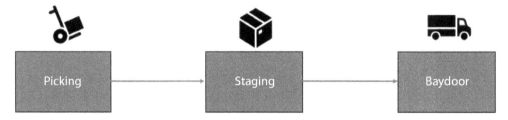

Figure 8.17 – Process flow of staging

In this case, we need to perform an extra pick-put pair. So, to set up this scenario, we need to do the following:

- **Work template**: Create a new work template with two pick-put pairs. In the first put, we must assign a directive code to represent the staging location. We will use it on the location directives. Remember to add a work class ID for sales order work. Another thing to activate here is the **stop work** option on the second pick line. This will allow the first worker to pick the items and put them in the staging location and the second worker to pick from the staging location to the bay door. As different workers will be processing this work, we can create different work class IDs to separate this work in the menu item. The first pick-put pair must have a location directive, and the second pick-put pair must have another one:

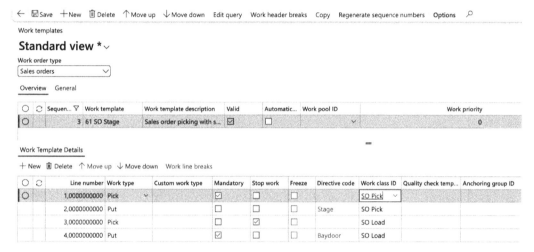

Figure 8.18 – Work template example for staging

- **Location directive**: We can reuse the same location directives we configured in the direct sales order scenario, but to direct the work to the staging locations, we need to add another location directive with the directive code of staging used in the work template and, in the location directive actions, click the **Edit query** button and filter the staging location. As the location directives work with sequences, the staging location directive must have a lower sequence number than the bay door directive:

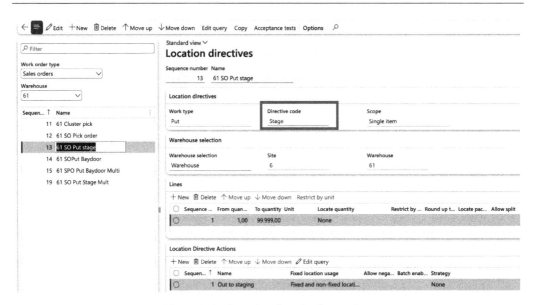

Figure 8.19 – Location directive for staging

- **Menu item**: We can reuse the same menu item as the previous example but add a work class ID of SO Pick, as shown in *Figure 8.14*. Then, we must create another one to process the put-to-bay door work with a work class ID of SO Load.

- **Wave templates**: We can reuse the same template we used in the direct sales order example.

When we create and release a sales order with a reserved inventory, the system will automatically do the following:

1. Create the wave.

2. Process the wave, creating the work.

3. Release the wave to the workers so they can perform pickings.

Once work has been released and created, the worker will perform the pickings in this way:

1. Enter the menu item for sales picking.

2. As with system-directed work, it will automatically show the created work for this sales order picking.

3. Perform the picking at the picking location.

4. Perform the put-away at the staging location.

5. The first work will be completed.

6. The second worker will enter the sales order in the **Put-away** menu.

7. As with system-directed work, it will automatically show the created work for this sales order put away.

8. Perform the picking at the staging location.

9. Perform the put-away at the bay door.

We can use the **Anchoring** option in **Mobile device menu items** when we use several staging locations. This is useful when a staging location is occupied by another load or shipping being completed, and workers cannot put the subsequent works in that staging location and must override it. We can find it here:

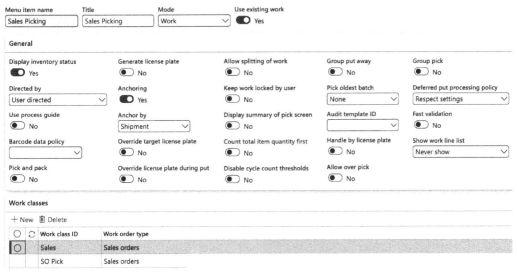

Figure 8.20 – The Anchoring option in Mobile device menu items

We must decide if we should anchor by shipment or load by modifying the anchor by option.

Packing and containerization

In various warehouses, picking work ends with a packing process where every product is put in a container. These physical dimensions need to be tracked down, especially in shipping processes. Dynamics 365 Supply Chain Management has a packing process that provides visibility to packing stations and calculates the appropriate container to be processed in every situation.

The first step of the packing process is to perform the picking work and move the items to the packing locations. Once there, the packing station will put the items into containers and give each container a number. If not every item fits into a container, workers could use another one until the order is fully packed. Then, a put-to-bay door process could be executed to move items to the bay door and then into the shipping truck.

To set up the packing process, we must create a packing location. We can do this by going to **Warehouse management** > **Setup** > **Warehouse location profiles**. Here, we can create a location profile for packing with the following parameters, understanding that packing location can mix products into location:

- **Use tracking of license plates** set to **Yes**
- **Allow negative inventory** set to **Yes**
- **Allow mixed items** set to **Yes**
- **Allow mixed inventory status** set to **Yes**
- **Allow mixed inventory batches** set to **Yes**

Next, we must create the location with this profile to process the packing work.

After that, we must create the container types to pack our items. Go to **Warehouse Management** > **Setup** > **Containers** > **Container types**. Here, we can create all our types of containers by inputting each type's dimension, maximum weight, and volumetrics.

The following setup will create the packing profile in **Warehouse management** > **Setup** > **Packing** > **Packing profiles**. In this form, we must define how the packing station will work, which assigns the container packing policy that controls the final location for shipment. Here, the options are the weight unit that's been designed, whether we are closing containers automatically or manually, how we are handling the manifest of the container – for example, if we need to print that manifest automatically – and the requirements to do that. Also, we can define printing a shipping label and a packing slip at the packing station. In the **Container ID mode** field, we can indicate if containers are labeled automatically or manually, and finally, the **Container type** value that will be assigned to this packing profile:

Standard view ∨

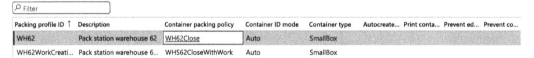

Packing profile ID ↑	Description	Container packing policy	Container ID mode	Container type	Autocreate...	Print conta...	Prevent ed...	Prevent co...
WH62	Pack station warehouse 62	WH62Close	Auto	SmallBox				
WH62WorkCreati...	Pack station warehouse 6...	WHS62CloseWithWork	Auto	SmallBox				

Figure 8.21 – The Packing profiles form

The last setup for manual packing is to assign the packing station to the worker. We can do this on the **Worker** screen. Here, we can set up the packing profile and the container packing policy in the **Profile** tab. This information is not mandatory because when we perform the manual packing process, we can log in and input this information.

Also, in the default packing station, we can set up the location where packing occurs for the packing worker.

When processing sales orders that need to be packed, warehouse workers will pick items, after which they will arrive at the packing station, and packing workers will start to pack them. Workers can log into the packing terminal by going to **Warehouse management** > **Packing and containerization** > **Pack**. The first thing they'll be asked is to complete their worker and packing station locations. If we defaulted this information in the worker form, this will be auto-completed.

When they hit **OK**, the workers can access the packing screen. Here, the workers need to scan the license plate or shipment that will be packed. **License plate information** will be displayed, showing which items need to be packed to complete the order. The worker must create a new container via the **New container** button (if created manually) and select which container type will be used. Then, they can start scanning the labels of the items. With each scan, the system will control that the weight does not exceed the container's maximum allowed weight:

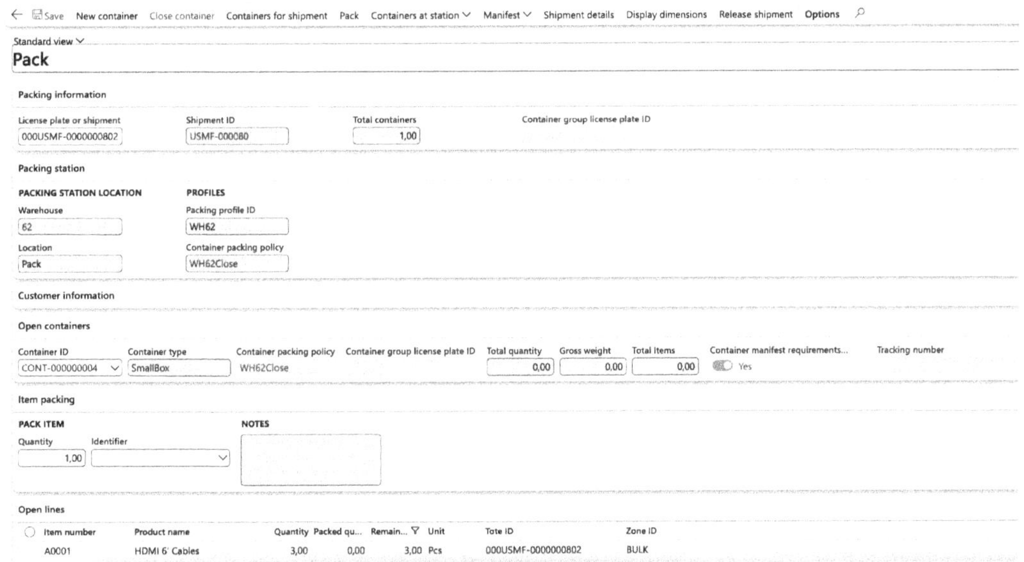

Figure 8.22 – The Packing station form

When the container is completed, we can print manifests and packing slips, and close the container with the Clos**e container** button. When this is done, depending on the setup of the container packing policy, items can be delivered automatically to the bay door, or a put-away work to move those containers can be automatically created.

At any time, the worker can select the **Available Container** option to review which containers are in the packing location and adjust, delete, reopen, or reverse the manifest. All unpacked items modified this way will be updated so that they can be packed again.

Automated containerization creates containers and the picking work once the wave is processed. To do this, we need to set up the following under the **Warehouse management** > **Setup** > **Containers** menu:

- **Container types** defines the physical characteristics of the containers.

- **Container group** groups the same type of containers that can be used for the same products. Here, we need to define the sequence in which container types are assigned. The system will assign the container closest to the item's size dimension, so it is recommended to arrange them from larger to smaller.

- **Container build templates** defines the rules of containerization:

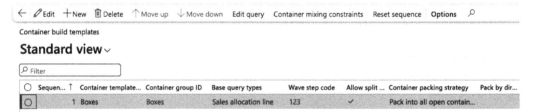

Figure 8.23 – Container build templates

Here, we set up a container build template by sequence number, and we must assign it to a wave step code.

> **Important note**
>
> Upon clicking the **Edit query** and **Container mixing constraints** buttons, we can filter up which shipments and items are assigned to this template and restrict items that can be packed together.

- **Wave template**: We can create or modify a wave template to process containerization. We must add the containerization method and a wave step code to process and create picking works to do this.

When we release the order to the warehouse, the following process will be executed, depending on the wave template (automated or manual):

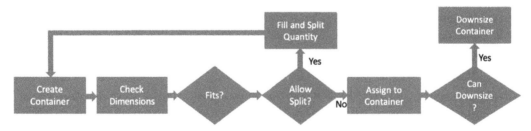

Figure 8.24 – Containerization process flow

We can describe the process shown in *Figure 8.24* in the following way:

1. The release wave will process the container build template with the matching wave step code.

2. If the criteria defined on the query of the build template are met, the template is selected a processed.

3. The system checks the highest physical dimension of the items against the container type's maximum allowed values.

4. The system checks the weight of the items against the maximum allowed weight of the container, considering the container use percentage.

5. The system can split items into multiple containers if the **Allow Split?** option is activated on the container build template.

6. The system will try to downsize containers into small ones. If this process fails, it will keep the container in the previous sequence. It's recommended to order containers from larger to smaller.

7. If the container build template fails – for example, the physical dimensions of the item are above the maximum allowed – it will assign the larger container and indicate that the container has an error that's enabling that field in the container. It will also send an error in the system.

8. The system will start over with the following line until no more lines are left to be processed.

Outbound sorting

This functionality allows workers to organize small containers in the packing process better. There are two ways to work on this functionality: sorting after packing and before packing, as shown in the following figure:

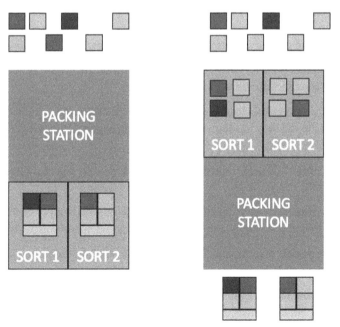

Figure 8.25 – Outbound sorting

Figure 8.25 shows that outbound sorting can happen when we pick up different items in the warehouse and all reach the packing station; then, they will be packed and sorted in different pallets for shipping. Alternatively, warehouses can have a sorting position before packing and sort into different pallets. This process is commonly called put-to-wall.

We can set up outbound sorting by going to **Warehouse management** > **Setup** > **Packing** > **Outbound sorting template**:

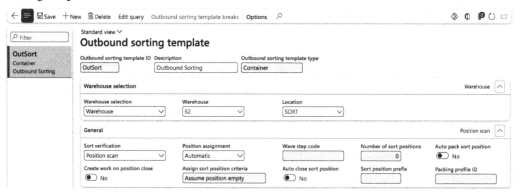

Figure 8.26 - The Outbound sorting template form:

In this form, we can create our sorting template, and we can decide how it is going to work:

- **Outbound sorting template type** controls which sorting we want to execute. **Container** means that we perform the de-containerization process first and then sort the containers into pallets, while **Wave demand** means we sort first in a sorting position and then process the packing.

- **Sort verification** defines if we need to scan the position or the license plate to verify that the items are being sorted in the correct locations.

- If **Create work on position close** is activated, this will create the put-away work from the sorting locations to the next location, which could be bay door or packing, depending on the sorting type.

- **Position assignment** directs the shipments to be sorted to a sorting location manually or automatically.

- **Assign sort position criteria** controls if positions are assumed empty or if the system must ensure that the position is empty. This is enabled on wave demand sorting type.

- **Auto close sort position** automatically closes the sorting position when all assigned work is completed.

- **Number of sort positions** and **Sort position prefix** name the sorting positions and define how many of them we can use. This is enabled on wave demand sorting type.

As with many other configuration forms in warehouse management, we also have the **Edit query** button, where we can filter the orders, shipments, or loads that will be applied to this template.

Here, we also have a button called **Outbound sorting template breaks**, which will break the coming items into different locations, depending on the setup. For example, we can break into sales orders or shipments so that each location will be assigned to a sales order or a shipment.

For example, two sales orders were created, one for SP-001 and SP-002 for 2 units each and another for SP-002 for 4 units.

If we set up a wave demand outbound sorting type, we can release an order to the warehouse and process the wave; the picking work may be created separately to address different zones in the warehouse. The first worker can pick 6 units of item SP-001 and leave it in the sorting location with LP number 001. The second worker can pick the 2 units for SP-002 and leave them in the sorting location with LP number 003-

As different workers do this, items arrive at different times in the sorting position. The sorter worker will pick LP 001, which contains 6 units of item SP-001, and the system will indicate that 2 units must go to sorting location C-1 and 4 units to location C-2. Then, it will scan LP 003, and again the system will indicate to put 2 units of item SP-002 into sorting location C-1. At this time, orders will be sorted. Order number 1 will be in location C-1, and order number 2 will be in location C-2.

This can be controlled by going to **Warehouse management** > **Packing and containerization** > **Outbound sorting position assignments**:

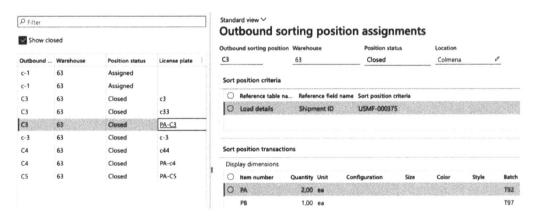

Figure 8.27 – The Outbound sorting position assignments form

Here, we can see the assigned sorting position, which shipment is sorted in that position, and which items are in that position

Cross-docking

In many warehouses, is a common practice to ship merchandise on the same day or the next day. With cross-docking, the system allows us to check in the items in the receiving docks, and instead of putting that inventory into a shelf or bulk position, immediately generate work to move it to the bay door and ship it. This is also known as the flow-through process, and it reduces several warehouse times when handling items.

The process in the warehouse is straightforward:

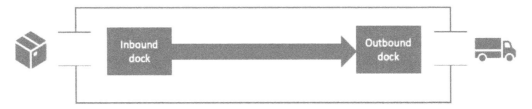

Figure 8.28 – Cross-docking

When items arrive at the inbound dock, we immediately send them to the outbound dock. In some cases, as shipments are not always so instantaneous, a flow-thru or cross-docking shelf exists in which the pallets enter from one side and are picked from the back, so the warehouse stores them for a little time, and they are shipped when the truck arrives to the outbound dock.

To set up this process in Dynamics 365 Supply Chain Management, we need to configure the cross-docking templates located at **Warehouse management** > **Setup** > **Work** > **Cross docking templates**:

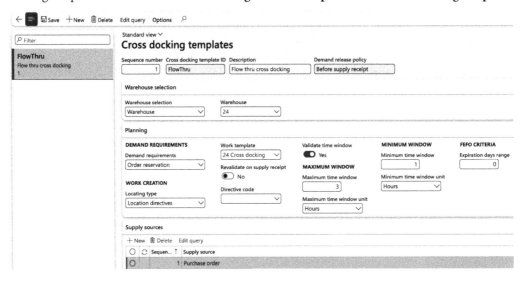

Figure 8.29 – The Cross docking templates form

In this form, we will create our template to control how cross-docking is going to work:

- **Demand release policy** controls when cross-docking is planned before supply receipt or at supply receiving. The first one will create work when the sales order is released, and the wave is processed. The **Supply receipt** option is used for production cross-docking.

- **Demand requirements** defines where demand is taken from. It could be an order reservation or marking.

- **Locating type** defines where the put work will be directed. If we select **Location directive**, we need to specify a location directive for cross-docking to specify the location, though we could inherit the location from the shipment.

- With **MAXIMUM WINDOW** and **MINIMUM WINDOW**, we can specify a time window for shipments to be processed by this template.

- The **Supply sources** tab indicates the sources for cross-docking. We can add purchase orders, transfer orders, and production orders.

We also need to create the following:

- A **Work class** to define cross-docking work.

- In case we set the locating type to **Location directive**, we must create a location directive to indicate which location will be directed to the put work.

- A **Device menu item** to execute the cross-docking work. We have two options: include the work class in the **Purchase Put-away** menu item or create a new one indicating work mode, use the existing work that's been activated, and include the cross-docking work class.

Once this setup is done, we can process the work in the following order:

1. Create a purchase order to supply the items.

2. Create the sales order where the items will be shipped.

3. Reserve or mark the items against the purchase order, depending on the template.

4. Release the sales order to the warehouse. This will create the shipment but not the work because no items are in the warehouse yet. We can confirm that it will be cross-docked if we enter the created shipment, scroll down to the **Load** tab, and click the **Planned cross-docking** button.

5. In the **Planned cross-docking** information area, we can see the order, shipment, and load ID. It also shows the quantities and the supply order number.

6. When the purchase order arrives, workers can receive it normally. Depending on the template, this will create the put-away work in the location indicated in the location directives or the shipment location.

7. Workers can process the put-away work, and the app will indicate to move it to the cross-dock assigned location.

8. The worker can go to the shipment, confirm it, and print the packing slip and required documentation.

Summary

This chapter examined inbound concepts and flows, as well as how to design and implement those processes in Dynamics 365. We also covered various outbound scenarios and provided suggestions on which options are best suited for each process. Additionally, we reviewed internal warehouse operations such as cycle counts and replenishments.

As this module is regularly updated with new real-world scenarios to expand its boundaries, it's up to us to keep up to date with these functionalities to learn and implement them in the right way. I recommend that you use this chapter as the beginning of your journey, as a base foundation of everything this module can accomplish, and discover new ways of implementing it.

Questions

1. You are implementing the warehouse management module. A warehouse worker informs you that every sales order created as urgent must be processed immediately.

   Which of the following configurations do you need to perform to address this problem?

   A. Filter urgent sales orders in the wave template, put them in the highest sequence, and set the automatic wave release option to **Yes**.

   B. Filter urgent sales orders in the work template, put them in the highest sequence, and set the priority to 1.

   C. Filter urgent sales orders in the work template, put them in the highest sequence, and set the priority to 100.

2. You are implementing the warehouse management module. You need to set up replenishment work. Which of the following configurations is not necessary?

   A. **Replenishment templates**.

   B. **Work templates**.

   D. **Load demand**.

   C. **Mobile device menu item**.

3. You are implementing the warehouse management module. When sales orders are released, and work is created, you detect that no location is assigned for moving the items to the bay door.

Which of the following configurations must you review to address the problem?

A. Review the shipment threshold in the wave templates.

B. Review the sales order pick location directive.

E. Review the sales order put location directive.

C. Review the bay door location profile.

Answers

1. Option B.

Priority is controlled by the work templates, sending the lower numbered priority first. This will allow the workers to receive first the urgent orders.

2. Option C.

All the other options are required to perform replenishment.

3. Option C.

The most common error is incorrectly assigning the location at the location directives. In this case, moving items to the bay door indicates that we need to review the put-away work, which is controlled by the sales order put location directive.

.

Transportation Management – From Planning to Execution

Transportation management (**TMS**) is a module that allows us to automate a huge part of the logistics of a company. This brings efficiency to the logistics process, serving as the vital link that bridges the gap between production and delivery. It is no secret that the transportation landscape has become increasingly complex, with global markets, diverse shipping options, and customer demands constantly evolving. In this dynamic environment, businesses need a robust solution that can adapt to change, optimize operations, and propel them ahead of the competition.

Our goal in this chapter is to fully equip you with the knowledge and skills to leverage this powerful tool. By the end of this chapter, you will be able to do the following:

- Understand TMS concepts and its workflow
- Set up parameters and the TMS engine
- Work with loads, rate, and route shipments
- Process automatic or manual reconciliation and generate invoices
- Set up and work with route plans, route and rate engines, and appointments

What is TMS?

This module helps us control a company transportation process by identifying vendors and routing solutions that help us select the best route with lower prices in each shipping use case.

The TMS process of a shipment starts with the planning step, which indicates which container items will be shipped, on which date, and on which dock door it will be prepared.

The most important part of the TMS module is defining each shipment's rates and routes. Once a load has been created for the shipment, we can rate it using a rate engine to identify better routes and lower prices. Each rate engine could define these rates based on multiple factors. For example, a **less-than-load** (**LTL**) shipment will have different costs than a **full load** (**FL**) for the same route.

TMS can help us control invoices for customers when we have transportation charges, and it also controls the freight reconciliation processes with the logistics providers.

First, it is important to know that the TMS module is designed for use in the following cases:

- When the company uses external providers for transportation, we can use TMS to control the inbound and outbound processes.

- When the company has its fleet available for delivery, and charges are invoiced to customers, we can use TMS to determine and invoice those charges.

- When the company uses its fleet for delivery, and charges are not invoiced to customers because the pricing of the items includes the TMS tariff, we can use the TMS module to determine transportation rates and adjust sales prices.

- Suppose logistics are handled for another legal entity in the same company. In that case, TMS can help us by planning and controlling the logistics of the other legal entity as it's a normal logistics provider. But those transactions cannot be automated as intercompany transactions. Therefore, it will be handled manually, for example, by creating a purchase order.

It is important to note that the TMS module is designed to plan, control, and execute logistics for goods of the legal entity that owns those goods. It is intended to be implemented on something other than logistics providers or carriers because it could lead to costing and inventory issues.

We'll start by understanding TMS concepts:

- Transit hierarchy

- Inbound transportation

- Outbound transportation

Let's get started.

Transit hierarchy

In Dynamics 365 Supply Chain Management, we can plan transportation based on orders or shipments. For example, if we had a sales order, a shipment could be automatically created, and we can process that delivery by the sales order or the shipment link to the order.

We can mention the transit hierarchy that defines this segmentation in the following way:

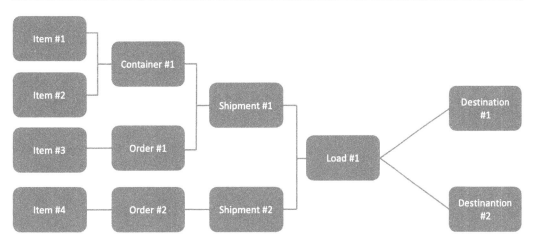

Figure 9.1 – Transit hierarchy example

This defines the following process:

1. Items are selected and grouped by order.

2. For example, if we create a transfer order, we must include which items we transfer from one location to another.

3. Items can also be grouped and put into containers.

4. Containers are a group of items put together for warehouse control.

5. Shipments group containers and orders.

6. Shipments are a collection of one or more orders and containers heading to the same destination.

7. Shipments are put into loads.

8. Loads are a collection of shipments that are transported simultaneously. At this level, we define pricing.

9. Each load is assigned to one or multiple destinations.

With these concepts in mind, let's review the inbound transportation and outbound processes.

Inbound transportation

When we receive items from a vendor to a company warehouse, and the company arranges the transportation of that load, we can use transportation management to plan and receive those items.

We can process this inbound transportation in the following sequence:

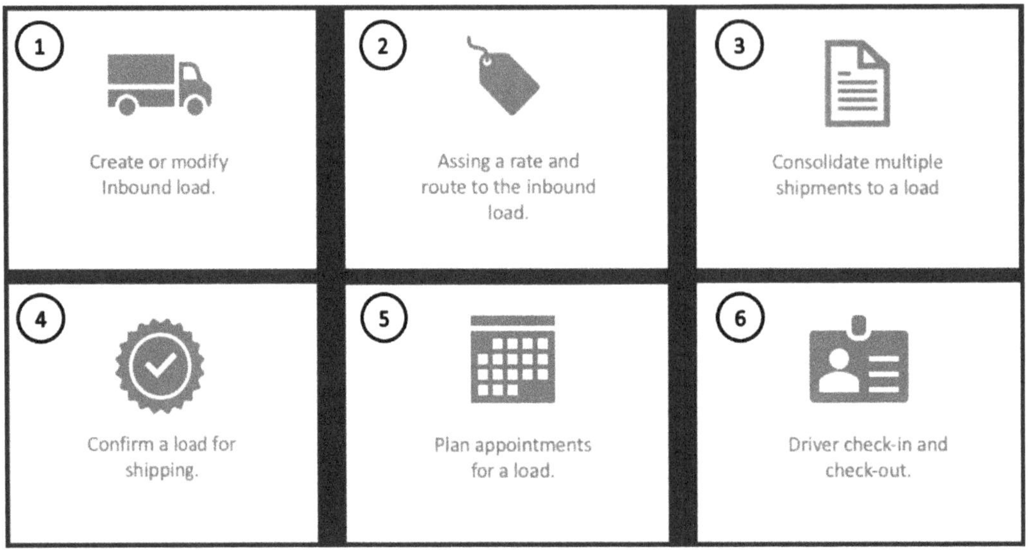

Figure 9.2 – Inbound transportation steps

Let's take a closer look:

1. The first step is to create the inbound load. This will create the entity to process the receiving process attached to that load.

2. Once a load has been created, we can define the rate and route of the inbound load. This will allow us to select the proper carrier to transport that load.

3. We can consolidate multiple shipments to the created load and control if those items fit the created load, specifying the truck container's weight and volume.

4. Following that, we can confirm the load for shipping, indicating that we have selected the carrier, shipment, route, and rate and completed all the needed information.

5. We can plan appointments for a load, indicating to the warehouse on which date and inbound dock the load will arrive.

6. Optionally, when the shipment arrives, we can process the driver check-in and check-out with all the driver's information if we have created an appointment. With this process, we can control and analyze warehouse unloading times.

Outbound transportation

When we need to ship our goods, we can use transportation management to control the shipping process. Outbound transportation allows us to follow and execute shipments from sales or outgoing transfer orders.

We can process outbound transportation in the following way:

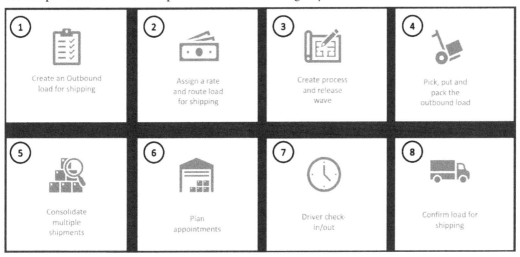

Figure 9.3 – Outbound transportation steps

Let's take a closer look:

1. First, we must create an outbound load and assign all the shipping from the orders. This will allow us to consolidate various orders and ship them together based on the capacity of the load.

2. Once we have the load, we can select the carrier we want based on the rates and routes we defined earlier. These rates are calculated based on the rating engine and, for example, on the truck's distance, fuel, and used capacity.

3. Then, we can release it to the warehouse and release the wave. This will allow warehouse workers to start the picking process.

4. As we saw in *Chapter 8*, once the picking work has been created, workers can pick, put, and pack the goods into the bay door.

5. We can consolidate various shipping into one load to maximize the load capacity.

6. Optionally, we can plan appointments for a load, indicating to the warehouse on which date and inbound dock the load will arrive.

7. Finally, when the shipment arrives, we can process the driver check-in and check-out with all the driver's information if we have created an appointment. With this process, we can control and analyze warehouse unloading times.

8. Once the truck has been loaded, we can confirm the load for shipping to end the process.

This is the full life cycle of a load in the TMS module. As we will review, we have multiple possibilities to control and manage those loads.

A crucial step in this process is to plan the shipments correctly. Let's review the load planning process.

Planning TMS

The transportation module is interconnected with the supply chain. This ensures that supply chain planning implements the correct flow of operations, maintaining an efficient and effective way to store, receive, and ship goods and information from the origin to the destination. This module will ensure the information flow at each point of the process.

For example, if we create a sales order, we can plan its shipment, pick and pack goods, and ship it, from sales order creation to successfully shipping to the destination. This is possible because all entities in Dynamics 365 Supply Chain Management are interconnected:

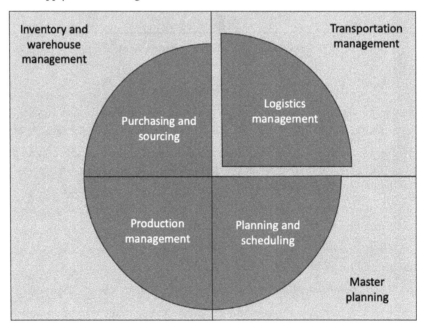

Figure 9.4 – Integration with TMS

With that, we have provided an overview of TMS. With this in mind, let's start by setting up this module.

Start with the basics – shipping carriers and carrier groups

Before jumping to forms and configuration, let's define a carrier. A **shipping carrier** is a company that transports goods on behalf of another company and charges by that service. For example, if we need to transport goods from point A to point B, we can ask a shipping carrier to move them for us, and they will charge for that service. We can also have our shipping fleet and do our shipping service internally, but this depends on the company.

Most companies have a fleet to transport goods and shipping carriers for specific routes or to handle emergency issues, such as broken-down trucks or fleet maintenance problems. To handle both scenarios, we can start by creating rate masters and rating profiles.

Rate masters and rating profile

We must set up a rating profile to define a carrier in the system. This functionality allows us to determine the shipping rates and compare carriers' rates.

Rate masters and rate bases are associated with the carrier profile in the rating profile. The following diagram will help us understand how to set up rate profiles for a carrier:

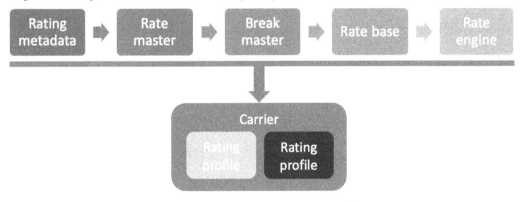

Figure 9.5 – Components of a rating profile

- In **Rating metadata**, we define which data in the system will be used for calculating rates. We can define this by going to **Transportation management** > **Setup** > **Rating** > **Rating metadata**:

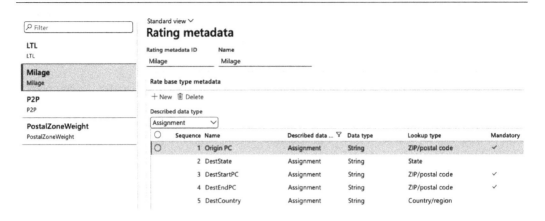

Figure 9.6 – The Rating metadata form

In *Figure 9.6*, the rating metadata is shown. Here, we define a metadata ID and name. In the **Rate base type metadata** tab, we can add how we assign and rate this type. *Figure 9.6* shows that **Mileage** rating metadata is assigned by origin and destination postal code; since fields are mandatory, that configuration works as lookup criteria to assign that rate to the shipment.

- The **Rate masters** form determines available rates for the shipping carrier. If we go to **Transportation management** > **Setup** > **Rating** > **Rate master**, we will see the following form:

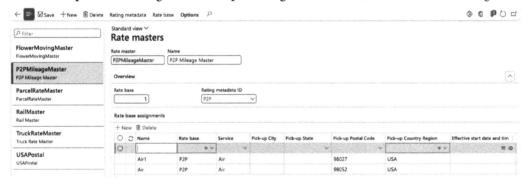

Figure 9.7 – The Rate masters form

Here, we can set up a rate master and assign it to a rating metadata ID. In the bottom part of the form, we set up **Rate base assignments**. Here, we can assign a rate base and a service for the rate master. As shown in *Figure 9.7*, we are assigning an **Air** service from the 98027 pick-up postal code. This means that every time we create a shipment from the 98027 (Washington) postal code with an **Air** service, this rate master will be assigned.

- **Break masters** allows us to create breakpoints to the rate master to assign values to rating categories. We are working with mileage master, which means, for example, that we will charge more for every number of miles. This form helps us with that, as shown here:

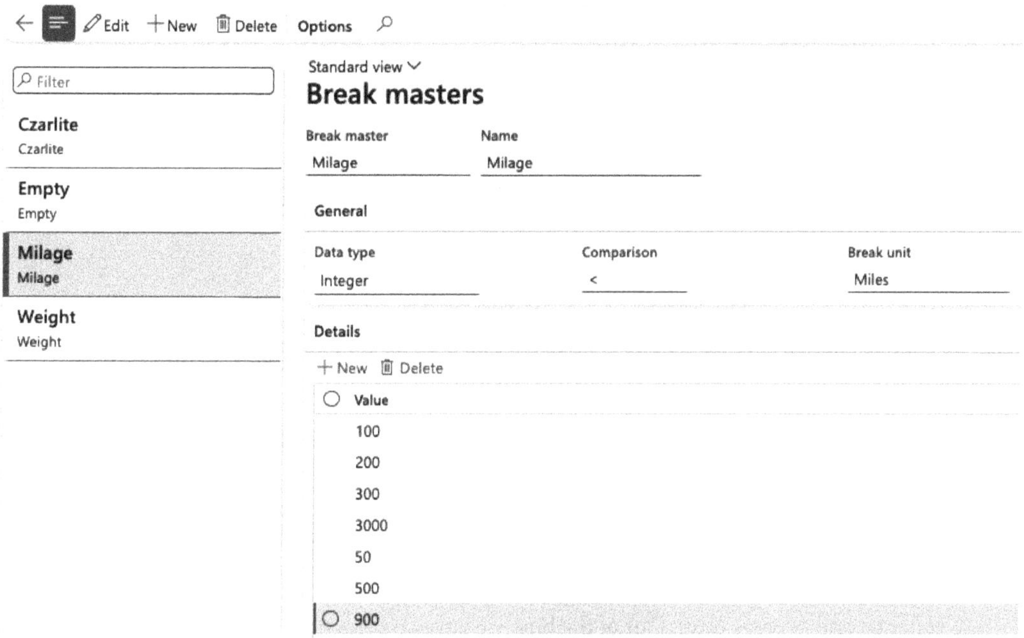

Figure 9.8 – The Break masters form

To reach the form shown in *Figure 9.8*, we must go to **Transportation Management** > **Setup** > **Rating** > **Break Master**.

Here, we define **Break master** and **Name**. We must define which data type we will work with within the **General** tab. For example, if we are working with milage, we define an integer as a data type. The **Comparison** field will work as a comparison between values. **Break unit** will work as a unit of measure for the rate, and in the **Details** tab, we add every breakpoint value.

To give an example, in the base rate form shown in *Figure 9.8*, the following values will be shown: < 50, < 100, < 200, < 300, < 500, < 900, < 3000, > 3000. This allows us to define a rate for those values.

- The **Rate bases** form allows us to combine **Rate master** and **Break master** to define a price for every breakpoint – in our example, this is **Mileage**. To access this form, select **Rate master** and click the **Rate base** button at the top. We will end up in the following form:

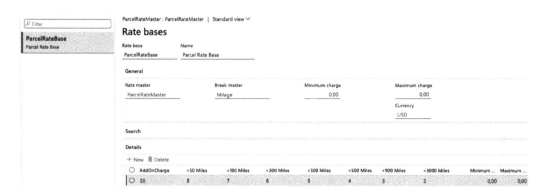

Figure 9.9 – The Rate bases form

As shown in *Figure 9.9*, the system combines the rate master with the break master to create this rate base. In the **Currency** field, we define US dollars as the currency of this rate base, and in the **Details** tab, the mileage breaks from the break master are shown.

Suppose we take *Figure 9.9* as an example, and we are working with a shipment that has 150 miles from the pick-up postal code to the destination postal code. In that case, it will fall under the < 200 miles bucket, giving it a value of 6 USD a mile, so 150 miles x 6 USD = 900 USD, with an add-on charge of 20 USD, totaling 920 USD for the full trip.

- **Rate engines**: TMS calculates tasks assigned to shipment rates using engines, which have logic to generate and process rates. Out of the box, we have engines that, for example, calculate the mileage between point A and point B, or that calculate transit times, and so on. Rate engines are associated to calculate rates with the configured metadata. We can see them by going to **Transportation Management** > **Setup** > **Engines** > **Rate Engines**:

Rate engines

Standard view˅

Rate engine	↑	Name	Rating metadata ID	Engine assembly	Engine class
LTL		LTL Rate Engine	LTL	Microsoft.Dynamics.Ax.Tms.dll	Microsoft.Dynamics.Ax.Tms.Bll.LtlRateEngine
Milage		Milage	Milage	Microsoft.Dynamics.Ax.Tms.dll	Microsoft.Dynamics.Ax.Tms.Bll.MileageRateEngine
P2PMileage		P2P Mileage Rate Engine	P2P	Microsoft.Dynamics.Ax.Tms.dll	Microsoft.Dynamics.Ax.Tms.Bll.P2PMileageRateEngine
P2PWeight		P2PWeight	P2P	Microsoft.Dynamics.Ax.Tms.dll	Microsoft.Dynamics.Ax.Tms.Bll.P2PByWeightRateEngine
PostalZoneWeight		Postal Zone Weight Engine	PostalZoneWeight	Microsoft.Dynamics.Ax.Tms.dll	Microsoft.Dynamics.Ax.Tms.Bll.PostalZoneWeightRateEngine

Figure 9.10 – The Rate engines form

This form is defined automatically as those engines are standard, but we can develop new ones via X++. To do that, we need to develop an extension from the TMS standard classes and assemblies. Once developed, we can deploy this third-party engine as a package.

We will not dive into how to create new engines, but it is essential to know that it is possible to do that, and we can alter how calculations are made if our implementation needs it.

For example, a customer asked me to rate shipments based on the number of units per kilometer. This means we have a different rate if I travel 100 km with 10 pallets or 100 km with 20 pallets. So, in that case, we must develop an engine that processes that metadata and set up a different rate master for that case.

As rating metadata is required before setting up a rate engine, we can go to **Transportation management parameters**, which is located under **Transportation management** > **Setup** > **Transportation management parameters**:

Standard view ∨

Transportation management parameters

General	**Set up parameters for Transportation management**
Reports	
Print management	**Default duration**
Number sequences	0
	Driver check-in and check-out
	Vendor invoice
	Hub type
	Shipment
	In transit planning
	Loads
	Direct delivery
	Engines
	Initialize base engine data

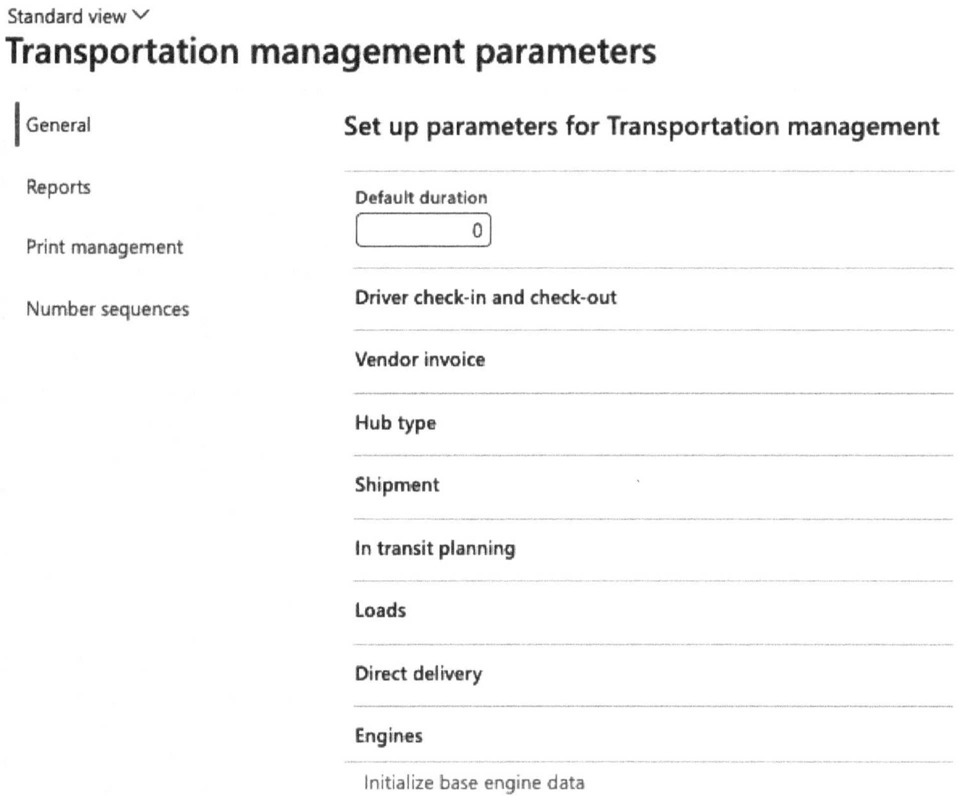

Figure 9.11 – The Transportation management parameters form

Here, under the **General** tab, we have the **Initialize base engine** data button in the **Engines** menu. With this option, Dynamics 365 Supply Chain Management will create the required metadata for the standard engines. However, if you are going to use the existing engines, it is not recommended to create your metadata. This will cause many errors, causing the engine to fail unless the rating metadata complies with the engine's rules.

Now, we are ready to create the rating profile. So, let's go to **Transportation Management** > **Setup** > **Rating** > **Rating Profile** to access the following form:

Rating profiles

Standard view ⌄

Rating profile ↑	Name	Shipping carrier	Site	Warehouse	Rate engine	Rate master	Transit time engine	Carrier fuel index
Air	Air	Air Cargo			P2PWeight	P2PMileageMaster	PointToPoint	
FlowerMoving rate	FlowerMoving rate	Flower moving			LTL	FlowerMovingMa...	PointToPoint	
LTL	LTL	LTL			LTL	FlowerMovingMa...	PointToPoint	
Ocean	Ocean	Ocean Carrier			P2PMileage	P2PMileageMaster	PointToPoint	
P2PMileageRating	P2PMileageRating	Point 2 Point Truck			P2PMileage	P2PMileageMaster	PointToPoint	
ParcelGeneral	Parcel General	ParcelCarrier			Milage	ParcelRateMaster	PointToPoint	
RailRatingProfile	RailProfile	RailCarrier			Milage	RailMaster	PointToPoint	
TruckRatingProfile	TruckRating	TruckCarrier			Milage	TruckRateMaster	PointToPoint	
USAPostal	USAPostal	Zone 2 Zone Truck			PostalZoneWeight	USAPostal	PointToPoint	

Figure 9.12 – The Rating profiles form

Here, we can create the rating profile, giving it a code and a name, after which we can link it to a shipping carrier (which we will be creating in the following sections of this chapter), a rate engine, a rate master, and a transit time engine.

With that, we have just created the rate structure of our TMS module. Before moving on, here are a few tips to keep in mind:

- Effective dates can be set in many of the forms we've seen but be aware of them because they can have undesired results. It is better to keep them blank until you have the desired result.

- We can set up rating profiles by site and warehouse. Again, it is better to start without those configurations until you have the desired outcome. Then, you need to set up one rating profile for each combination.

- Verify rating metadata when setting up rate masters.

- Choose the right data type for units when configuring break masters. If you're working with weight, choose kilograms, pounds, tons, and so on. If you're working with distance, choose miles or kilometers.

Now, we can configure the transportation standards, which are codifications for international transportation of goods such as classes, STCC, and NMFC codes.

Transportation standards

The transportation industry has standards, classifications, and notations that we can manage under the transportation management module.

LTL specifies **less-than-truckload** and is used when we ship various pallets but not enough to fill a truck and is a **National Motor Freight Classification** (**NFMC**) code that categorizes freight. There are 18 freight classes, ranging from 50 to 500, and every item shipped under the LTL class relates to one of those categories.

For example, if we ship wine cases on an LTL class shipment, we must categorize them as class 100.

This differs from **FTL**, which means **full-truckload**, and is used when we ship a dedicated truck full of pallets. In this case, we don't need to assign an NFMC code to that shipment.

We can assign the LTC classes in Dynamics 365 Supply Chain Management. Navigate to **Transportation management** > **Setup** > **Transportation standards** > **LTL Classes**:

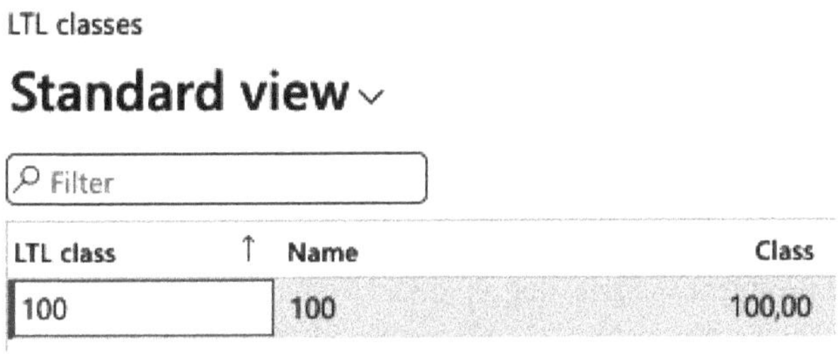

LTL classes

Standard view ⌄

LTL class ↑	Name	Class
100	100	100,00

Figure 9.13 – The LTL classes form

Figure 9.13 shows an example where we set up an LTL class for wine cases as 100.

Another transportation standard has to be with the **Standard Transportation Commodity Code** (**STCC**). This is a seven-digit number that represents the commodity within a shipment. Related to this STCC code are two corresponding codes: the harmonized commodity description coding system and a **Standard Classification of transported goods** (**SCTG**) category.

By navigating to **Transportation Management** > **Setup** > **Transportation standards** > **STCC** codes, we can create STCC codes, as shown in the following figure:

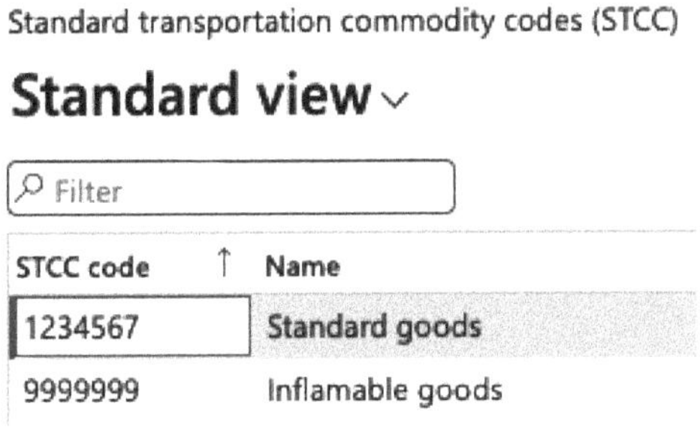

Standard transportation commodity codes (STCC)

Standard view ⌄

STCC code ↑	Name
1234567	Standard goods
9999999	Inflamable goods

Figure 9.14 – The Standard transportation commodity codes (STCC) form

In this case, we can specify a code and a description to fill that list.

We also can set up the **National Motor Freight Classification** (**NFMC**) code in the TMS module. This will complement the LTL class code we set up earlier. The NFMC code is classified based on various factors related to the shipped goods. For example, if we ship steel pipes, we will have an FTL class of 50 and an STCC code of 51200. This can be set up by going to **Transportation management** > **Setup** > **Transportation standards** > **NFMC codes**:

NMFC codes

Standard view ⌄

NMFC code ↑	Name	LTL class	BOL handling unit
100	Standard goods	100	Units

Figure 9.15 – The NFMC codes form

In this form, we can relate the NFMC code with the LTL class and the bill of lading handling unit.

Finally, we can associate those codes with a product by navigating to **Product information management** > **Products** > **Released products** and selecting a product from the list. On the selected product, we can go to the **Warehouse** tab and enter the NMFC code and the STTC code, as shown in the following figure:

Product details | Standard view ⌄

0002 : Adult Helmet Accessory Combo Set

General

Warehouse

NATIONAL MOTOR FREIGHT CLASSIFICATION	ADDITIONAL CODES
NMFC code	STCC code
100 ⌄	1234567 ⌄
	Harmonized system
	⌄

Figure 9.16 – Inputting transportation standard codes on the Product details form

Now that we have set up the rate parameters, we can move on to creating shipping carriers.

Shipping carriers

As we mentioned previously, shipping carriers are the companies that ship the companies' goods by charging their transportation services. In Dynamics 365 Supply Chain Management, we need to create those carriers and their services to perform rate and route activities on the TMS module.

To create a shipping carrier, we must go to **Transportation management** > **Setup** > **Carriers** > **Shipping carriers**:

Shipping carriers

Shipping carrier	Name	Mode
ParcelCarrier	The Parcel Carrier Company	TL

Overview

Activate shipping carrier	Tracking URL	Transportation tender type	Pro number sequence	Average container weight
Yes		None		0,00
Website URL	Vendor account	SCAC	Activate carrier rating	
	ParcelCarrier	PARCELSCAC	Yes	

Services

+ New 🗑 Delete

	Carrier service	Name	Load template ID	Transportation met...	Mode of delivery	External code	Billing group ID	Volume fac...
○	STD	Parcel Ground	Stnd Load Template	Ground	Parce-STD	PCG0001	Freight	0,00

Addresses

Rating profiles

+ New 🗑 Delete Rate master Transit time engine

	Rating profile	↑ Name	Site	Warehouse	Rate engine	Rate master	Transit time engine	Carrier fuel index	Effective
○	ParcelGeneral	Parcel General			Milage	ParcelRateMaster	PointToPoint		

Figure 9.17 – The Shipping carriers form

In this form, we've got a lot of information to input. Let's explain the most important sections and fields of *Figure 9.17*.

In the header section, we must set up the shipping carrier code and name.

Then, we have to select a shipment mode, which can be created by going to **Transportation management** > **Setup** > **Carriers** > **Mode**. In this example, we have selected TL mode.

In the **Overview** tab, we can specify the carrier details. If the **Activate shipping carrier** slider is set to **Yes**, it will let us use this shipping carrier on the shipments. The **Vendor** field relates this carrier to a vendor account to generate invoices and payments. Activating the **Carrier rating** slider will enable automatic rating for this carrier. We also have the **Transportation tender type** field, enabling the system to update the document manually or automatically via EDI.

In the **Services** tab, we can enter the carrier services details. Carrier services define the services offered by the shipping carrier. For example, a shipping carrier can offer ground service, next-day delivery, or second-day air service.

This tab allows us to enter a carrier service ID. The transportation method can be set up by navigating to **Transportation Management** > **Setup** > **Carriers** > **Shipping carriers** > **Transportation methods**.

We can also assign this service a mode of delivery and an external code related to the shipping carrier service code. Finally, we can associate a billing group with this service to group the billing activities of the carriers.

If we refer to *Figure 9.17*, The parcel carrier company offers a service named **Parcel Ground**, which has a **Ground** transportation method, and its mode of delivery is coded as Parce-STD. It also has defined a load template, which defines the load dimension that this carrier will use.

In the **Rating Profiles** tab, we can see the rating profiles associated with this shipping carrier. Those fields are the same as what we discussed in the **Rating Profiles** section.

We can group carriers by going to **Transportation Management** > **Setup** > **Carriers** > **Carrier groups**, as shown in the following screenshot:

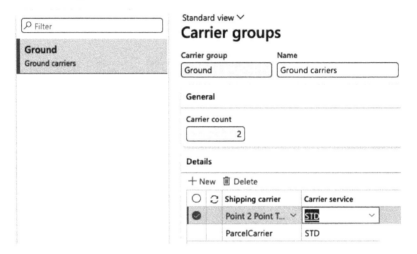

Figure 9.18 – The Carrier groups form

By doing this, we can group shipping carriers with their corresponding services, allowing them to also group transactions and functions in the TMS and WMS. For example, we can set up sales order consolidation policies by carrier group, grouping various shipments that are handled by those carriers.

With the carriers put in place, let's continue by reviewing how to plan and execute loads and shipments.

Build loads and plan shipments

As part of the transportation process, companies should consolidate shipments to build loads and deliver them to their customers. Consolidating shipments will help companies lower costs as they reduce the number of shipments. As we reviewed earlier, planning the loads is the first step of the transportation process.

As an important concept, a load is a group of goods transported together. It may be from different orders or shipments, so companies must optimize their loads into the right containers to save time and money.

To do so, Dynamics 365 Supply Chain Management has load templates.

Load templates

We can assign load templates to new loads to give that load information about equipment and measures such as height, width, depth, and volume. We can create templates to define the capacity of a container that carries goods. For example, if we are shipping frozen food, we can use a load template for that shipment with a refrigerated container and specific weight and volumetrics.

Navigating to **Transportation management** > **Setup** > **Load building** > **Load templates**, we can create different templates to apply to our loads, as we can see in the following form:

Standard view ˅

Load template ID	Equipment	Load height	Load width	Load depth	Max. allowed load volume	Max. allowed load weight	Max. allow...	Stack load ...	Allow load...	Maximum ...	Maximum ...
20' Container		120,00	100,00	240,00	2.880.000,00	15.000,00	0 ☑		☐	0,00	
40' Container		120,00	100,00	480,00	5.760.000,00	20.000,00	0 ☐		☐	0,00	
40' Frozen container	CFF ˅	120,00	100,00	480,00	5.660.000,00	20.000,00	0 ☑		☐	0,00	˅
Stnd Load Template		0,00	0,00	0,00	10,00	1.000,00	0 ☐		☐	0,00	

Figure 9.19 – The Load templates form

In this form, we can define the template ID and equipment. Then, we can define volumetrics such as height, width, and depth. Two other important fields are **Max. allowed load volume** and **Max. allowed load weight**, which will control that our goods fit into the container by volume and weight.

Now that all the setup is complete, we can continue with rate and routing, which is part of transportation planning.

Routing

Routing is one of the main components of the transportation process. It is used to plan the best shipping routes to deliver on time and with the best rates. Routing has several complexities and different approaches on a day-to-day basis.

To comprehend the routing process, TMS has two approaches – **static** and **dynamic** routing:

- **Static routing** is a fixed plan with predefined routes that are executed on specific days. For example, a company could ship to western warehouses on Monday and Tuesday and to eastern warehouses on Thursday and Friday. All orders are categorized and consolidated by that agenda, and picking is made the day before the shipments.

- On the contrary, **dynamic routing** has temporary breaks to consolidate shipments of the day and then execute picking works. For example, from 12:00 to 16:00, orders are accumulated. Then, we execute the route plan, consolidating all shipments and processing the wave release. The warehouse picks up those orders delivered the same or the next day.

In Dynamics 365 Supply Chain Management, there are four main components in routing:

- Routing guide
- Route plan
- Segments and route schedules
- Hubs and routes

These can be seen in the following figure:

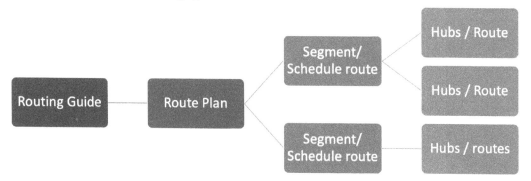

Figure 9.20 – Relationship between routing components

As shown in *Figure 9.20*, a routing guide has one route plan. A route plan can have multiple segments and route schedules. Segments and schedule routes can have multiple hubs and routes. We're going to break down these concepts into subsections.

Routing guide

Routing guides work as filters for the system to select the best routing plan for our shipments. It is the top of the pyramid when we're defining static routes and it will relate to shipment information to assign the route that complies with our shipment.

To define a routing guide, navigate to **Transportation management** > **Setup** > **Routing** > **Route guides**. We will find this form:

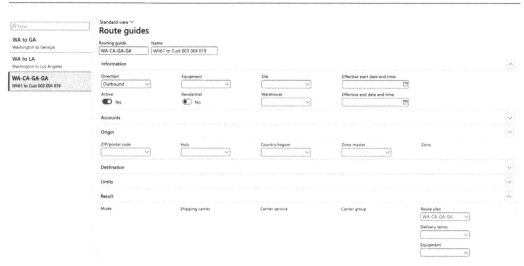

Figure 9.21 – The Route guides form

In this form, we can create a routing guide by clicking **New** and giving it an ID and a name.

In the **Information** tab, we can select **Inbound** or **Outbound**. This will filter up when working with rate and route processes, depending on the direction of the shipments. There is a third option called **None** that could work for both directions but is not recommended as it creates more processing for the routing engine.

The active slider can turn this route guide on and off, but as we mentioned when we talked about rate profiles, we can define a site/warehouse and effective dates for this route guide. Again, starting this setup by restricting this configuration is not recommended. It's better to leave those fields blank and then, if needed, create various route guides by site or warehouse.

Then, we have the **Accounts** tab, where we can restrict by customer or invoice account.

All the other tabs work the same as filters for assigning routes to the shipments: the **Origin** tab will let us filter by postal code, hub, country, and zone, the same as the **Destination** tab. The **Limits** tab can filter shipments by volume, weight, and number of containers.

The **Results** tab is mandatory as it will link this route guide to a mode, shipping carrier, service, group, and route plan. Attaching a route plan to this route guide will assign our load to the desired route.

Route plan

The route plan contains specific segments, stops, carriers, and information about the route. For example, if we need to define a route from Washington to Los Angeles, we can use a hub to store the items midway and then another trip to the destination. This could be executed by different carriers with different services. In the same example, we can ship our goods by train to San Francisco and then use a ground service to Los Angeles.

We can access the route plan from the route guide form by viewing the details of the route plan field or by navigating to **Transportation management** > **Setup** > **Routing** > **Route plans**, where we can access the following form:

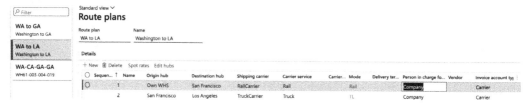

Figure 9.22 – The Route plans form

Here, we can create a route plan, and we can add each trip segment in the **Details** tab. Those segments detail the route and carriers used to transport the goods. We can specify the hubs that are used to unload the cargo or container on each segment. Those hubs can be vendors, customers, or even a company warehouse. If we click the **Edit hubs** button, we can create the hubs we need and assign them to a vendor or a customer. Each hub had a specific type, a rate master, and an address.

We can also specify rates for those segments by clicking the **Spot rates** button. Those rates can be charges related to the hubs, for example, an unloading charge at the dock or handling rates of the hub. Using this route plan will add the spot rate to the transportation rates.

Once our route plan is finished, we must create the route schedule.

Route schedule

This schedule works with the routes that use static routing and occurs regularly. For example, every Monday, we ship to LA. To do this, we can enter the route plan form right into the route schedule at the top of the screen. We will see the following form:

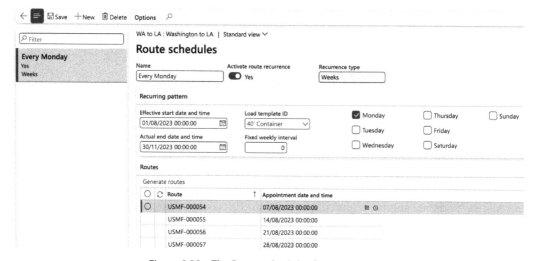

Figure 9.23 – The Route schedules form – example

In *Figure 9.23*, we created a route schedule for the WA to LA route plan. In the **Recurring pattern** tab, we must specify the start and end dates and the recurrency that's needed. As shown in *Figure 9.23*, we set up a route every Monday from August 1 to November 30. When we hit the **Generate routes** button, this will create every route with an appointment.

We can create these as scheduled routes, and loads can be assigned using the load building workbench form. This will suggest loads that can be assigned to the route based on addresses and delivery dates.

On the contrary, non-schedule routes are created from the rate route workbench, and loads are assigned manually on the same form.

Let's continue by discussing the load planning workbench and load building workbench.

Load planning workbench

The load planning workbench is a form in the system that allows us to plan our loads so that we use fewer freights to deliver our goods. This form will take everything we've set up earlier to consolidate our shipments as best as possible.

One thing to notice is that the load planning workbench is universal, meaning we can use it for sales and transfer shipments and purchase orders. This book will center on sales orders, but the same process applies to every order type.

This functionality best suits dynamic routing as we construct the loads when the orders arrive, and we can consolidate shipping using the load templates and, once confirmed, release picking to the warehouse. For example, we can access the load planning workbench, identify all sales order lines that need to be shipped to Los Angeles, and consolidate them together, assigning them to a container and shipping them.

As a requirement for using this workbench, we need to have sales orders created before we can create the loads.

Let's create a load and process the shipment. For this example, we created two sales orders for a customer located in Georgia from our warehouse in Washington.

We must navigate to **Transportation Management** > **Planning** > **Load Planning Workbench** to access the **Load planning workbench** form:

Figure 9.24 – The Load planning workbench form

This form shows all sales order lines (or shipments) that have to be delivered on a certain shipping date. The information is taken from each sales order line. The top of the form has various controls to filter the information, such as the supply and demand filter, which can be preset and selected for quick filtering. There is also a site and warehouse filter to group by location and, finally, ship and receipt date to filter orders by date.

In the first table, we can see all order lines yet to be assigned to a load. We can select the lines and navigate to the **Supply and demand** tab, click the **Add** button, and go to a new load option to do that.

Once there, we must select a load template. Which is the container where the cargo is assigned. In this dialog, we can control the container's weight and volume and see if they fit into that container, as shown in the following figure:

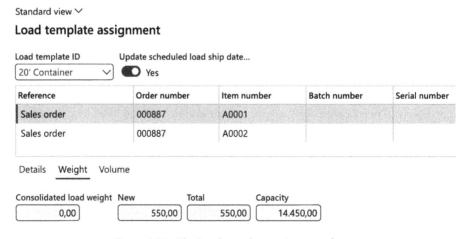

Figure 9.25 – The Load template assignment form

Once the load template has been selected and the load is OK, we can click **OK** to create the load.

This will bring us to the load template workbench again, and both order lines will disappear. At the bottom of the form, as shown in *Figure 9.25*, a new load will be created with the shipping information, and the load will have an **Open** status. From here, we can click on **Release** > **Release to warehouse** to send the information to the warehouse, where workers can start the picking work. This will change **Load status** to **Posted**, and once the wave is released, it will change to **Waved**.

Parallel to that action, we can rate and route our load by navigating to **Rate and routing** > **Rate route workbench**.

This will navigate to a new form that searches for all the routes and ratings this load can use. We will see the following form:

Figure 9.26 – The Rate route workbench form

We will find four options to work with this form:

- **Rate**: This option will search for all carrier services and return the lowest possible rate for our load.
- **Rate shop**: This will search for all carrier services and return all possible options for this load. We can select the ones that are the best suited here.
- **Route**: This will show all available routes for this shipment.
- **Rate and route**: This will search and return all available routes and their corresponding rate.

The TMS module works with three planning scenarios:

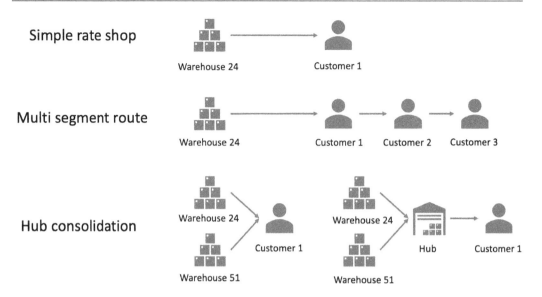

Figure 9.27 – Load planning scenarios

- **Simple rate shop**: This will rate a shipment from the warehouse directly to a customer

- **Multi-segment route**: This will rate a route that has different drop-off points for different customers.

- **Hub consolidation**: We can consolidate different loads into one truck or a hub and then ship it to the customer

Simple rate shop

We can work with the rate and route workbench for the simple rate shop scenario. As it is a manual option, we can aboard this option the best way we consider. For example, it is better to try the **Route** or **Rate and route** option in **Static routing** as it will be assigned to a previously created route. On the contrary, it is better to use the **Rate** or **Rate shop** options for dynamic routing to control shipments by rating them.

Be aware that we have a **Criteria fast** tab that can filter rates and routes from the search. In our example, we can assign an LTL mode because our shipment only partially fills a truck. This will reduce our shipping costs.

The returned information will be shown in the following tabs when we click any of the four options:

- The **Route results** tab will show rates and routes available for this shipment. Selecting the **Hide exception** option will only show the available information and hide the routes unsuited for the load.

- The **Segments** tab will show the segments for the selected route. For example, *Figure 9.24* shows the segments for the route from Washington to Georgia.

Once we have decided on a route and rate, we can click the **Assign** button, which will bring the rate and route to the selected load to the load planning workbench and create the route. We can see this in the following form:

Figure 9.28 – The Routes form

As shown in *Figure 9.28*, a route was created for our load; it has a rate of 1,300 USD, an appointment date on August 18 at 7 A.M., and the two segments in sequence:

1. First, it will travel from our warehouse to the San Francisco hub by RailCarrier.

2. Then, it will travel from San Francisco to Georgia via TruckCarrier.

Multi-segment route

As we have seen, a multi-segment route refers to a unique load with multiple drop-off destinations. To use it, we have to create a route plan with the customer we have scheduled to visit. We did this setup earlier when we discussed the route plan, but as a reminder, we can navigate to **Transportation management** > **Setup** > **Routing** > **Route plans** to reach the **Route plans** form:

Figure 9.29 – Multi-segment route plan example

As shown in *Figure 9.29*, we defined a multi-segment route plan that has three customer directions:

- From warehouse 61, which is in WA, to LA

- From LA to GA

- From Abbeville, GA to Alpharetta, GA

The origin and destination hubs have the postal codes and cities configured, so if we need to deliver a product into those postcodes, it will be assigned to this.

It is important to note that because we can create a route plan by postal code and map all deliveries in a scheduled route, the transportation management module will assign those shipments automatically to this route. We can go to **Route schedules** and give a recurrence. In this example, I've generated routes every Tuesday, as we did in the schedule routes segment of this chapter.

To test this out, I've created the following sales orders as an example:

Customer	Order	Item	Quantity	Shipping Date	Route Plan
US-003	000894	A0001	55	This Tuesday	1
US-003	000895	A0001	30	Next Tuesday	2
US-003	000896	A0001	13	This Tuesday	1
US-004	000897	A0001	25	This Tuesday	1
US-004	000898	A0001	34	Tuesday in 3 weeks	3
US-005	000899	A0001	21	This Tuesday	-
US-019	000900	A0001	100	This Tuesday	1

Table 9.1 – Sales orders line example

Given these seven orders, we want transportation management to group orders in the first week with route plan 1, which will be shipped this Tuesday.

Let's navigate to **Transportation management** > **Planning** > **Load building template** to process the shipments of those orders:

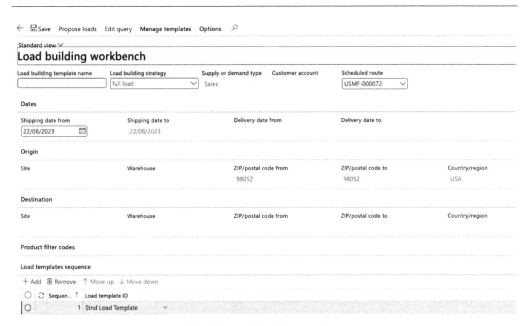

Figure 9.30 – The Load building workbench form

As shown in *Figure 9.30*, we start by selecting the load-building strategy, which is a full load, and then the scheduled route. Those scheduled routes were created when we generated routes in the route plan we created in the previous step.

Is mandatory to add a load template in the **Load templates sequence** tab. This will review each sequence and locate the best load template for our shipments.

Once this form is completed, we can click the proposed **Loads** button; it will show the proposed load for orders 000894, 000896, 000899, and 000900, which are shipped on the first Tuesday:

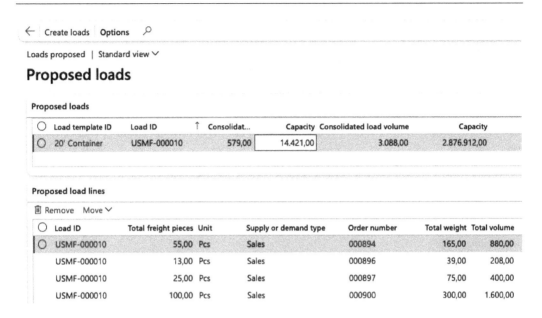

Figure 9.31 – The Proposed loads form

Once we have confirmed the load, we can hit the **Create loads** button to create the load for shipment. Here, we can release work to the warehouse to start the picking work.

Hub consolidation

Hub consolidation is the process of shipping from different warehouses to a hub, then consolidating the loads into a new one, and finally shipping to the customer.

To archive this process in the TMS module, we need to activate the **In transit planning** option from the **Transportation management parameters** page. Then, we need to create the hubs where consolidation will occur.

This process starts the same as the previous ones, where we navigate to the **Load planning workbench** form and create new loads for each order to be consolidated.

Once loads have been created, and before shipping, we can select the load and click on the **Transportation menu > Hub consolidation** option. This will allow us to change the destination to the consolidation hub or warehouse. This will create transportation request lines on the **Load planning workbench** form, as shown in the following figure:

Figure 9.32 – Transportation request lines

We can select those transportation request lines and create a new load to ship to the final customer.

To review this last process, if we ship from warehouse 21 to an LA customer and form warehouse 61 to an LA customer too, we will create the following:

1. The first load from warehouse 21 to LA.

2. The second load from Warehouse 61 to LA.

3. Perform hub consolidation to an LA hub.

4. Create a third load from the LA hub to the LA customer.

Let's move on to the remaining steps of the transportation process.

Appointment scheduling

We can schedule an appointment for the drivers to pick up the load at a certain time and date.

To do so, we can navigate to **Transportation management** > **Planning** > **Load planning workbench**, select the load, and choose the **Transportation menu** > **Appointment scheduling** option, as shown in the following figure:

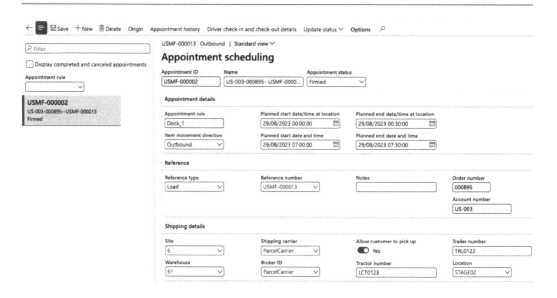

Figure 9.33 – The Appointment scheduling form

This will have two main objectives:

- Plan order preparing works to locate the cargo in an outbound dock at a certain time
- Register driver check-in and check-out information

When we release the picking work, we can configure warehouse management location profiles to deliver those goods to the appointed dock.

We can also create warehouse management menu items to perform driver check-in and then driver check-out activities and control how long it takes for the workers to load certain trucks.

With the truck loaded, we can print the bill of lading from the **Load planning workbench** form and click the **Generate** button or navigate to the shipment. Finally, we can confirm the shipment to end the transportation process once the truck has been loaded and is ready.

Now, we're going to move on to the freight reconciliation process, where we will match vendor invoices with each route.

Reconciling freight bills and invoices

When we confirm our shipment, a freight bill is generated with the estimated costs calculated by the rate engine. As this bill is estimated, we can have differences between what is charged on the bill and what comes in the shipping carrier invoice, which could affect the costs of the sales order, for example.

Not to mention that, daily, companies receive tons of carrier invoices that need to be matched with every associated shipment.

This is commonly known as the **freight bill reconciliation** or **matching process**. There are two ways to perform freight reconciliation: manually or automatically. We must set up parameters to use automatic reconciliation to define the criteria that match bills with invoices.

For a better understanding, the TMS within Dynamics 365 proposes the following process for freight reconciliation:

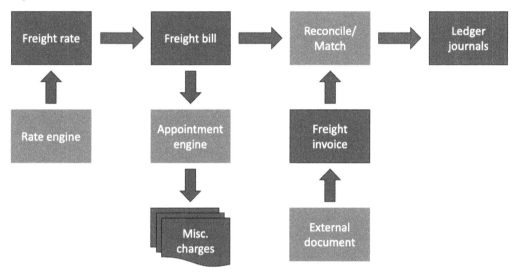

Figure 9.34 – The freight reconciliation process

The freight rate is calculated by the rate engine and is associated with the shipping carrier. Once the load has been confirmed, a freight bill is generated containing the rates calculated in the previous step. These are the estimated values for the freight. This bill updates the related order miscellaneous charges – it could be a purchase order, sales order, or transfer order.

Then, an external document, such as an invoice, arrives from the shipping carrier with the actual values and is created as a freight invoice to the system. Here, we can start the reconciliation process, where we match the invoice received with the freight bill. And finally, this reconciliation ends up in a ledger journal that updates the financial module.

Let's begin by setting up the module parameters for this feature.

Configuring freight bill reconciliation

The first thing we must do is activate the freight bill reconciliation parameters. Navigate to **Transportation management** > **Setup** > **Transportation management parameters**. Under the **General** tab, we will see the following:

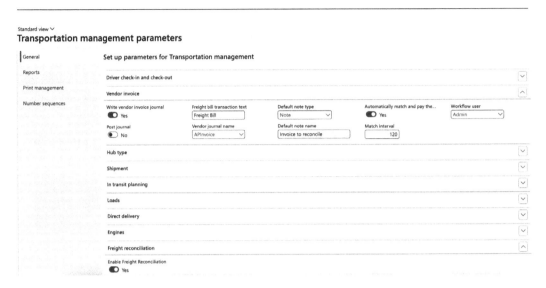

Figure 9.35 – Freight reconciliation options under Transportation management parameters

Enable freight reconciliation parameter must be activated to use this feature in the TMS module. Under the **Vendor invoice fast** tab, we have several options to control the freight reconciliation process, such as the vendor journal name, which will be used for matching the vendor invoice. The first two options, **Write vendor invoice journal** and **Post journal**, will control the vendor journal's behavior on the reconciliation's automatic pay process. Finally, the **Automatically match and pay the freight invoice** option will activate automatic reconciliation. It is recommended to start by doing the manual process; once we've checked that the freight reconciliation is working correctly, we can activate it and monitor its behavior.

Another mandatory setup is **Billing groups**, which we can find under **Transportation Management > Setup > Freight reconciliation > Billing groups**.

This is a very basic setup; we have to create a billing group ID and a name, as shown in the following figure:

Standard view ⌄

Billing group ID ↑	Name
Freight	Freight
Fuel	Fuel

Figure 9.36 – The Billing groups form

It is recommended to create billing groups based on how our carrier bills us and which categories carriers are invoicing. This will ease the reconciliation process.

Then, we can set up the freight bill types by navigating to **Transportation Management > Setup > Freight reconciliation > Freight bill types**. This form will set up the required fields matching the carrier invoice and our bill. As shown in the following figure, we added two fields – **Billing group** and **External code**:

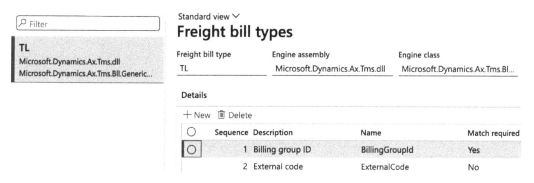

Figure 9.37 – The Freight bill types form

There are two important things to notice here. First, the freight bill types are validated by an engine that is initialized with the engine parameters under **Transportation management parameters**. Also, you will notice the **Match required** field, which controls, for example, if the billing group ID is required to be the same between the invoice and the freight bill. We must have one **Match required** field in the sequence, but if we create another one with **Match required** set to **No**, the engine will use them to help match information between documents.

The freight bill assignments will assign the direction, mode, and shipping carrier to a freight bill type, so when we perform the reconciliation, it will use the fields that have been set up in the freight bill type to control the shipping carrier and mode. We can set up this parameter by going to **Transportation management > Setup > Freight reconciliation > Freight bill type assignments**:

Freight bill type assignments

Standard view ⌄

🔍 Filter

Direction	Mode	Shipping carrier	Site	Warehouse	Freight bill type
None	Ground	Flower moving			TL
None	Ground	Point 2 Point Truck			TL
None	Ground	Zone 2 Zone Truck			TL
None	TL	ParcelCarrier			TL
None	TL	TruckCarrier			TL
None	Rail	RailCarrier			TL

Figure 9.38 – The Freight bill type assignments form

As shown in *Figure 9.38*, we can filter up by site and warehouse, but leaving them blank is recommended for easier reconciliation.

In case there's a variance between the freight bill and the carrier invoice, TMS will register a journal with the variances. This journal will use the accounts that have been configured in the **Reconciliation reasons** form, which we can find by going to **Transportation management** > **Setup** > **Freight reconciliation** > **Reconciliation reasons**:

Reconciliation reasons

Standard view ⌄

Reconciliation r... ↑	Description	Debit account	Credit account	Pay the freight vendor	Override accounts
Approved	Approved	211650--		✓	
Damage claim	Damage claim	211650--	200110		
FB Underage	FBUnderage	211650--	200110		✓
FBMapping	FB Mapping	211650--		✓	

Figure 9.39 – The Reconciliation reasons form

Here, we have to set up a reason, debit, and credit account. However, if we activate the **Pay the freight vendor** option instead of using a credit account, it will charge the variance to the vendor.

To do this, the shipping carrier must be related to a vendor in the shipping carrier master.

The last parameter is **Audit masters**, which we can find by navigating to **Transportation Management** > **Setup** > **Freight reconciliation** > **Audit masters**:

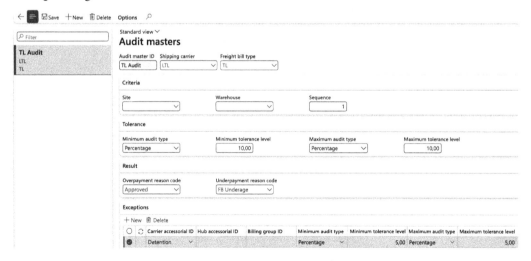

Figure 9.40 – The Audit masters form

Audit masters controls the tolerance amount or percentage of the variance between the carrier invoice and the freight bill. In the **Result** tab, we can associate the reason codes for overpayment and underpayment of the system to use those financial accounts.

Finally, we can add accessorial IDs with different tolerance levels in the **Exceptions** tab.

Manual reconciliation

To do the manual reconciliation process, we must confirm our shipment. This will generate our freight bill with the carrier rates. We can see this information by navigating to the load, and then going to **Transportation > Related information > Freight bill details**:

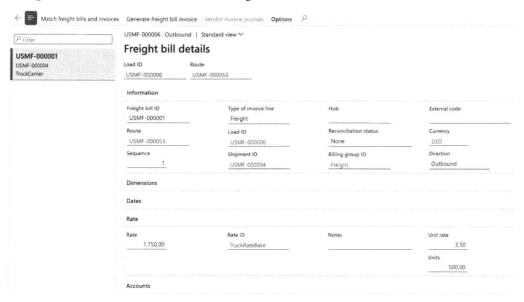

Figure 9.41 – The Freight bill details form

Here, we can find the bill's details, along with rates and vendor accounts. We can register the carrier invoice from here by clicking **Generate freight bill invoice** at the top of the form.

This will show a dialog box asking for the carrier's invoice number. Once completed, we can hit **OK**. This will process the invoice creation and allow us to review the information and register any extra charges, as shown in the following figure:

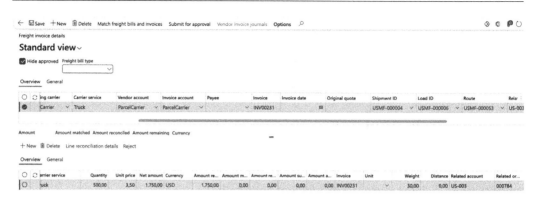

Figure 9.42 – The Freight invoice details form

To perform manual reconciliation, we can navigate to **Transportation management** > **Freight bills and invoices** > **Match freight bills and invoices**. This will open a dialog where we can filter all bills and invoices by any information we want. For example, if we want to filter by carrier and date, we can do so to have less information in the form. Once confirmed, we will end up in the following form:

Freight bill and invoice matching

Show submitted or approved   Freight bill type
● No

Invoice header   ∨

Invoice details   ∧

	Workflow status	Internal invoice ↑	Net amount	Currency	Amount re...	Amount m...	Amount re...	Shipping carrier	Type of invoice line	Freight bill type	Invoice	Unit price	Quantity	Unit	:
○	None	USMF-000000002	1,750.00	USD	1,750.00	0.00	0.00	TruckCarrier	Freight		INV00231	3.50	500.00		

Matched freight bill details   ∨

Unmatched freight bill details   ∧

Match   Freight bill details   Discard

	M...	Freight bill ID	Route	Sequence	Shipping carrier	Direction	Type of invoice line	Freight bill type	Rate	Currency	Amount re...	Amount m...	Rate ID	(:
○		USMF-000001	USMF-000053	1	TruckCarrier	Outbound	Freight		1,750.00	USD	1,750.00	0.00	TruckRateBase	500,0(

Figure 9.43 – The Freight bill and invoice matching form

This form is divided into two parts. At the top, we have the invoice details, and at the bottom, we have the unmatched freight bill details.

What we have to do here is select the invoice and the bill and click on the **Match** option to reconcile both documents. Then, we can submit it for approval, and the journal will be posted.

If any differences occur between both, we must select a reason for the difference that determines how this difference will be posted in the general ledger.

If multiple reasons exist, we can split the difference and assign different reasons, which will be posted to different accounts in the general ledger. Once the complete amount has been reconciled, we can submit it for approval, and the journal will be posted.

Automatic reconciliation

Once the freight bill and invoice have been registered, we can activate the **Invoice is ready for automatic matching** option in the **Freight invoice details** form.

We must navigate to **Transportation management** > **Freight bill and invoice** > **Auto match batch to process automatic reconciliation**. Here, we can process the automatic reconciliation by demand or schedule a periodic batch to process automatically.

Once this process has been executed, we can go to the **Freight bill details** form to see the results of the auto-match batch. The workflow status of the invoice will change to **Ready to process** when matching occurs, and we can see the amount reconciled and the remaining. If everything is OK, we can submit it for approval.

Advanced TMS parameters

To close this chapter, we will discuss a few advanced parameters, tips, and tricks that are important to understand when working with the TMS module.

Defining constraints

We can define constraints to control items, shipments, or carriers to apply restrictions. For example, certain carriers won't ship hazardous materials, so we can set up a constraint there.

Another example could be a carrier that is not allowed to visit certain customers. We can navigate to **Transportation management** > **Setup** > **Routing** > **Constraints** to set up constraints:

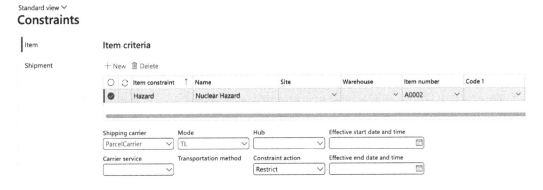

Figure 9.44 – The Constraints form

In this example, we are configuring a hazard constraint to **ParcelCarrier**, on item **A0002**, and restricting the creation of loads with this combination.

Transportation tender

A transportation tender is a document for keeping track of the dates and rates that have been approved for customers, vendors, and the shipping carrier. We can create this document on various entities – for example, from a route, a load, or a route segment.

By navigating to **Transportation management** > **Planning** > **Transportation tenders**, we can create the transportation tender and keep track of the updates, as shown in the following screenshot:

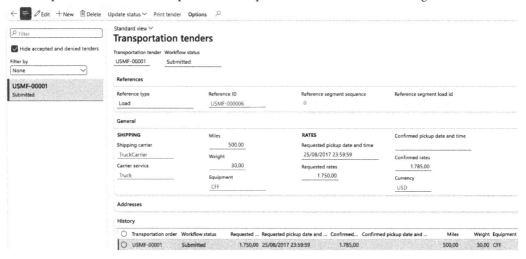

Figure 9.45 – The Transportation tenders form

Once confirmation of the carrier arrives, we can modify the transportation tender with the confirmed details, such as rate and pickup dates. Under **Update status**, we can confirm or deny this tender.

Small parcel shipping

Small parcel shipping is a functionality that enables direct communication with carriers via API to send sales orders. It is not recommended to use it when you're shipping containers or LTL services.

When we activate this functionality, we can interact with our carrier with a dedicated rate engine that we need to develop. It is not out-to-the box functionality.

To activate it, we first need to develop or obtain a dedicated rate engine. Microsoft provides an example rate engine for small parcel shipping on GitHub: `https://github.com/microsoft/Dynamics-365-FastTrack-Implementation-Assets/tree/master/SCM/SPS`.

Once we've downloaded that rate engine, we need to save it in the Supply Chain Management server, in the `\AOSService\PackagesLocalDirectory\ApplicationSuite\bin` folder.

Once we've saved the engine, we need to create a new rate engine by navigating to **Transportation management** > **Setup** > **Engines** > **Rate engine**.

As we are working with a new engine, in the **Engine assembly** field, we need to enter the DLL of the new engine. In our example, this is `TMSSmallParcelShippingEngine.dll`.

The same happens for the field rate engine class as we need to enter the class of the new engine: `TMSSmallParcelShippingEngine.SmallParcelShippingRateEngine`.

Once the rate engine has been created, we need to set up a new carrier that works with the created rate engine.

Tips and tricks

Let's look at some helpful tips and tricks for working with this module.

Rating

- Leave the site and warehouse blank on the rating profile setup to ensure inventory dimensions do not filter rating profiles. Also, leave effective dates blank in rate base and rate base assignments.
- Verify the metadata on the rate master to ensure a proper rating.

Routing

- Define the direction of the routing guide. This will help with the performance of the routing engine.
- Populate the address on hubs to ensure routing will validate the customer address against hubs.
- Activate recurrence on route schedules to create routes periodically.

Freight reconciliation

- Remember to configure billing groups based on carriers. This will help with automatic matching.
- Leave the site and warehouse blank when setting up freight bill-type assignments. This can help with understanding matching logic.
- Set manageable tolerances on audit master. If we set tolerances to low, auto-matching will need to approve every difference before processing, which will take a lot of effort.

Summary

In this chapter, we covered the steps in configuring a TMS module, enabling a company to manage its shipping operations efficiently.

We started by defining rating parameters to ensure precise rate calculation. Then, we explored route planning via both static and dynamic routing methods, such as simple rate shop, multi-segment route, and hub consolidation. Finally, we discussed the freight reconciliation process, which verifies that carrier invoicing matches route execution.

With the knowledge you've gained from this chapter, you will be able to set up and execute inbound and outbound transportation processes, rate and route load internally and for carriers, and work with advanced TMS processes such as multi-segment routes and hub consolidation.

In the following chapter, we're going to start reviewing the master planning module and dive into how companies plan their item requirements and ensure they receive, stock, and process them on the planned dates.

Questions

Answer the following questions to test your knowledge of this chapter:

1. You are implementing the TMS module.

    You need to explain to workers what the rating process does to a load. Which of the following statements is correct?

    A. The rating determines the load costs and methods of delivery for a load.

    B. The rating determines the sequence and path a load will take to reach the destination.

    C. The rating will use appointment scheduling and freight reconciliation.

2. You are implementing the TMS module.

    The warehouse manager asks you to manage the dock doors properly, not only to assign the shipments to a dock but also to track loading times. Which functionality is recommended?

    A. Driver check-in.

    B. Appointment scheduling.

    C. Warehouse receiving.

3. You are implementing the TMS module.

    You need to propose a routing method to ship goods from different warehouses, then group those goods into a new container and ship them to the final destination. Which routing planning method do you propose?

    A. Simple rate shop.

    B. Multi-segment route.

    C. Hub consolidation.

Answers

Here are the answers to this chapter's questions:

1. Option A. The rating determines the load costs and methods of delivery for a load.
2. Option B. Appointment scheduling.
3. Option C. Hub consolidation.

10
Master Planning Implementation – A Guide to Streamlining Operations

Master planning, also known as **material resource planning** (**MRP**), is a process that allows companies to plan all materials and manage stocks according to the company's needs to improve the manufacturing or distribution of their product and services. The main objective of MRP is to ensure that the company has all the required materials to address manufacturing and customer demands.

MRP methodologies came to address a common problem at companies: stock breaks. At first glance, it seems as simple as someone saying, "Let's raise stock levels to ensure we never run out of stock." But this solution is too costly as we need tons of inventory, a lot of warehousing space, and a lot of money invested in rarely used inventory.

To be cost-efficient, MRP reduces the stock level by raising the level of service to reduce manufacturing and delivery times, and it gives vital information to the company so that it can address different types of problems, such as delays in purchase deliveries or production lines that cannot work due to a machine breakdown.

In this chapter, we will dive into the master planning module, the solution that Dynamics 365 Supply Chain Management proposes to implement MRP methodologies and techniques in a company.

In this chapter, we're going to cover the following topics:

- Understanding the master planning scope and advantages of planning optimization
- Setting up coverage groups and master planning parameters
- Understanding forecast plans, master plans, and continuity plans
- Running a master plan, reviewing its orders, and working with messages

Introduction to master planning

An MRP system or module works to determine the need for material requirements and the organization's capacity to meet the company's goals. By measuring the level of complexity, we can distinguish different types of master planning.

MRP works tightly with the manufacturing area and can calculate item requirements to meet demand-based production goals. MRP II has a broad scope that considers the market demands and makes plans based on the company's departments' requirements. It also considers procurement, sales, QA, and finance.

Demand Driven Material Requirements Planning (**DDMRP**) is another type of master planning that upgrades the MRP II type by considering dynamic demands and having stock buffers to ensure inventory despite market fluctuations.

All these types help companies assess the following information:

- Production materials and resource capacities that are needed.

- Materials that are currently available.

- Operations and materials that are needed to meet goals. These can be translated into purchase, manufacturing, and transfer orders.

To be able to propose this information, Master Planning takes data from different areas:

- Demands from sales orders

- Demands from sales quotations

- Demands from production orders

- Demands to meet safety stocks

- Demands from sales and procurement forecasts

Dynamics 365 Supply Chain Management introduces a master planning module that has been around for a while.

The master planning module was introduced in earlier versions of Axapta and was kept as-is for a while. However, in late 2021, planning optimization was introduced to replace the classic master planning engine. The difference between the classic master planning engine and planning optimization varies in where it runs.

We, the oldest of the consultants, remember that implementing master planning in Ax2012 was quite a headache because we had to make a lot of volumetric considerations when running a master plan.

Most of the time, master planning runs had a 4 to 6-hour execution. So, we recommended scheduling master planning runs outside office hours. On a day-to-day basis job, this was problematic because we wouldn't be updated on modifications to the plan until the next day.

This problem is no longer an issue with planning optimization because it has improved performance and minimal impacts on the SQL database during master planning runs. The following figure explains the difference between both architectures:

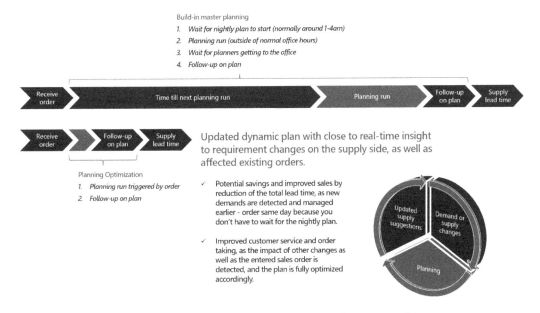

Figure 10.1 – Planning optimization architecture from Microsoft Learn

As shown in *Figure 10.1*, the classing, or built-in master planning, receives an order, and we must wait until the next planning run. This was commonly scheduled off office hours. Then, there was the planning run, where we had to wait for planners to follow up on the plan.

With planning optimization architecture, master planning runs are executed outside Dynamics 365 Supply Chain Management as the planning optimization service is located in the same data center or region as the supply chain instance. This allows for faster processing, reducing planning times from 4 hours to approximately 10 seconds.

> **Note**
> The downside of planning optimization is that it won't be available for on-premises implementation or cloud-hosted environments.

I strongly recommend using planning optimization, as well as Microsoft does. The main reason is that you can run master plans and see results within seconds, instead of getting results the next day. This allows planners to react quickly to demands or parameter changes.

How can we activate planning optimization?

As a prerequisite, this environment must be a tier-2 or greater environment and a Power Platform integration should be enabled for this environment:

1. We must access LCS, sign into the desired environment, and then go to the Full Details option. Under the Environment add-ins fast tab, we can click the Install a new add-in button and select Planning Optimization.

2. We must follow the installation guide and agree to the terms and conditions there. After that, we must select Install. This will trigger the installation, which we can control the progress of in the Environment add-ins fast tab. After a few minutes, planning optimization will be installed in the environment.

3. Then, we must log into Dynamics 365 Supply Chain Management and navigate to Master Planning > Setup > Planning Optimization parameters to activate planning optimization.

Now, let's start by explaining plans and master planning strategies.

Master planning concepts and setup

Master planning has multiple concepts and parameters to discuss. As we explained previously, this module allows companies to plan suggested orders or planned orders as a result of the inputted demands.

To understand how master planning works, let's look at the following diagram:

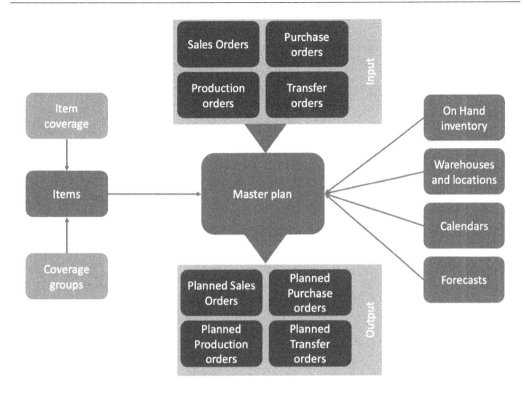

Figure 10.2 – Master planning flow

As shown in *Figure 10.2*, master plans are affected by various sources of information:

- **Item coverage and coverage groups**: These are the basis of item planning and control of how we cover our stocks. For example, we can cover all the demand for an item monthly or by each requirement that the item has.

- **On-hand inventory**: This affects the master plan and specifies if we need to re-stock our items.

- **Warehouses and locations**: Depending on how we set up coverage, we can control our stock by site, warehouse, or location. This is useful to prevent movements between those entities.

- **Forecasts**: If we set up a sales forecast, this will add the forecast demand to the plan and calculate the items needed for those items.

The inputs are all the placed orders that a master plan covers. For example, a sales order adds for demand to be covered, and a purchase order decreases that demand because it is taken for inventory to be received in the near future.

The results of the master plan are shown in the **Output** area of the preceding figure and are the proposed or planned orders to be executed to achieve demands.

In a nutshell, master planning groups all demands that come from placed orders or the forecast and, depending on the coverage setup in the items, returns the planned orders to be placed and executed. Let's break down these concepts in order and learn how to set them up in Dynamics 365 to understand how they work.

Coverage groups

Coverage groups define how the demand for items is covered. Here, we define how to replenish, manufacture, or buy products. For example, we can create a planned purchase order for each sales order we had to cover that demand, or we can go with 30 days of stock to cover all the sales order demands.

This can be set up under **Master planning** > **Setup** > **Coverage** > **Coverage groups**:

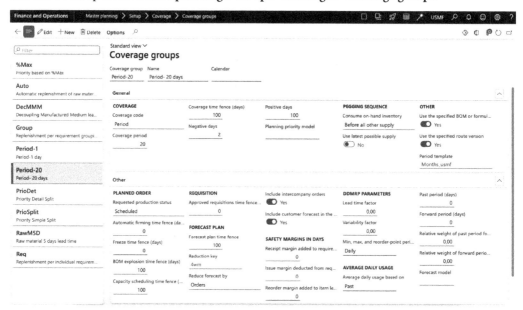

Figure 10.3 – The Coverage groups form

There are six types of coverage groups:

- **Manual**: Here, we don't plan the coverage of the items. This means that the master planning module won't create planned orders for items with this coverage group.

- **Requirement**: This type defines that for each demand we have, the system will plan an equal planned order to address that demand. For example, if we have a sales order next week for 10 units of item 1, master planning will suggest a planned purchase order for 10 units of item 1. We can see an example of this in the following figure:

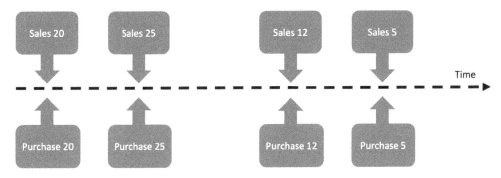

Figure 10.4 – Requirement coverage group example

- **Period**: Here, the system will create one planned order for the sum of every demand in the given period. For example, if we set up a period coverage of 30 days, and when we have a demand of 10 units of item 1 on day 10 and 5 units of item 1 on day 15, master planning will create one planned purchase order of 15 units of item 1 to cover the cumulated demand. When we work with this coverage type, we need to input a coverage period in days to define the coverage of the items:

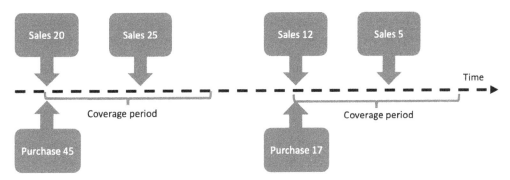

Figure 10.5 – Period coverage group example

- **Min/max**: This type will have a minimum and maximum quantity setup by item. When demands in place drop the stock levels under the minimum, the system will create a planned purchase order to raise that inventory level to the maximum. For example, if item A0001 has 5 units on hand with a minimum of 10 and a maximum of 30, master planning will place a planned purchase order of 25 to raise the stock to the maximum:

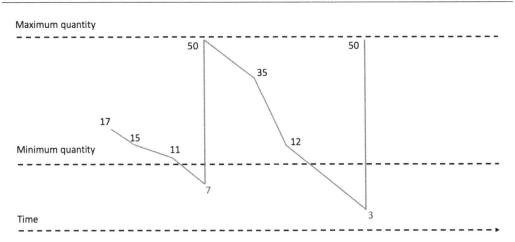

Figure 10.6 – Period coverage group example

- **Priority**: This type of coverage group works with DDMRP and instead of working with requirement dates, it will prioritize orders to generate planned orders. We will discuss this type of planning in the next chapter when we talk about DDMRP.

- **Decoupling point**: As before, the decoupling point is a coverage group that works under the DDMRP methodology and will measure stock levels in a certain period to cover dynamic demands.

When we set a coverage type in our coverage group, we must define how we want the items to be covered by master planning. We can have different scenarios for different items.

For example, if we have to store liquids in a silo, a min/max coverage group is recommended because we cannot store more than the silo's maximum capacity. Alternatively, if we have multiple low-quantity demands for an item, it is better to work with periodic coverage to group those demands in a unique purchase order and have discount benefits with our vendors.

If we look at the coverage form in *Figure 10.3*, we can mention various fields:

- In the **Coverage time fence** field, we set the days the system will look up demand to create planned orders. In the example, it is set to 100 days, meaning that it will plan for the demand of those 100 days.

- **Positive days** defines how far in the future the system will consider the inventory on hand to fulfill a demand. For example, if we have 10 units of item A0001 in our inventory and the coverage group has 100 positive days, it will consider 10 units for the following 100 days. If a demand appears on day 101, a planned supply order will be created to address that demand, and on-hand inventory won't be considered.

- **Negative days** defines how late a supply order will be considered to fulfill the demand. For example, if we have a sales order 14 days from now and a purchase order 16 days in the future, we can use that purchase order to fulfill the sales order if we set up 2 or more negative days. Before configuring this field, we need to ask ourselves if we want master planning to consider those existing supply orders, even if they are after the requirement date of our demand.

- The **Consume on-hand inventory** field controls when we plan to consume on-hand inventory, before or after all other supplies. In most cases, it is recommended to consume before all other supplies so that we use the inventory in stock first.

In the **Other** tab, we can find the following relevant fields:

- **Requested production status**, which controls which status the production order will be created when the planned order is firmed.

- **Automatic firming time fence**, which will automatically firm planned orders when they reach that time fence.

- **Time fence**, which will block planned orders on the defined days; this cannot be modified by any user. This is useful when working with long lead times.

- **Bom explosion time fence**, which explodes the bill of materials of the manufactured items that are in the defined time fence.

- **Capacity scheduling time fence**, which schedules manufacturing resources when the orders reach the time fence.

- **Safety margins**, which will add or deduct days on the planned orders for the internal jobs to handle orders and inventory. For example, if our warehouse has a working day to process the receiving orders, we need to set up one day in the **Receipt margin added to requirement date** field of the coverage group.

It seems to be too much information in one little form but coverage groups are the beating heart of the master planning module. Understanding this part will give us a complete understanding of the module. Let's look at a full example. We are going to plan for item A0001. This item is purchased and sold directly in one warehouse to make things easy.

We will set up the following coverage group:

- **Coverage type: Requirement**
- **Coverage time fence: 100** days
- **Negative days: 2** days
- **Positive Days: 50** days
- **Receipt margin added to requirement date: 2** days

We have the following orders:

- On-hand stock for 50 units

- A purchase order on day 10 of 15 units

- A sales order on day 20 of 45 units

- A sales order on day 55 of 100 units

When we execute the master planning, this will happen:

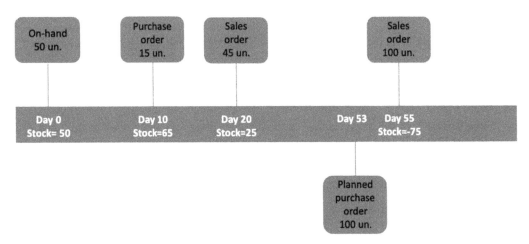

Figure 10.7 – Coverage group planning example

As we can see, with this information, the system knows that the first sales order is going to be covered by the on-hand stock and the purchase order, so there's no problem there, but to cover the sales order on day 55, we will not have available stock, so we need to purchase more. Master planning will propose a planned purchase order of 100 units to cover the sales order requirement. But why 100 and not 75 units? This is where positive days come in place. Positive days have a time fence of 50 days, and our sales order is on day 55, so the system cannot use the on-hand stock available to cover that order. That's why it will plan a purchase order of 100 units, raising the stock from 25 to 125 units, and after the sales order is delivered on day 55, the stock will drop to 25 units.

As we are not working in this example with lead times, the planned purchase order is created 2 days before the sales order because we set up a receipt margin, and that is deducted from the requirement day.

But what will happen if a sales order of 55 units is created on day 5?

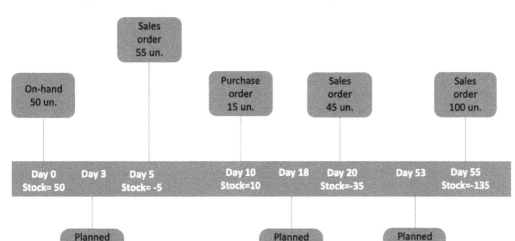

Figure 10.8 – Coverage group planning example

When we add those sales orders and run the master planning process, it will create two new planned purchase orders, as shown in *Figure 10.8* – one on day 3 to cover the stock needed for the sales order on day 5 and another planned purchase order on day 18 for 30 units to cover the sales order on day 20. As order placing is a dynamic process, changes may occur, so it's important to run master planning periodically.

Another thing to notice is that as we plan with a requirement coverage group, demands are evaluated separately, so the system creates three purchase orders. If we plan with a periodic coverage group of 50 days, demand will be added, and a purchase order will be created on day 3 for 35 units to cover the three sales orders on the 5th, 10th, and 20th days.

Associating a coverage group with an item

Associating a coverage group with an item is mandatory to plan the item the way we want. To do that, we must navigate to **Master planning** > **Setup** > **Item coverage**, where we will find the following form:

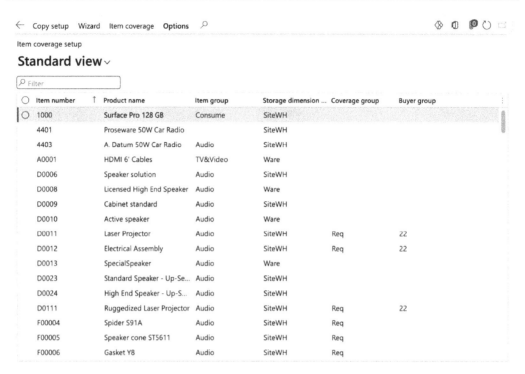

Figure 10.9 – The Item coverage setup form

Here, we can associate an item with a coverage group. To do that, we have two options. Looking at *Figure 10.9*, we have the **Copy setup** button. This will copy the setup of another item to the selected items. For example, if we need to copy the item's D0011 coverage group to item D0023, we must first select item D0023 and click on **Copy setup**, and then, in the dialogue that appears, select item D0011 to copy from.

If we click on **Wizard** instead, the system will guide us to configure coverage groups for sites and items across our company and to new coverage rules, such as overriding the coverage code or periods for the selected items and setting lead times and inventory levels. We will dive deep into these options in the next section. Once completed, the selected option will apply to all items.

Planning parameters on item master

Navigating to the released product form, we will find a plan section at the top of the form that will allow us to set up specific configurations for our items. Let's click the **Default order settings** button. We will find the following form:

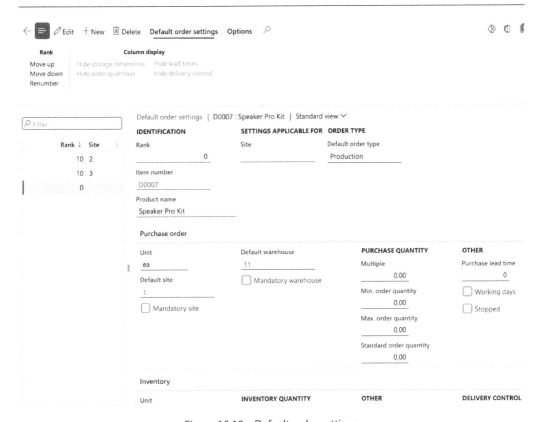

Figure 10.10 – Default order settings

In this form, we will define the default order configuration for the item. This is item-specific.

Here, we have a header in which we can set global parameters, and for each type of order (purchase, inventory, and sales), we can default specific information.

We have a vital field in the header: **Default order type**. This controls the supply order that master planning will create when run; it could be a production order, a purchase order, or a Kanban.

Then, moving to the **Purchase order** tab, we can find the default warehouse and a section for purchase quantity, which will control how quantities are managed when creating an order.

Here, we will find the following fields:

- **Multiple**: The default quantity in which an item is purchased
- **Min. order quantity**: The minimum quantity allowed for the order
- **Max. order quantity**: The maximum quantity allowed for the order
- **Standard order quantity**: The quantity we to default when a purchase order line is created manually

These quantities are used when we run master planning. For example, if we set **Multiple** to 10, **Min. order quantity** to 50, and **Max. order quantity** to 100, and we need 35 units, the system will create a planned order of 50 because the minimum order quantity is 50; if we need 67, it will create an order of 70 because it has a multiple of 10.

Moving on to the next important field, we have **Purchase lead time**, which is the time between an order being placed and the item arriving at our warehouse. The master planning module takes this information to calculate when the order needs to be created to arrive on the required date at the warehouse. If we activate the **Working days** option, lead time days will be only working days.

Finally, the **Stopped** option will block purchases for this item. The same fields repeat on each section of the form.

> **Note**
> It is important to note that production orders will be controlled by the **Inventory** parameters set in the **Default order settings** form.

As shown in *Figure 10.7*, to the left of the form, we have a rank that we can create to disaggregate those settings. Another planning parameter to be aware of is the item coverage on the item master.

If we navigate to **Coverage** > **Item coverage**, we will find the following form:

Item coverage, Site: 2, Warehouse: 24 | D0007 : Speaker Pro Kit

Standard view ⌄

Overview   General   Lead time   Min./Max.   Dimension   Buffer values   On-hand

○ ↻	Site	↑	Warehouse	CW minim...	Minimum	CW maxim...	Maximum	Coverage group
	1				0,00		0,00	Req
	2		21		100,00		500,00	Req
✅	2	⌄	24 ⌄		50,00		100,00	Req
	3		32		75,00		150,00	Req

Figure 10.11 – The Item coverage form

In this form, we can set up, for example, different coverage groups for sites and warehouses in our company. For example, let's say we need to plan by requirements in one warehouse and by period in another one. If we click on the **New** button, we can create that setup, and the setup created by the item coverage wizard will be stored here.

If we move to the **General** tab, we will have access to the specific information about the coverage of the item in the selected inventory dimension:

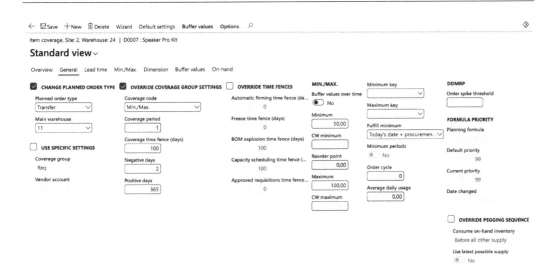

Figure 10.12 – The Item coverage form, the General tab

In this form, we can override certain parameters we set up in the **Default order settings** form. One of the main parameters here is the planned order type for this specific warehouse. For example, if we purchase the item in a specific warehouse and then distribute it to other facilities, we can override the order type to transfer. This will create a transfer order instead of a planned purchase order.

We can also modify the coverage group, the coverage group settings, and the time fences that this item has inherited from the coverage group.

Here, we have a crucial field called **Minimum quantity** that works as a safety stock, meaning that the quantity that's configured here is held in the inventory to prevent running out of stock. The **Minimum key** and **Maximum key** fields are used to control the seasonality of an item when using a min/max coverage group. For example, T-shirts are sold better in the summer seasons, so with those keys, we can modify the minimum and maximum values depending on that.

Another important field is the **Fulfill minimum** field, which is also used when using a min/max coverage group. This field defines the period during which the inventory level must meet the minimum quantity. In this form, we can define parameters for DDMRP runs, such as **Order cycle** and **Order spike threshold**. We are going to focus on DDMRP in the next chapter.

Configuring a master plan and master planning module

Now that we've set up coverage groups and items, let's focus on the master planning module's configuration. First, we need to create master plans. A master plan is an organization's requirements planning and has the setup to guide the system in calculating those requirements.

We can create any number of master plans that we want in Dynamics 365. For example, if we want to have an optimistic view of a sales forecast and a pessimistic one, we can create two master plans to focus on those views. To create a master plan, go to **Master planning** > **Setup** > **Plans** > **Master plans**; you will find this form:

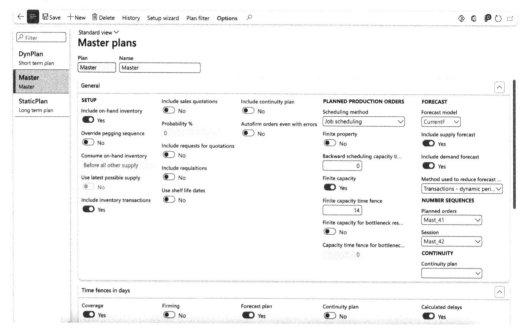

Figure 10.13 – The Master plans form

Master plan configurations are divided into various tabs. In the **General** tab, we have the setup segment, in which we can configure the general behavior of the master plan:

- **Include on-hand inventory**: If activated, the master plan calculation includes on-hand inventory of the item. If deactivated, the master plan will create planned orders for items already in stock.

- **Include inventory transactions**: If activated, the master plan calculation will include all transactions, such as inventory journals, sales, purchase, production, and transfer orders that are not yet physically registered.

- **Include sales quotation**: If activated, it includes a sales quotation in the master plan calculation. Once enabled, the **Probability** field will be cleared, and we can select a probability percentage. Those sales quotations with a probability percentage equal to or higher will be included in the calculations.

As master planning connects with production modules, we have parameters that control how planned production orders will be created:

- **Scheduling method**: Select the scheduling method for planned production orders generated by the master plan. Operation scheduling will give us scheduling without assigning resources, and job scheduling will provide scheduling in detail.

- **Finite property**: When creating planned production orders, master planning will validate that the resource property matches the planned production order.

- **Backward scheduling capacity time fence**: This defines a period in days from the requirement date, in which master planning will search for available capacity. If no capacity is found, it will be scheduled forward from the requirement's date.

- **Finite capacity**: Planned production orders will be created while considering the resource capacity.

- **Finite capacity time fence**: This defines a period, in days, in which master planning will schedule planned production orders with finite capacity. Forward from that time fence, infinite capacity will be used.

Another segment in the master plan form is **Forecast**, which controls how we can include forecast provisions in the master plan's calculation:

- **Include supply forecast**: This will include the supply forecast in the master plan calculations. This supply forecast must be defined in the forecast model that's been selected for this plan.

- **Include demand forecast**: Same as the supply forecast, this will include the demand forecast in the master plan calculations.

- **Method used to reduce forecast**: This controls how planned orders will be planned when there are firm orders. For example, if the sales department inputs a quantity of 10 of item A0001 for January in the forecast model, and a sales order for item A0001 of 3 units in January is created, what will happen with the quantities in the forecast plan? We have the following options:

  - **None**: Quantities will not be reduced. It will keep creating planned orders for 10 units in the forecast plan and also for the 3 units that we have in the sales order.

  - **Percent – Reduction key**: This will reduce quantities based on the percentages defined in the reduction key. In this example, if we have a reduction key of 50% in January attached to this product, it will plan a quantity of 5.

  - **Transaction – Reduction key**: This will reduce quantities based on the transaction in the periods. Following the same example, this will be for January.

  - **Transaction – Dynamic period**: This will reduce quantities by transaction based on the periods, but those could be Dynamics 365 – for example, 5 days or 3 weeks.

- In the **Time Fences in Days** tab, we can control time fences for the calculations. Each time fence will have an activation button to override the coverage group's time fence. Let's review some examples:

  - If a coverage group has a 100-day coverage time fence, and the master plan has an activated coverage time fence of 30 days, 30 days will be planned

  - On the other hand, if we define a coverage group with a 100-day coverage time fence, and the master plan has an activated coverage time fence of 150 days, then 100 days will be planned

The **Calculated delays** tab controls until which point in the future master planning will detect and notify delays in planned orders. If the required date for an order cannot be met, the order can be fulfilled at the earliest requirement date based on factors such as lead times, material availability, and capacity.

All the options in this tab have an **Add the calculated delay to requirement date** option. This option works in the following way:

- If set to **Yes**: The delay is added to the requirement date. This means that if a delay is detected, a new date is calculated automatically for the planned demand. This option is recommended when we use the capacity to promise date calculation in the orders because those orders depend on the manufacturing process.

- If set to **No**: The requirement date is maintained. However, if action messages are activated, this planned order will receive messages to alert the delay to the planner.

Select the **Update postponed date as requirement date** option under the **Action message** tab to automatically update planned purchase orders with the proposed action date. The action date must not be later than the requirement date.

The **Safety margin in days** tab works the same as what we reviewed in the coverage groups. In this case, **Safety margin days** will be added to the ones on the coverage groups:

- Adding days to the **Receipt margin added to requirement date** field will add days to the requirement date of the supply orders. If we set 5 days in the receipt margin and 3 days in the coverage group, a purchase order with a receiving date on the 10th of the month will be planned for receiving on the 18th (10 + 5 + 3 days).

- In the same way, the **Issue margin deducted from requirement date** field will deduct days from the requirement date of the issue orders. If we set 5 days in the issue margin and 3 days in the coverage group, a sales order with a delivery date on the 10th of the month will be planned for delivery on the 2nd (10 - 5 - 3 days).

If we need to create a master plan, we can create one manually or we can execute the setup wizard, which will guide us through the fields in an explanatory way for a better understanding of what we are configuring.

Once our master plan has been set up, we can follow the **Master planning parameters form** to define how the master planning module behaves. Navigate to **Master planning** > **Setup** > **Master planning parameters**. You will reach the following form:

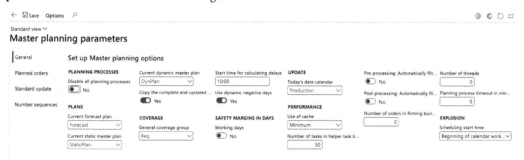

Figure 10.14 – The Master planning parameters form

As shown in *Figure 10.14*, we can set up options to control how master planning works. In the **General** tab, the first option is to disable all planning processes. This works as a master switch that deactivates all the master planning runs. Then, we can define the default master plans – the forecast plan to calculate forecasts and the static and dynamic master plan to calculate requirements. We have the option to copy the complete and updated master plan to the dynamic master plan; this will copy the static plan to a dynamic plan every time we run the static plan. When planning with a two-plan strategy, static plans are used for long-term planning, and dynamic plans are used for everyday planning. Copying static to dynamic plans will help keep both plans current.

> **Important note**
> Planning optimization does not support copying static to dynamic plans. Even if we set it up in this form, because of the speed of the planning optimization, we can configure each plan separately.

There are some other important fields here:

- **General coverage group**: This will default to the coverage group when creating a new item. It is used automatically if we don't specify any coverage group for an item.

- **Dynamic negative days**: This is used to include the remaining item lead time in the negative day calculation.

- **Working days and Today's date Calendar**: This defines the calendar that's used to run master planning. It also controls if we plan only working days or a full week. Remember that each coverage group can have a different calendar to work with.

In the **General** tab, we have a segment where we can control configuration that affects performance – for example, the number of tasks in helpers or the number of threads. Also, pre-processing and post-processing will ease the weight of the master planning run.

If we move to the **Planned orders** tab, we will find the following setup:

- **Find trade agreements**: When working with planned purchase orders, it will find valid trade agreements to apply to the planned purchase orders

- **Search criterion**: If multiple trade agreements apply, it will be selected depending on this criterion: *minimum lead time or lowest unit price*

In the **Standard update** tab, we have the following:

- **Update marking**: This defines the inventory policy when firming orders. If we select **No**, no marking is made. Selecting **Standard** will mark inventory according to the pegging, and if we select **Extended**, the requirement order and the fulfillment order will be marked.

- **Stop firming if an error occurs**: This will stop the firming of an order in case of an error. If we are firming more than one order, it will stop firming all orders.

The four following fields are for grouping planned orders on firming. **Group by vendor**, **Buyer group**, or **Purchase agreement** will consolidate orders that are from the same vendor, buyer group, or purchase agreement. **Group by period** will consolidate transfer orders of the period defined here.

Now that we have most of the module set up, I want to dive into the action messages that master planning gives the planner.

Action messages

These messages are generated in the master planning calculation and warn the planner when it has changed requirements. For example, the quantity or delivery date of a sales order that we already created in the fulfillment purchase order might change, so master planning gives the planner one or more action messages to update the purchase order. However, it is up to the planner to modify the suggested changes.

Action messages are activated in the coverage groups under the **Action messages** tab, as shown in the following screenshot:

Figure 10.15 – Action messages in the Coverage groups form

As we can see, **Action messages** can be activated by setting its parameter to **Yes**. It also works with a time fence. For example, if our coverage group is set to 100-day coverage, but we only want to have action messages for the first 50 days, we can set the action time fence to 50. As with every time fence in the master planning module, the same is defined for **Postpone margin** and **Advance margin**.

Basis date is from the date the action messages are calculated. We can select **Requirement date** or **Delayed date**. Then, we can activate or deactivate which messages we want to receive for this coverage group. To understand them, let's look at the following table:

Message	Description
Advance	Upon selecting this option, master planning will generate a message to request moving orders to an earlier date. In the Advance margin field, we can specify a time fence to receive those messages.
Postpone	Upon selecting this option, master planning will generate a message to request a moving order to a later date. In the Postpone margin field, we can specify a time fence to receive those messages.
Decrease	Upon selecting this option, master planning will generate a message to request a decrease in the quantities of supply orders to prevent an excess in inventory levels.
Increase	Upon selecting this option, master planning will generate a message to request an increase in the quantities of supply orders to prevent a break in inventory levels.
Derived actions	Upon selecting this option, master planning will generate a message to request modification for derived requirements – for example, actions in purchase orders that fulfill a production order.

Table 10.1 – Action messages

These messages appear in the master planning run and we can accept or ignore the suggestion. Let's move on and learn how to run a master plan and work with planned orders.

Running a master plan and working with planned orders

We've been talking about master plans, calculations, coverage groups, and multiple other concepts, but we've not seen how Dynamics 365 shows planned orders. So, let´s dive into it.

With the created plans and coverage groups, I will first explain the process of running a master plan. Then, we will review which information the orders will give us and how to work with those planned orders.

Master planning will generate supply orders to address the demand. To understand these concepts, we must state that the demand can come from different sources, with the most known being sales orders. However, forecast demand, transfer orders, sales quotations, and project item requirements contribute to the demand. To address those orders, master planning creates planned purchases, planned productions, planned transfers, and planned Kanban orders.

For example, if a forecast is created for an item we store in a different facility, a planned transfer order could address that demand.

Running a master plan

To run a master plan, we need to go to **Master Planning** > **Run** > **Master plan**. The following dialogue will appear:

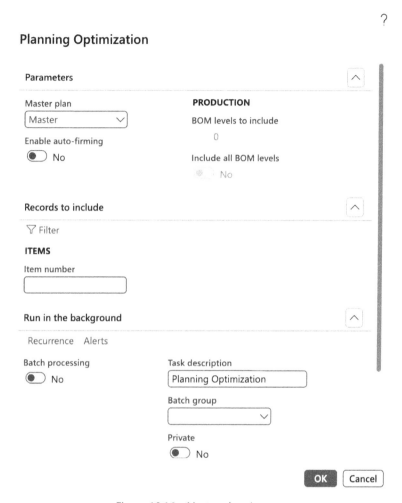

Figure 10.16 – Master planning run

As shown in *Figure 10.16*, we can select a master plan to run, and then we can choose **Enable auto-firming**. If we do, it will automatically firm the orders that fall into the firming time fence.

We can also set batch processing for the master plan. Remember that it will take a long time to process if we don't activate the **Planning optimization** feature, so **Batch processing** is recommended.

> **Important note**
>
> Note that in the figures and examples of master planning provided, I have the **Planning Optimization** feature activated, as shown in *Figure 10.16*. If you are working with the deprecated master planning engine, some calculations may differ.

Once we hit **OK**, the master plan will be executed. When the process has ended, it will show a notification in the Action Center at the top of the screen marked with a bell icon.

Running a master plan for a subset of items

Master planning lets planners set up filters to limit the set of items included in a planning run. To do this, we can identify two types of filters:

- **Plan filters**: We set up these filters in the master plan
- **Runtime filters**: We can set these up in the planning optimization run dialogue, as shown in *Figure 10.16*

To set up a plan filter, we can navigate to the master plan form by going to **Master planning** > **Setup** > **Plans** > **Master plans**. Then, we can select the plan and click on the **Plan filter** button at the top of the form. Here, we can limit the set of products that are included in the master planning run.

A runtime filter is set up when running a master plan. We can filter an item or group of items in the dialogue box by clicking on the **Filter** option. When setting up a plan filter and a runtime filter and combining them, only the intersection of both filters will apply.

For example, let's say we set up a plan to include items A, B, and C, and we run master planning filtering for the following scenarios:

- **Scenario 1**: Runtime filter includes item D

  Result: No items are planned because there is no intersection between filters.

- **Scenario 2**: Runtime filter includes items A and D

  Result: Only item A is planned. Item D is not in the plan filter.

- **Scenario 3**: Runtime filter includes item B

  Result: Item B is planned. All other items are not planned because they are included only in the plan filter.

- **Scenario 4**: Runtime filter includes all items (blank filter)

  Result: Items A, B, and C are included, but item D is not planned because only the first three items are in both filters.

Now, let's review the planned orders.

Planned orders

We can see the results by navigating to **Master Planning** > **Master planning** > **Planned order**. We will find this form:

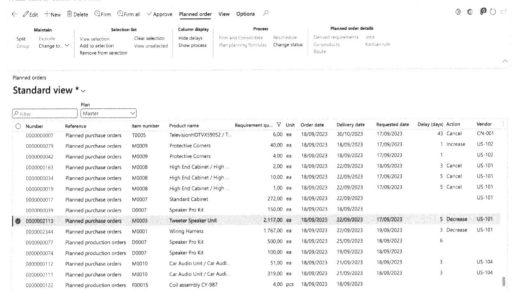

Figure 10.17 – The Planned order form

Here, we will find all the planned orders created by the master plan run. The first thing to notice in this form is that we can select the plan to filter the planned orders. If we work with a static and a dynamic plan, we can change the plan from the filter and the different orders will be shown.

In the grid, we can view the planned orders. We can differentiate them via the **Reference** field, which indicates the planned order type. Then, we can see the item, quantity, and unit of measure of the order. Here, we have three important dates:

- **Order date** is the date that the order needs to be firmed.

- **Delivery date** is the date that the order will be delivered.

- **Requested date** is the date that the system requests to move the order to. This can be for advance or delays.

Then, we can see the order delay in days and the action message. If we select this order, we can access detailed information, as shown here:

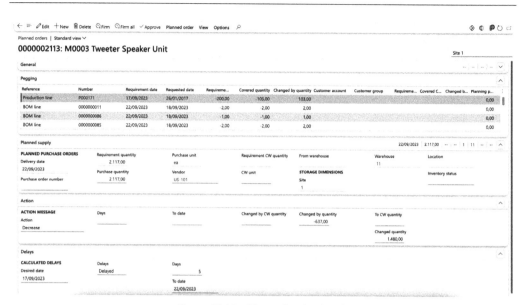

Figure 10.18 – Planned order details

As shown in *Figure 10.18*, we can see the order's detailed information:

- First, in the **General** tab, general details are shown, such as the planned order number and item information, such as number, variant, and name. Then, the requirement, scheduled, and order dates are shown. One important field here is **Status**, which will control what happens with this planned order. In this case, it is unprocessed, meaning it will be erased once the following master planning run is executed.

- Moving on to the **Pegging** tab, we can see which demand or demands the master planning considers for creating this planned order. *Figure 10.18* shows that a production order and BOM lines need this item to be purchased.

- The **Planned supply** tab shows information about the quantity and dates of the planned order. For example, **Requirement quantity** is the needed quantity, while **Purchase quantity** is the quantity that will be planned to be purchased. They can be different if we set multiple and minimum order quantities in the default order settings of this item.

- Finally, the **Action** and **Delays** tabs show the messages of this order. *Figure 10.15* shows an action message of decreasing the quantity of 637 units, totaling a quantity of 1,480 units. Also, it suggests delaying the date by 5 days from 09/17/2023 to 09/23/2023.

> **Important note**
>
> It is important to note that every planned order is no more than a plan or suggestion the system proposes to the planner. But none of these orders will modify or block any of the processes related to master planning. For example, if we don't firm these orders, nothing will happen with purchasing orders. We can create them manually as well.

Viewing and editing planned orders

If we go back to the planned orders form, as shown in *Figure 10.17*, we have various buttons to process these orders:

- **New**: This lets us create a planned order. First, we must select the type and fill in the remaining mandatory fields, such as order date, item, and quantity.

- **Delete**: This will delete a planned order. However, if we run the master plan again, it may be created because a demand requires it.

- **Firm**: This will firm the order and create it in the correct module. For example, if we firm a planned purchase order, a purchase order with the same information will be created and the planned purchase order will be erased.

- **Firm all**: This will firm all planned orders.

- **Approve**: This will approve the order and change its status to **Approved**. This will ensure that the approved orders will not be erased when running the master plan again. For example, if we modify a planned purchase order of 10 units to 20 units and approve it, when running the master plan again, this order will not be erased or modified in any way, and it will remain with the 20 units.

These buttons help us control the planned order life cycle, as shown in the following figure:

Figure 10.19 – Planned order statuses

When the master plan runs or we create a new order, the status given to that order is unprocessed and will be deleted the following time the master plan is run. We can manually change its status to **Completed** to indicate that the planned order has been reviewed and modified if necessary. However, we must keep in mind that completed orders will be treated as unprocessed and erased on the next master plan run. If we approve an order, we are indicating that the order has been approved for firming. If an order has the approved status, it won't be deleted the next time there's a planning run. It will be copied exactly from the old plan version to the new one during master planning. Once an order has been firmed, it will be deleted from the master plan version and created in the related module.

There is no defined flow for these statuses. We can move from unprocessed to approved or directly firm the order. We can maintain the order from the **Planned order** form. If we navigate to the **Planned order** tab, we have the following options:

- **Split**: We can split the order into multiple ones. For example, if we have a planned production order of 1,000 units but can process only 100 units with our current stock and capacity, we can split this order into one of 100 units and another of 900 units with this function. In the dialogue, we need to input the delivery date for the split order.

- **Group**: We can group various orders into one, but we must consider certain requirements. For example, if we need to group two planned purchase orders, they must be from the same vendor, and the same item number can be grouped.

- **Explode**: If we select a planned purchase order, we can explode and plan its components. The requirement for this option is that the planned order must be approved.

- **Change to…**: we can change the planned order type in this option. For example, if we have a planned production order and we cannot produce it, we can change that order to a purchase order and process it with a local vendor.

Planned order inquiries

We can view information about the order if we navigate to the **View** tab in the **Planned orders** form. By clicking the **Gantt chart** button, we can access the following form:

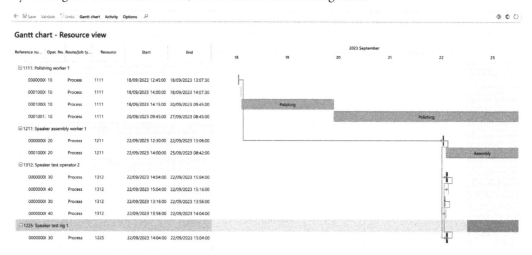

Figure 10.20 – Gantt chart view

Here, we can see the resource planning for a planned production order and the time each operation and resource takes place in a calendar view. By entering the **Gantt chart** option, we can customize this report to change the view's content and the time scale.

Entering the **Requirements** profile under the **Requirement** section, we can review the net requirements of this item, as shown in the following figure:

Figure 10.21 – Requirements profile

This inquiry lets us filter by plan. In the first part of the form, each warehouse and site has coverage setups, such as coverage group and planned order type.

Down to the second grid, we have all the firm and planned orders arranged by requirement date. If we look at the **Accumulated** column, we can see how the stock moves between orders. When this quantity falls below zero, we have a stock out, meaning we must take action to restore that stock. The last grid in the form shows the pegging demand related to the selected order in the second grid. This helps us trace the demand behind the orders. If we make some changes, at the top of this form, we have an **Update** button that lets us run master planning without leaving this form.

Last, but not least, we also have the **Explosion** inquiry in the **Requirements** section of the **Planned orders** tab:

Figure 10.22 – Explosion form

Here, we can see a planned purchase order explosion, which means we can drill down by its bill of materials and understand if the inventory needed to manufacture that order will be on the production order's requirement date.

In the first part of the form, we can see the different levels of the bill of materials. The ones that are written in bold letters are still planned, so we need to firm or work on the planned orders. The other ones have on-hand inventory ready to use or depend on a firm order.

When we click on a line in the bill of materials, the other two grids will look up the information related to that line. The first grid shows the related order or on-hand inventory. The second grid shows the pegging information of the order. This form gives the planner a 360-degree view of the materials needed for the order.

If we move to the **Critical on-hand inventory** tab, we will see if we have critical inventory to consider; for example, we have on-hand inventory, but another order reserved it.

Now that we understand the master plan's behavior, let's review the safety stock functionality.

Safety stock journals

Safety stock journals are part of the functionality to review the minimums of an item and calculate it based on historical transactions. Multiple times, due to stationary demands, minimums rise and fall and we need to update those minimums to feed master planning with accurate information.

We need at least 3 months of historical data to work with this journal because less information is not considered meaningful.

To create a safety stock journal, we need to navigate to **Master planning** > **Master planning** > **Run** > **Safety stock calculations**. Upon clicking **New**, we will reach the following form:

Figure 10.23 – Safety journal example

Under **Journal lines**, we can click the **Create lines** button. This will open a dialogue that asks us for a time frame to use as historical data. Then, an option to calculate standard deviation can be activated. This option is mandatory if we want to calculate safety stock based on the level of service.

After clicking **OK**, the grid will be populated with the items that had movements between that time frame, and the current minimum will be shown in the proper column. Then, we can click on the **Calculate proposal** button to calculate the new minimum inventory level. Again, a dialogue will appear, asking you to choose between two calculations:

- **Use average issue during lead time**: This will calculate the new minimum values based on the average issue during the period specified. In the **Multiplication factor** field, we can adjust the result. Upon entering **1.0**, it will use the exact calculated quantity; using 1.2 will add a 20% buffer.

- **Use service level**: We can set a percentage of service level to set our minimum.

We can use the calculated minimum as the new minimum quantity. This will replace the new minimum column with the calculated minimum on the form.

Then, we can click **OK**. As shown in *Figure 10.23*, the calculated minimum will be populated. When we post this form, the minimum quantities of the item will be replaced by the new minimum on the item master.

Demand forecast lines

Most companies set a sales goal for the year or a period, which is translated by a demand forecast. Here, sales departments declare how many quantities for an item they are willing to sell; this can be the main input for master planning.

We can create the forecast demand by navigating to **Master planning** > **Forecasting** > **Manual forecast entry** > **Demand forecast lines**. We will reach the following form:

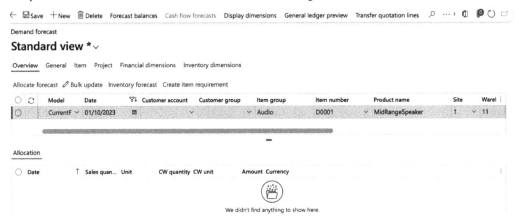

Figure 10.24 – The Demand forecast form

We can input one line for each item and date. For example, if we look at *Figure 10.24*, we can see that for 10/01/2023, we plan to sell 550 units of item D001. This will impact our forecast plan and our master plan calculations because we will have a demand of 550 units in October.

We can allocate forecasts to expand our forecasted units into more than one period. For example, we can repeat 550 units every month until the end of the year. This will display the following forecast balance:

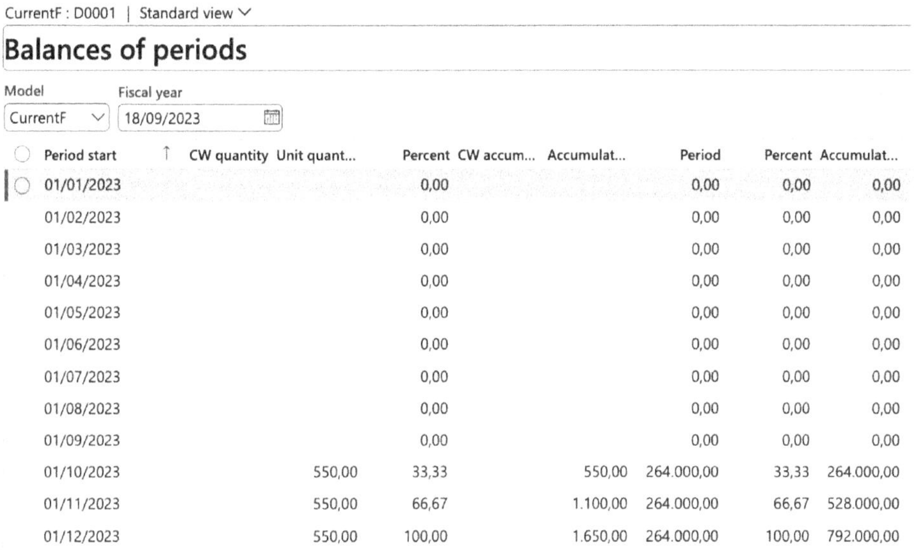

CurrentF : D0001 | Standard view ∨

Balances of periods

Model

CurrentF ∨

Fiscal year

18/09/2023

Period start ↑	CW quantity	Unit quant...	Percent	CW accum...	Accumulat...	Period	Percent	Accumulat...
01/01/2023			0,00			0,00	0,00	0,00
01/02/2023			0,00			0,00	0,00	0,00
01/03/2023			0,00			0,00	0,00	0,00
01/04/2023			0,00			0,00	0,00	0,00
01/05/2023			0,00			0,00	0,00	0,00
01/06/2023			0,00			0,00	0,00	0,00
01/07/2023			0,00			0,00	0,00	0,00
01/08/2023			0,00			0,00	0,00	0,00
01/09/2023			0,00			0,00	0,00	0,00
01/10/2023		550,00	33,33		550,00	264.000,00	33,33	264.000,00
01/11/2023		550,00	66,67		1.100,00	264.000,00	66,67	528.000,00
01/12/2023		550,00	100,00		1.650,00	264.000,00	100,00	792.000,00

Figure 10.25 – Forecast balance

We can allocate forecasts via the allocation key. This will help predefine a trend on the allocation key and apply that trend to our forecast. By navigating to **Master planning** > **Setup** > **Demand forecasting** > **Period allocation categories**, we can define those trends.

We can create them manually or via the **Wizard** button, which will guide us through the creation process. A trend will look as follows:

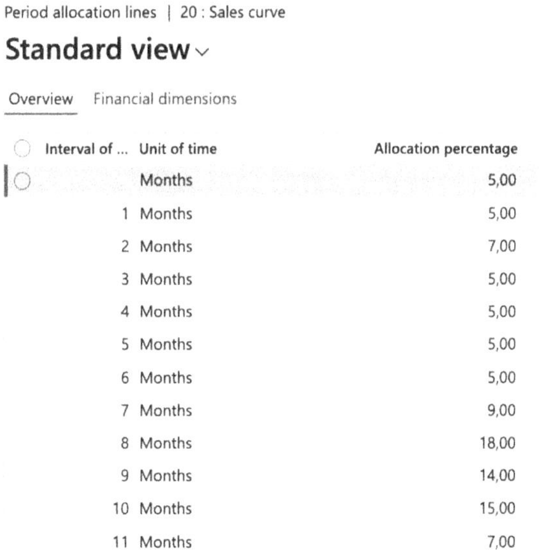

Period allocation lines | 20 : Sales curve

Standard view ∨

Overview   Financial dimensions

Interval of ...	Unit of time	Allocation percentage
	Months	5,00
1	Months	5,00
2	Months	7,00
3	Months	5,00
4	Months	5,00
5	Months	5,00
6	Months	5,00
7	Months	9,00
8	Months	18,00
9	Months	14,00
10	Months	15,00
11	Months	7,00

Figure 10.26 – Period allocation key example

As shown in *Figure 10.26*, a sales curve is defined for this period allocation key when, in the first 7 months, we have a low sales percentage that spikes in months 8, 9, and 10.

After manually entering our demand forecast, we can run master planning to update the planned orders. New planned orders will be generated for items in the forecast plan, as shown in the following figure:

Figure 10.27 – Planned order from a forecast demand

Now, let's review the supply schedule to overview current demands.

Supply schedule

This form helps planners overview an item's current demand and supply based on selected criteria. We can view the product supply information filtered according to our needs. We can analyze the supply of an item and make the proper changes to this planned supply.

To access the supply schedule form, we can navigate to **Master planning** > **Supply schedule**. Once we enter the filters and the item to evaluate, we will reach the following form:

Supply schedule

D0001

Expand   New ∨   Master planning   Max. report as finished   Update planned orders   Level   Material plan policy by location   Kanban rule

	Backlog	Monday	Tuesday	Wednesday	Thursday	Friday
PERIOD START INVENTORY	11,00	-945,00	-708,00	-708,00	-708,00	-708,00
PERIOD END INVENTORY	-945,00	-708,00	-708,00	-708,00	-708,00	-705,00
PERIOD END PEGGED INVENTORY	-945,00	-708,00	-708,00	-708,00	-708,00	-705,00
PERIOD NET SUPPLY	-956,00	237,00				3,00
[+] DEMAND	956,00					
[+] SUPPLY		237,00				3,00

Period end inventory

Figure 10.28 – The Supply schedule form

Here, we have a view of the planned supply of our item. In columns, we have the backlog values, representing the sum of the transactions until today, the days of the following week, and the following weeks and months.

Each row represents a transaction quantity that helps planners understand and balance stock quantities.

From this form, we can create new orders to control the demands of this particular item, such as a planned order, a purchase, or a production order. We can also click on **Update planned orders**, which will bring us to the **Planned orders** form filtered by this item. Here, we can modify, create, and approve planned orders and then review the supply schedule again.

This is a different way to view the master planning orders and control the supply schedule.

Tips and tricks

I would like to take this opportunity to recommend some real-world tips and tricks when working with planning optimization. These are from my own experience:

Start small and evolve your parameterization.

> This is a key tip when working with this module. Start simple: define one coverage group, and then iterate and increment your parameters, for example, by adding another coverage code with a different type, or adding freezing times and working with more complex scenarios. This will help you understand what the MRP engine is calculating and how it is doing it. By doing this, you can compare expected results with real results.

1. **Don't forget about dates.**

   It is essential to plan quantities first and understand how many units the MRP is ordering to supply, but it is vital to have them on the proper dates. Make sure that lead times are correct and in place when working with master planning. Don't forget to add handling times as safety margins.

2. **Define the level of coverage you want to have.**

   It is different to work by site, warehouse, or location. You need to understand the level of depth a company has before starting with parameterization. If you decide to work by site, none of the transfer orders between warehouses will be planned. On the contrary, if you decide to work on location level, every location and warehouse transfer will be planned by the MRP, creating several planned orders planners must review. Remember that how master planning creates the order is determined by the storage dimension group under the coverage plan by dimension field.

3. **Inventory, inventory, inventory.**

   On-hand inventory is vital information for master planning. Based on that information, every calculated supply order is created. Having an accurate inventory is going to save you time and money because you will plan what you need to re-stock.

4. **Avoid using blanket orders.**

   A common practice is creating a purchase order for quantities that will be acquired in a year, to obtain vendor discounts. This will create issues when you're running master plans because dates will not match with demands, and not all quantities will be needed on a particular date. To perform this action, creating purchase agreements that work as a blanket order is better. This will allow the master planning module to search for a purchase agreement with those prices and discounts and, with the help of master planning, at the correct times.

5. **Understand your demand.**

   The planning process is based on addressing our demand. One of our most important jobs when working with master planning is understanding how our demand behaves. For example, in a clothes company, seasonality dramatically impacts our demands, because swimsuits sell differently in January or June. We can declare seasonality by working with allocation keys in Dynamics 365 and adding forecasts that represent that seasonality.

Summary

In this chapter, we reviewed the basics of the master planning module, starting by explaining the objective of master planning or MRP techniques such as MRP I, II, and DDMRP.

Then, we dived into the planning optimization enhancement that was released in Dynamics 365 that optimizes master plan runs from hours to seconds. After that, we defined coverage groups and master plans and looked at how they interact with all of the modules we previously reviewed and with the orders of the corresponding modules.

Next, we reviewed the coverage or replenishment methods, such as by requirement, period, min/max, priority, and decoupling point. Then, we learned how to set up a master plan from start to finish and reviewed action messages and how to interpret them.

We also reviewed how to work with planned orders, which options the planner has, and how to interpret the information generated by master planning runs in different ways and from different forms. Finally, we reviewed the demand forecast and forecast plans and how to control supply by analyzing the supply schedule form.

As you can see, master planning is an extensive module that allows for personalization and multiple configurations. We will continue reviewing some advanced planning techniques in the following chapter.

Questions

1. You are implementing planning optimization. A planner needs to group demands of a month and create planned purchase orders for every item's demand.

Which of the following configurations do you need to perform to address this problem?

A.   Create a requirement coverage group, then select and group all generated planned purchase orders.

B.   Create a period coverage group. Set the period time fence to 30 days and assign it to the items.

C.   Create a min/max coverage group. Assign it to the item. Set minimum and maximum levels of the item and set the lead time to 30 days.

2.   You are implementing planning optimization. A planner sets a plan filter for items A and D. They only need to plan item A on the next master planning run.

Which of the following configurations do you need to perform to address this problem?

A.   Create a new master plan, set the plan filter for Item A, and run the master plan.

B.   Run the master plan and set a runtime filter for item D.

D.   Run the master plan and set a runtime filter blank.

E.   Run the master plan and set a runtime filter for item A.

3.   You are implementing planning optimization. A planner modifies the quantity of a planned purchase order and must keep it the same after the next master plan run is completed.

Which of the following configurations do you need to perform to address this problem?

A.   Leave the status set to **Unprocessed**.

B.   Change the status to **Completed**.

F.   Approve the planned purchase order.

Answers

1.   Option B.

The period coverage group consolidates demands by periods of days, accumulating the demands and creating planned supply orders for that demand.

2.   Option D.

When setting up plan and runtime filters, the intersect values are planned.

3.   Option C.

Approving the planned order is the only way that the master planning run will not delete the order. Planned orders with unprocessed and completed statuses will be erased.

11

Master Planning Implementation – Advanced Scenarios

When working with master planning, companies do not always have simple scenarios such as the ones we saw in *Chapter 10*. Multiple warehouses and sites often come into the equation, which obliges planning transfer orders and replenishments. Consider, for example, one facility that manufactures semi-finished items delivered to other facilities that produce the finished goods. Times and dates are crucial to address that problem. When shipping items overseas, longer lead times are needed, and replenishment or purchase orders cannot be modified. This brings up the importance of the freezing time of the coverage group.

The post-pandemic world brings other problems into the master plan, such as demand's dynamism. Some companies cannot plan this dynamic demand, so they rely on demand-driven planning techniques where a stock buffer is placed in some warehouses and demand is calculated daily. This allows facilities to have the needed stock and not understock or overstock the warehouse.

In this chapter, we will dive into these advanced scenarios, including multi-warehouse and multi-site planning, activating AI models to calculate demand, and working with **Demand Driven Materials Requirement Planning** (**DDMRP**) to place decoupling points of stock and work with priority planning.

In this chapter, we're going to cover the following topics:

- Understanding DDMRP and using it in Dynamics 365
- Understanding multi-warehouse and multi-site planning
- Setting up and planning intercompany orders

Multi-warehouse and multi-site planning

When working with several facilities across multiple countries or regions, planners must consider longer times to ensure the proper delivery of their stocks at the right time. To address this problem, we must understand how to work with multi-warehouse and multi-site planning in Dynamics 365.

The following figure shows a real-life scenario:

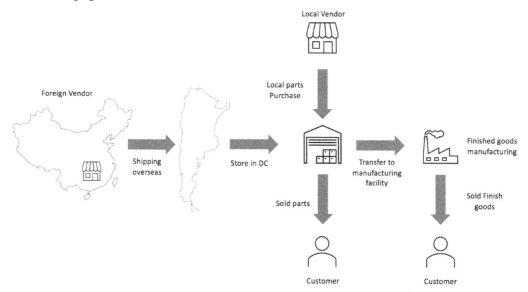

Figure 11.1 – Real-life scenario multi-warehouse planning

Figure 11.1 describes the process of a company that manufactures mountain bikes and sells bike parts. This company is located in Argentina, and bike parts, such as bike frames and handlebars, are imported from China and shipped overseas. This shipping has a lead time of 25 days, and parts are stored in the distribution center. The remaining parts are purchased from local vendors and stored in the distribution center.

From here, the inventory has two destinations: parts can be sold directly to customers or transferred to manufacturing facilities, where the finished goods are built and then sold to the customers.

As we can see, multiple orders intervene in the process – purchase orders for the parts, transfer orders to the manufacturing facility, and sales orders to the customer. A forecast must be created as this company works on a sales plan to import the bike frames and handlebar.

To replicate this scenario in Dynamics 365, we must first define the items we must work with. To keep this example easy, we will work with the following items:

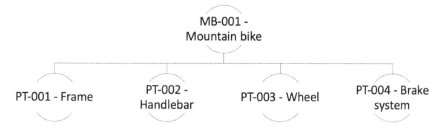

Figure 11.2 – Example of the bill of materials (BOM)

As seen in *Figure 11.2*, we have the following items:

1.   **MB-001 – Mountain bike** (finished goods item):

    A.   **PT-001 – Frame**: With a quantity of 1 unit in the BOM

    B.   **PT-002 – Handlebar**: With a quantity of 1 unit in the BOM

    C.   **PT-003 – Wheel**: With a quantity of 2 units in the BOM

    D.   **PT-004 – Brake system**: With a quantity of 1 unit in the BOM

Once items have been created and the BOM has been defined, we need to define and create the coverage groups for the items.

Setting up the scenario – coverage groups

It's time to define and set up the coverage group for each item. We can segregate them into three types:

* Item MB-001 can have a coverage group called **Production per requirement** (**ProdReg**) with a requirement type to address each forecast and sales requirement to create one production order. This can be seen in *Figure 11.3*:

Coverage groups

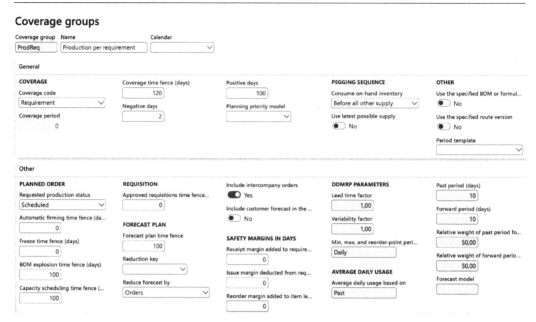

Figure 11.3 – Import per requirement coverage group

- Items PT-001 and PT-002 must have a period coverage type with at least 90 days of coverage; we can call it **Period with Freeze time** (**PeriodF**). This is because the lead time for ordering frames and handlebars from China is 25 days. Also, we need to set up a freeze time of 30 days to freeze the created purchase orders and not allow changes to be made to them. This can be seen in *Figure 11.4*:

Coverage groups

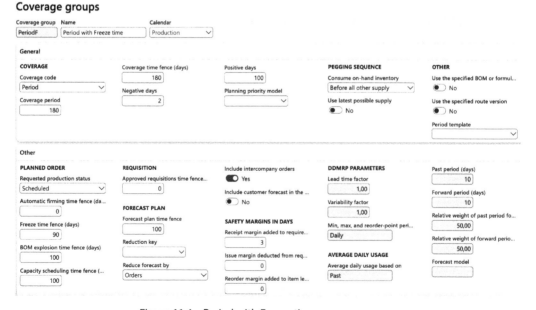

Figure 11.4 – Period with Freeze time coverage group

- Items PT-003 and PT-004 could use a period coverage type of, for example, 30 days to bulk order to local vendors to obtain purchasing discounts per quantity; we can call it **Period 30 days (Period-30)**. No freeze-time fence is required for this operation:

Coverage groups

Coverage group	Name	Calendar
Period-30	Period 30 days	Production

General

COVERAGE	Coverage time fence (days)	Positive days	PEGGING SEQUENCE	OTHER
Coverage code	100	100	Consume on-hand inventory	Use the specified BOM or formul...
Period	Negative days	Planning priority model	Before all other supply	● No
Coverage period	2		Use latest possible supply	Use the specified route version
30			● No	● No
				Period template

Other

PLANNED ORDER	REQUISITION	Include intercompany orders	DDMRP PARAMETERS	Past period (days)
Requested production status	Approved requisitions time fence...	● Yes	Lead time factor	10
Scheduled	0	Include customer forecast in the ...	1,00	Forward period (days)
Automatic firming time fence (da...		● No	Variability factor	10
0	FORECAST PLAN		1,00	Relative weight of past period fo...
Freeze time fence (days)	Forecast plan time fence	SAFETY MARGINS IN DAYS	Min, max, and reorder-point peri...	50,00
0	100	Receipt margin added to require...	Daily	Relative weight of forward perio...
BOM explosion time fence (days)	Reduction key	0	AVERAGE DAILY USAGE	50,00
100		Issue margin deducted from req...	Average daily usage based on	Forecast model
Capacity scheduling time fence (...	Reduce forecast by	0	Past	
100	Orders	Reorder margin added to item le...		
		0		

Figure 11.5 – Period 30 days coverage group

Looking back at *Figure 11.3*, we also set up a safety margin for the coverage group to handle the receiving times of the warehouse. Now that we've defined the coverage groups, we must set up each item's particularities. Let's dive into default order settings setups.

Setting up the scenario – default order settings

Let's start with item MB-001. As it is a finished goods item, we must change the default order type from purchase order to production under the default order setting. This will create a production order instead of a purchase order when running master planning. We can see this setup in the following figure:

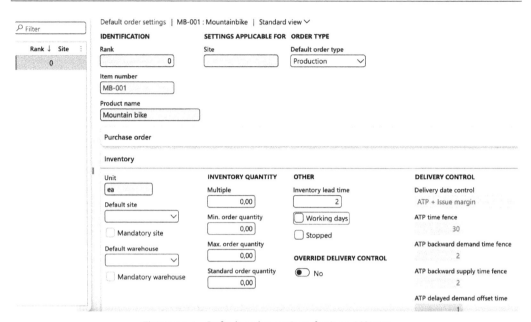

Figure 11.6 – Default order settings for item MB-001

Another thing to set up here is the inventory lead time for this item. This will reflect the manufacturing lead time in the master plan. In our case, we set this up in 2 days, as shown in *Figure 11.6*.

> **Note**
>
> If we use the manufacturing module and set up production routes, the manufacturing lead time is calculated based on the active route times for the item.

Looking at the default order settings for items PT-001 and PT-002, they are imported from China, so they have a lead time of 25 days. As shown in the following figure, we have set up the lead times under the **Purchase order** tab:

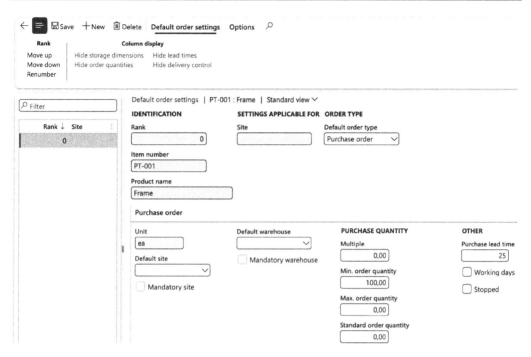

Figure 11.7 – Default order settings for items PT-001 and PT-002

We also create a minimum order quantity of 100 units because, as those items are shipped overseas, we must ensure we purchase a considerable quantity to justify the shipping.

As items PT-003 and PT-004 are purchased in the local market, we only set up a lead time of 3 days.

Now that we have configured everything related to items and coverage groups, we can move on to demand. As the company works with a sales plan, we must create the forecasts to input the sales projections.

Setting up the scenario – demand forecast

As we discussed previously, demand forecast refers to sales projections made by the sales department in which they define the goal for the next periods. To the MRP, those projections feed the stock and date calculations and help have the items when the sales projections need them.

For this example, the sales department assumes that it will sell 150 units of the mountain bike (item MB-001) and that it will also sell 55 units of the brake system (item PT-004) for the next month.

To create that demand, we must navigate to **Master planning** > **Forecasting** > **Manual forecast entry** > **Demand forecast lines**. We will find the following form:

Figure 11.8 – Manual forecast entry example

As shown in *Figure 11.7*, we have set up the forecast for next month (December) as the sales department projects. Two important things to consider when creating manual forecasts are that we need to assign each line to a forecast model. Those models refer to a sales plan (for example, current, optimistic, or pessimistic) that can be assigned to a master plan.

Another thing to know about demand forecast is that we can allocate demand on periods. This translates to assigning demand to each period or bucket of a pool of demands. To explain it better, let's say that the sales department projects sales for 12,000 units of a T-shirt all over the year. But demand changes between summer and winter as we can sell more T-shirts than in winter. So, we can assign a period allocation key with the allocated forecast to our demand forecast. This will allocate our demand periodically to a previously defined period key such as the following:

Period allocation lines | 20 : Sales curve

Standard view ⌄

Overview   Financial dimensions

○ ⟳	Interval of ...	Unit of time	Allocation percentage
		Months	5,00
	1	Months	5,00
	2	Months	7,00
	3	Months	5,00
	4	Months	5,00
	5	Months	5,00
	6	Months	5,00
	7	Months	9,00
	8	Months	18,00
	9	Months	14,00
	10	Months	15,00
⊘	11	Months ⌄	7,00

Figure 11.9 – Period allocation key example

Figure 11.9 shows the period allocation of a sales curve of a year, where we project higher sales in the 8th, 9th, and 10th months.

If we allocate demand under this sales curve, demand will be divided under those 12 periods, with each period having those percentages.

Returning to our example, we have the sales projection for next month, so we are ready to execute our first master planning run.

Executing the scenario – master planning run

Let's follow by navigating to **Master planning** > **Master planning** > **Run** > **Master planning**. Here, we can execute our master plan, and once run, we can navigate to **Master planning** > **Master planning** > **Planned orders**. We will find the following form:

My view ∨

Number	Reference	Item number	Product name	Requirement quantity ▽	Unit	Order date	Delivery date	Requested date	Delay (days)
0005000002	Planned production orders	MB-001	Mountain bike	200,00	ea	29/11/2023	01/12/2023		
0005000110	Planned purchase orders	PT-002	Handle Bar	200,00	ea	30/10/2023	24/11/2023	24/11/2023	
0005000111	Planned purchase orders	PT-003	Wheel	400,00	ea	24/11/2023	29/11/2023		
0005000112	Planned purchase orders	PT-001	Frame	200,00	ea	30/10/2023	24/11/2023	24/11/2023	
0005000113	Planned purchase orders	PT-004	Brake System	255,00	ea	24/11/2023	29/11/2023		

Figure 11.10 – Planned orders

In *Figure 11.10*, we can see the created orders for our example. Let's analyze the results.

First, we have a planned production order for the mountain bike that starts 11/29 and ends 12/01 and will deliver 200 units. As the demand forecast plans to sell 200 units by 12/01, to cover that demand, the master planning is creating that planned production order.

The same happens with all the raw materials. Master planning has created a purchase order covering the needed items for mountain bike manufacturing. We need 200 units of handlebars, 200 units of frames, 200 units of the brake system, and 400 units of wheels. If we look at the planned quantities of the brake system, we can see that for the needed 200 units, the master planning created a planned purchase order of 255 units. This is because we created a demand forecast line of 55 units for selling that item in December. As the coverage group for item PT-004 is for 30 days, both demands (manufacturing and demand forecast) are summed together to calculate the planned purchase order.

When we analyze dates, we can see, for example, that the mountain bike delivery date is planned for 12/01. This is the day when the demand is placed. To address that date, master planning suggests firming this production order by 11/29. With this, we ensure to end by the expected date, as the inventory lead time for this item is 2 days.

Planned purchase orders follow the same pattern. For example, PT-001 is the frame shipped from China. As the shipment has a lead time of 25 days, we need to create the purchase order on 10/30. Doing that, items will arrive 25 days later, on 11/24. We have a weekend and then a receipt margin of 3 days. This will add 5 days to reach the required date of the production order, 11/29.

If we select the planned production order and click the **Explosion** button, then navigate to the Gantt chart, we will reach the following figure:

Explosion

Planned production orders, number 0005000002, item MB-001, Site 1, Warehouse 11

Overview   Gantt   Action   Critical on-hand inventory   Explanation

Timescale   Colors   Setup

Reference	Number	Item	2023 October								2023 November										
			28	30	01	03	05	07	09	11	13	15	17	19	21	23	25	27	29	01	03
Planned productio	0005000C	MB-001																		MB-001		
Planned purchase	00050001	PT-003															PT-003				
Planned purchase	00050001	PT-004																PT-004			
Planned purchase	00050001	PT-002							PT-002													
Planned purchase	00050001	PT-001							PT-001													

Figure 11.11 – Gantt chart of the planned production order of the scenario

In *Figure 11.11*, we can see the orders from the order date to the delivery date in a time scale. Here, we can see that every order aligns with the requested pegged demand. Master planning tries to have the items needed just in time as the demand associated needs to consume it.

With that, we understand how master planning works. Returning to *Figure 11.1*, where we explained our case scenario, one key part is missing: all inventory is first stored in a DC, and then only the production necessities are transferred to the manufacturing facilities.

To reflect this, we need to configure some things:

1.   Modify the demand forecast for the mountain bike to the manufacturing facility.

2.   Configure the BOM to consume items in the manufacturing facility.

3.   Set the manufacturing facility to refill from the DC.

Let´s define the manufacturing facility as warehouse 13 and DC as warehouse 11. With that in mind, we must modify the demand forecast as we now sell manufactured items from warehouse 13. Once again, navigate to **Demand forecast** under **Master planning** > **Forecasting** > **Manual forecast entry** > **Demand forecast** and modify the warehouse for the MB-001 demand, as shown in the following figure:

Figure 11.12 – Demand forecast with a modified warehouse

Now, let's navigate to the BOM of item MB-001 under **Product information management** > **Product** > **Released products**, search for MB-001, and then, in the **Engineer** tab, click the **BOM versions** button.

We now need to set the warehouse of each line to the manufacturing facility (in our case, warehouse 13), as shown in the following figure:

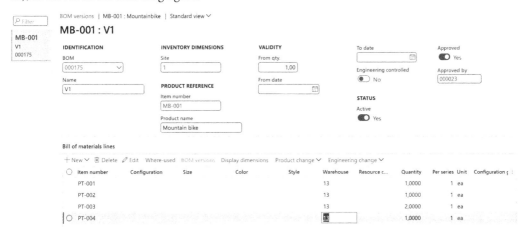

Figure 11.13 – Mountain bike BOM

If we leave this as-is and run a master planning, every planned order will be created in warehouse 13, except for the planned purchase order of the brake parts since its demand is set in warehouse 11, making it available to purchase and receive from each facility. This is unreal because we don't receive purchase orders in every facility. The supply flow starts in warehouse 11, then the raw materials needed in manufacturing are transferred from warehouse 11 to warehouse 13. So, now, we need to set up that supply flow.

To do that, we must configure warehouse 13 (manufacturing facility) to refill from warehouse 11 (DC). To do so, let's navigate to **Inventory management** > **Setup** > **Inventory breakdown** > **Warehouses**. Here, we'll select warehouse 13 and, under the **Master planning** tab, activate refilling and assign warehouse 11 as the main warehouse, as shown in the following figure:

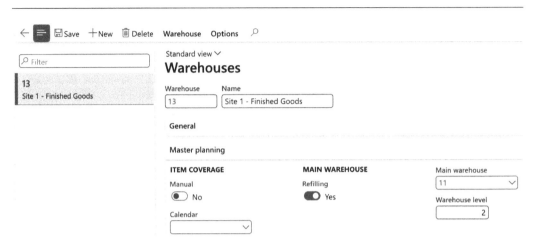

Figure 11.14 – Warehouse refilling setup

One last detail is to handle the mountain bike coverage. If we run master planning now, Dynamics 365 will assume that, as every item is received in warehouse 11, we can manufacture there, so we need to force master planning to create the planned production order in warehouse 13. Let's move to **Product information management** > **Products** > **Released products**, select **MB-001**, and then, under the **Plan** tab, select **Coverage** > **Item coverage**.

In this form, create a new coverage for warehouse 13, and in the **General** tab, activate the **CHANGE THE PLANNED ORDER TYPE** option and select **Production**, as shown in the following figure:

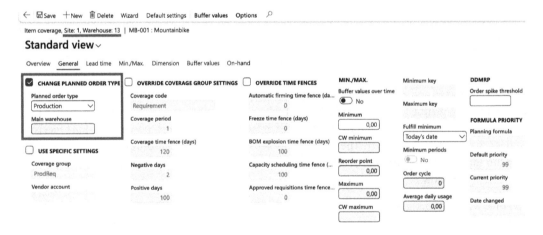

Figure 11.15 – Item coverage for the mountain bike in warehouse 13

And that's it. Now, we can rerun the master planning and navigate to the planned orders form to find the following:

Planned orders

My view ⌄

	Number	Reference	Item number ▽	Product name	Warehouse	Requirement quantity ▽	Unit	Order date	Delivery date	Requested date
◉	0009000003	Planned production orders	MB-001	Mountain bike	13	200,00	ea	29/11/2023	01/12/2023	
	0009000043	Planned transfer	PT-004	Brake System	13	200,00	ea	29/11/2023	29/11/2023	
	0009000044	Planned transfer	PT-002	Handle Bar	13	200,00	ea	24/11/2023	24/11/2023	24/11/2023
	0009000045	Planned transfer	PT-003	Wheel	13	400,00	ea	29/11/2023	29/11/2023	
	0009000046	Planned transfer	PT-001	Frame	13	200,00	ea	24/11/2023	24/11/2023	24/11/2023
	0009000047	Planned purchase orders	PT-003	Wheel	11	400,00	ea	24/11/2023	29/11/2023	
	0009000048	Planned purchase orders	PT-002	Handle Bar	11	200,00	ea	27/10/2023	21/11/2023	21/11/2023
	0009000052	Planned purchase orders	PT-001	Frame	11	200,00	ea	27/10/2023	21/11/2023	21/11/2023
	0009000081	Planned purchase orders	PT-004	Brake System	11	255,00	ea	24/11/2023	29/11/2023	

Figure 11.16 – Planned orders form

Looking at *Figure 11.16*, we can now see that master planning has suggested planned transfers from warehouse 11 to warehouse 13 to move that inventory. As the planned production order is in the manufacturing facility, every raw material needed for that order is moved from the distribution center. Another thing to look at is that the brake system was purchased for 255 units, but it is only suggested to transfer 200 units to the manufacturing facility because the demand forecast takes the 55 units remaining in the DC.

Analyzing the dates, all purchases must be done earlier than the first planning because of the handling times of the warehouse reflected in the safety margins. As we set up 3 days of receipt margin, this will add those days to every reception 3 days in the distribution center, and another 3 days for the manufacturing facility.

This setup reflects the real-life scenario described at the beginning of this chapter. But what will happen if we need to manufacture in a different legal entity? We'll review that scenario in the following section.

Intercompany planning

In some cases, companies have different legal entities for different business purposes. For example, for the car manufacturing business, we can have a legal entity that buys and sells car parts, another legal entity that manufactures and sells cars, and a third company that handles car repair services.

Extending our scenario, we can have segregated operations as follows:

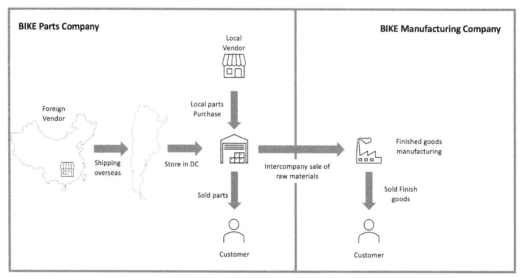

Figure 11.17 – Intercompany planning scenario

This scenario is the same as what was described in the previous section, but now, the manufacturing process is done by another legal entity of the same group, forcing intercompany planning.

From the bike manufacturing company, we will create or plan production orders, and that demand will be transferred to the bike parts company, which will plan their purchase accordingly.

We need to start by configuring the following:

- Intercompany planning groups
- Intercompany trade
- Demand forecasting/or sales order creation

First, we must create the intercompany planning groups accordingly. To do so, navigate to **Master planning** > **Setup** > **Intercompany planning groups**. Following that route, we will reach the following form:

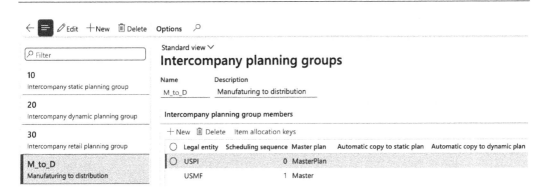

Figure 11.18 – Intercompany planning groups

Here, we can create an intercompany planning group. This will schedule the sequence in which companies' master plans must be run to create the intercompany orders.

In *Figure 11.18*, we can see that the first in the sequence is the USPI master plan and then the USMF master plan. This is because USPI-generated demand will impact the USMF purchase process downstream.

For example, if we demand a mountain bike from the USPI company, USMF will manufacture and sell it to USPI. USMF will also need to create purchase orders to stock warehouses to manufacture those finished goods.

As the second step, we must set up intercompany trade between the companies. To remember this process, you can refer to *Chapter 4*, where intercompany trade was explained. But, for a quick reminder, we need to create a customer in the USMF company and relate to a vendor in the USPI company by going to **General** > **Intercompany**.

Once we've done that, we can generate demand for the USPI company. Navigating to **Demand forecast**, we will create the following line:

Figure 11.19 – Intercompany demand forecast

When we run master planning after this, it will create a planned purchase order for this material. If we enter the USMF company, the demand will be reflected. We can see it by navigating to **Master planning** > **Inquiries and report** > **Intercompany master planning** > **Incoming planned intercompany demand**:

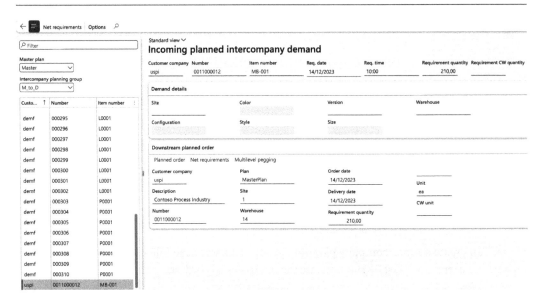

Figure 11.20 – Incoming planned intercompany demand

Figure 11.20 shows the incoming demand from USPI for the 210 units that we need to manufacture for USMF. Once we firm this order and rerun master planning on USMF, our planned order will show the following:

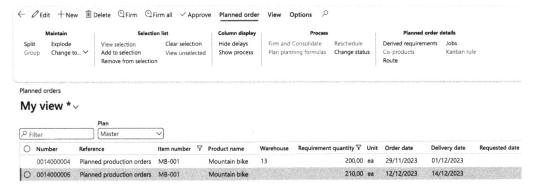

Figure 11.21 – Planned order in the manufacturing company

Here, we will see the reflected demand from USPI on USMF and it will calculate the requirements to address that intercompany demand.

We reviewed multi-site, multi-warehouse planning, and intercompany planning with these two examples. It is important to remember that these processes can be modified according to our business scenario, but both examples' structure applies to every business process.

Now, we can review another piece of advanced functionality: DDMRP.

DDMRP

In this ever-changing world, MRP techniques fall short when planning dynamic demands. In most cases, demands are not fixed, and companies tend to have stock shortages or overstock, which brings serious cost and storage problems. Under this reality, DDMRP is created as a methodology to address this problem.

DDMRP is a planning framework that's used to protect and promote the flow of the supply chain by strategically placing stock buffers in critical locations. This method also combines relevant methods from MRP and DRP with the pull and visibility we can find working with the Lean methodology.

DDMRP can be summarized in its three pillars: *position*, *protect*, and *pull*: position the relevant inventory as decoupling points in our warehouse, protect that inventory by quickly reacting to the demand, and pull the inventory by driving the demand under the planning.

DDMRP methodology is disseminated worldwide by the Demand Driven Institute. You can access their website at www.demanddriveninstitute.com for more information about this methodology. Dynamics 365 Supply Chain Management is certified by the Demand Driven Institute as software that complies with demand-driven methods.

What DDMRP is trying to mitigate is the bullwhip effect shown by the following figure:

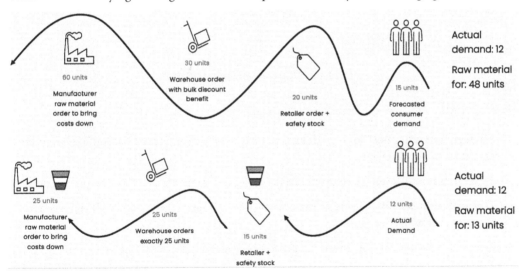

Figure 11.22 – Bullwhip effect

In *Figure 11.22*, looking at the first example, we can keep short or pass over the actual demand when we forecast the consumer demand. As we don't know the exact demand, we must order the stock plus safety stock. This will be passed through to the warehouse, which orders more production inventory and produces their economic batch to reduce costs. To address those 12 units of actual demand, as we cover issues, we pass through the linked parts of these stock variations and end by ordering 48 more units than needed.

If we strategically place inventories – the decoupling points – in some of the supply chain points, we can stop these variations, as those decoupling points disconnect one entity from another and make it independent of its inventory.

A decoupling point compresses the lead times and allows us to rely on accurate demand if it's within a sales order visibility. DDMRP has five components that align with its pillars of *Position*, *Protect*, and *Pull*, as we can see in the following figure:

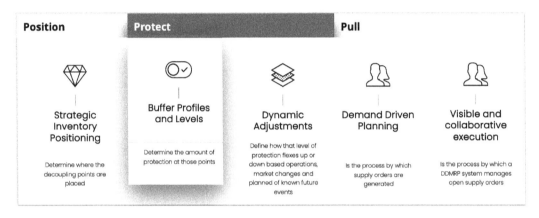

Figure 11.23 – The five components of DDMRP

As shown in *Figure 11.23*, we can describe the five components or steps of DDMRP as follows:

- **Strategic inventory positioning**: This refers to determining where the decoupling points are placed in the supply chain

- **Buffer profiles and levels**: These determine the protection we need to give those decoupling points

- **Dynamic adjustments**: These refine how that level of protection can be flexed based on operations or market changes

- **Demand-driven planning**: This is the process by which supply orders are generated

- **Visible and collaborative execution**: This defines how a DDMRP system manages open supply order

This feature is activated by default in Dynamics 365 Supply Chain Management, after version 10.0.35. Let's start by breaking down setups and processes from DDMRP.

Strategic inventory positioning

The first step of DDMRP is to determine where we can place a decoupling point in our supply chain. A decoupling point is where we can have an inventory buffer to help compress lead times and absorb shocks on the supply chain.

To know where we should place a decoupling point, we can enumerate the following tips:

- **External variability**: To mitigate the effects of supply variability beyond our control, we can add buffers

- **Inventory leverage and flexibility**: We can add buffers to prioritize components used in multiple products

- **Critical operations protection**: To prevent the idling of operations due to insufficient raw materials, decoupling points can be added before critical operations or bottlenecks

- **Customer tolerance time**: Buffers can be added at stages where customers expect a short delivery time for the item

- **Sales order visibility horizon**: Buffers should be added at points where we must react quickly to meet new demand

- **Potential market lead time**: Buffers should be added at points where items can be sold at a higher price if the lead time is longer

For example, let's say that we have the following BOM to produce an aluminum window:

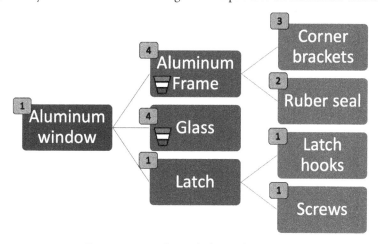

Figure 11.24 – BOM with decoupling points

As shown in *Figure 11.24*, we have defined an aluminum window composed of semi-finished and raw materials. The numbers at the top of each part describe the lead time of that particular piece. If we calculate the accumulated lead time of the aluminum window, we need to add the pieces representing the longest lead time. For example, if we have aluminum window (1) + aluminum frame (4) + corner brackets (3), this will give us an accumulated lead time of 8 days.

If we place decoupling points (inventory buffers) where they're marked in *Figure 11.24*, now, the decouple lead time is aluminum window (1) + latch (1) + screws (1), giving us a total of 3 days.

You might be wondering why the lead times are reduced. This is because inventory is available on hand where decoupling points are placed, so no lead time is added to the product.

We can define this in Dynamics 365 by first creating the BOM of this aluminum frame. Then, we must create a coverage group by navigating to **Master planning** > **Setup** > **Coverage** > **Coverage groups**. We will reach the following form, where we can create a decoupling point coverage group, like so:

Figure 11.25 – Decoupling point coverage group example

As shown in *Figure 11.25*, the coverage code is the decoupling point, meaning that this coverage group will be used to place strategic inventory in our supply chain.

Marked by the red square in *Figure 11.25*, we have the DDMRP parameters that control this group. Let's explain them:

- **Lead time factor** is a decimal value given to the lead time. If a lead time is longer, the lower the value will be. The demand-driven institute recommends the following ranges:

  - Long lead time from 0.20 to 0.40

  - Medium lead time from 0.41 to 0.60

  - Short lead time from 0.61 to 1.00

- **Variability factor** is a decimal value to evaluate a product demand's variability. The higher the variability, the higher the value will be. The demand-driven institute recommends the following ranges for this factor:

  - Low variability from 0.20 to 0.40

  - Medium variability from 0.41 to 0.60

  - High variability from 0.61 to 1.00

- **AVERAGE DAILY USAGE (ADU)** is the average consumption of an item per day. We can calculate this in three ways – past, which will average the quantities used on certain days in the past; future, which will do the same, but in future demand; or blended, which will calculate both and then average both results.

- **Min, max, and reorder point period** will determine the periods to calculate the buffer levels. The two options are days and weeks.

- **Past period (days)** and **forward period (days)** will determine how many days in the past, and in the future, we will evaluate demand to calculate the ADU.

We will revise these concepts later when discussing buffer levels.

Once our coverage group is in place, we can assign them to our item. But is important to know that decoupling points are placed in an item's specific site and warehouse. We cannot assign them directly in the released product form because we must define a decoupling point to an item, plus an inventory dimension where that buffer will be placed.

First, we need to navigate to the released **Products** form, select an item, and then navigate to the **Plan** tab > **Coverage** > **Item coverage**.

Here, we will create a new item coverage and ensure we set up a site and a warehouse at a minimum. Then, in the **General** tab, we will activate the **Use specific settings** control and select our coverage code, as shown in the following figure:

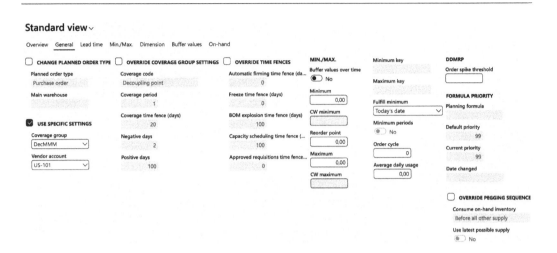

Figure 11.26 – Item coverage with a decoupling point placed

Once we've set up all our decoupling points, we can select the manufactured item (aluminum window, in our example) and navigate to the **Plan** tab > **Coverage** > **Item coverage**.

Then, we can select the coverage and, in the **Buffer values** tab, select the **Decoupled lead time** option. We will reach the following form:

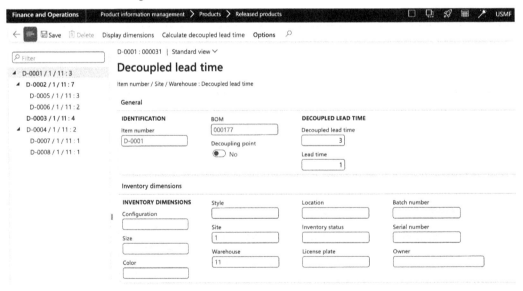

Figure 11.27 – Decoupled lead time for the BOM item

By clicking the **Calculate decoupled lead time** button, we can see the product's and its components' decoupled lead time in the BOM, as shown in *Figure 11.27*. On the left of the form, the items marked in bold are the decoupling points.

In short, we can place decoupling points in Dynamics 365 Supply Chain Management by determining a decoupling point coverage code under the items coverage code for a specific site and warehouse.

Buffer profiles and levels

After determining the decoupling points in our supply chain, we need to define how much stock we will store in those points. DDMRP defines items in buffer-level zones as red, yellow, and green:

Figure 11.28 – Buffer-level zones

As shown in *Figure 11.28*, the buffer level is categorized as follows:

- **Green zone**: Determines the average order frequency and specific order size. The top of the green zone is the maximum stock allowed.

- **Yellow zone**: Determines the inventory coverage. We want our inventory levels to be in this zone. The top of the yellow zone is the re-order point.

- **Red zone**: Determines the safety stock for eventualities. The more variability the item has, the greater the red zone is. The top of the red zone is the minimum stock.

To calculate those three zones, DDMRP has the following equations:

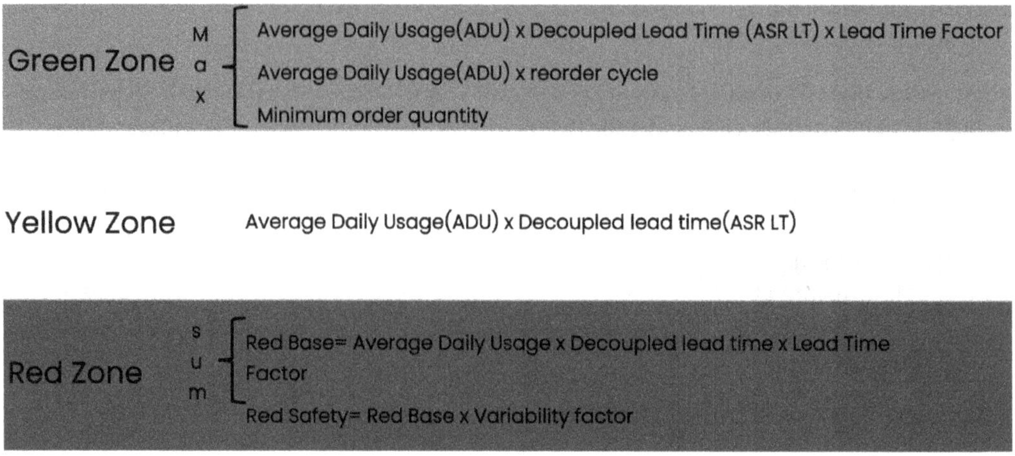

Green Zone (Max) of:
- Average Daily Usage(ADU) x Decoupled Lead Time (ASR LT) x Lead Time Factor
- Average Daily Usage(ADU) x reorder cycle
- Minimum order quantity

Yellow Zone = Average Daily Usage(ADU) x Decoupled lead time(ASR LT)

Red Zone (Sum) of:
- Red Base= Average Daily Usage x Decoupled lead time x Lead Time Factor
- Red Safety= Red Base x Variability factor

Figure 11.29 – Buffer zones calculation

To simplify this, we will consider an example regarding the following item:

Item	Glass Panel
ADU	15
Decoupled lead time	8 days
Lead time factor	0.5
Variability factor	0.5
Reorder cycle	0
Minimum order quantity	75 units

Table 11.1 – Glass panel example for buffer calculation

In *Table 11.1*, we have defined the values for calculating the buffer zone. The simplest way is to start from the yellow zone.

Yellow zone = ADU x Decoupled Lead Time = 15 x 8 = **120 units**.

Now, we can follow by calculating the red zone. Here we've got two parts – red base and red safety:

- **Red base** = ADU x Decoupled Lead Time x Lead Time Factor = 15 x 8 x 0.5 = 60 units

- **Red safety** = Red Base x Variability Factor = 60 x 0.5 = 30 units

The red zone translates to the sum of red base and red safety:

- **Red zone** = Red Base + Red Safety = 60 + 30 = **90 units**

Finally, the green zone has three different equations, but we have to choose the one with the maximum value:

- **Green zone**:

  - ADU x Decoupled Lead Time x Lead Time Factor = 15 x 8 x 0,5 = 60 units

  - ADU x Reorder Cycle = 15 x 0 = 0 units

  - Minimum Order Quantity = **75 units**

As we can see, the greater value between the three is 75 units. So, the zones for the glass panel are defined in the following way:

Figure 11.30 – Example of a buffer-level calculation

As you can see, buffer levels are tightly tied to demand. As every time demand changes, the average daily usage will modify every calculation.

We must go to the coverage group to input that information in Dynamics 365 Supply Chain Management, as we saw in *Figure 11.25*. Those fields control the buffer level, calculations like we did in the previous example.

Once we have set up our coverage group and assigned it to our item coverage group, we can start our calculations. Let's go back to the item coverage group's **General** tab, as shown in the following screenshot:

Figure 11.31 – Items coverage group for a decoupling point

We have two ways of calculating buffer levels: we can calculate them manually by demand or calculate them over time. This is controlled by the **Buffer values over time** parameter, as seen in *Figure 11.31*. If you leave it set to **No**, it will calculate the **Minimum**, **Reorder point**, and **Maximum** fields based on the average daily usage placed manually. But if that field is set to **Yes**, calculated fields will gray out and it will activate the **Buffer values** tab.

In this example, we will calculate buffer values over time. So, we can move to the **Buffer values** tab and we will reach the following form:

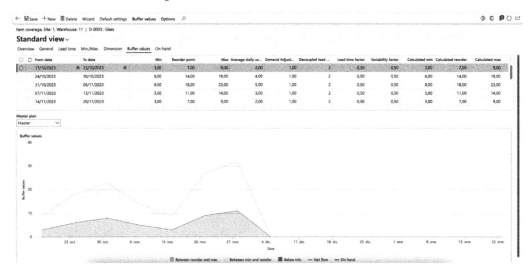

Figure 11.32 – Buffer values

Figure 11.32 shows the form with calculations made, but the first time you access the form, it will be blank. The first step is to create the periods for calculation. If we look at *Figure 11.32*, we'll see that periods are defined weekly. To add periods, select the **Buffer values** tab > **Periodic setup** > **Add period**.

Once periods have been populated, you will notice that the values are zero. This is because we need to calculate buffer levels for each period, so the first thing to do is calculate the decoupled lead time of the period. Again, select the **Buffer values** tab > **Calculate** > **Calculate decoupled lead time**. This will populate the **Decouple lead time** field.

Next, we need to calculate the average daily usage for that period. Select the **Buffer values** tab > **Calculate** > **Calculate average daily usage**. This will populate the **Average daily usage** field. This calculation depends on the demand of the selected period. Remember that, in our coverage group, we defined how the average daily usage will be calculated (past, forward, or blended).

After that, we must calculate the min, max, and reorder point to define our zones. Select the **Buffer values** tab > **Calculate** > the **Calculate min**, **Calculate max**, and **Calculate reorder** quantities to do that. This will populate the **Calculated min**, **Calculated max**, and **Calculated reorder** fields.

Once there, we can analyze those values and accept or discard calculations by selecting the **Buffer values** tab > **Take Action**.

If we approve the calculations, the graphic at the bottom of the form will reflect the values and we can start planning to meet those values or change those values with dynamic adjustments.

Dynamic adjustments

As we've been discussing, demand and plans can change over time, so it is important to have a tool to make adjustments and tune some factors so that we have the right calculations and disrupt the least possible supply chain.

Many factors can change our calculations but DDMRP classifies them into three groups:

- **Demand adjustment factor** (**DAF**): We can use this when variability tends to surpass the buffers and potentially have a stock break. Buffers are designed to absorb variability but with this adjustment type, we can control them.

- **Zone adjustment factor**: we can use this adjustment type to modify a zone or part of it. Remember that each zone has a function, as we explained earlier when we talked about buffer profiles and level segments. Here's a reminder:

  - **Green zone adjustment**: To adjust order size and frequency

  - **Yellow zone adjustment**: To adjust the response to planned short-term promotions or supply disruptions

  - **Red zone adjustment**: To adjust the response to a temporary volatility change, where a change in buffer profile is not warranted

- **Lead time adjustment factor**: Used when a lead time increases or decreases the normal lead time for a period (For example, road works that increase transportation time).

We can adjust those factors in the buffer levels form we've been working with:

Item coverage, Site: 1, Warehouse: 11 | D-0003 : Glass

Standard view ⌄

Overview   General   Lead time   Min./Max.   Dimension   Buffer values   On-hand

	From date	To date	Min	Reorder point	Max	Average daily us...	Demand Adjust...	Decoupled lead ...	Lead time factor	Variability factor	Calculated min	Calculated reorder	Calculated max
	17/10/2023	23/10/2023	3,00	7,00	9,00	2,00	1,00	2	0,50	0,50	3,00	7,00	9,00
	24/10/2023	30/10/2023	6,00	14,00	18,00	4,00	1,00	2	0,50	0,50	6,00	14,00	18,00
	31/10/2023	06/11/2023	8,00	18,00	23,00	5,00	1,00	2	0,50	0,50	8,00	18,00	23,00
	07/11/2023	13/11/2023	5,00	11,00	14,00	3,00	1,00	2	0,50	0,50	5,00	11,00	14,00
	14/11/2023	20/11/2023	3,00	7,00	9,00	2,00	1,00	2	0,50	0,50	3,00	7,00	9,00

Figure 11.33 – Dynamics adjustments factors

We can adjust our calculations if we modify the columns marked in *Figure 11.33*. Once we modify those, we can recalculate the min, max, and reorder points and accept calculations to reflect those changes. The next step is to execute demand-driven planning.

Demand-driven planning

Before executing planning, we must understand how demand-driven planning suggests planned orders. It works with two main concepts: **qualified demand** and **net flow**. To explain them better, we will work with the following example:

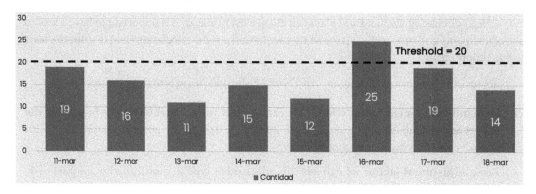

Figure 11.34 – Example of an item demand

In *Figure 11.34*, we can see an example of a demand for one item over time. There is also a threshold marked indicating a demand out of the ordinary on March 16.

The concept of qualified demand is all demand until today plus the spikes, meaning demand that surpasses the threshold. In our example, if we say that today is March 11, qualified demand is calculated by the following equation:

Qualified Demand = Demand Past Due + Today's Demand + Spikes = 0 + 19 + 25 = 44 units

That's the demand that demand-driven planning is going to focus on. But to calculate and propose a planned order, it will use the net flow, which compares the qualified demand with the on-hand inventory and the upcoming orders. To extend our example, if we have 98 units of stock, we can calculate net flow in the following way:

Net Flow = On-Hand + On Order - Qualified Demand = 98 + 0 – 44 = 54 units

Now that we have our net flow, we need to compare that with our buffer levels. If that net flow surpasses the reorder point, a planned supply order will be generated of the maximum stock (top of green) minus the net flow.

The orders will be generated in Dynamics 365 if we run master planning, which we can do by navigating to **Master planning** > **Master planning** > **Run** > **Master plan**.

Once executed, we can review the net requirements by navigating to the **Released product** form, selecting the item, and then going to the **Plan** tab and choosing **Requirement** > **Net requirement**:

Figure 11.35 – Items net requirements

As shown in *Figure 11.35*, we can review net requirements and planned orders. You will see a column reflecting the spikes of orders surpassing the threshold. We can define the threshold in the item coverage group in the **General** tab.

Finally, the last step of DDMRP covers having a tool with collaboration and visual indicators that helps the planner review and place orders.

Visual and collaborative execution

This last step is covered in Dynamics 365 by a series of reports and forms that help planners know exactly what is happening with their stocks without diving into calculations.

The first thing we can mention is the **Demand driven MRP** workspace, as shown in the following figure:

Figure 11.36 – The Demand driven MRP workspace

This workspace helps us control the related process of demand-driven planning easily. If we look at the first square, we can run the master plan and gain information about the last run, including if it had warnings or errors on that run. Going to the left, we can see the decoupling point's status by net flow. Each square gives us the number of decoupling points in that status; if we select any status, we can see all related information about them.

We can also calculate buffer values via the **Calculate buffer value** button. To the left, we have the decoupling points status by on-hand.

Down, we can see the planned orders for decoupling points, and we can see them segmented by decoupling point status:

Standard view ˅

	Item number	Product name	Site	Warehouse	On-hand stat...	On-hand	On-hand status	On-hand status color	On order	Qualified d...	Unit	Net flow	Net flow status
◎	D-0003	Glass	1	11	500,00	15,00	On-hand higher than averag...		0,00	98,00	ea	-83,00	Below minimum
	F00001	Magnet Assembly AX-21	1	11	0,00	0,00	On-hand critically low		0,00	0,00	pcs	0,00	Below minimum
	F00003	Basket assembly BA0193	1	11	0,00	0,00	On-hand critically low		0,00	4,00	pcs	-4,00	Below minimum
	GA0001	SpeakerSet Highline-41A	1	11	0,00	0,00	On-hand critically low		0,00	0,00	pcs	0,00	Below minimum
	GA0001	SpeakerSet Highline-41A	1	11	66,67	210,00	On-hand critically low		0,00	10,00	pcs	200,00	Below minimum

Figure 11.37 – Decoupling points by on-hand

Figure 11.37 shows us the status of the on-hand inventory in the decoupling points. Again, a color scheme shows us the status:

- **Red**: On-hand critically low

- **Yellow**: On-hand low

- **Green**: On-hand on the average range

- **Violet**: On-hand higher than the average range

If we navigate to **Master planning** > **Master planning** > **DDMRP** > **Decoupling points status by net flow**, we will see the following form, which gives us information about the net flow of the decoupling points:

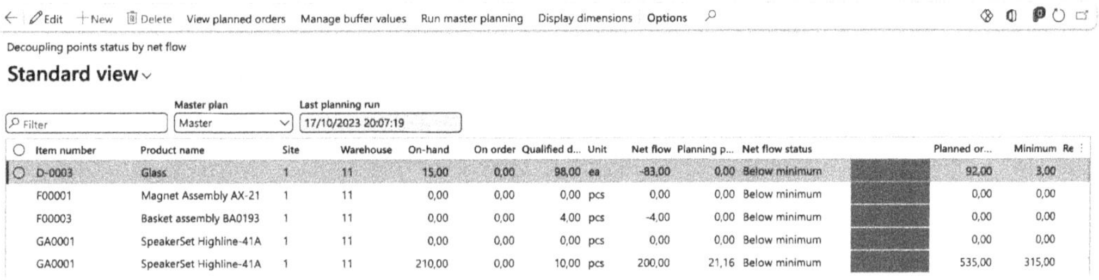

	Item number	Product name	Site	Warehouse	On-hand	On order	Qualified d...	Unit	Net flow	Planning p...	Net flow status		Planned or...	Minimum Re
○	D-0003	Glass	1	11	15,00	0,00	98,00	ea	-83,00	0,00	Below minimum		92,00	3,00
	F00001	Magnet Assembly AX-21	1	11	0,00	0,00	0,00	pcs	0,00	0,00	Below minimum		0,00	0,00
	F00003	Basket assembly BA0193	1	11	0,00	0,00	4,00	pcs	-4,00	0,00	Below minimum		0,00	0,00
	GA0001	SpeakerSet Highline-41A	1	11	0,00	0,00	0,00	pcs	0,00	0,00	Below minimum		0,00	0,00
	GA0001	SpeakerSet Highline-41A	1	11	210,00	0,00	10,00	pcs	200,00	21,16	Below minimum		535,00	315,00

Figure 11.38 – Decoupling points by status

Looking at *Figure 11.38*, we can quickly watch the status of each decoupling point. The first thing that came to our attention is the colors of each line representing the status where they were placed:

- **Red**: Below minimum. This represents the red zone.

- **Yellow**: Between min and reorder. This represents the yellow zone.

- **Green**: Above reorder point. This represents the green zone.

We also have significant information, such as on-hand inventory, on-order inventory, qualified demand, net flow, and planned orders.

Another important field in this inquiry is **Planning priority**. This field tells us the importance of the demand or supply. It is ranked from 0 to 100, with 0 being the most important.

Navigating to **Master planning** > **Master planning** > **DDMRP** > **Decoupling points status by on-hand**, we can see the following information:

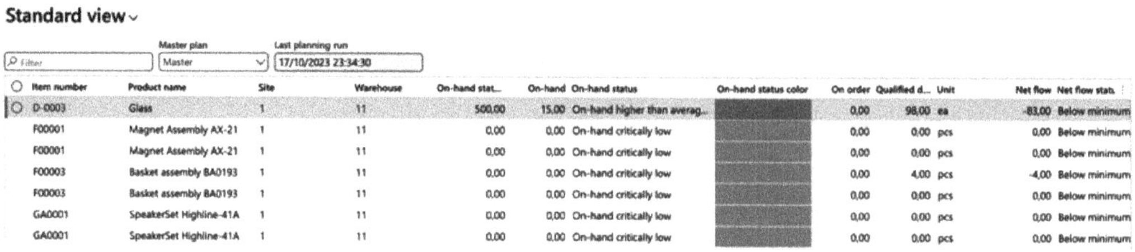

Standard view ⌄

Figure 11.39 - Decoupling points by on-hand

If we select a product and click on the **Manage buffer values** button, we will navigate to the detailed coverage information of that item, as we saw earlier in *Figure 11.32*.

To close this section, we can mention the benefits of implementing DDMRP based on information from the Demand Driven Institute:

Benefit	Impact
Better customer services	Companies raise the constant on-time delivery rate by 97–100%
Lead time shrink	There have been cases where companies lowered their lead times by 80% in various industry segments
Right inventory sizing	Companies lowered their inventory levels by 30–40% while upgrading their customer service
Lowered total costs of customer service	Costs related to accelerated activities and fake signals are mostly eliminated
Easy and intuitive	Planners can see priorities instead of constantly struggling with MRP messages

Table 11.2 – Benefits of implementing DDMRP

As shown in *Table 11.2*, DDMRP methodology helps companies address customer demand, with the least inventory on hand. This will significantly reduce costs, not only item costs but also related costs regarding operation and indirect costs.

It also helps planners easily know which orders have higher priority compared to others. This means they don't have to look at and analyze thousands of orders and understand which will have a higher impact on operations.

Summary

This chapter focused on two main topics. First, we covered advanced MRP scenarios, such as multi-warehouse and intercompany master planning, which opens the umbrella of many different company configurations and setups.

We dove into an example so that we could work with those topics and set up all MRP configurations and executions.

We also reviewed DDMRP methodology, how it affects today's world, and how we can benefit from it. Then, we covered the five steps of DDMRP and set up Dynamics 365 to apply the methodology to various real-world case scenarios. These helped you understand how the DDMRP methods apply to real-world problems and how Dynamics 365 addresses them.

Congratulations on finishing this book! I hope you enjoyed reading it as much as we enjoyed writing it. Now that your journey to learn and master Dynamics 365 Supply Chain Management has started, I recommend that you use this book as a guide to expand your knowledge and, day by day, try to learn a little more. Investigate and test as much as you can. Dynamics 365's ecosystem is ever-changing and evolving, keeping solution consultants alert to keep learning and evolving their methods. Stay motivated, and learn by doing.

Questions

1. You are implementing planning optimization. A company needs to transfer inventory from one warehouse to another to continue with the manufacturing process.

   Which parameters in the warehouse setup do you need to take care of?

   A. In the **Master planning** tab, turn the manual slider on.

   B. In the **Master planning** tab, set **Refilling** to **Yes**, and select the main warehouse we will transfer to.

   E. In the **Master planning** tab, set **Refilling** to **Yes**, and select the warehouse we need to transfer from.

2. You are implementing DDMRP. You need to explain the function of the red zone to the planners.

   Which of the following is the right answer?

   A. Determines the safety stock for eventualities.

   B. Determines the average order frequency and specific order size.

   C. Determines the inventory coverage.

3. You are implementing DDMRP. You need to explain to the planners how to calculate the net flow.

   Which of the following is the right answer?

   A. It is the difference between the on-hand stock and the qualified demand.

   B. It is the qualified demand plus the on-hand stock.

   C. It is the on-hand stock plus the upcoming order minus the qualified demand.

Answers

1. Option C.

    Setting **Refilling** to **Yes** activates planned transfer orders and the main warehouse is the warehouse we transfer from.

2. Option A.

    Determines the safety stock for eventualities. The more variability there is, the greater the red zone is.

3. Option A.

    It is the on-hand stock plus the upcoming order minus the qualified demand.

Index

Packtpub.com

Subscribe to our online digital library for full access to over 7,000 books and videos, as well as industry leading tools to help you plan your personal development and advance your career. For more information, please visit our website.

Why subscribe?

- Spend less time learning and more time coding with practical eBooks and Videos from over 4,000 industry professionals

- Improve your learning with Skill Plans built especially for you

- Get a free eBook or video every month

- Fully searchable for easy access to vital information

- Copy and paste, print, and bookmark content

Did you know that Packt offers eBook versions of every book published, with PDF and ePub files available? You can upgrade to the eBook version at packtpub.com and as a print book customer, you are entitled to a discount on the eBook copy. Get in touch with us at customercare@packtpub.com for more details.

At www.packtpub.com, you can also read a collection of free technical articles, sign up for a range of free newsletters, and receive exclusive discounts and offers on Packt books and eBooks.

Other Books You May Enjoy

If you enjoyed this book, you may be interested in these other books by Packt:

Becoming a Microsoft Dynamics 365 Marketing Functional Consultant

Malin Martnes

ISBN: 978-1-80323-460-1

- Create and manage marketing forms and pages
- Write good emails and use analytics to measure their effectiveness
- Explore outbound and real-time customer journeys
- Use Power Pages for real-time marketing events
- Create surveys to send to your customers with Customer Voice
- Exploit the Microsoft ecosystem to get the best results

Becoming a Dynamics 365 Finance and Supply Chain Solution Architect

Brent Dawson

ISBN: 978-1-80461-149-4

- Design an architectural solution for Dynamics 365 with the Fasttrack method
- Discover potential issues that occur while integrating D365 Finance Supply Chain Management
- Set up industry-standard yet customized security configurations
- Scope license requirements and apply license rules during deployment
- Plan and test for successful data migration and system integration
- Identify required tools, applications, and methods for ALM
- Explore different aspects of human change management in D365 F projects

Packt is searching for authors like you

If you're interested in becoming an author for Packt, please visit `authors.packtpub.com` and apply today. We have worked with thousands of developers and tech professionals, just like you, to help them share their insight with the global tech community. You can make a general application, apply for a specific hot topic that we are recruiting an author for, or submit your own idea.

Share Your Thoughts

Now you've finished *Becoming a Dynamics 365 Supply Chain Management Functional Consultant Associate*, we'd love to hear your thoughts! Scan the QR code below to go straight to the Amazon review page for this book and share your feedback or leave a review on the site that you purchased it from.

https://packt.link/r/1804618004

Your review is important to us and the tech community and will help us make sure we're delivering excellent quality content.

Download a free PDF copy of this book

Thanks for purchasing this book!

Do you like to read on the go but are unable to carry your print books everywhere?

Is your eBook purchase not compatible with the device of your choice?

Don't worry, now with every Packt book you get a DRM-free PDF version of that book at no cost.

Read anywhere, any place, on any device. Search, copy, and paste code from your favorite technical books directly into your application.

The perks don't stop there, you can get exclusive access to discounts, newsletters, and great free content in your inbox daily

Follow these simple steps to get the benefits:

1. Scan the QR code or visit the link below

https://packt.link/free-ebook/9781804618004

2. Submit your proof of purchase

3. That's it! We'll send your free PDF and other benefits to your email directly

www.ingramcontent.com/pod-product-compliance
Lightning Source LLC
Chambersburg PA
CBHW060649060326
40690CB00020B/4571